THE TRUTH ABOUT FIREARMS AND CONCEALED CARRY

THE TRUTH ABOUT FIREARMS AND CONCEALED CARRY

Daniel R. Engel

1603 Capitol Ave., Suite 310 Cheyenne, Wyoming USA 82001
1-888-980-6523 | admin@urlinkpublishing.com

URLink Print and Media is committed to excellence in the publishing industry.

Published in the United States of America
ISBN 978-1-64367-903-7 (Paperback)
ISBN 978-1-64367-902-0 (Digital)
02.10.19

NEW ADMINISTRATIONS CHALLENGE THE US CONSTITUTION AND THE SECOND AMENDMENT INTENTIONALLY.

Too many people try to reinterpret the meaning of the US Constitution, but mostly the anti-gunners are looking to take away your guns. It was written with very clear intent and not subject to be re- deciphered by every new administration we get in the White House. We must stand firm to protect it!

Dedication

I would like to dedicate this book to America the Free and to those brave individuals who served honorably in every branch of the United States Armed Forces to help maintain our freedoms that we so much enjoy. I'd like to make a special honorable mention of our combat veterans, including our disabled American veterans. To belong to the disabled American veterans, you have to have a service-connected disability, that is, the disability occurred during your military service, whether wounded or injured. Sometimes they say the greatest and most seriously devastating scars are those emotional scars we cannot see, but there are also those with physical damage—damage that leaves many veterans living the lowest quality of life with seriously impaired bodies and continuous daily pain and their scars incurred for freedom all the way to the end of their life. It seriously offends me that politicians try to reduce their disability compensation, where no price can equal their continuing sacrifice, and they should be listed as WAR casualties. We respectfully thank these veterans, no matter how they were injured, whether it was combat or serving wherever they were assigned and needed. There are so many who have never returned from WAR, whether killed in action or POW/MIA, which means prisoner of war/ missing in action, no matter what the US Government called such action—a police action or any such conflict because we fight and die for freedom just the same, and we are sent to our final resting place equally covered with American flag-draped caskets, symbolizing our service in the armed forces of the United States. The UNION always covers the LEFT shoulder or the HEART.

We also thank our policemen, firemen, and emergency workers for putting their lives in the face of danger each and every day, right here at home throughout America to save the lives of fellow Americans. We hope we'll always have sufficient number of required personnel to assist their local communities created due to local governmental cutbacks that leave Americans vulnerable.

Let's have a special moment in remembering ALL those who have given the ultimate sacrifice of their lives in the line of duty, with the utmost respect, no matter what the cause was while they were doing what they believed in doing, and while protecting the country they loved, for the rest of us to be able to continue to live in freedom. Those who came home must never forget those who could not. In addition, a special honorable mention in remembrance of those who were awarded the Purple Heart. While many have multiple Purple Heart awards issued, it could have been their death each and every time. We wish to further this honor to those who have been awarded special medals for valor due to their courage, bravery, and heroism, especially the Medal of Honor, our nation's highest award.

Due to so much misinformation throughout America regarding firearms, I got tired of seeing innocent people die each and every day at the hands of criminals. I've come to take this poor information and loss of innocent lives in this great country very personally, and I decided to put together a book that very thoroughly explains the way firearms and ammunition work and why they do what they do. With extensive information, I hope to further your knowledge and teach you many things to help save your life one day.

This book is intended for those with absolutely no experience in firearms and also for those professionals who carry a gun every day for a living. It covers certain specific information to help every household in America to become familiar with firearms, including the most commonly owned firearms, so that nobody will be left owning a gun they cannot or should not use, and prevent as many injuries as possible. Also, it assures that you will learn considerable information and be much more prepared to maintain your life in addition to maintaining FREE America.

I'd like to specifically thank 5 colonels who dedicated their life to the lives of the American people, including extensive combat (and wounds) from Vietnam through Iraq and Afghanistan. While three of them are personal friends, the other two are someone I very highly respect. I'd also like to thank a friend, a federal judge and veteran for his commitment to justice for the people, and another friend who was the district attorney and veteran for his equally dedicated service. Furthermore, I'd like to thank all my friends in the veteran's community, especially the Vietnam Veterans of America, my era, for their service to America in its time of need. And, lastly, a special "thank you" to the veterans service officers who fight to get disabled veterans their rightful disability compensations to try to help them meet their needs through their daily struggle and to maintain their life with the many disabilities they obtained in their military service—disabilities that prevent them from working and cause such losses of income, wives, and families while they lose their own self-respect, failing in life, which is all beyond their personal control as they continue their physical and emotional struggles.

We hope that all our presidents as commander and chief will help develop laws that prevent taking away and/or reducing the very disability compensation that becomes the sole support of those with these many disabilities that they incurred when our country needed them and promised them, but, sometimes the later, newer administrations say they have changed the rules which should never be allowed once earned.

God bless America!
Respectfully,

Daniel R. Engel, US Navy Retired

Disabled American Veterans, LIFE Member
Vietnam Veterans of America, LIFE Member
National Rifle Association, LIFE Member

Should I Decide to Carry?

IF THIS WAS YOUR FAMILY, WHAT WOULD YOU DO IF SOMEBODY KILLED THEM INTENTIONALLY?

With the current crime rates in the United States, there's been a great deal of controversy between anti-gunners and those who don't want to give up the guns protected by the Second Amendment: the right of the people to keep and bear arms shall not be infringed.

It's unfortunate that there are so many thugs and killers living among us while those who insist on removing our guns and weapons have most likely never been assaulted. In 1960, the number of MURDER in the US was 9,110, and for 31 years, it continued to climb, where it peaked at 24,700 in 1991, but with the ever-increasing concealed carry permits issued, the number of MURDER started to decline from 1991 to 14,612 in 2011. In 2010, 67.5% of all homicides in the United States were perpetrated using a firearm. I guarantee that people who have been on the wrong end of a gun barrel will support those who want to prevent it because it's not a good feeling. I grew up in drive-by shootings, gang and drug-related killings, and fistfights to resist being beaten. I had 5 guns pulled on me and was lucky enough to live through them and took one with a gun grab, aside from being hit with clubs, bricks, and other things, but there are people who will cut you up and put you in trash bags. They *don't care* about your life! Some gang members will kill for initiation or *be killed* themselves as a penalty, while innocent people die just because others are trying to be the two toughest kids on the block. I decided not to include any graphic pictures of victims due to their nature, but I assure you that if you watched the video that I saw while drug cartels kidnapped a pretty young woman and they used a razor to hack the head off of her conscious body while she was kneeling outdoors, they also filmed it to make their video very effective so their future victims will do anything and everything they want them to, but if you saw this, you'd certainly pay attention to everything in this book and never have to make up your mind to own and carry a gun for survival. Remember, they killed her after they were finished with her. DEATH comes around only once!

I've had broken and shattered bones and scars and been shot, so you can understand my lifetime of studying to stay alive. I don't trust thugs of any kind once they direct their attention to me. I've come to my brother's rescue at times and he has come to mine other times; it was a way of life, but the thugs eventually become hardened criminals and killers. Unfortunately, many breed new criminals, and because of what I was exposed to in life, I decided to write a book to help teach what so many people don't know about firearms and about protecting themselves. So there might be a word or two about me here and there throughout the text to explain things in reference, but very minimal once past the first few pages. I'd never hesitate to protect my life or the life of an innocent person if I'm able. I learned it at a very young age when I came home crying one day. A big guy beat me up, and my father, a World War II army veteran who had traveled the South Pacific and Japan and had no sympathy for thugs, sent me out to beat him up, or I'd have to deal with him. So just before I beat the daylights out of this thug, I apologized and then found that the guy twice my size became limp on the ground while he cried this time. I think my dad was sorry because once my fear was broken, I never backed down from a fight the rest of my life, if it was obvious that I was being forced to fight, and I put down some real bruisers out of necessity. The point in my mentioning this is because I've talked to adults who have never been in any kind of fight in their entire life and those who have a great fear of it happening. They don't even have the knowledge of using any firearms but find themselves looking to learn. There are too many with opinions other than the true facts. You can *learn* to overcome your fears, and you can learn to defend yourself. Somehow, I figure you're going to pay very close attention throughout the rest of this book. If you do, you won't be sorry.

Due to my lifetime of dealing with thugs, and the residual aches and pains that linger on for life, I learned to be wise and do my best to outsmart them, which doesn't always work. Fear keeps people from protecting themselves and their families, but everyone is very capable of confronting what comes to them in some way and not just allowing killers to do them in by *KILLING* them and wasting their life, just so the punk gets his kicks or initiation. One fellow was confronted by a killer with a gun, and he said, "In the name of God, your gun won't fire," and so the thug decided to put it to the test, and bullets ripped through the victim's body. Don't get me wrong, some are bad hombres, but many don't want to die either, while some of them just may stand their ground, so you have to understand this and stand your ground too if you want to stay alive. "Never tempt a thug to shoot you because they just might." Some travel in groups and many fight in groups, so there's no way to try to rethink or come to any terms with this breed; you have to learn to deal with them and fight back, but you have to learn to recognize the right time to react and the severity of the threat.

If you read this book, it will give you your money's worth, I assure you. You'll learn all about firearms and what to do to be able to react in a timely manner and fend off the threat to save yourself or a loved one, maybe even another innocent person. I'm giving you a book full of facts, and you have to decide what to do with your newfound knowledge. There's a great deal of information regarding various firearms and assorted sights, but I feel most households can use a copy of this book because it covers many firearms owned in American households and clarifies specifics while doing away with many myths. Any safety benefit gained from carrying a firearm depends on the owners having appropriate training and understanding of developing the skills, abiding by the rules, and learning to compensate for varied conditions! While so many people are killed every day, if you learn one thing in this book that might help you save your life, then it was well worth the money.

If you already have your concealed carry permit—just because a person is legally authorized to carry a weapon—it does not mean you have the proper training and judgment to use it during an emergency or crisis. If you obtain your concealed carry license or permit (and I hope you do), there's a BILL before Congress, HR822 for national concealed carry reciprocity between states. Under the house legislation, HR822 will authorize people with a concealed carry permit in one state to carry a concealed weapon in every other state that gives people the right to carry concealed weapons. If this bill gets passed, you can travel nationwide without fear of being a victim because the other states will honor your license. Presently, you can already obtain licenses in several states, and many states will honor the license of other states on their list. Check the states that your state will honor, with your attorney generals, and make sure you study the laws in every state you plan to travel, including your own.

Don't become a dead victim because you deny the fact that you can be next on the list of those being killed! Guns don't kill people, but people certainly kill people!

It's time we take America back from the criminals who have no value for life other than their own. They get a free ride in jail with housing, food, medical care, pay, rest, and relaxation, and when they get out and kill someone, they get free representation while the innocent people who *try* to save their own lives and the lives of their families have to face the law for practicing self-defense and hurting these criminals who are often repeat offenders and always claim that their rights were violated, but what about yours?

You will find information here for rifles, shotguns, handguns, how to use them, and how to stop a threat as fast as you can. We'll cover sights, scopes, targets, and shooting procedures for handguns, including the way it all works, in addition to holsters and the best one for your needs and so much more. Within a few days, you will have a great deal of more knowledge than you could ever imagine, and this book can be used to train people for the things they might not be aware of, and it would be a great purchase for those wanting to learn their way, including for concealed carry protection.

UNITED STATES CRIME RATE 1960—2011

	1960	1991	2011
OK PUNK	31 YEAR RISE	PEAK	CONCEALED CARRY CRIME RATE
MURDER	9,110	24,700	14,612
FORCIBLE RAPE	17,190	106,590	83,425
ROBBERY	107,840	687,730	354,396
AGGRAVATED ASSAULT	154,320	1,092,740	751,131
BURGLARY	912,100	3,157,200	2,188,005
PROPERTY	3,095,700	12,961,100	9,063,173
VIOLENCE	288,460	1,911,770	1,203,564
POPULATION	179,323,17	252,177,000	311,591,917

FACTS!

GUNS INCREASE & CRIME DECREASES

Study the chart, where the crime went up steadily for 31 years, peaking in 1991, and, with so many guns being increasingly carried, the crime had gone down steadily!

(Crime rate verification: http://www.disastercenter.com/crime/uscrime.htm)

While your knowledge of firearms may be somewhat nonexistent today, by next week, you'll know more than so many walking the streets who think they do. This book is all facts, but you have to be able to use them! A couple of reading references will be mentioned for other books that have nothing to do with firearms, but just bear with me as we go from the basics to the advanced. Various firearms will be mentioned throughout the book for references. This book will give you your money's worth, I assure you.

The Powers of Observation

There are many things we can study to try to recognize something improper, but we must learn to *think properly* first to effectively communicate. While we're sure we figure we've confirmed one thing, it just might actually be different. In one incident, a man was taking his young son in the car to run a few errands, and he was preparing to back up out of the driveway, so he asked his son if there were any bicycles behind the car, and the boy looked around and said no. The father very confidently backed up the car over some toys and a wagon while he heard them crunching under his wheels. While he immediately shouted at the boy and blamed him for this incident, and while he was claiming that the boy had told him there was nothing in the driveway behind him, the boy who was very upset and confused told his father that he never said that. The boy did, however, say that the father had asked if there were any bicycles, and there were no bicycles. The boy said there were many other things in the driveway, but the father never asked about any of those items, just bicycles. You can see how thinking properly of the way we do things in our life, including someone asking such simple questions properly, directly affects the outcome or the results. Such simple errors in our everyday thinking causes so many situations like the bicycles, which is also responsible for many misunderstandings between a husband and wife where they may tend to argue about what they said or what they meant, but the fact is that it happens every day, and by simply making an honest and conscious effort to say exactly what we mean, life may improve a hundredfold for many of us.

Honesty is *always* the best policy (unless confronted by a thug). So many people try to create the illusion of being a good person, very honest and very truthful, while they might be stabbing you in the back or about to at that very same instant. They might volunteer certain information that has nothing to do with the current conversation by cleverly slipping it in, and, to those knowledgeable in such things, it stands out like a blinking light. A person who might get involved in occasional illegal practices may buddy up to you, thinking this will throw any improper thoughts of them getting involved in wrongdoings out the window, but people experienced in these matters of observing might suspect *them* of being deceptive, depending on how much they try to influence or impress others. A person who goes overboard and brags about his extensive military knowledge or actions while in the military service may not even be a veteran, and many phonies misconfigure the uniform protocol, but someone knowledgeable sees these things as clearly as knowing his name, especially where so many military phonies brag about being trained for so many numerous jobs, but the military trains for certain specific jobs to get exceptional knowledge and skillful abilities. Can you imagine an infantryman (foot soldier) flying the space shuttle because his side jobs are being astronaut and electronic technician to repair satellites? The more lies that are told, the better his memory better be, because the stories start breaking down, but if it's the truth, there's no problem remembering it. Sometimes it's so easy to pick out numerous lies in a single conversation between those knowledgeable and those thinking they're really making a big impression, but let me explain techniques that may help you before we move on.

While there are many people, even some you might know who get to be known as professional liars, especially criminals, I used to study what they call body language (a science of nonverbal communication), which is used to analyze commonly used gestures made by millions of people every day. I figured it might help me a great deal throughout my life. At one time in my life, I applied to the FBI and the US Secret Service for anti-terrorist work who study body language extensively. I was always studying unusual things that most other people don't while constantly becoming much more observant of people who unknowingly speak a silent language that is unknown to the majority of the population. Many politicians spend a lot of money, being instructed in depth on body language and avoiding directly addressing specific subjects of discussion for every reason. When the president of the United States addresses the nation and offers tax cuts to some groups, he says so, but to avoid saying increases, he says adjustments, and when the cost of Medicare and the health care for the retired and disabled is going up and the benefits they will pay out are going down, he says reform so that even though he says these things to the nation, he feels he did his job by telling them what they need to know, and, surely, he felt he didn't lie, but the actual truth is, many of the people who heard him speak still have no idea what's happening or do not know that their benefits are even being cut due to his *bending the truth* with clever word manipulation and word play. So after being told of his plan of reform, they clap for him, not knowing they are losing. With the US military interaction going on in Iraq and Afghanistan, he says he's withdrawing 10,000 troops as if it's really significant, but then everyone asks how many military personnel are in a troop. But to clear up this question, I say a troop is only (one) man, so ten thousand troops is exactly 10,000 men, not the millions so many people perceive. Similarly, when the politicians say improved gun safety, they don't mean technologically or mechanically advanced devices or laws to make safer guns, their definition of safety means "by disarming us."

If the *criminals* know they speak only with their body actions in many ways despite what they're saying, they will only lie if their lips are moving. Salesmen and business executives study body language to read and understand when people are more interested so they can make more sales and increase their income. Studies have taken place among thousands of people who attended seminars where the discussions were specifically arranged differently and the speaker was using certain specific gestures in his speech and displayed prearranged hand interactions in motion while speaking to his audience, and the results confirmed the already proven facts. The very reason a candidate for office, even for the White House, gets the popular vote and the trust of the people is due to his performance, but then he turns the country upside down when it's time for reality because he was tutored on how to get your attention and gain your confidence (and therefore get your vote), but he still doesn't have the proper knowledge or experience to go beyond his so-called popularity that was otherwise gained by actual deception while everyone then says that, well, more than half the country voted for him, so he *must be* good. There's no room for assumptions when it's LIFE or DEATH! Even a lie, to those who listen and *believe it*, becomes true. By studying body language and observing what you encounter in everyday life, you will start tuning your brain to alerting *you* to what's happening that you already see but were never aware of. A book on body language would be good reading, so you can adapt it to *never trusting your killers* while they say one thing and mean another, but review the books before you buy one. Some are good and some are not. You will start understanding how to interpret such things and learn to adapt a great deal of what you learn from your everyday life.

I also studied the attention span of an average person including the established fact that you have 30 seconds or less to get someone's attention, or they lose interest and move on. If you try to sell someone something, they take a genuine interest and know if they want something within the 30 second-time frame or even much less, and, in many situations, it is a great deal less. Once you become accustomed to the routine, it becomes much easier to do and understand more around you. No expression and no reaction from you will definitely keep a salesman confused. Put the 30-second claim to the test for yourself.

Try it when you go to a store or to a mall and when you see something that catches your attention; observe the time it takes you to decide if you like it or not. The more you do it, the more you will realize how quickly mental decisions are actually made. People know whether they are or are not interested in mere seconds, so no matter how long they stand or sit there, trying to justify the money, the decision was made long before they bought it or moved on. While 30 seconds seem like so little time to some people, once you're aware of it, you realize how long 30 seconds actually is. Lives are taken in mere seconds, so you have to learn to respond in a timely manner. If someone says he's going to kill you, it shouldn't take you any longer than the time it took him to speak those words to understand what it means. If someone were to say he or she is going to kill you, your first thoughts should be to never again trust this person in any way while your defensive tactics should be immediately in thought while you watch and observe to see what the person has up his sleeve.

Combining your new awareness with possible threats and common crime will not only make you recognize the things that are abnormal but also will allow you to be on the ready for danger (without premature reactions), which could otherwise result in the *appearance* of YOU being the bad guy, possibly getting shot by another good guy responding to your lack of confidence. Training and patience to wait for the proper response time to make sure it's an actual lethal threat to *you* is necessary, but you have to learn to evaluate the circumstances because I don't want you to wait too long and get attacked or shot because of it. We have to respond as soon as possible, but we don't want two good guys shooting each other due to FEAR by their nerves coming unraveled and both thinking the other is a thug.

Should You Trust Your Killer?

Is this really a necessary question? Criminals KILL for no reason, so I NEVER TRUST THEM, and neither should you! One thug shot his girlfriend in the face "because he was mad at her." Killers kill for sport, lust, and greed. There have been many other situations where the criminals had told their victims to follow their instructions and not to resist in any way so that they wouldn't hurt them. However, while many claim this was to their advantage, or they thought it was, and they actually survived, some of the thugs lied and killed their victims anyway before escaping into the night. You must decide, but be cautious! When a policewoman tried to talk an armed thug into giving up his gun, she knelt down and set her gun on the ground to show him that she didn't want to harm him, and then he laughed and shot her. Never give up your GUN! There are people who offer advice on being attacked and say that you should never resist and should always do everything the perpetrator tells you to do, no matter what (these are probably people who have never been attacked). But then with my own experiences in life and then with the assailants who made such promises to their victims and then killed them anyway before fleeing, I would never advise not considering defending yourself when the opportunity presents itself if you are capable. You are the only one who can make this decision based on the circumstances at hand since every situation is different. (You will obviously be thinking, *LIVE or DIE*). I know because I've been there many times. Statistics are there to show past experience, and although many people have survived by doing what they were told, the cemetery is full of people who made the wrong decision because some criminals don't like leaving witnesses despite what they tell you, while many criminals have no value for life. Many people live in denial, thinking that an assault won't ever happen to them, but if they're prepared for one, they stand a much greater chance of living on through old age, having made a decision to "trust or not to trust a criminal who is already breaking the law and already threatening your life," but you will have to decide what that decision is. For me, it's always survival! I'll NEVER trust anyone who makes any threat upon me (while never allowing him the option to know what I think), and I'll maintain possession of my gun at all costs.

Firearm Operation and Selection

You might wonder why some information is in here; it's to help you understand the mechanics and fundamentals of the operation for bullets and firearms, most importantly handguns for your defense to stay alive, but also including other firearms such as rifles and shotguns as well. Some of what you read in this book may contradict what some people teach, but, regardless, these are the facts!

Live or Die? It shouldn't take very long to make this decision. Die for nothing or learn to protect yourself. Life is precious and not repairable once it's gone. DON'T THROW IT AWAY!

An important part of owning a gun is maintaining it and being knowledgeable about how it works. If you ask 25 people about their opinion on a personal defense handgun, or any gun for that matter, it'd be like asking a group of politicians and you may get 25 different answers. If you ask the technical specifics, you still get 25 different answers. If you ask a firearms instructor, you would think you are more likely to get some reasonably proper information, but even then, some of them might be more biased toward his own preferences. I am too, but you're getting the facts! While I've seen some firearms instructors who were totally wrong in some of their information and tactics, which is sad but true, I wondered how this can happen. While your mental conditioning (your mental ability to fight for your life) is absolutely necessary for a confident and defensive use of a firearm, many people avoid the technical aspect or hardware. So since we are preparing in advance, it is an equally important consideration, even though there are reported occasions where granny, with no experience, no training, and not even a technically superior gun, pulls out her Old Family Heirloom .22 and drops the KILLER dead in his tracks!

Your mental mindset has to be to do whatever it takes to survive, even if it means the taking of someone's life. If you cannot do this, then you have no business carrying a gun because in the mishandling of a situation in which you're not being sure you *can* do this, long before you start carrying your gun, you may fumble your own chance at survival and DIE or accidentally KILL some innocent bystanders. Know your capabilities, and if you're certain of your ability to KILL (or be KILLED), then read this book for a solid foundation on how firearms work to build your skills on or to understand the way it all works for you to decide better. Mental strength and *your* mental capabilities (called mindset) are your first consideration, and then there are your choice of weapons and the development of the necessary skills. In that order, your skills have to be developed with *your choice* of firearms. Once you have them all in the proper order, that is, (AFTER you read this book), you will learn to integrate them into your defensive routine as you practice what you learn. If you never practice what you will do in a counterattack against your KILLER, you certainly will never do it under the stress of reality (with a *real* gun pointed at you). Recently, a concealed carry firearms instructor who qualified hundreds of people for their concealed carry licenses was charged with illegally authorizing his students for concealed carry due to *his* not fulfilling the state requirements to teach such classes, thereby with improper knowledge, capability, and authorization resulting in the nullifying of the license of every student he taught! Upon selecting your school for such a permit or license, make sure you check the instructors (legal), authorizing credentials *before* you lay down your cash. He may have *taught* students, but by his not being state-certified, he does not have the right (and the required skills) by your state law to pass the much-needed knowledge onto you. The only reason you are doing this is to save your life and the lives of your children and family who count on you for their safety because they cannot do it, and even though getting a concealed carry license gives you enough knowledge to pass the *basic* test as far as your required state laws and the ability to hit a stationary paper target up close, it's only the beginning, and you should further continue with your learning of the proper skills; it's absolutely necessary.

If you are going to use a gun to defend your life, you should also understand very thoroughly how they *work*. Nobody needs help in dying, but we need all the help we can get to stay alive. Not knowing what to do in such an emergency is a terrible feeling and can cost a life, maybe YOURS! Facts are what's needed, not opinions, guesses, or the local neighborhood know-it-all, who's more BS than knowledge, so once you know the facts, you can better determine *your own needs*, whatever works best for *you*, no matter what anyone else suggests according to *their own* likes. While this book is going to teach you how handguns, rifles, and shotguns work, it also covers some information on assault rifles, clearing up many myths. This information was put in here because so many households have one. You need to know what they *won't* do, but you need to know in general how firearms work so that you will further understand how to defend yourself and be capable of making all your own decisions. After reading this book, you will have more knowledge than the average person who thinks he knows, but this book just might save your life, and that's what it's all about. The FBI, in reviewing a high number of law enforcement shootings, suggests that regardless of the number of rounds fired in a shooting, only one or two solid torso hits can be expected. This is very realistic due to the nature of shooting incidents and the extreme difficulty in shooting a handgun with precision under such conditions. The probability of multiple hits with a handgun is not high. Experienced officers recognize that fact, and when potential violence is anticipated, their preparations are characterized by obtaining as many shoulder-fired weapons as possible. Since most shootings are not anticipated in the first place, the officer cannot be prepared with heavier armament. As a tactical principle, no one should ever plan to meet an EXPECTED attack armed *only* with a handgun. The handgun is the primary weapon of choice for an UNEXPECTED attack since the majority of shootings occur under circumstances in which you do not have any other weapon available, or cannot get to it, while a shotgun will make them turn and run the other way. Make sure this happens in this way, or they might shoot you first.

The Taurus Judge revolver above left shoots a 410 shotgun shell or a 45 Long Colt. The Smith and Wesson Governor above right shoots the 410, 45 Long Colt, or the 45 ACP (Automatic Colt Pistol), using moon clips shown on the far right. A moon clip holds semiautomatic rounds in place to fire in revolvers that have a relief at the back of the cylinder to insert the moon clip. A moon clip loaded makes easy reloading. They also have half-moon clips for some revolvers.

These are half-moon clips above. In the center is a tool for de-mooning the rounds, and on the right is a revolver capable of using moon clips where it is machined in the back of the cylinder. Unless a moon clip is preloaded, it's NOT a speed loading process.

Although we're going to address many firearms throughout the book, the handgun must be relied upon and must prevail. When the FBI determined by experience as mentioned above that if attacked, only one or two torso hits to your killer can be reasonably expected in a handgun shooting incident, it's based on law enforcement officers who are trained for this, so for those new to self-defense, you might be only skilled enough to even get one such hit, and, if that, the ammunition used must maximize the likelihood of immediate incapacitation, so we'll be looking at everything that comes into play and how it all works in a very coordinated effort to stay alive. While there are many different handguns, they are different in type and operation. There are revolvers and semiautomatic pistols, but we're going to add the newest design in semiautomatic pistols separately as striker-fired pistols, even though they have been around for the past 27 years or so due to differences.

While they have personalized guns otherwise known as smart guns that will function only for the owner due to fingerprint recognition (otherwise called biometric or by whatever other means since they use different technology), they aren't proven for public use yet, so just the mention of them is all we're going to do. Up front before we get into selecting your preferred style of gun for defense, I want you to understand that it takes ACCURATE SHOOTING to *stop* your assailant. Very cheaply made high-production guns, or junk guns as I call them, might only be accurate only to a certain degree with very limited operating reliability, which is not something to trust for gunfight survival, but the name-brand manufacturers, not necessarily being higher priced, usually perform so much better. Even then, due to the cheaper manufacturing practices for high-volume sales, you still have to sort them out. A good shooter may not hit the side of a barn if the gun is junk, and a poor shooter certainly won't hit the side of a barn even with a good gun if his skills aren't good enough. While there are many fine makes and models of guns available, guns that are often referred to as junk or Saturday night specials are among the many poorly made guns that are more likely to misfire or malfunction. The only time I see justifying a junk gun is like the time when a teenage assailant bought one for $40, and when it *didn't work* and he got caught because his murder attempt failed, he was puzzled as to why his gun didn't work. But since the criminals are going to get their guns regardless of the laws, it would be nice if all the junk guns went to the criminals so they could all malfunction when they try to use them on innocent people like this moron did before he questioned it. If YOU were using that junk gun to TRY to save YOUR life when it didn't work, you'd be pushing up daisies, that is, lying in the cemetery. Guns don't do their intended job just because you put bullets in them and pull the trigger. When deadly force is justified, you have to perform within seconds to stop the threat as soon as possible! LIVE OR DIE, no way around it, and that's the way it is! Guns are not magic and are not guaranteed to hit your assailant just because you pointed the gun in his direction and fired. It may completely miss! If you don't study and get things in the proper order, this just might be what happens to you. Remember, a shot that misses is the same as no shot fired!

Some people think the probability of an attack happening to them is not very high or even unlikely to happen. They live in denial, but remember that since it *will* happen to somebody, there's nothing keeping YOU from becoming one of their victims rather than your own proper preparation to prevent it. With all the guns I've had pulled on me, five to be exact, none of them were expected until they suddenly appeared.

When I was 15 feet from my truck at 25 minutes past midnight, there was a gang forming less than 75 feet away from me when sudden gunfire broke out, leaving three shot, one dead, and

30 thugs scattering while three were running from the shooting scene. While seeking immediate cover, I was grasping the grips of my .45 under my jacket, and on the ready to respond, my other hand had my phone while I called 911 and reported everything that was happening to the police as it unfolded. It *will* happen; the only thing we can do is to try to prevent you from becoming a statistic. The most ideal circumstances would be in making the local police department gifts of all those new handguns that were never fired and dropped only once; that is, we beat the punk to the draw or we were better trained than he was. While we don't want to support anti-gunners in any way, probably the only thing they had on track was when they said that allowing people to carry guns will be like going back to the old west, but first hear why. In the old western movies, they were always afraid of the fastest gun, or should I say they were afraid of the person who was the fastest at drawing his gun and placing a kill shot or even many kill shots while sometimes the other guy never even got a single shot off. Guns and threats today are somewhat similar in some ways that I'll teach you as you read through the information regarding the speed at presenting your sidearm and the speed at which your bullets hit your would-be killer; we also have an advantage that they didn't have back in the old days, that is, finely tuning your gun for the best performance in the fastest time. Don't figure you need to be a gunslinger because once you have the proper sidearm and learn to use it at your own pace, it will undoubtedly surprise you in an emergency, but you need to be able to respond to a life- threatening emergency in mere seconds. One of the things they would always forget to do in the movies though was to reload their gun since the cowboys would shoot all day without ever thinking to reload, and while their gun was only a 6 shooter, they somehow made you believe it was a 600 shooter, but we'll study everything that comes together to make it all work. To give you an example of what I mean by fast and effective gun presentation, a few days ago, a local policeman was attacked by three thugs, who pulled their guns and shot him, while he managed to pull his own gun and return fire simultaneously, hitting two of them. This wasn't a bad result for the way it unfolded, but the police officer was lucky to have survived. If he didn't have more skills than those who surprised and wanted to kill him, he'd have definitely been dead, so pay attention to what you read in *this* book! All FACTS! Ignore those who say it's not necessary; YOU are responsible for YOUR life!

Sometimes the thugs are women. What if you think she's pretty? Hesitation at that critical moment may cause you to lose that few seconds of valuable time that you need to survive a deadly encounter! The same applies to both men and women here.

We are going to start examining the way bullets and firearms work. Much of the information provided in this book will teach you much more than the average person currently knows about firearms and ammunition. While some people might think they really don't need to know all this, we're going to address many things to make you familiar with them whether you think you need it or not, so a few hours of your time to read this book will prepare you for saving your life. And, remember, if you fail to read and to learn the actual facts, then you may fail to survive a deadly encounter. Knowledge outweighs chance! Understanding how the gun works will help YOU understand *how to use it* and why it does what it does, not just because it's popular or cool. *Cool* and *popular* have no place in this book, and neither does an *ego*! *Proper* and *effective* do!

The earliest successful propellant for firearms was a combination of potassium nitrate, charcoal, and sulfur that has come to be known as black powder or gunpowder. Gunpowder is always used to define a bullet propellant, no matter what type of powder it is, black powder or smokeless powder, so you always have to be specific in what type of powder or gunpowder you're referring to. Early firearms used gunpowder (the black powder) since it was the only propellant available at the time, and due to its chemical makeup, it was considered very unstable for handling. When the firearm was discharged, it smoked a great deal, showing the location of where it was actually fired from. In 1884, there came the invention of our modern-day gunpowders called smokeless powders, which are very stable for handling, compared to the original black powder. The smokeless powder provides three times the power and smokes very little. There are currently well over a hundred smokeless powders available—142 that I'm aware of at the time of this writing—which all burn at a different rate of speed due to their chemical design for combustion; modern ammunition cartridges are loaded with smokeless powders which are made up primarily of nitrocellulose or some of nitrocellulose and nitroglycerin. The US Navy demonstrated nitrocellulose burning under water, so unlike many other flammable materials, nitrocellulose does not need air to keep it burning as the chemical reaction produces oxygen. Once burning, it is extremely difficult to extinguish, so some modern gunpowders may be perfectly capable of igniting even in damp or wet environments. Hand reloaders (people who reload their used cartridges to fire again) still use black powder for shooting old-style cartridges, but if you put smokeless powder into an old firearm, into an older bullet cartridge, or into a muzzle loader instead of the intended black powder that they were originally designed for, it would be a very serious error and mistake because the gun would blow apart due to the severe pressure increase from the more powerful powder. So now we can certainly understand our need to know enough about firearms so that we don't accidentally kill ourselves either. Modern black powders are actually a black powder substitute but are made for greater stability in their handling as compared to their original chemical makeup.

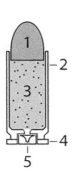 

A cartridge or round is actually an assembly of bullet.

1. *A cartridge case 2*
2. *Propellant 3*
3. *A base or rim 4 for extraction*
4. *Primer 5 to ignite the propellant 3 through the flash hole above the primer*
5. *The bullet 1 seals the cartridge opening to build pressure to launch the bullet.*

While bullets themselves are measured by their outer diameter, measured decimally in inches or in millimeters, the metallic cartridge case that holds the bullet is measured and sized so the bullet fits snugly on the inside of the cartridge neck opening, and the cartridge for each and every caliber has its own various dimensions. The cartridge length is measured from the base to the end of the cartridge neck, not to the end of the bullet, but the bullet is also located at a specific depth in the cartridge for optimal results, giving the cartridge *assembly* an overall length. A completely assembled modern cartridge consists of a cartridge case, a primer, a smokeless powder charge, and a bullet which has the neck of the cartridge crimped slightly into a groove (called the cannelure) on the bullet. It holds the bullet in place until sufficient pressure builds to launch it while also assisting in keeping the bullet in its proper place while handling it so it does not get pushed further inward or move further outward (called bullet pull). Otherwise, the bullet itself (not the assembly) is also called a projectile. Some specialty bullets don't have a cannelure. A completely assembled cartridge is often technically (improperly) referred to as a bullet, but the proper term would be to call it a *cartridge* or a *round* while the term *bullet* is very commonly used. While these terms apply to all firearm rounds, shotgun ammunition is also quite often referred to as shells or shotgun shells. Brass cartridges vary in wall thickness, depending on the manufacturer and the caliber. Military brass cartridges are slightly thicker in places. A bullet does its damage due to impact and penetration.

The cannelure is the crimping groove in bullets to hold them in place and prevent them from sliding into or out of the cartridges while holding it until greater pressure builds to force it out of the cartridge and down the barrel.

There are many bullet designs for different purposes. The actual firearm chamber has a specified internal dimension measured in thousandths of an inch larger than the outer diameter of the cartridge case for easy insertion and extraction. When the primer in the cartridge is struck, it ignites the gunpowder charge through an internal flash hole inside the cartridge. While the burning powder builds internal pressure due to the expanding gas, it expands the case tightly against the chamber walls, and then the pressure escapes by forcing the bullet out of the cartridge case toward the only opening available, which is down the bore of the barrel.

Cartridges with different length and diameter use different powders which burn at different rates of speed to control the amount of pressure that builds and the speed of the bullet exiting the barrel. Fast-burning powders reach maximum pressure and launch the projectile quickly with the available power at hand, but slow-burning powders allow more pressure to build before the bullet is forced out. Many people often misuse the term *faster powder*, thinking it launches the bullet at a greater rate of speed, but, technically, it doesn't work that way, although everyone seems to refer to it the same way. A fast-burning powder charge is generally used in handguns and shotguns and will reach maximum pressures and launch the bullet quickly, but slow-burning powders used in magnums and rifles will allow it to build more pressure before launching the bullet. Due to the greater pressures, it will reach much greater velocities. If you said a specific powder gives you a faster bullet, you would be more on track than claiming it has a faster powder. Specific powders are chosen to get the maximum desired benefit whether it's a handgun cartridge or a rifle or a shotgun cartridge. The longer the barrel, the greater the bullet velocity, such as in a rifle, because the pressure of the expanding gas is still building as the bullet travels the longer path before exiting the barrel. There's much more science to this than we are going to address here, including where excessive barrel length can start to change the desired results due to vibration or the cartridge's ability to continue to build pressure before it maxes out, reaching its maximum potential. A bullet seated too deep into a cartridge may cause excess pressures due to the smaller confinement of the charge; in the same way, excess space by volume may give less than desired pressures, depending on the speed of the powder used. This is why the .380, which is a shortened 9mm Kurz, and the .45 GAP (Glock Automatic Pistol), which is a shortened .45 ACP, work well. Either one, changing the volume and/or powder speed, will affect velocity and accuracy. Hand loaders again are people who reload cartridges by hand at home with reloading equipment designed for it, and they often eliminate the crimping process on their bullets while sometimes using bullets with no cannelure to improve accuracy, but while some of them think it to be an advantage, it may have its disadvantages too, depending on the round, the firearm, and your knowledge. By using an uncrimped bullet, the bullet starts to leave the cartridge case as soon as the pressure becomes sufficient to push it out. If the case was crimped, it would hold the bullet in place longer, requiring greater pressures to launch it down the barrel. Having no crimp causes a reduced velocity that some shooters may consider insignificant, but experienced reloaders understand what they want. While all this sounds complicated due to so many speeds, it all happens so fast in milliseconds (thousandths of a second) that most people have no idea about so many different gunpowder speeds, which are technically called burning rates.

For handguns, you always want to crimp your cartridge case against the bullet *to avoid* having the bullet slide inward or outward in its case due to the recoil of the previous round being fired. You should never experience this in commercially manufactured ammunition, which is crimped or glued in place. For revolvers, an uncrimped bullet may slide outward due to the rearward momentum of the recoil and jam your cylinder in rotation. That's right, if you're not fully aware of what ammo you put in a revolver—meaning, properly crimped, it could jam the cylinder against the barrel due to a bullet protruding.

BULLETS HITTING BARREL CAN JAM THE CYLINDER AND THE GUN WON'T FIRE BULLETS MUST BE CRIMPED
BULLETS MUST BE CHECKED BEFORE CARRYING FOR DEFENSE

Protruding bullets, generally caused by no crimp (which some hand reloaders do), can hit the protruding end of the gun barrel and jam the revolver. This can cause your death in a confrontation shooting for your life, and the gun simply hangs up because the cylinder cannot rotate due to the bullet jammed against the edge of the barrel. Beware of what you carry for self-defense! It MUST work! DEAD OR ALIVE!

I've read where people said in their factory ammunition, the bullets jumped the crimp quite often, but I've shot assorted ammunition including many magnum calibers (most powerful loads) all my life, and *I never experienced a factory loaded round* with a bullet that moves in its cartridge, and if I ever do, I'll never use their ammo again. Ammunition has to be reliable! If a bullet did move forward and outward in its cartridge, this would change the pressure and complicate the function of the round. I don't think the manufacturers want a liability suit on their hands for making dangerous commercial ammunition, providing they are US manufacturers, and can be held accountable as compared to imported ammo. In semiautomatic pistols, the bullets will be subject to forward and rearward bumping in the magazine. In tubular fed firearms, no matter if it shoots handgun calibers or rifle calibers (some have even claimed that in pump action rifles too), the inertia of all the bullets bumping each other during recoil can drive the uncrimped bullets further into their case, *and* pointed bullets in a tubular fed firearm may accidentally fire the primer and discharge the round in front of it, setting off a chain reaction through every round in succession all the way down the tube. CRIMPING IS NECESSARY FOR HANDGUNS OR TUBE FED FIREARMS, but there are several types used. Roll crimping should not be used for semiautomatic rounds that are what they call head-spaced, that is, cartridge uniformity to maintain consistent safe pressures by the cartridge length such as 9mm or .45 ACP, so taper crimping is used instead. Taper crimping is crimping the edge of the cartridge case over the curve of the bullet nose (the ogive, which is the curved shape of the nose of the bullet).

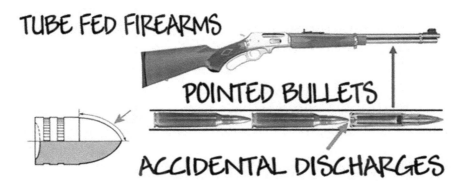

The arrow on the left indicates the bullet ogive, which is the curved shape of the bullet nose! The arrow on the right shows pointed bullets against the primer of the bullet in front of it in a tube fed rifle.

Materials that *detonate*, which explode faster than the speed of sound or are supersonic (called detonation), are considered high explosives as compared to materials that flagrate, which explode slower than the speed of sound or are subsonic (called deflagration) and are considered low explosives such as those used in small arms, that is, rifles, shotguns, and handguns. For the purposes of this book, the Offices of the Chief of Ordnance of the US Army define small arms as those weapons of calibers of .60 or less. Even though small arms' smokeless powders cause deflagration, they are capable of propelling a bullet at supersonic speeds. Hand loaders experiment with their reloads by sometimes changing the type of powder and gradually adjusting the amount of the powder charge (up or down) to improve accuracy (but within manufacturer's recommendations), especially for competition shooting—just the opposite of what some people improperly claim by stating that *any* factory ammo is far better than any reload. Their lack of knowledge is responsible for such claims. By now, I hope you understand that you never carry un-crimped bullets in a handgun, especially for self-defense! It's your own responsibility to have a very effective and fully operational carry gun as compared to fumbling the job and DYING due to your own negligence. That's right, your own negligence, which might be hard for some of you to swallow, so you need to understand that I'm providing the facts for you to assess your own circumstances and try to determine what you might be able to do about your own protection. Remember, LIVE OR DIE!

While we look for effectiveness, sometimes we get confused, trying to understand why criminals might be shot in the chest several times and still continue to advance on their victim. A survey on police shootings proves that accurate head shots effectively stop the threat 100% of the time, even though they do not always cause death. FBI studies (on real police shootings) proved the only way to consistently stop a threat as soon as possible is to severely damage or sever the central nervous system. A head shot to the center of the nose allows little resistance for the bullet to reach the part of the brain to spinal cord connection that can immediately shut down an attack; otherwise, you rely on their loss of blood or broken bones to shut them down, and even if the blood supply is completely cut off from the brain, technically they claim the brain contains enough oxygenated blood for 10 to 15 seconds of willful action; that is, a wounded assailant can still KILL you, which seems consistent with strangleholds designed to render an assailant unconscious if applied properly in 7 to 14 seconds, or even up to a minute if not experienced in how to apply one, by depriving the brain of the oxygenated blood. FBI statistics (on real police shootings) reveal that 70% of all police shootings over the last 40 years are between 5 to 10 feet. Unfortunately, many policemen have also been shot with their own guns when a confrontation occurs at such close range, so we will also address close quarter confrontations later. Another study by the FBI stated that *most* attacks *on individuals* from assailants with a gun are generally 21 feet or less, with a very small percentage being beyond 21 feet. Therefore, there is no need for a barrel length delivering a great deal of extended range accuracy while most handgun barrels average from 1½ inches to 5 inches. This is very sufficient, considering that we anticipate attacks to happen from 5 to 21 feet. For close encounters, if you have a long barrel, you must be capable of drawing and shooting it effectively if needed, as well as having the same capabilities if you're using a short barrel. The majority of personal carry guns have barrels of about 3 inches; we'll address these issues soon.

A handgun is a gun designed to be used by one hand. While we learn different ways to use them, both hands obviously become involved, but we must still maintain the ability to use it single-handedly. With picking a carry gun for concealment, there are many factors you need to study and question as to whether you're disabled in any way and/or able to use your hands properly and be able to see sufficiently. Many people have arthritis, fibromyalgia, or many other problems including impaired vision, so YOU ARE RESPONSIBLE to study and evaluate your own circumstances. Being armed isn't magic, and it also makes you as dangerous as your assailant if you lack the skills to use it. I've read such statements in articles that say even if you're disabled, it won't make any difference (don't you believe it) because the first concern is YOUR SURVIVAL followed by the legal interaction afterward. YOUR LIFE COMES FIRST! We certainly don't want you to try to use a gun that you are not capable of using and accidentally shooting yourself or some innocent bystanders. There are many gun styles, sizes, and calibers available, but different physical limitations may restrict what your capabilities are, and they may require you to select a specific style of gun. This is an area where we need to be true to ourselves because we don't want the big giant gun that we cannot properly use just because it makes us feel powerful. Those who say they need a big chrome one so the killers will get scared when they see the flash of the shiny gun don't believe that either because many things can happen including a flash of chrome in the midst of a potential gunfight, and it may make the other person think it is a muzzle flash and you may get yourself killed instead. You will see the muzzle flash *before* you hear the report, which is the bang from the gun going off. Having a sidearm of the proper size and caliber that you can handle quite effectively with whatever your health status is at the moment is the one that's going to save your life, especially if the killer is not scared at the sight of a chrome finish or big gun; that is, you might have to use your gun to stop him, and if so, you are going to need the necessary skills.

In the picture, the gun above is my Kimber 1911, compact stainless II in 45 ACP with a compact grip and a 4-inch barrel, and my Kimber Solo Carry in 9MM at the bottom.

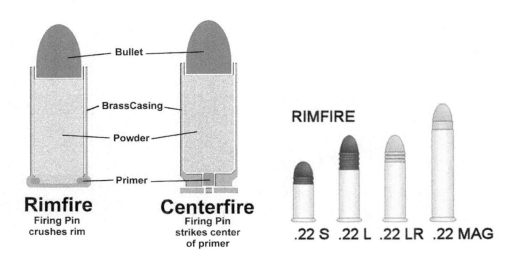

The illustration above shows the .22 caliber Long and Long Rifle having different case lengths, and some have different bullet lengths, but the overall length of some rounds are actually shorter on many .22 Long rounds; that is, they are shorter than the .22 Long Rifle. Make sure of your firearm requirements because a cartridge case too long can cause misfeeds and jamming problems, just the same as a cartridge case too short or even too little in velocity, which may be insufficient velocity to cycle the action in certain semiautomatics, especially in the .22 calibers. Manufacturers vary, so always beware.

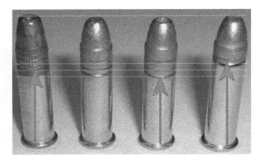

The illustration above shows the difference between the rimfires having no primer cup in the center of the base compared to the centerfire. Note the .17 caliber comparison to the .22 caliber. Just like the popular .22, handguns and rifles are chambered for the .17. Beware of different manufacturer's length of .22 cartridges, which can cause feeding and jamming problems.

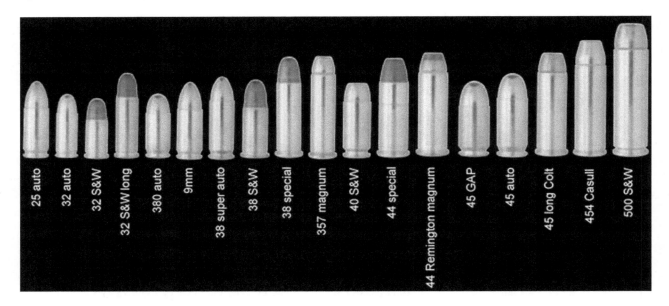

Here are some centerfire cartridges, although they are not all shown here.

To name a few handgun calibers, we have .17 Rimfire, .22 Short Rimfire, .22 Long Rimfire, .22 Long Rifle Rimfire, .22 Magnum Rimfire, .25 ACP, .32 ACP, .32 Colt, .327 Federal Magnum, .380, 9mm, .38 Special, 10mm, .357 Magnum, .40 Smith and Wesson, .41 Magnum, .44 Magnum, .45 ACP, 45 GAP, .50 AE, .50 GI, and .500 Smith and Wesson. Although there are many more, those above are the most common ones with ammo readily available, while some are more of a hunting round, so anything not mentioned may not necessarily be suitable for a self-defense round. Bullets such as the .22 Short (.22S), the .22 Long (.22L), the .22 Long Rifle (.22LR), or the .22 Magnum (.22WM) are all called rimfire due to the cartridge design, where the primer, which is the source of ignition that ignites the powder charge in the bullet, is chemically based in the .22 and any sufficient impact on the rim of the .22 may cause it to fire, but it's generally fired in a gun by impacting the rim. Calibers ranging in size from .25 and above have a separate primer designed to cause a small internal explosion called flagration to ignite the larger powder charge for a controlled burning. This separate primer is inserted into the center of the cartridge base, thereby being struck by the firing pin in the center, which is called centerfire. Centerfire primers are also chemically based but have to be capable of greater power as compared to the rimfire due to the more powerful powder charges, which need a more powerful source of ignition. Although both primers are chemically based, the rimfire is considered less reliable than its centerfire counterpart. Some of these large calibers do not really qualify for concealed carry due to the physical size, mass, and weight of the guns necessary to fire them because I don't see many ways to conceal them, let alone find proper holsters for such guns other than designs for hunting purposes. Manufacturers are making them though. I might continue to mention a few assorted guns along the way, but you must make up your own mind while knowing your own preferences and your own personal capabilities (or inabilities), due to possibly being physically impaired, but you may be able to develop or improve some of your abilities by studying the way it all works and what is available.

Recoil

All I ever read is about people and recoil. I've read an article in a magazine where the person says shooting a .38 revolver is like getting hit in the hand with a baseball bat, so he says, "Don't do it." This is nonsense! The recoil is not that dramatic unless you've never fired a gun before, and it scares people who are new to firing, but some guns are too uncomfortable for some people, so read the book first and then make your own decisions. Another article said that if you fire any caliber as large as a .38 Special even once, it will cause permanent hearing damage. While we know prolonged exposure to very high noise levels can damage hearing, I always recommend wearing hearing protection to *prevent* hearing loss *due to extended and prolonged exposure*, but you cannot walk around all day with ear plugs in your ears, anticipating hurting yourself from a lethal encounter with an assailant. Many of these claims come from the inexperienced. You want to overcome your fears, NOT to create new ones! If you are ever confronted and are forced to fire in defense, similar to my having to suddenly take immediate aim and fire a snapshot (even with very large calibers with loud reports) while hunting in mountain wilderness areas, you most probably won't even notice having fired the weapon (the way hunters never fear having to fire) as compared to being unnecessarily scared just from the thought of doing it. Assailants are KILLERS! Just be happy about still being alive! To save yourself, you do whatever is necessary! I never heard the blast from the shotgun that shot me from 5 feet away, but in the tense circumstances, it knocked the hell out of me while blowing out muscle and shattering my bones with no recollection of the sound. The bullet will usually always hit before the sound reaches the ears as long as you're shooting within its capable range and not shooting 500 to 1,000 yards or more, but simple math could quickly determine this. Your focus should be on the KILLER and *stopping* him! When you read items somewhere that are written to cause such concern over possible hearing loss, claiming such excessive recoil, you must understand not everyone writing these articles are all knowledgeable and experienced and some are writing from assumptions, not their experience. If you are familiar with specific firearms and you very well know what the recoil is like from these particular guns, then you are able to sort through these and be more selective. Use commonsense because you very well know you need to DO OR DIE!

On the left are hearing protectors and on the right are electronic hearing protectors, which can be used while you practice shooting and are adjustable to block out certain noise levels.

Everyone says to use the .38 Special. As far as the .38 Special is concerned, it actually is used to be more potent and equivalent to what is now called +P, but, in 1972, SAAMI (Small Arms and Ammunition Manufacturers Institute) pronounced Sammy, a nongovernmental agency who maintains the specifications and guidelines for firearms in the US, and revised their guidelines on the .38 Special, reducing its power. Even though some government and military personnel carried the .38 Special for certain use, even before its power was reduced, it was considered by the US military that carrying it as a sidearm in the Philippine-American War from 1899 to 1902 to be quite ineffective as a defense or combat round. In the United States, firearms and ammunition specifications *are not* overseen by the Consumer Product Safety Commission or any other branch of government. The Federal Consumer Product Safety Act, which imposes health and safety standards on consumer products, exempts firearms and ammunition from its requirements. Federal law *does not* even set any design or safety standards for domestically manufactured firearms, and it does not prohibit unsafe domestically produced firearms from entering the US market. Consumers should be aware that only manufacturers that are members of SAAMI are informed of the institute's suggested guidelines, and we have no agency, not even the ATF to protect us against unreasonable risks or injuries associated with firearms and ammunition. Safety guidelines for firearms and ammunition are specified by SAAMI if you're a member but are not written into law. While some people claim that the federal law prohibits the importation of junk guns through a ban on the importation of firearms not suited for sporting purposes and the BATFE licenses companies to sell in the US, there are no safety regulations regarding the safety of their firearms. There are rules and laws prohibiting certain types or functions in firearms that are mostly due to regulating the prevention of them, but some are allowed if you pay special fees and registration of these differences. Here's a link to these if you'd like to explore: http://en.wikipedia.org/wiki/National_Firearms_Act. I recently read, since the US Government doesn't regulate the safety of firearms and ammo, some states are now starting their own requirements but again mostly to prohibit. Eight states try to regulate junk guns now through handgun design and safety standards, which *sounds* somewhat technical, where three require a drop-and-firing test, a few use a melting-point test, a few require safeties, chamber load indicators, and magazine disconnects, but beware that a magazine disconnect safety *prevents a* semiautomatic *pistol from firing* if the magazine is removed. The US state of California passed legislation in 2006, requiring magazine disconnects on all new handgun designs sold in the state starting January 1, 2007, which has resulted in their widespread availability in other jurisdictions as well. Only three states allow the sale of handguns that the *state* preapproved, and they have them printed on a list of the states' choice of gun, and you are only allowed to buy, not your choice! But I thought this was America. SAAMI does not list any NATO (North Atlantic Treaty Organization) information, and neither does many of the reloading manuals, so saving brass from NATO rounds for reloading may become a quite complicated issue unless you have sufficient experience.

I have read countless articles about not going above a .380 due to recoil, but remember the .380 is actually a shortened 9mm, which is otherwise known as 9mm Kurz. Some people, and even a book or two, get this issue confused and say Kurtz, but it's Kurz. I've personally shot what many people, especially hunters, consider cannons due to far too much recoil. I would head out to the range before going up into the mountains with my deer, bear, and mountain lion tags. I'd shoot many boxes of ammo through my 8mm Remington Magnum rifle in which very few people, even hunters, would even try to shoot, but the real problem is people are scared of recoil and afraid to pull the trigger mainly because of being inexperienced, but too many rounds from such a powerhouse can definitely get the shoulder aching. This also accounts for poor marksmanship due to self-induced fear. I do have to admit that the 8mm Remington Magnum is a real mule though, and it was eventually discontinued. Such powerful firearms may be considered uncomfortable for many people, but I chose it for my wilderness hunting based upon its bullet size, power, trajectory, and downrange (power on impact, being the delivered kinetic energy including its terminal ballistics), a few hundred yards away as compared to other available calibers. I'd also carry my .44 Magnum Ruger Red Hawk holstered diagonally across my chest in case I get unexpectedly jumped by a bear along the way since many people including park rangers have been found dead with their hands pinned down where they were trying to pull the gun that was holstered on their hip out of the holster, but with the weight of a huge bear standing on their chest, pinning them to the ground, they couldn't get to it or even get it out of the holster, so this is an example of wrong equipment causing failure since the hip holster was the wrong choice. In my studies on numerous human deaths by bear, I chose to holster my .44 diagonally over the chest, which should assure my access. The biggest battle with shooting, especially with a newbie or newcomer, is the fear of recoil and their complaints of poor performance with the handgun they are using. Poor performance can be attributed to their own fear of the recoil in handguns (or rifles and shotguns) and the shooters' anticipation of the gun firing, thereby causing you to flinch and jerk as you pull the trigger, resulting in improper use of the gun. As the bullets are extremely fast, by jerking the trigger, the gun is pulled away from its aim point *before* the bullet actually fires and the difference is magnified downrange in distance. A great deal of the fear in recoil is self-induced from constantly hearing others complain about it, but I've taken small women out to the range and let them shoot 9mm and .357 Magnums while putting their group in the center of the target—and even .45 ACPs while doing the same—but I clearly instructed them as to what to do and not to fear. Of course, afterward they knew they could do it, and I called them dead-eye and was sure glad that they were on my side! Even teenage girls shoot the .45 ACP out at the firing range, claiming it's a lot of fun. If you're afraid and anticipating the gun firing and being afraid of it kicking you from recoil, you will undoubtedly flinch, jerking the trigger and pulling your gun off the intended target. This definitely causes a miss! This is the shooter's poor performance, not the gun. This is caused from not only fear but inexperience and improper knowledge, possibly improper mechanical actions in your particular gun.

Another major factor contributing to the recoil of a handgun is the weight of the gun (steels as compared to polymers). Heavy is easier to handle the recoil than light, but even then it depends on the type and size of the gun and what caliber it's shooting. If you have handled a light gun for very long and suddenly changed to a heavy gun, you may not be effective with it until you adjust to the heavier weight difference in its handling. You will find that once you learn properly, most guns become very controllable and your marksmanship will improve a great deal. The only difficulty you might actually encounter as somewhat of a problem but still very workable if your life is threatened is heavy derringers that have a very short barrel. Some shoot a 45 Long Colt or a .410 shotgun shell. Even though these guns are made of steel, you will find a lot of power in the palm of your hand and a grip that is not sufficient in size *or shape* to hold onto it securely enough. This *will* have a great deal of felt recoil, and it might rap the web of your hand a bit, but don't be afraid. If a small gun with a large caliber has a properly sized and shaped grip, it makes shooting it so much easier and controlled. It's like pulling the stock of a magnum caliber rifle tightly into your shoulder before firing, making it much easier to shoot and hit the target, compared to holding it too loose and getting whacked in the shoulder or the jaw and missing the target, causing even more fear, especially causing you fear of firing the next shot. The massive large bore derringer is one type of gun I definitely wouldn't recommend for the elderly or the disabled. If you really like derringers, there are plenty with smaller calibers that are more compact and more easily used, but if your life is threatened and the heavy derringer is all you have on hand, then *remember* that the first shot is the easiest one since you're not trying to recover from the recoil and not trying to reacquire the sight picture again for another shot like you would be trying to do if you had already fired the gun. Always make the first shot count, and derringers are single-action (SA) firearms, requiring you to pull the hammer back into a cocked position before you can fire it (for each shot including the first), so the large bulky but powerful derringers with rounded grips that promote muzzle flip can only be effective if you can manage to handle it, at least for that first shot which may be all you need in such a gun, if you can hit the target or assailant, but remember that the derringer is going to have only 2 rounds available, so you have to remember to pull the hammer back for the first shot and back again to fire the second shot. A person who experiences body or hand tremors may opt for a gun just a little bit heavier than a light one intentionally to help act as a stabilizer, where the heavier weight will not move and shake as quickly when aimed at a target.

While many people love this big derringer, the power and recoil are really something for the elderly and disabled to avoid unless they try shooting it and feel they can handle it.

Balance and Center of Gravity of a Handgun

Any particular gun you consider for a carry gun, no matter what the caliber or bullet capacity is, should have a natural balance (a proper center of gravity). An empty gun with a grip equal to the length of the barrel creates a natural point of balance, and you will naturally point the gun more easily than if the gun had a barrel twice as long as the grip. The longer barrel will have a counteracting leverage applied to your wrists with the tendency to dip the muzzle due to gravity while you are struggling to maintain its proper point of aim, especially with a heavy—or steel-framed gun. If you are very experienced with a hunting handgun, you will already have the toned muscle strength to maintain the more rigid hold required, but for a gun needed in an immediate lethal encounter, you need instant access and the immediate pointing ability of your gun, which naturally balances into and through the moves necessary to draw to present your gun and to make a quickly *aimed* shot. For example, if you had a gun with a 3-inch barrel and a 4-inch grip, it would be easier to naturally balance and aim in a fast encounter as compared to a gun with a 7½-inch barrel and a 3-inch grip. While in semiautomatics the grip also holds the loaded magazine of cartridges, the weighted end of the gun in your hands assists in holding the lighter end (the barrel muzzle) upright at your assailant, and you may feel as if there's less recoil transferred to your hands. You should find this proper balance with the gun being empty (meaning, unloaded), and a naturally balanced carry gun will assist in handling recoil and hitting your target. Lighter guns are usually preferred, but they increase the felt recoil energy as compared to a heavier gun that will act as a stabilizer helping to absorb recoil. Guns with accessories mounted under the muzzle such as lights and lasers, even though these accessories are very lightweight, become more muzzle-heavy than normal and need more of a proper grip to maintain its upright position through actual firing but will have a tendency to drop the muzzle too low in the attempt to recover for the next shot. Lasers that replace the original grips (laser grips) help to maintain or restore the natural balance of the gun by redistributing the weight into your hands. Revolvers place the ammunition above and forward of your grip in the cylinder, adding the weight of the ammo to the counteracting leverage that is trying to dip the barrel and, thereby, trying to naturally point the barrel downward, and the revolver may feel as if there's more recoil transferred to your hands. Some carry guns or pocket guns are small in caliber and physical size and can usually fit into the palm of your hand; they generally don't fall into the question of balance and center of gravity as compared to a full-size model 1911 .45 ACP with a steel frame and a 5-inch barrel. The engineers that design handguns take these factors into consideration to make it most effective, but each and every person has his or her own hand size, finger length, and arm and gripping strength and will find that even the same gun in different hands will feel quite different in their handling ability and controllability.

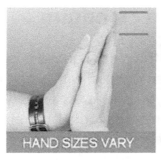  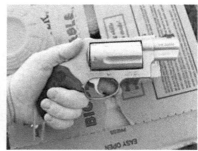

Due to various hand sizes between men to men and women to women, let alone men to women, gun grip sizes also vary. It's very important to have a sidearm that fits your own hand comfortably. Larger grips open your hands more, and whatever size you settle on, remember you need to maintain proper control.

An important thing to know is when you look at various handguns for proper selection to suit you, many people immediately say the polymer gun is so much lighter, but what people don't know is that you really need to know the actual weight of each and every gun that you consider. Keep a pocket-sized notebook because sometimes the heavier aluminum-framed gun might be lighter than the polymer gun in its overall assembly, and some polymer guns are actually heavier than some of the metal guns they were supposedly designed to replace due to the metal guns' claimed weight. Remember too that the lightweight polymer may already be heavier, but then they usually provide a higher magazine capacity for cartridges, so up goes the weight again! You might be starting to understand that there's quite a bit of technicalities here that nobody ever considers. Another modification that some manufacturers offer is slots machined out of the top of the slide on semiautomatic pistols, claiming that the large hole is to reduce the weight of the gun, maybe improve balance, but *beware* of anything that could allow any kind of debris or *anything* for that matter that can fall into the open hole machined into the slide because it could cause a jam immediately by altering the operation of the slide. For a defensive sidearm, I would make sure that the slide has no openings whatsoever that are not necessary for their operation. There's no room for ego's here; we don't want to try to look cool by purchasing something we saw in the latest movie or to impress people. We want to stay alive; remember granny! A fine gun for a person who works out at the gym or works a very strenuous physical job and has a superior grip may actually be a total washout for someone who works behind the desk and never does anything other than pushing a pencil, but you can learn, and it can be improved. It's not advisable to buy a handgun for another person for that person's own defense unless you take *them* into the shop and sort through the dozens of possibilities until *they* feel right about one that will work in every other aspect, after the means of operation is clearly explained to them. Not to mention buying a firearm for another individual is highly illegal in many states due to required background checks. Most people are ready to buy their gun, go in to gun shops, and ask for a recommendation on a carry and defensive sidearm, and many of them are sold something completely inappropriate as I've personally seen happen several times while some of the salesmen quote, "These are very popular guns," aside from questioning what the gun is going to be used for, who is going to be shooting it, if there are any physical impairments or disabilities, and a list of your needs versus sales popularity. A major concern is that people buy guns without *ever* working the mechanics of it in the gun shop before they buy it. Guns of different models have different tension on the slides, the triggers, and even the more simple parts like the slide stop and release or the magazine release. While the slide stop is so easily released on a full-sized .45 caliber 1911-style gun, some of the polymers in even smaller calibers have little buttons to release the slide, and some are actually very difficult for some people to press. No matter how popular the gun is, *the lack of ability*, either the gun's or yours, leans more toward losing the gunfight! If you like two different guns, then cycle the action and go through all the functions in each one right there in the gun shop to *compare* them. Physical disabilities even like arthritis in the hands can prevent you from operating the necessary functions so if you're carrying a gun that you cannot safely operate, this is a certain disadvantage and you may get your gun taken away from you and killed too. Since there are over 100 types of arthritis which are all disabling in their own way, you have to be your own boss here (a judgment call). Even if you don't have any disabilities, by putting the guns through a proper evaluation by cycling their actions and comparing them, you will know what it's like and whether you feel comfortable with it. But a word to your advantage here is, trying to cycle the slide on a *specific* semiautomatic pistol for the first or the second time may seem a bit more difficult than it really is, so make sure you try it several times just to be certain because it's new to you, but if it's definitely too hard, then don't figure you'll grow into and adjust to it because you might not, and you could be killed. Then, study and know the way *it all works*, preferably before you go into the gun shop, and then you will more than likely get what you need on your first purchase rather than your second or third purchase because sometimes you learn that the first ones you bought were not suited to your situation if you didn't do your homework, and you'll probably take a *heavy* loss on trading them back, even to the same people who initially sold them to you, and you will find yourself being stuck with them even if they take them in trade. Remember that if you have a gun you cannot get any significant money back in trade, you can always make it a part of your emergency bag that you can carry in your trunk in case you ever get shanghaied and locked in your own trunk. You will have a gun for when they open the lid! There's *nothing* like the element of surprise! But be alert and aware of who might open that trunk lid because the people that locked you in might not be the same people who let you out. They might be emergency responders, police, or innocent bystanders trying to come to your rescue, so don't shoot until you know for certain! Never shoot unless you know your target!

These hand exercisers are great for exercising the fingers for proper grip and control of your gun. The one on the left allows for individual fingers to be exercised.

Reducing Recoil

There are ways to reduce recoil in guns today. If it's a revolver, they cut a compensating port on the top of the barrel at the muzzle, and if it's a semiautomatic, then they do the same and sometimes they also cut the vents in the slide. This allows the burning gases that are under extreme pressure and pushing the bullet out of the barrel to escape through the vent on top and help keep the muzzle from flipping up so high, but you still have to learn to control your gun. It's like having a small *jet* action venting from the top side of the barrel with the firing of each round thrusting the muzzle downward and counteracting the recoil. So far, while there are dozens of designs available, I've always shied away from ever using these compensating ports on any of my guns because even though some shooters claim that they are getting to be pretty good shots by using it, it actually reduces your bullet velocity, giving you the equivalent of a shorter barrel due to the vent. So if you have a 4-inch barrel and the vent starts 1 inch or more from the muzzle end, then you will get a reduced bullet velocity equivalent to a shorter barrel. For competition or target shooting, this is fine because you have nothing to worry about as far as the target is *shooting back* at you, but since MY LIFE DEPENDS on my *weapon*, I personally want full velocity, maximum impact, and full penetration downrange rather than my intentionally reducing all of it. For competition shooting, handguns are often referred to as *race guns* which are used for action shooting (competition shooting with points for accuracy and minimal elapsed time), but target hand loads are generally already reduced in power for less recoil and faster recovery. People claim the loss in velocity is negligible, but I would prefer to see expanded hollow points shot into ballistic gelatin with certain muzzle brakes first. Handguns are mostly short barrels, and some are already somewhat lower in velocity than we might prefer, but for concealed carry, I feel that a compensating port in a defensive handgun, sort of, defeats my whole ability here like an Indianapolis racer running a small emergency donut spare tire on a drive wheel and trying to run a race. It might work somewhat but very inferior and not as effective as it could (or should) be. While the driver will obviously lose the race, I don't plan on losing my life. In an actual encounter, if you get only ONE shot, *it better work!* Reality where you are being attacked by moving target(s) is very different from target shooting. While some people try to shoot *moving targets* for more realistic practice, it's even better than still targets, but those targets are still not shooting back! In reality, you may have to counterattack, fire, and seek immediate cover because you may not be sure of even getting a hit on your killer, so we certainly don't want to give *him* an easy shot, let alone *any* shot. If you have some specific guns in mind for your sidearm, you can actually calculate the recoil energy of each gun with a little math and see in comparison which one you might prefer, but even this is good only for a comparison to what you might already know on a specific firearm where all these figures may otherwise just confuse you. I would find the best gun for my preferred cartridge, firearm design, and functionality and get used to the recoil which can also be adjusted by choosing specific rounds.

Using the following formulas, you can determine your recoil energy (kinetic energy). According to forensics, the recoil velocity of the gun equals the bullet velocity, times the bullet weight, and is divided by the weight of the gun.

$$V \frac{FT}{M} \text{ or } FT = VM$$

where *M* is the mass of the gun or bullet, *F* is the force in pounds, and *T* is the time in which it acts. During the period in which this force is acting on the bullet, it is, therefore, also acting with an equal degree of force on the gun. If the velocity of the bullet is *v*, the mass of the bullet *m*, the rearwards velocity of the gun *V*, the mass of the gun *M*, and the time during which the force acts *T*, it, therefore, follows that the forward motion of the bullet will be *FT = vm*, and the backward motion of the gun will be *FT = VM*.

This also tells us that *vm = VM* or, by rearranging the equation, we have

$$V = \frac{vm}{M}$$

In other words, the recoil velocity of the gun equals the bullet velocity, times the bullet weight, and is divided by the weight of the gun. If, for example, we have a gun weighing 2 lb firing a 158 gr. bullet at 860 feet per second and there are 7,000 grains in a pound, we have the following formula:

$$\frac{860}{2} \times \frac{158}{7000} = 9.7 \text{ feet per second}$$

This is the velocity of the recoil of the weapon.

Further, the applied energy of the recoil is calculated by using this next formula.

$$KE = \frac{1}{2} MV^2$$

The kinetic energy (*KE*) of the recoil or the recoil energy clarifies the actual forces involved. The recoil energy of a weapon and the kinetic energy of a bullet are calculated exactly the same way and are measured in foot pounds.

$$\frac{1}{2} \times \frac{2}{32.2} \times 9.7^2 = 2.9 \text{ foot pounds}$$

Formulas can continue by adding the weight of the propellant to the weight of the bullet, but this is somewhat negligible for simply estimating the power in your hands.

If you think you've found a possible sidearm and you're trying to determine how effective your potential sidearm may be to suit your needs, look over some boxes of personal defense ammunition in the caliber you're considering and read the specifications on the box in velocity and foot pounds to help you determine whether your potential choice may be capable of delivering sufficient stopping power (kinetic energy) for the target to absorb an impact while creating a permanent wound cavity, but be sure to look over a few different rounds that claim to be effective to see which ones even offer higher velocities and more foot pounds per specific bullet weight as we'll later discuss, which will help you to analyze the option of using a smaller caliber sidearm if you have to, with personal defense rounds in the smaller caliber actually capable of delivering somewhat comparable energy. While recoil is more a scare due mostly to inexperience and possibly having a disability regarding your dexterity, that is, the ability to handle the firearm with a coordinated effort due to *your* capabilities. Once you understand the way it all interacts upon your own *personal* ability to operate a suitable firearm, it will be much easier for you in your decision-making, but the one major and true fact regarding the recoil is that the person who can effectively control the recoil, or the ability to recover from the recoil for the next follow-up shot, is the person who can operate that particular sidearm most effectively and who will undoubtedly outshoot anyone else in actual rounds fired and accuracy—better than those who cannot master this—but who will also and most hopefully be your killer *on the losing end!* Once you're familiar with the true recoil without the fear of it, then you're in the best position to decide whether it's acceptable or a bit too much for you to handle.

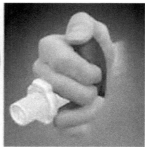

A person with arthritis, above left, is shooting a .22 caliber revolver, while, above right, a person is shooting a Palm Pistol! The Palm Pistol® is an ergonomically innovative single-shot defensive firearm chambered in .38 Special that may be fired using either hand without regard to orientation of the stock. Suited for home defense, concealed carry, or backup gun, it is also ideal for seniors, disabled, or others who may have limited strength or manual dexterity. Using the thumb instead of the index finger for firing, it significantly reduces muzzle drift, one of the principle causes of inaccurate targeting. Point and shoot couldn't be easier.

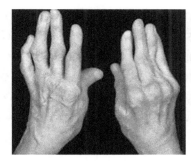  

Here's the Palm Pistol with its action open and closed.

The Russian AK-47 was adopted for combat use by Russia in 1947. Another version was later revised in 1959 with an angled muzzle, designated as an AKM. While not specially suited for target shooting, it does not reduce the barrel's effective length (and no loss of velocity) due to the angle being located at the very crown of the barrel and allows the expanding gas, which is under extreme pressure, to start to escape from the top side of the projectile first, giving the barrel muzzle a natural downward thrust from each round fired while helping to maintain a steady hold on target. The downside to this is that any deviation at the crown of the barrel, which is at the very end where the bullet exits, should have an even gas distribution around the back of the bullet while the bullet leaves the barrel, or it may cause the bullet to be unstable or inaccurate. There are attachments for some handguns such as the 1911 that extend the length of the gun by adding the compensating port to the end of the barrel, but then it makes the gun even longer and maybe more difficult for you to draw in a hurry in addition to requiring a holster capable of the additional firearm length. The more you complicate things, the tougher it will be to make it all work properly. I say study, think it through, look at available models, see how they feel in *your* hand, know their means of operation, *test-fire them if you can*, and then decide.

Wound Ballistics

According to the FBI studies on wound ballistics that I read very thoroughly, which were put together by a team consisting of the FBI, coroners, and other medical doctors, while many people argue the differences in what causes actual damage in a bullet wound, some of them even try to use assorted mathematical formulas to theorize what will and will not happen, but the information in this report was written on *actual facts* from the dead bodies studied after being shot. There is no theory here, just the facts! There are a couple of factors of importance when using a bullet to stop a lethal threat, but the main consideration is the actual size of the bullet across its cross section, that is, the size of the caliber, which is the outer diameter of the bullet. The bullet weight of any caliber is based upon its length in grains. The bullet weight is measured only by the bullet itself and does not include the weight of the cartridge, the powder, or the primer. While there are 7,000 grains in a pound, there are 437.5 grains per ounce, so remember this while learning the effects of bullet weight being influenced by velocity. The bullet when passing through flesh creates what they call a permanent cavity, that is, like drilling a hole the actual size of the outer diameter of the projectile through the flesh. A smaller bullet obviously creates a smaller permanent cavity. This hole, the permanent cavity, is where the blood will exit the blood vessels, the organs, and the body, reducing the blood pressure, so the larger the hole, the faster we might be able to incapacitate the threat. There is also what they call a temporary cavity, which is where the permanent cavity originally or initially stretches and expands many times its size due to hydrostatic shock, which is a shock wave created in flesh due to the flesh actually containing a lot of water; where the shock wave is created due to the impact and velocity of the bullet.

While the temporary cavity is actually the permanent cavity (temporarily *expanded*), which is so many times larger than the actual size of the inside diameter of the actual permanent cavity due to the shock wave of the projectile impacting and penetrating due to the velocity of the bullet used, the temporary cavity quickly returns in milliseconds to its original size as it quickly retracts, still meaning that the permanent cavity is the only hole left and the one wound we really need to rely on. Sometimes the temporary cavity rips and tears other blood vessels and tissues in addition to other permanent damage due to the momentary shock wave which assists in bleeding the killer down. The temporary cavity is the largest cavity in ballistic gelatin that you see in the first half of the bullet's travel, looking like a ballooning effect, but the gelatin does not contract like the elasticity of body flesh, so you have to understand the way it really works so you don't think that massive hole ballooning in the photographs shown in the first half of the penetration viewed in the gelatin is the actual damage or hole like so many people seem to think it is, unfortunately. Comparing what you see in ballistic gelatin, if it were in actual flesh, the larger ballooning tunnel in the first half of its penetrating path would immediately retract back to the size of the smaller permanent hole that you see in the second part of the bullet's path as the bullet slows down in velocity, which reduces its kinetic energy as it passes on through the rest of the length of the gelatin block where all you see is the round hole passing on through. One major discrepancy in the way many people seem to think of the permanent and temporary cavities is mostly associated with rifle rounds, where they make a diagram and create a chart, showing the ballooning temporary cavity we already explained, but too many have the misconception that the bullet that hits human body mass starts its journey through, then yaws (or tumbles end over end) many times, and somehow miraculously straightens itself out and exits in the same stable path that it had when it entered, thereby leaving an exit wound similar to the entry wound; some wounds might need to be observed to determine which end was the entry versus the exit. Many people don't exactly understand the explosive effect the bullet actually has on the body by hitting it dead, on which it creates the temporary cavity before it runs out of sufficient kinetic energy (the momentum of the weight of the bullet driven by the velocity). If you had a way to record the way the bullet had actually traveled through human body mass, I'm sure you'd be quite surprised to find that many of these bullets are still flying true to their original flight path upon their exit wound. The odds of any bullet, especially FMJ rifle rounds used by the US military which are pointed, entering, then yawing (tumbling end over end), and then straightening itself out again back on its flight path either forward or backward in time to exit, would probably be in the area of 1 in 100 million or greater, but there are many bullets that do yaw, and when they do, they are most likely to exit somewhere else on the body OR to leave a *much larger* exit wound, indicating that the bullet may have been sideways upon its exit, which is called key-holing due to its lengthy or oblong exit hole—the same as on a target if an unstable bullet hits the target sideways. Two holes of somewhat similar wounding effects, entry and exit from the same bullet, would more than likely indicate a clean shot through and through. I saw an emergency room video where some young doctors with no gunshot wound experience were having trouble in trying to treat a male victim who had an entry wound and another wound elsewhere on his body, so they were trying to figure out why the bullet never came out, but they lacked the knowledge that the other wound was the actual exit wound elsewhere on the body due to the bullet's ability to yaw and then travel in a different direction. I immediately knew what happened, but they were young, and I'm sure by the end of their day, they figured it out. Further, if you had one entry wound and two or three smaller exit wounds, it would most likely indicate the bullet breaking apart on its way through. If someone showed me a graph illustrating the destructive path of a bullet from entry through the temporary cavity into the deeper portion of the permanent cavity with a very irregular exit path of much greater proportion than anyone ever lists on a graph, then I'd say here's a man that understands much more of what's going on.

Since I have my own wounds, I study others, so one thing that I've studied on my own due to my own curiosity is the way wounds would stop one assailant but would not stop another assailant, even though some of the wounds might be nearly the same. I naturally have a curious mind and sometimes take enough interest to find answers. Even multiple wounds in the same assailant, where one wound bled so much and the other wound didn't bleed anywhere near as much while I wondered why some of the wounds appeared to be very effective, didn't necessarily incapacitate the threat. In my thoughts, I came up with something that I've never before heard of, nor that anyone else has ever mentioned or considered as far as I know. I wondered about how a wound *might be* cauterized the way they would normally try to do by applying a very hot object or blade against the wound to coagulate and seal the wound. While it takes 107.6°F to start coagulating proteins in the body, it takes 120.2°F to start burning human flesh, which will actually melt as the temperature increases, and the melting flesh melts quickly and has a very distinctive smell that any welder can vouch for. In probably hundreds of situations where killers were shot repeatedly by civilians, police, and military alike, it was never clearly understood why sometimes it took so many shots to stop someone, and the question always comes up is whether they were hopped up on illegal drugs or whatever the case may be. So due to my curiosity, I did a little research on my own and I've come to my own conclusions that sometimes we may actually be unknowingly and accidentally treating the new wound that we just created, and then we wonder why the rounds seemed to be ineffective. Let me explain. Sometimes a person would get shot numerous times and survive while at other times somebody might get shot only once but didn't make it or bled to death, but again with similar wounds. I've read many wounds that were treated in Vietnam seemed to coagulate the blood, but in my studying and trying to understand what was actually happening, I sorted out a few items that seemed somewhat unrelated to me, like having two or three different people study the same thing; each one might separate some things or add a few others, so I looked further for my own answers. I started looking to find temperatures of the actual rounds fired from weapons and found that when a military 5.56 caliber NATO round is fired from an M16, its temperature at a distance of 10 feet from the muzzle reads 513°F, so it appears that sometimes the bullets we fire into an assailant to stop him may actually be somewhat sterilized and partially cauterizing the inner walls of the permanent cavity, going through the body mass, and if it is, then some of the wound channels may be less effective than originally thought or planned to be since the 513°F greatly exceeds the temperature required to burn human flesh. But maybe this hot temperature combined with the speed at which the bullet passes through the body mass may somewhat cauterize the wounds and reduce the bleeding. Since different calibers and different powder charges vary, as well as there is resistive friction due to different barrel lengths, assorted rounds will obviously reach different temperatures. That is why different people live or die from similar wounds, but it seems that if we used a bullet that somewhat absorbed the temperature into the projectile while retaining a cold outer jacket, then it could be possible that when we see someone shot 6 times and he bleeds from all 6 wounds, it's letting us know that the bullet probably isn't internally cauterizing the cavities we are trying to create, although even partially cauterizing may help the victim to retain more blood that he would have otherwise lost. I'd like to see the US military research on this possible situation in depth since it could change the way a lot of projectiles are made and used. In thinking that this could be happening to some degree at least, it would probably be best to use certain hollow point ammunition that provides sharp scoring or tears around the inside diameter of the permanent wound channel to assist in less probability of any smooth surfaces like those on full metal jacket (FMJ) ammunition used extensively by our armed forces. So if *we used hollow points*—the military is not allowed to use them due to NATO agreements—and if the hollow points expanded with sharp points like some designs, the wound channels cannot snap back together as smooth and tightly as they otherwise would and might help in our preventing of the possible sealing (or cauterizing) of the permanent cavity in any way or form.

Handgun projectiles or bullets as commonly referred to, compared to rifle bullets (not to be confused with hunting handguns that shoot rifle rounds), generally don't produce enough velocity to create much of a temporary cavity at all, so the report considers the temporary cavity insignificant when using a handgun, thereby bringing the attention specifically to what kind of bullet we can use to create a more effective permanent cavity. The FBI suggests that a minimum penetration of 12 inches is actually preferred with 14 inches being more ideal due to the many variations in what may impair the bullet's path, including larger body mass and allowing angled or side shots. In addition, they also say that 18 inches is too much and undesirable for safety factors. The military uses FMJ or ball ammunition. It was *once* almost exclusively a military term; most refer to it with the round balls used during the civil war era, but it is now frequently used in a civilian context as well. It means *a bullet that is solid or non-expanding in nature*. Ball ammo in rifles *usually* means FMJ, so ball ammunition means that the bullet inserted in its metal cartridge is actually covered in a smooth round-nose metal covering for handguns and pointed for rifles for several reasons, and the metal covering (or jacket) is usually copper. One reason for using copper is it is a normal alloy; lead surfaces on bullets leave lead residue (called leading or fouling) in the barrel, and it causes undesired problems and destroys accuracy since each round has to force its way through such fouling residue, but, just as important, a major reason for the metal jacket on a bullet is for actually controlling the bullet shape during penetration. The high temperatures of the burning propellants against the back of the bullet cause it to leave traces of lead or copper in the bore of the barrel by actually melting traces of the metal while depositing it throughout the length of the bore, and it also erodes the integrity of the bore, eventually making it ineffective and further destroying accuracy, and is in need of replacement. While fouling can also happen with copper, it's a much stronger material that holds up incredibly well for this purpose, so the actual fouling happens very little for the average shooter unless you're shooting lead bullets or you shoot quite a bit, leaving copper deposits. Although lead and copper may be dissolved chemically while cleaning the bore properly, the inside of the bore erodes and wears due to the internal friction from normal wear and tear while being seriously affected by the jacket material used on the bullet. Nothing is forever. While we use rifling, the rifling was first developed to give the lead fouling somewhere to go in an attempt to reduce or eliminate the problem, but it was immediately discovered that rifling increased the accuracy of the firearm incredibly as compared to firearms without it. Some big game calibers such as the .458 Winchester Magnum rifle rounds that use a steel jacket instead of copper have been found to shoot out the barrel; that is, its maximum life for accuracy has been depleted in as few as 200 rounds, so steel jackets or such hard materials are very destructive to the rifling inside the barrel. Military sniper rifles with stainless steel barrels that have been put to the firing test have been reported to shoot as many as 10,000 rounds and still maintain its accuracy, but I certainly wouldn't count on one doing this that wasn't submitted, especially for testing purposes, due to the probability of getting the best firearm they had available to send for evaluation as we might all be inclined to do to generate sales. And then I might even question it when it does come in, but the materials used today are far superior to those used even ten years ago due to trial and error where questionable materials failed earlier tests, demanding longer life, higher quality, and better reliability. While a target or competitive shooter would be concerned with the life of the barrel since they might shoot 100,000 rounds a year, most hunters will never shoot so many rounds in his entire lifetime or even very few rounds in his hunting or personal defense rifle. Hard barrels and soft-jacketed bullets are ideal. While a soft lead bullet will expand, but again according to its design and velocity, an FMJ will go through the KILLER as it is intended and designed to do with its round nose (RN), or pointed nose, but we're not in the military with more enemies standing behind the intended target, nor as civilians are we committed to NATO rules. So we have to consider innocent bystanders, preferably not behind the KILLER, when we shoot and a proper backstop because we don't want to hurt anyone else in the process. We should know that there are also hard lead bullets that may not be designed to, but may actually, penetrate completely through the assailant similar to an FMJ. It happens, so *anything can actually happen*, depending on everything coming into play when the round is actually fired and depending on where and how it hits the KILLER.

Since the bullet may pass through the KILLER and hit whatever is behind him, we must shoot at the most proper time and direction and with proper ammo, always being conscious of bystanders behind or in close proximity. This will become more instinctive with proper practice. A hollow point, which some states are trying to successfully outlaw, is actually safer to use for concealed carry than an FMJ round. Outlawing hollow points would favor the criminal who is in the wrong and out to harm an innocent person. The hollow point will (hopefully but not always) expand upon penetration, causing a larger permanent cavity and tearing flesh along its path while going through the body mass because its expansion actually shortens the length but enlarges the outer diameter of the bullet, creating a larger passage for draining blood in an attempt to incapacitate and eliminate the threat. A common myth is that a hollow point bullet will expand to the size of a quarter, *but this is not true*. View the image with many rounds circling the quarter, and you'll understand that this is just a myth. Although the hollow point can expand to be much larger than normal (the reason being its design), the actual caliber determines the size of the permanent cavity which is increased only by the amount of expansion of that particular bullet.

In the comparisons above, you can clearly see the bullets are much smaller than a quarter and even compared to smaller coins; they don't get the fantastic expansion that you often hear in rumors, but they do expand considerably larger. Look at the crosscut profile of a hollow point, but keep in mind that they are made by different manufacturers in different designs and materials.

According to the FBI report, many bullets have been fired into criminals and have actually been recovered (even hollow points expand only 60 to 70 % of the time), but it is much safer than using ball ammo called FMJ, which may distort but generally does not expand. As far as overpenetration with FMJ, since the jacket is hard and smooth, it continues to penetrate through the body mass while it retains sufficient energy, compared to the individual hollow point, which causes much more damage than the round nose. According to the hollow point's specific design, it abruptly expands and delivers its energy to the body mass, which absorbs the remaining energy until the round comes to a halt. Those who try to outlaw the hollow point need to be properly schooled on ballistics because some of them call the bullets cop killers, but the criminals who want to kill innocent people are going to find what they want anyway like they always seem to do. Why keep safer bullets from those who are trying to protect themselves and at the same time are being conscious of others who are also innocent and might be in the vicinity or behind an aggressive attack? Those who say that a specific hollow point bullet is a cop killer argue that this particular bullet should be outlawed (any bullet can kill a cop) just like it will kill anyone else, so is it OK for a criminal to shoot a cop if he shoots him with a different bullet? This is nonsense and a definite lack of knowledge generally brought on by anti-gun groups or by politicians like a popular senator who initiated bill S555 to outlaw "cop killing bullets." These particular bullets, he stated, were designed to kill cops, but he is lacking in the knowledge that some of the great penetrating bullets such as the KTW Teflon-coated brass were not designed to kill cops. But they were designed by cops to penetrate through car doors and the like for such survival needs against the criminals to save cops. Being a US Army veteran of 2 years and a Harvard graduate should have taught this senator to research the issue *before* acting upon his bill. There has never been a reported incident of a cop being killed with the bullets he successfully outlawed, but the majority of the general public doesn't have this knowledge available to them when a politician gets their attention, and the people tend to support those whom they like because they obviously trust his knowledge, but then when you try to educate those very people of the inaccuracy of the claims made by those who lack the proper knowledge, they resist and say we just don't like the person who initiated the BILL, or they say we just want our guns. In another situation, a woman politician was arguing against guns while she was unknowing of anything about guns; she was all worked up against the heat-seeking bullets that she had apparently seen in the same movie that I had seen; they don't exist. If they ever had such a bullet, we would live forever in peace since nobody could ever escape such a bullet, and we would obviously never have to fight a ground war anymore. This is a clear example where education and wealth do not mean knowledge; experience is always valuable. All this prevention just prevents the innocent citizens from self-protection, but it *always* protects the criminals who really don't have much to fear while carrying out their crime spree because those who are not lawbreakers won't be able to shoot back, especially with the proper and effective ammo. But we're slowly gaining in our rights to defend ourselves and our families. Unfortunately, we're gaining very slowly while those writing the laws that allow carrying concealed sidearms constantly try to include numerous technicalities in the laws that just may allow the removal of your own personal gun rights, even though you thought you were acting within the law or, in other words, using the law to allow your firearm ownership. But writing ridiculous conditions into such laws then further allows the taking away of all your gun rights if you were to violate any such conditions. That is, since they were an unknown attachment to the provisions of the law passed, you then had violated the gun laws. So they are in effect, legally taking away the greater rights while retaining those lesser rights they just allowed. This is a major reason to study the laws in your own state and in every other state you might be passing through in addition to voting. We should all understand how every single vote counts, or the wrong person just may win, and we all know that has happened.

There are also many other types of ammo available. One among them is the Glaser Safety Slugs that are very much identical to the military bird shot rounds used in WWII, but have a round and/or soft nose that will disintegrate upon contact with any object so they don't pass through the KILLER or through the wall and into the neighbors' house and so forth. Since we have many commercial ammunition companies answering the call to personal defenders, we have quite a few different defensive rounds available to choose from. I've noticed that when I buy a box of 20 specially designed .45 ACP 230 grain hollow points at a gun shop and a box of 50 Winchester 230 grain hollow points at Walmart for almost the same price (which my .45 seems to love), they both appear to get the very same results in ballistic gelatin with 30 extra rounds left to go, but some of the higher-priced rounds may have a higher velocity and more kinetic energy, *which is your bullet's striking potential.* So you really need to study what you want before you buy because the prices continue to climb. As Winchester provides the US military with billions of rounds for the defense of our country, in addition to supplying our allies, it's no wonder they are so accurate and so very reliable. I can personally vouch for their reliability since I shoot thousands of them. There are many different types of hollow points though that are actually designed quite differently, including an all-copper hollow point bullet other than just a copper jacket. While there are many calibers with the +P designation, that is, a slightly more powerful round, in 9mm Luger, .38 Special, and .45 ACP, the +P results in about a 10% increase in pressure as compared to the .38 Auto and .45 Colt, which are substantially more. Sometimes being more powerful *doesn't mean* more effective. While most metal jackets are copper, some are made now of many other materials, including tin or brass jackets, or plated to resemble them, but, years ago, the actual brass bullets coated with Teflon such as the KTW mentioned above, among other designs, were outlawed due to their incredible penetration, but some of the newer ones are just jacketed hollow points, so we'll see where they go. No matter whether your ammo is a flat point, soft point, or hollow point, they are designed to increase in diameter after impact, where the hollow point actually delivers about 70% of its energy into the target due to the rapid expansion while slowing down as the body mass absorbs the delivered kinetic energy, preventing overpenetration; whereas ball ammunition (FMJ), like we use in the military, delivers about only 50% of its energy into the target and just may use the rest of it to find its way all the way through. We're purposely addressing these issues so you understand bullets and their operation for what we're leading into to better help you in the eventual selection of your carry or defensive guns and the best ammo for your own needs.

All bullets are designed to do a specific job, no matter what their design is, but their job is to always stop the bad guy!

Another factor in ammunition selection is bullet weight and velocity. Velocity is the speed of the bullet. While I got tired of reading Newton's laws of physics every time, someone had their own theory. Years ago, I used to have my own preference that I personally devised for my .44 Magnum in case I might get jumped by a bear while being out in the mountain wilderness. But as the time of year was fall, a bear had about 3½ inches of body fat at the surface, and many handgun bullets may not penetrate deep enough to damage the vitals properly, if at all, especially if they abruptly expand upon impact with the body fat and never actually reach the vitals. So I had my own system with 3 different bullet designs and loads for three different depths and capabilities, and then I'd repeat the same bullet sequence. To me, a KILLER intending to kill *me* with a gun might be more dangerous than hunting grizzly bear in the wilderness.

It's a known fact that a heavy bullet hitting a killer is going to create a heavy shock wave and give sufficient penetration. It is also known that a lighter bullet with a higher velocity will also have a heavy shock wave while giving sufficient penetration. The claims of the heavier bullet resulting in more foot pounds due to its weight can also be challenged by the same caliber, but a lighter bullet is pumped up to a higher velocity so that it equals the same foot pounds or even greater foot pounds than the heavy round (even in handgun ammunition). Either way, the velocity combined with foot pounds equals your kinetic energy that's delivered to the target. In a test where a .45 Winchester Magnum, which is a stretched version of the .45 ACP, was fired into Level IIIA body armor with two different rounds, the heavier bullet, a 350 grain load at 950 feet per second, failed to penetrate, while the lighter round of 260 grains at 1,250 feet per second completely penetrated the armor. While 1,250 feet per second seems a bit light on velocity for such a round to penetrate the IIIA body armor, which is supposed to resist a .44 Magnum at

1,430 feet per second, the armor was taped to a wood backing. Maybe that is why the round penetrated because the armor is designed to be cushioned by the body to allow the armor to do its job, but then the rounds used were round nose like FMJ or target ammo, so maybe this also, or both, contributed to the armor failure, which is claimed to stop a flat nose or hollow point. Obviously better armor is always better to have, even though the cost is higher since *we get* only *one unrecoverable mistake.* US Army research stated that decidedly, impact velocity is the most important factor in creating a bullet casualty. They demonstrated that it takes 170 feet per second for a ¼-inch diameter projectile to penetrate human skin and muscle tissue, not including clothing, and they say that very few wounds are caused by projectiles less than 500 feet per second (which is usually shrapnel) while most battlefield wounds are created by projectiles two and three times greater than that. Wounds created from low-impact velocities are cleaner and free of the so-called explosive effect, while medium-velocity wounds are more extensive with considerable tissue destruction with more explosive effects when conditions are favorable. High-impact velocities result in many so-called explosive wounds with a maximum of tissue destruction. Everyone argues about which one to use, rather than trying to rewrite the laws of physics, or gets out the scientific calculator or even confuses you. The way many buddies confuse each other, my best advice is to use the largest caliber bullet that you can properly handle and use heavy hollow point ammunition, at the highest velocity (delivering the highest amount of kinetic energy) at least until you've learned enough to decide for yourself, but make sure you check your *state laws* regarding illegal ammunition to make sure of what you're allowed to use. The easiest way to find out what ammo is legal is to ask which ammo is *illegal*, which leaves the rest available for your use. It sure is sad that if someone wants to kill us with whatever he decides to use, we're only allowed to *try* to prevent dying if we kill him with the proper bullet. So if a killer attacks and tries to kill us but we beat him to the gun, we better have the proper bullet because if they find that we have used the wrong one to save our life, according to the state laws, *we* go to jail for being lucky enough to survive. In all respect to those who insist on bullet weight as the most critical factor and the FBI considering the velocity (insignificant for handguns), "technology and test results over the years bring the velocity factor into the picture as very significant," but again, handguns with reduced barrel length solve the easy weapon draw problem but limit the velocity factor. In my .45 carry gun, I've been known to alternate different rounds in my magazine like I did in the cylinder of my .44 Magnum when I was hunting bear. If you're recoil-conscious, you could work up magazine loads; for example, the first round fired was a 230-grain lead hollow point at a speed of 900 feet per second and hitting with 415 foot pounds, which was slower than the second follow-up round with a 165-grain all-copper hollow point at 1,100 feet per second, hitting with 443 foot pounds with a third of 200 grains at 1,080 feet per second, hitting with 518 foot pounds. This might give you an advantage with the first and second hit reaching the KILLER at almost the same instant when microseconds count, allowing for a third shot if needed. But all three rounds were arranged according to the slight increase in recoil (velocity and weight) for each successive round, allowing for the fastest recovery between shots, so study the ammo box for factory specs, but a little math can clearly show where the heaviest round does not always produce the most recoil (or kinetic energy), but a combination of bullet weight and, again, the velocity of the round will determine this. If you find this microsecond advantage a bit hard to swallow, then you can advise those who make custom $3,000 + handguns designed to operate faster by using (lighter) hammers and other lighter parts in motion to throw their knowledge of the way things work out the window and offer them $50 for one of their finely tuned pieces of self-defense, but I assure you that they will certainly get a good laugh. One thing for certain is that surviving a lethal encounter is definitely going to require preparation of ½ real world and ½ science, and sometimes even the best on paper doesn't work in real life. If you are used to your gun and are not afraid of slight differences in recoil, you might wish to load the highest velocities first to strike your killer *before* he gets his shot off at you! Back to the disbelievers! A main advantage gained by the US Armed forces is the speed at which they execute their actions *effectively*, which means shutting down the enemy and winning (while living to tell the story). Every second counts even if we have to cheat by modifying our equipment or by loading the proper sequence in our ammo to *gain* that extra fragment of time! Remember one thing: the first bullet to hit its mark just may shut down the one coming back toward whoever fired it, whether it might be you or your killer. There's no such thing as cheating when it's life and death. We want to win by any means necessary! We don't want to hear your name on the news when they identify the bodies. So we certainly want to make sure we give him the *disadvantage* here rather than the advantage.

The ammunition that breaks apart by design upon contact with or passing through just about any building materials is called frangible. It is actually preferred by many people as a safety factor in their homes or apartments in the hopes of doing the maximum amount of damage quickly, providing it holds together long enough while it passes deep enough into the intended killer. It's not structurally sound enough to hold together to cause overpenetration, going completely through, which would then endanger more people behind the intended target. While this ammunition has a thin jacket and is designed to disintegrate upon contact with and not to penetrate any hard object to avoid going through the neighbors' house if you miss, it delivers 100% of its energy upon impact, but its penetrating depth and damage is very little, compared to personal defensive rounds. The frangible round might not even stop the threat and may be lacking in sufficient penetration. The other side of the situation might be a problem if your killer is pursuing you and hides behind anything for defensive cover, where a frangible round will disintegrate upon contact rather than going through the killer's cover and stopping *him like you need to* and might make *you* vulnerable to *his* counterattack while he doesn't care about who he hurts. And he's going to use the most lethal and deadly ammunition he has available regardless of any laws or prohibitions. It's important to understand that every round fired that does not hit the killer is 100% ineffective, but various types of ammo have their proper place and use, so make sure you have your thinking cap on when you devise your plan of defense. If frangible ammo catches your interest, make sure you study the different manufacturer's specifications and capabilities, which may vary no matter whether it's for a handgun or a rifle, so that you can determine the most suitable rounds for your needs. While there are also rifle rounds designed as frangible rounds, any non-frangible rifle round just may break apart anyway, including a military round since the velocities are upwards or above 2,000 feet per second, but it depends on what kind of materials it hits. Since non-frangible handgun bullets don't normally reach such high speeds, they may or may not break apart on impact, depending on their speed, their weight, their material, and their design and shape. Remember to study frangible before you buy it because anything *can* happen! Planning is required!

Effective Barrel Length versus Velocity

Although short snub-nosed handguns are used all the time, the velocity of the round fired from a snub nose (meaning, a very short barrel) is going to be minimal at best. The longer the barrel, the more the pressure builds; the pressure pushes the bullet toward the end of the barrel before it exits, giving you much higher velocities, but technically speaking, if you use a longer barrel, a rifle for example, the pressure and velocity will almost max out to the bullet's maximum capability at about 20 to 22 inches of barrel length, and it will start to add a reduced foot per second gain for every inch beyond the 22 inches. The heavier calibers will add less feet per second for each inch beyond the 22 inches than the lighter ones. This is most likely the reason why the military M16 had a 20-inch barrel, and the M60 machine gun and the minigun, which is an electric-driven Gatling gun, use a 22-inch barrel. Here is an example. When this test was done on .9 calibers ranging from .223 Remington to .460 Weatherby, the pressure increase in the .223 went in two-inch increments to +48 feet per second, then for 2 more inches, it only added +42, then +38, and so on, *averaging* a gain of only +21.75 feet per second per inch. Each of the heavier calibers showed a greater reduction in gain, and the .460 Weatherby added +36, then +27, and then +24, respectively, *averaging* a gain of only +15.12 feet per second per inch. The test was done only for the extended barrel lengths of up to 8 inches, so there will be a much greater drop-off beyond this figure. The final results of the testing showed that at 20 inches, the velocity started to change in transition, but once the barrel reached or exceeded 22 inches, the gain slowly diminished. So for most of our own personal use, the longer barrels are the most effective, but only up to 22 inches, and give excellent speed downrange. The US ARMY and the NAVY (I didn't leave out the Marines; they are also included in the Department of the Navy) have several sniper rifles in 7.62 × 51 among other calibers with 22-inch barrels. There are a few rifles with 24- to 26-inch barrels and even the .50 caliber BMG, which uses a 29-inch barrel, but it's a scaled-up round, making the increased barrel length similar in performance. Many military sniper rounds are hand loaded for maximum effectiveness in the particular firearm and barrel being used. All this technical information can be very well used to scale any firearm up to as large as you want, such as the 16-inch guns on a US Navy Battleship that can easily send their rounds downrange 24 miles away!

Every increase in barrel length will increase the velocity of the round as it builds pressure, but when it reaches 22 inches, it will start to fall off in its feet per second gain as the pressure starts to diminish at this point. The flash suppressors don't count in measuring the length of the barrel. The longer the barrel, the more accurate the result, but too much of barrel length will start to add undesired vibration and undesired results.

For a concealment gun, you have to make sure you're capable of concealing whatever gun you choose and able to draw it fast enough in an emergency. I say fast because his is probably already on its way, if not already facing you, so you have to not only catch up but beat him to the shot, so careful thought must be given to the actual barrel length. While handguns also give more velocity per inch of barrel length, it's important to remember that the real concern is they respectively give less velocity per inch for shortening the barrel length. I personally think 3.5

inches is the most ideal barrel length, but some guns are a bit longer, which is OK, and many guns are just a bit shorter, which could be OK too, providing you can use it properly. Many dozens of new gun models are being produced with 3-inch barrels, which will shoot fine out to 25 yards (with sufficient practice). But while they're not going to be very tight groups, hitting the target and/or bull's-eye will be good but should be practiced and refined. While I mention "out to 25 yards," it means your ability to hit the intended target at that range, *not* the bullet's actual ability, which may be thousands of yards (not to be confused with the bullet's effective range), depending on the caliber. So if you miss the target, there may be no way to tell where that bullet is going. Many people really don't realize how far a bullet actually travels. The reason you don't fire warning shots is because you may unintentionally kill an innocent person, and while you're busy firing the warning shot, the killer is firing a round *through* you, so your first shot must always be at the killer's center mass or your own choice of target, depending on the particulars. Remember that every shot you fire that doesn't hit your target diminishes your ammunition by a percentage taking 100 and dividing it by the number of rounds you have available. You're most probably going to be shooting within 21 feet, quite possibly 5 to 10 feet, or it might get scary and be within arm's reach, but you must decide on what you feel you should do and remember that *each and every situation is different* and might even involve two or more assailants instead of one—another reason for practice and learning, in addition to developing the necessary skills. No matter how many assailants there are, always avoid letting them get behind you. If you feel uncomfortable, you can step into any doorway and, while turning in a circle, draw your firearm to be ready, but only you will know whether it's called for. Many home invasions are by 2 to 4 thugs. I've been attacked by several at one time, several different times over the years with no indication that it was going to happen and no way to prepare for the immediate circumstances unfolding rather than to be prepared in advance in the event that such a situation might occur.

Last week, while I was out on the range shooting a course of silhouette targets with the pictures of bad guys with assorted guns in their hands pointed at me, there was a guy shooting the course with a 5-inch barreled Colt .45 semiautomatic 1911 pistol. He was drawing it and getting a confirmed kill shot faster than I was, and I had my 3-inch barrel .45, lightweight 1911. During discussion, he said he was practicing the draw for the past 7 years steady. That's dedication in wanting to survive. While we were on the clock, he was a half second faster than me with a 2-inch longer barrel and a much heavier gun, so it goes to show you that practice enough *with (your) equipment* and you will develop the necessary skills. Even though it had more barrel length and weight, he desired maximum accuracy and velocity for distance. It also shows that if he were the bad guy, I might be dead in a real lethal encounter because that half-second advantage he had might have placed the shot into the central nervous system, shutting me down completely and saving *his* own life, even if he was the bad guy! Skills and experience definitely outweigh the lack of knowledge and the inability to perform on demand. Would you feel comfortable if a nurse was going to fill in for a doctor who called in sick and she was going to perform your open-heart surgery to fill in for his absence? Some people may laugh and disregard microseconds, such as a few hundred feet per second in a faster bullet as insignificant, combining this micro-advantage with other factors such as the actual speed in your ability to make a coordinated effort to draw and place a kill shot. The proper tuning of your gun might allow it to function a bit faster and a little more accurate than the thug's gun. Due to your carefully perfected improvements, it just might add up to enough time to total a full-second *or two* advantage in a real-life encounter, most probably ensuring your success of survival (if you hit your target). The whole encounter is over in seconds, so cheat as much as you can. Several policemen have died due to their inability to reload their revolver as quickly as the killer's semiautomatic pistol. Do whatever you feel proper for *your* protection and don't worry about what other people might think about all your preparation. Otherwise, what's the use of even having your own thoughts? You should practice until you can hit your target, again and again and again. They can laugh all they want about technical differences and the tuning of your gun while you know that by accumulating up to a few seconds in elapsed time through a responsive sequence of proper moves, ammunition (and/ or custom parts) will most likely put the other guy down, lying on the ground (being the loser), who might have been one of those who initially laughed at such things too. We get to lose only once! Remember that failure is not an option! Popular gun magazines on the newsstand make it a big deal if someone can make a fast draw with a personal defensive carry gun in .6 seconds, but *if, in addition to their draw*, they had to reach into concealment, under the cover of their jacket or shirt to expose and get their gun out, then they made an aimed (and successful) killing hit on a target in .6 seconds. It would be something to be a real bragging issue other than to be prepared for the timer and just to draw his gun from an open and unconcealed holster, which is really quite easy to do without having to follow through and make a *real* shot. You don't want to develop overconfidence in your abilities; you need to practice the way you will carry your gun, whether from under a shirt, jacket, or wherever you decide to put it, but keep in mind you might want the very same spot for concealment if you wear different holsters or clothing or even a different gun because it's not a good feeling to reach for your gun and discover you're carrying it in another spot today! Be coordinated and prepared!

There are numerous arguments as to whether a hollow point will expand sufficiently from a short barrel, but there are also bullets designated as SB on the box for short barrel; that is, they are designed to perform from a short barrel. So if you're not sure, again, I would avoid the argument and move ahead with your hollow points for now, remembering their required legality within your state and laws. No matter what caliber you actually use, the diameter of the permanent wound cavity is already very helpful, but any bullet expansion at all improves it by that much more. Another thing that always comes to conversation is what type of clothing the bullet might have to go through before the bullet actually gets into the KILLER. Even a .22 caliber short, the weakest of your bullet, will easily go through clothing other than body armor. Many people misunderstand this issue, thinking that the clothing reduces the power of the round, but it certainly doesn't have much of an effect here. In testing the effects of clothing, several layers of denim, 3 and 4 to be exact, are attached to ballistic gel, which is used for studying the bullet's effectiveness in comparison to body flesh; the fragments of denim were pulled all the way through the ballistic gel with the projectile.

Great moments of distraction, including being on the phone, are ideal times for kidnappings, carjacking, and more, so beware because it could cause your death!

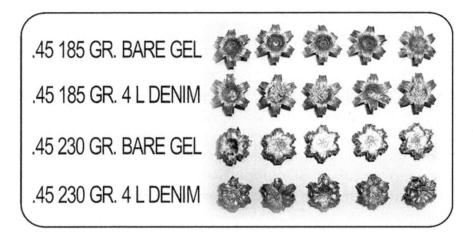

.45 185 GR. BARE GEL

.45 185 GR. 4 L DENIM

.45 230 GR. BARE GEL

.45 230 GR. 4 L DENIM

Notice the second and fourth rows horizontally were shot through four layers of denim and still performed as expected.

The real concern with clothing is not whether a bullet will go through the clothes (because it will), but the concern is whether the clothing material, no matter what type of clothing it is, will clog the hole in the nose of a hollow point and cause the hollow point to do an inferior job of expanding, or not even expanding, or changing the expansion without stopping the KILLER, but you can never establish the exact results, depending on all the variables in your encounter. So do the best with what's available. If the clothing filled the hole in the hollow point completely before coming into contact with flesh and body mass, then it has the potential to give more than desired penetration *as if there were no holes to initiate the beginning of the expansion.* So this is why there are always questions regarding the clothing issue. Many hunting rounds have hollow cavities in the nose, even shotgun slugs and some rounds with a plastic insert to cover the hole which disintegrates the insert before or on impact while some may blow out. I would ignore the clothing factor and just move ahead with a reliable hollow point, which is easy enough to compare manufacturer's specifications. Focus your attention on your handgun and the ability to use it properly and effectively while at the same time being safe, and the personal defense ammunition designed by engineers specifically for this purpose will do its job. Remember, if you *must* use a smaller caliber, a well-placed shot in the proper place is much more of a critical and beneficial issue than the inferior caliber or how effective your round actually is upon impact since you've established that it's all you're capable of doing. It's absolutely essential for proper shot placement, or you die! A .22 caliber round in the vitals as compared to a .45 or .50 caliber that missed the target is definitely the winner, but it all depends on you. A .22 can definitely kill, and we have history and statistics to prove it. Once you know how it all works, there's nobody to blame other than YOU if you fail to prepare to defend yourself, but remember that personal defense ammunition is available in most calibers from .22 and above.

Notice the variations in design between these three hollow points! The one on the left has an empty cavity for expansion. The one in the center has a plastic ball inserted into the hollow point where the round nose helps it function in semiautomatics. The right has a plastic insert that blows out when fired.

What Happens When a Gun Is Fired?

One of the biggest misunderstandings in firearms is the way they work. Although it's clearly understood by some people, so many others argue about what happens first—the recoil or the bullet leaving the barrel. It's like trying to solve the problem of what came first—the chicken or the egg. Now that you understand some of the way bullets work, there's something else, but we want to set our knowledge of physics aside, especially any reference to bullet weight or firing in a vacuum since this is something that we will never be doing. Heavier bullets over distance drop more (due to gravity), or, let's say, it drops faster than a lighter bullet in the atmosphere. This rule applies even if two different bullets of the same caliber and powder charge are used, but one bullet is heavier (more grains in weight). In addition, you must also understand that with everything else being identical, the heavier bullet will travel a shorter distance than the lighter bullet. This is physics, but to compensate for the additional weight, a heavier round may have more or a different type of propellant to maintain its power of flight sufficiently.

Normal Trajectory

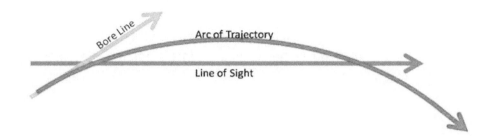

This arc of trajectory is to make you understand that the further away from the target, the higher the arc and mid-range trajectory are. Different bullet designs and weights have different trajectories.

The angle of the bullet in flight from it being fired to its impacting the ground downrange is called the trajectory, but it is pretty much negligible for (most) handgun defensive shooting, especially due to the majority of it being at such close range. A bullet *fired* horizontally and one dropped from the same height, both at the same exact time and both of the same weight, will hit the ground simultaneously, even though one is accelerated at a great speed. Since so many people didn't believe this, to confirm it for a full-scale testing, the Myth-Busters TV show started at a firing range and used a .45 caliber pistol to measure the distance a bullet would travel before hitting the ground. Since the ground there was not leveled, they set up a second test at Fort Mason. Once they had properly fine-tuned their mechanism to fire and drop the bullets at the same time, they found that the two bullets landed within 39.6 milliseconds of each other (thousandths of a second). Commenting that this difference was less than the duration of one film frame (shot at 24 frames per second) and thus short enough for the human eye not to notice, they declared the myth as (confirmed to be true) they both hit the ground simultaneously (considered to be at the same time). The 39.6 milliseconds may be negligible to account for the reaction time of the mechanical devices used for firing and dropping the bullets.

While we'll mention more for a proper understanding, firearms typically show a rise in the trajectory generally plotted on a graph due to the bullet's flight path. In reference to the line of sight, many people believe a bullet flies straight from the gun to the target, but it doesn't. Many others believe that bullets rise, but bullets don't rise; they drop. Let me explain. Bullets are of different size, shape, mass, and surface area, which is all aerodynamically affected by the air resistance surrounding them. Once fired, all bullets accelerate with a steady loss in their elevation and speed, eventually hitting the ground at its maximum distance due to the gradual loss in velocity and the power of gravity pulling it down.

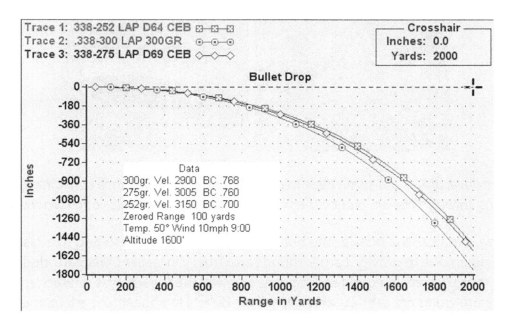

In the chart above, it shows three different bullets being fired out to 2,000 yards, but as you can see, the lightest projectile had the least bullet drop while each of the heavier bullets dropped more respectively. While this chart is only for your understanding, the trajectory of various bullets might be considerably different on the graph, showing a wide variation in the trajectory curve.

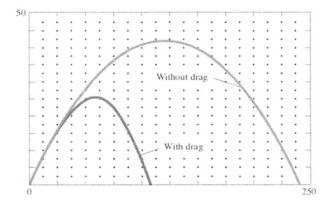

In the trajectory chart above, it shows that the bullet flying through the air develops air resistance, which has effects on the projectile's flight.

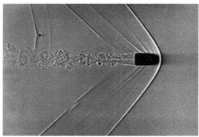 

In the images above, NASA did some tests to determine the air resistance called drag on the effects of a bullet flying through the air. Notice the pointed projectile flies easier and is more aerodynamic.

All things being identical, the heavier the bullet, the slower it goes, resulting in a faster drop and a shorter range, again due to gravity. Larger rounds are usually in larger brass cartridges to hold more propellant for more power and greater distances. The way the trajectory is referenced on charts and the way the firearm works are actually what causes the bullets to appear to rise to some degree due to the effects of the firearm firing the cartridge. This is affected by the propellant which is a gunpowder charge in combination with the bullet weight and the actual velocity, so all different bullets will give different results, and if you use a different caliber, then you have to refigure all the rounds again for that particular caliber because different weights and velocities will perform differently.

Firearms have a chamber and a barrel. The chamber completely surrounds and contains the cartridge containing the bullet, and the bullet is pointed to the only opening available, down the bore of the barrel. When the gun is fired and the firing pin strikes the primer, the primer ignites the explosive powder, causing a sudden burning of the powder and converting it into a gas that is rapidly expanding into the containment of the bullet cartridge. The extreme pressure building behind the back of the bullet forces the outer walls of the cartridge to expand by several thousandths of an inch, pressing the cartridge walls against the chamber walls to contain the extreme pressure, but it also makes the open path down the bore of the barrel its weakest point. Due to the extreme pressure still building, this energy forces the bullet out of its crimp and out of the cartridge, and as the pressure works against the back of the bullet to start pushing it through the bore and down the barrel, it also exerts this pressure against the back of the cartridge case in the opposite direction (a counteracting force). This initiates the very beginning of the recoil. Every action has an equal and opposite reaction. As these two opposing forces work internally inside the gun (called internal ballistics), they cause the firearm barrel to start an upward rise at the muzzle end and a downward thrust at the opposite end of the firearm while pivoting in a rotation at the point where the hands and wrists grip the firearm due to the firearm being above the hands and the axial rotation of the wrist. It is this counteracting force against the back of the cartridge case from the momentum that is driving the bullet down the bore of the barrel that eventually causes the recoil. As the bullet is traveling further down the length of the bore, the momentum in an upward rotation is raising the muzzle (muzzle rise) until the bullet finally exits and the gas is exhausted from the muzzle which causes the recoil kick or jolt (like a jet action driving the firearm toward the shooter), which then thumps you on the shoulder or handgrips. Once the bullet leaves the barrel, the technological term for study then becomes *external ballistics*, between the barrel and the target.

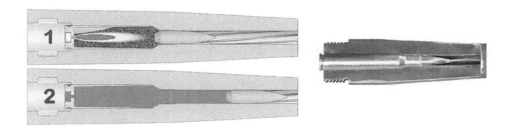

1. *The firing pin impacts the primer and sends a flash into the gunpowder which ignites in an enclosed cartridge assembly.*
2. *The burning gunpowder in a confined space builds extreme pressures, and, while the pressure expands, it forces the bullet out of the cartridge assembly and down the barrel. If there was no opening in the barrel for the bullet to escape the pressures, such as a blockage, the chamber or barrel would literally explode. See the cutaway view of chamber on right.*

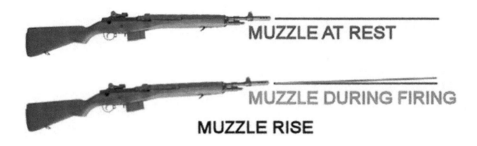

The level line indicates the axis of the bore without reference to sighting in or trajectory. While there is generally very little muzzle rise, the raised line indicates the rise at the muzzle when you fire the weapon. When you use sights of any kind, the level line will be elevated at an angle to illustrate compensating for bullet drop.

Once the bullet hits the target, the technical information then becomes terminal ballistics, that is, what actually happens to the target by this particular bullet. As the bullet is traveling down the bore during the period in which the barrel is lifting, when it exits the barrel, it will strike the target at a point above the point where the barrel was actually pointed when the trigger was pulled. This does have an effect on the striking point of the bullet since only *a minute of barrel lift*—(1/60 of one degree) known as arc minute but commonly referred to for firearms as minute of angle or MOA—will change the impact point by 1.047 inches at 100 yards. One MOA is actually 1.0471975511966 but most times rounded to 1 inch for fast calculations and always referred to at 100 yards as a standard rule. For a 1-MOA rifle, this small deviation from the barrel's original point of aim, down the centerline or axis of the barrel, would only measure to be a muzzle rise of .005820 inches from a 20-inch barrel if the bullet traveled a straight path, but, with all firearms, the bullet exits the barrel during the muzzle rise, and after the bullet leaves the barrel, the muzzle rise continues while the pressure is then exhausted at the muzzle. So you get the rest or the majority of the muzzle rise and recoil, but the bullet has most probably already hit the target and you're trying to physically recover for the next shot. The figures used above will actually be more in actual rise due to bullet drop and will vary according to the specific round used but are only given to show that it doesn't take much movement at all to change the point of impact, especially over distance where the difference is magnified. To compensate for this, the sights are calibrated or sighted or adjusted (called zeroed) to impact at the desired point of reference on the target.

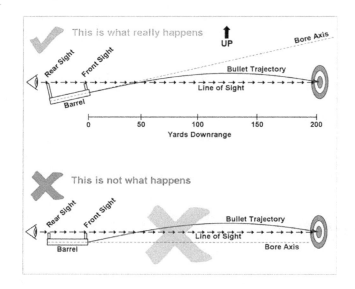

A shooter can easily readjust their rifle scope by measuring the distance in inches the bullet hole is from the desired impact point and adjusting the scope that many MOA in the same direction, but some scopes such as target shooting scopes have adjustments in 1/8 or 1/4 MOA clicks. One eighth minute of angle is about one eighth inch at 100 yards or one inch at 800 yards. This does NOT mean that just because you adjust the scope for a specific distance, the bullet will hit there; the scope adjustment is specifically dependent upon the caliber and round capability, which you need to know before extended distance shooting or making scope adjustments (and your knowledge of what you're doing).

While a firearm capable of 1-MOA will shoot a group of 1 inch at 100 yards, one capable of 2-MOA will give a 2-inch group at 100 yards. For a firearm that shoots *under* 1-MOA, the firearms manufacturers often use the term *sub-MOA* or target barrels claimed to be .25 MOA *capability* (not to be confused with ¼ MOA adjustments) on your scope. Firearm MOA capability and scope MOA capability are two opposites; that is, you want less MOA capability for the rifle but more MOA capability for the scope, which means sufficient adjustment positions or clicks to refine your point of impact over great distances due to bullet drop. Some scopes are suitable for shooting close or far, but know what you have. Obviously, higher quality gets better results, which is the very reason some firearms cost more, but different calibers and barrel lengths also affect this. The longer the bullet is in the bore, the more time the recoil has an effect on the hand and the greater degree of barrel swing or rotation (muzzle rise). If you fire a heavier bullet, the heavier bullet will require greater pressures to build enough energy to push it through the bore, but it will be slower than the lighter faster bullet and will stay in the barrel longer. The heavier bullet will result in more of an upward barrel swing in rotation, striking higher on the target (within a reasonable distance before gravity pulls it down), but a lighter bullet will actually impact lower due to less muzzle rise and the sights being above the axis of the bore. This is exactly the opposite of what you would expect using common knowledge. So bullets don't rise, but the simultaneous rotating action (muzzle rise) of barrel up and stock or grips down places the centerline or axis of the barrel at a higher point by the time the bullet exits the bore. Studying a graph on bullet trajectory will show the slight increase into an arc with its highest point in the arc called mid-range trajectory and a drop-off at the other end, where the barrel's upward rotation is the actual cause of the slight upward motion or bullet rise. But the drop-off is due to gravity pulling the weight of the bullet back down while it's running out of velocity due to air resistance (drag or ballistic coefficient) and losing its power of flight, so it drops to the distant target or eventually to the ground. To simplify the ballistic coefficient, it is the ratio of the bullet's sectional density to its coefficient of form, which directly affects its ability to overcome air resistance in flight due to its weight and shape. The air density has a great effect on the air resistance, being denser at sea level as compared to less dense at higher elevations. The higher the BC number, in comparing .12 to .23, or .454 to .550, the greater the number, means the greater the ability to overcome air resistance. If you buy a specific manufacturer's ammunition, make sure of understanding their coding for the BC indicating greater or less ability which may be of the manufacturer's own reference. Ballistic coefficient generally increases in number to coincide with increased weight, but it sometimes changes up or down on some bullets of the same weight due to their physical design aerodynamically, so two bullets of the same caliber and even the same weight may have a different BC. In addition, in selecting BC, it is best to consider it to be caliber-specific due to the slight variations such as a larger caliber having less BC than a smaller caliber on a particular round. So for each and every caliber, you need to reassess and start over at zero, looking for the best one. This also applies to handgun bullets, so always reassess from rifles to handguns and for every caliber. Different bullet sizes and powder charges (easily identified by the size of the caliber and cartridge case) control the trajectory and downrange power—the reason for why a hunter or military sniper may have several rifles in his collection due to different capabilities. Further, while the propellant continues to expand and the energy pushes the bullet down the bore, as the bullet exits the barrel at the muzzle, you get a visual (muzzle flash), especially in low lighting due to the burning propellant, which finally relieves its pressure from the barrel, and you also get an audible report or bang. Military rifles have a flash suppressor mounted on the muzzle to try to hide the source of flash reference as much as possible when firing in combat so the enemy cannot easily locate you visually (not to be confused with the movies where they *increase* the flash for visual effects).

The Clock System

For shooting purposes, we're going to assume the same coordinates for incoming wind that the military uses to call many things that happen according to the simple face on a clock, which is otherwise called the clock system but not to be confused with the 24-hour clock time reference or the MGRS (military grid reference system), which are different animals. Think of yourself standing dead at the center of the clock with all twelve numbers around you in a circle. A target is said to be at the twelve o'clock position since it is directly in front of you; this would then make directly behind you the six o'clock position, then 90 degrees to your right would be the three o'clock, and 90 degrees to your left the nine o'clock position, and so forth, while using the entire numerical clock face for reference. Further, if you had an incoming right wind at about 45 degrees from the 12, it would correspond to the coordinates on a clock face between 1 and 2 or otherwise called the 1.30 position. Similarly, it would be called the 10.30 position if it were a left wind and directly overhead would then be twelve o'clock high, six o'clock low, and so forth while the three o'clock and the nine o'clock positions will be in exactly the same place. But for wind reference for shooting, we generally don't need to consider anything such as high or low. So if you refer to a point between 2 and 3, it would be 2.30 or between 9 and 10, a 9.30 position.

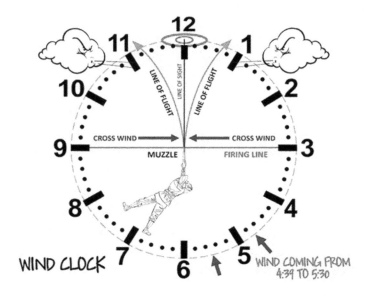

Note the wind clock for shooting purposes. With the wind coming in from 4.39 to 5.30, a 6-mile-an-hour wind would be considered a 3-mile-an-hour wind due to the angle having half the effect on the projectile. The target is always considered to be at twelve o'clock, no matter where it is, and you are always in the center of the clock where the firing line is. Winds from the left blow the bullet to the right, and winds from the right blow the bullet to the left.

Wind Deflection (Wind Drift)

While we've explained the way the firearm and bullet work together in elevation, the bullet is also affected from each side of its path by crosswinds at any given distance, called wind deflection. For serious shooting, you also have to understand what crosswind deflection is and how to correct where your shot will actually go, so if there's a wind coming from the right of your muzzle at 90 degrees, it is called a right wind, and from 90 degrees to the left, it's called a left wind, but the wind coming in from different angles and directions all have different effects on the bullet. For proper correction of a projectile which is being forced laterally from side to side by a crosswind and deviating off what would otherwise be its normal flight path, there are formulas to assist in trying to decipher the effects of the crosswind against a certain round, considering the power of the round or the velocity and the caliber and the weight of the projectile while determining the wind speed against the amount of surface area of the projectile in flight.

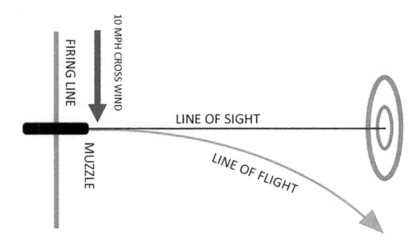

The crosswinds at the muzzle causes the bullet to deflect from side to side along the direction of the wind. The further the shot, the greater the deflection.

We'll also be addressing and working into MILLs soon, but we're going to touch on the subject briefly. Competitive champion shooters repeatedly prove the established fact that a crosswind of each mile per hour creates a 10-inch drift in the bullet's path at 1,000 yards or a 3-mph crosswind, causing the bullet to impact 30 inches to the side of the bull's-eye at 1,000 yards. One shooter consistently puts the bullet in a 10-inch circle. A US Army sniper using a 7.62 caliber and a crosswind of 2 to 2.5 miles per hour put 7 rounds by rapid-fire into a somewhat small group in the center of the bull's-eye at 1,000 yards by using a ¼ MIL wind correction. So for your knowledge, 1 MIL = 3.6 inches at 100 yards × 10 = 36 inches at 1,000 yards / 4 (4 is a constant) = 9 inches, and dividing it by 10, (1,000 yards divided by 10) equaled .9 inches per hundred yards, making the 1 mile per hour wind deflection per hundred yards between the two shooters within .15 hundredths of an inch apart from each other's results at 100 yards and very similar results at 1,000 yards, which makes the 1-inch drift per mile per hour at 100 yards somewhat true (in general), but the caliber, the bullet weight, and the velocity will all alter these results, and there are mathematical formulas used to calculate the shot based on the actual wind drift. Although the 1-inch rule is well known to those who shoot at such distances, everything beyond 500 yards changes the constant values in several formulas used, but it's always nice to see it happen and to have actual facts to back it up, and while it takes 6+ weeks for Sniper School, 25% of those being trained to understand all these effects fail to succeed. If you're uncertain on the exact wind estimation, it's best to error by estimating less wind speed since so many people have so much difficulty estimating the *actual* wind speed. The further the shot, the more critical the crosswinds are in having an effect on the bullet impact to either side of the bull's-eye. Fortunately, manufacturers have come to our rescue and sell small inexpensive pocket-sized wind meters that will sample the wind and give an immediate digital readout. While theory always claims that a heavier bullet will be affected less than a lighter one by any crosswind (wind deflection), it would be easy to test if both of their physical sizes were the same, but since this can't happen, due to the heavier weight, there's more surface area. In a test of .12 calibers, the difference in results between the best and the worst was only 2.5 inches at 300 yards. The .458 Winchester Magnums with a 500-grain bullet drifted twice as much at 300 yards as any of the other rounds studied. While the larger bullet has more surface area for the wind to act on, it deflected it more than the others, but these rounds varied in velocity, so even a large heavy bullet may be deflected more than others if it's traveling at a slower speed. The final results proved that even though the heavier weight has more surface area, and the heavier bullet can overcome air resistance better than a lighter one, the *fastest* bullet allowed less time for wind and gravity to work against the bullet in flight. The slower the bullet becomes, the more the wind deflection works against it. It's important to remember that while warmer temperatures offer less air resistance to the projectile, this makes the bullet faster and less sensitive to the crosswinds. It takes experience and knowledge to properly estimate your crosswind deflection, and normal statistics are based on the wind coming from a 90-degree angle to either side, so if you have a wind coming from any other angle, say 45 degrees or so, it would be wise to use half the estimated wind speed. For better understanding right winds, if coming from the three o'clock position or anywhere from about the two o'clock to the four o'clock position, we would consider it to be of a full-value wind, and the same from about the 8 to 10 left wind. While headwinds may slow the round and tailwinds speed them up, headwinds from the 11.30 to 12.30 and tailwinds from the 5.30 to 6.30 give no value, while right winds from the 12.30 to the two o'clock and the four o'clock to the 5.30 or left winds from the ten o'clock to 11.30 or 6.30 to eight-o'clock would be half-value winds; that is, if you had a 4-mile-per- hour wind coming from a half-value direction, we would divide it by 2 and use a 2-mile wind other than 4 because they have only half the deflecting effect on the bullet in flight from that particular angle.

Bullets are designed differently, and some called boat tails (BT) have a more rounded base of the bullet, which makes it more aerodynamic than the others that have a flat base. Further, pointed bullets cause less drag than rounded bullets, and rounded bullets cause less drag than flat-nose bullets. If you have 3 separate but identical cartridges, all containing the same primer, the same powder, and the same caliber bullet, but of three different bullet designs, the sectional density and the weight of the bullet are identical in each, but the ballistic coefficient is different; the greater or highest number will be your best choice. Based on the manufacturer's data and the test results above, I would simply combine them both. If one of the three mentioned of the same weight has a greater velocity, I would definitely choose it. If putting out wind flags to practice, estimating wind speed and direction, it's very important to be sure every single flag is of the very same material and cut exactly the same in size and proportion so they are all equal in weight, balance, and wind resistance, which will allow the most accurate determinations with all flags being identical. Purchasing wind flags manufactured identically would be the best bet.

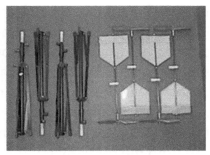

Two types of wind flags and a pocket-sized wind meter in the center to estimate the wind speed.

Trajectory

If you zero the sights or scope for a certain bullet at a specific distance or range, if you then try to shoot an identical bullet at a longer range at the longer distance, the effects of gravity will cause the bullet to impact lower than it is sighted for, so you have to visually, with no mechanical adjustments, lift and aim your sight or crosshairs higher in elevation vertically above the bull's-eye (called holdover) to compensate so that when it is fired, the bullet will drop to impact the target at the desired point. Holdover and aim points become specially important as ranges increase while shots displaced vertically are referenced as shot dispersion.

Drop in MOA vs Zero Range for 7mm Rem Mag

	Zero Range			
	100	200	275	300
100	0.0			
200	1.2	0.0		
300	3.0	1.9	0.5	0.0
400	5.2	4.0	2.6	2.1
500	7.5	6.3	5.0	4.5
600	10.0	8.9	7.5	7.0
700	12.8	11.6	10.2	9.7

The custom ballistics card is made and laminated while being attached to the scope cover for fast visual indication of bullet weight, yards, MOA, and bullet drop to eliminate the guesswork when needed quickly. The shooter should have placed the card on the inside of the scope cover, facing him when open, for bullet drop at various ranges. Always think and rethink your planning!

Since most hunters are not mathematicians to try to calculate bullet trajectory, many skillful shooters and hunters are knowledgeable in sighting in for a particular bullet and the way trajectory works, especially for that particular round. They often tend to sight in (called zeroing), for a longer range, say two hundred yards, knowing that the same bullet will impact approximately 1 inch higher at 100 yards due to its trajectory, but doing the same in reverse *might* get you on paper (I said *might*). It requires refining due to variations unless you carefully calibrate your scope, which we'll address soon. A round capable of such a slight rise for an extended range before it finally falls severely is generally referred to as a flat shooter; that is, the arc from the muzzle to the target is much smaller or flatter than other calibers. The further away the target, the higher the muzzle has to be when the gun is fired, but even though the trajectory might only be an inch or two different within the first 100 to 200 yards, it may be a drastic change at 300. While I used to prefer a scope zeroed for 200, sometimes more, I used to zero my all-purpose rifle for 200 yards, then aim, and shoot dead at the bull's-eye at 100 yards and measure the distance from the bull's-eye to the bullet hole, and this is my mid-range trajectory. So I was always prepared in knowing the bullet rise at 100, but it's important to know that the further the distance you zero your rifle for, the higher the mid-range trajectory between the muzzle and the zero distance. This is because of the greater arc. This is where a flat shooter gains in popularity. Each caliber, propellant, and bullet weight in combination with its barrel length all gives different results. An example using a .30 caliber carbine with an 18-inch barrel, shooting a 110-grain bullet at 1,990 feet per second and zeroed for 100 yards, will impact the target at -12.8 inches at 200 yards and will impact at -48.5 inches at 300 yards. Bullets continue to drop due to gravity while the air resistance and gravity combined cause the bullet's velocity to gradually diminish to 0, so the further the bullet gets from the muzzle, the more velocity it loses while gravity is still pulling the bullet down, so looking at a chart for the bullet trajectory, it shows a continuous drop in flight from muzzle to target. This bullet drop is not to be confused with reading a graph showing a particular bullet trajectory where it shows -1.5 inches at the start or at the muzzle. This -1.5 shown at the start is a figure used, assuming you have an optically scoped firearm, and the muzzle is -1.5 inches in reference to or below the line of sight through the crosshairs of the scope and accounts for the centerline or axis of the bore of the barrel being 1.5 inches below the centerline of the scope where the crosshairs meet, the line of sight or *your aim point*. This is NOT a -1.5-inch drop in the bullet's trajectory from the muzzle. This same reference may be written as Sight-Above-Bore (in.) +1.5, that is, sighted from a scope +1.5 inches above the bore centerline. Rifles and guns will generally have a similar designation of -.8 on a chart in reference to their iron sights; that is, the center of the bore is 0.8 inches below the sight picture. Manufacturers may differ!

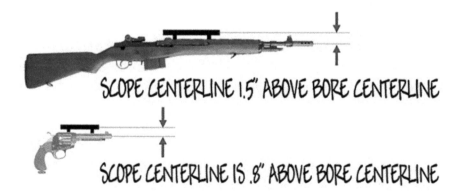

SCOPE CENTERLINE 1.5" ABOVE BORE CENTERLINE

SCOPE CENTERLINE IS .8" ABOVE BORE CENTERLINE

Although most firearms will have a predictable and comparable trajectory based on the round used, each individual firearm will have its own variations that affect the point of impact (its accuracy), no matter whether it's a handgun or rifle, depending on manufacturing techniques and tolerances which may be several thousandths of an inch in difference here and there as compared to the engineer's required design measurement specifications on the blueprint. But it's close enough to function safely and pass inspection. These are the very reason you have sub-MOA, 1-MOA, and 2-MOA firearms due to tolerance differences, including the reason for custom parts and barrels from after-market suppliers. This is also why sometimes you might buy a firearm right out of the box that drives tacks, so to speak, while some don't. Another reason to understand is, cheaply manufactured guns are not necessarily held to close tolerances as long as they work good enough to pass *the manufacturer's own allowances* and increase production. They may be intentionally manufactured cheap without regard for accuracy or functionability, hence the term *Saturday night specials*. When the so-called tack driver was made (meaning, it could hit the head of a tack at shooting distances), figuratively speaking, the tolerances were right on or very close to specifications called for. Due to the slight differences in accuracy between identical firearms and major differences in bullets and their trajectory from different rounds, this is why it is always recommended to practice with the round you will be shooting with, hunting with, or carrying for self-defense. KNOW YOUR GUN AND KNOW THE ROUND YOU WILL BE SHOOTING. If you bought 3 of the same make and model guns which are identical in every respect, the accuracy of each one may or may not be much of a difference. In addition, manufacturers that downgrade their firearms such as grade 1, grade 2, and so forth for the very same gun on the assembly line due to actual gun quality and how close the tolerances are at the time of inspection send the grade 1s to firearm and sporting goods stores, and the lower grades get sent to the discount-type stores. This could mean the difference between a sub-MOA and a 2-MOA capability or even more in the same design and model firearm and actually being sold within a few dollars of each other at two different stores according to the manufacturer's suggested retail price. Custom gun makers make all grade 1 firearms. Professional shooters sometimes even try to enhance their grade 1 firearm to try to improve accuracy or functionability. You will never be disappointed for buying a little bit better, but you will certainly curse yourself repeatedly for not buying good enough! So the reason people buy after-market custom parts and barrels is because they are made to exact tolerances, offering better accuracy, and maybe made out of more superior materials than the factory would normally use for a high-production gun on an assembly line in an effort to keep their costs down, and the improved tolerance and materials may even come with other enhancements or modifications that would otherwise be too costly to consider on a production line where they don't necessarily think they might need such improved accuracy or the extra work to keep the tolerances so close to design specs because then they couldn't get enough sales for an *average* firearm due to having to charge above average or higher prices. Personally, if I'd taken the time and the effort to set up and manufacture firearms, I'd make nothing but quality grade #1 and please my valued customers while building the reputation in business for a better quality firearm. I do tend to complain to top-notch manufacturers who even made a marketing decision to eliminate the iron sights on their fine rifles to save a buck because I loved the rifle and wanted to buy one, but their marketing department saved them a whole couple of dollars by eliminating the iron sights and lost the sale of such rifle at a few thousand dollars because personally, I won't buy anybody's rifle with no iron sights available, if they were not even available as an option.

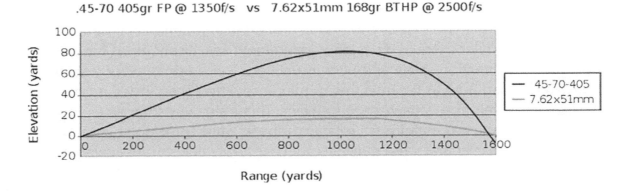

.45-70 405gr FP @ 1350f/s   vs   7.62x51mm 168gr BTHP @ 2500f/s

Notice the comparison between two calibers, the 45-70 and the 7.62 × 51. The firearm shooting the heavier 405-grain bullet has to be zeroed with the rifle muzzle pointed much higher to reach the same point on the target 1600 yards away. All calibers and bullet weights vary in their trajectory. Compared to the 45-70, the 7.62 × 51 would be considered a flat shooter.

Barrel Twist and Barrel Whip (Not the Rifling!)

When studying rifles to select one for your shooting hobby, or hunting, or whatever the need may be, "we're always concerned with the accuracy, no matter what we're going to do." Target rifles are made to specifications with very close or tight tolerances including the chamber. A couple of items we haven't mentioned yet directly concern the barrel of your firearm, which means it affects the accuracy. While everyone is always concerned with the type of steel the barrel is made from, generally looking for the more suitable material to hold up internally, everything comes into concern such as the rifling, the chamber, and the crown of the barrel, which all affect the accuracy of the fired round. While we understand that the way the rifling works is by the internal spiral controlling the bullet's path through the bore, we also have what is called *barrel* twist, which is the counteracting force trying to twist the material of the barrel in the opposite direction of the rifling, as if trying to untwist it, under extreme pressures as the bullet travels the length of the bore. This causes excess vibration throughout the length of the barrel as the bullet rides through the bore while the bullet holds the pressure back behind it and causes another effect called barrel whip where the actual length of the barrel flexes momentarily through its length while the pressure is held behind the bullet and snaps back when the bullet exits the bore, exhausting the trapped gas which causes more undesired vibration. The *barrel twist* (NOT the rifling or the twist rate of the rifling), but the steel barrel attempting to flex in a counteracting direction of the rifling due to the trapped pressure behind the traveling bullet, in addition to causing barrel whip, the barrel takes on a momentary slightly bowed or arced shape, again due to the pressure, both have an effect on the stability of the bullet being fired which directly affects the accuracy of the projectile in flight. Heavier barrels are used to try to overcome these problems, such as a varmint rifle with the heavier barrel, even though it shoots a somewhat small caliber, but heavy barrels will help overcome such difficulty in all calibers.

Mil-Dot and Minute of Angle

Clearing up the confusion and the myths!

Some scopes are made with dots equally spaced in increments vertically and horizontally on the crosshairs. This system was originally developed for the US Marines and is used by the military for range estimation, trajectory correction, and wind deflection correction. While they are called MIL-DOT scopes, they are referred to as MIL, and the term is not an abbreviation used to define military, but it is in reference to the MILLIRADIAN. While there are oval or round dots for MIL-DOT reticles, they are made using either the round or the oval on a specific reticle and they are not intermixed, so the scope will either have one or the other. Neither one is superior to the other, but the round dots are the most widely preferred and used by the military and law enforcement. So that's what we're going to refer to.

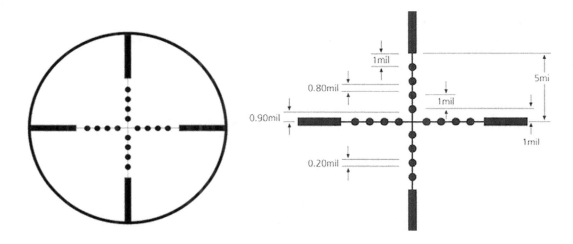

The Mil-Dot reticle above. The assorted measurements are shown on the right, but the distance between the dots from center to center is all you need to worry about unless you're very dedicated to your shooting.

Angular Mills are used for this purpose, and the scopes are referred to with the milliradian. While there are originally 6,283.19 milliradian to a 360-degree circle, the military decided that to use such figures for targeting purposes. The math would be too complicated so they shrank the value of the milliradian for military small arms ballistic purposes to 6,400 to a 360-degree circle (which means there are more in the circle so they are smaller), which is more easily mathematically divisible and corresponds to the primary directions on the compass similar to the compass Mil. The *adopted* MILL equals 3.43774677078493 MOA, which is 21.6 inches at 600 yards or equals to 3.6 inches at 100 yards (3.6 × 6 = 21.6 inches). Some people constantly argue the true dimensions of the milliradian and continued controversy and confusion over what dimensions to use. According to Leupold, who makes so many of the US military's rifle and sniper scopes, their engineers at Leupold say the 3.6-inch MILL at 100 yards is the rule to go by while they clearly explained that years ago, the military changed these values to suit their own needs and for their use. Even though 1.02 military mills = 3.375 MOA, for small arms ballistics purposes, 1.00 MILLIRADIAN = 3.43 MOA, which corresponds to the 1,000 to 1 ranging ratio which the military wanted, so 3.375 actually subtends (meaning, stretched to) 3.6. The incremented dots referred to as MIL-DOT means they are spaced 1 milliradian apart from center to center (3.6 inches), which has nothing to do with the size of the dot in the scope. While MOA (MINUTE of ANGLE) is always referred to as 1 inch at 100 yards as a standard, the MIL-DOT is always referred to as 3.6 inches between the dots from center to center of each dot as a 100- yard standard. MILLs and MOA are two different means of measurement, but while MOA is always used for reference in accuracy capability of rifles and scopes, MILLs and MOA are used together to determine proper shot placement.

There are 10 Mils horizontally placed and 10 Mills vertically placed in a specific MIL-DOT scope reticle between the posts, which are the thick lines on each side of the thin line on the crosshair. The math in yards by 100s works perfectly as it was designed to do; otherwise, if you tried to use 3.375 × 10 for 1,000 yards, the figure would be 33.75 per MILL, and while the 2.25-inch difference doesn't seem like much at all, using the full 10 MILL reticle, it would be 337.5 inches rather than the 360 inches the 3.6-inch MIL-DOT system provides for quick calculations. The 22.5-inch difference both vertically and horizontally would affect a serious competitive shooter or sniper, but for those shooting at normal hunting distances, the 3.6 system equals 7.2 inches, minus the 3.375 difference of 6.75 inches difference at 200 yards, equaling .45 inches difference but still being 6.75 inches. A MIL-DOT scope will allow you to take quick accurate shots once familiar with the system without taking your eyes away from the scope for any adjustments. So, remember, 1 MILL = 3.6 inches at 100 yards or progressively in 100-yard increments all the way to 1 yard or 36 inches at 1,000 yards, so 2 MILLs at 100 yards is 7.2 inches or 72 inches at 1,000 yards. This MIL-DOT reference works the same whether it's vertical or horizontal. All this information is accurate and works properly, providing your scope is zeroed for 100 yards, so you can visually aim your sights one dot down, which raises the elevation for bullet impact up an extra 3.6 inches at 100 yards to compensate for bullet drop or for a longer shot, say 200 yards, or 7.2 inches at 200 yards. You need to know the bullet's normal trajectory or you have to adjust for your determination of the distance, but you still get only 3.6 inches between each dot at 100 yards. While US Army, Marine, and Navy SEAL snipers use the 3.375 for calculations, they are of no concern here, but *if YOU* buy a Mil-Dot scope, you must know *which Mil measurement is used*. If you know the approximate size of an object or target, you can use the dimensions between the dots from center to center, adding them together to estimate the distance further downrange because it gives you a means of measurement. You can do the same for windage (side-to-side point of impact) by the same MIL-DOT measurement. Leupold also offers the MIL-DOT standard in TMR (tactical milling reticle), and there's TDMR (tactical distance milling reticle), which expands on the existing MIL-DOT reticle by using various sized and spaced lines (called hash marks) on the vertical and horizontal stadia for increased ranging precision and accuracy, where you can now get a more precise measurement in the portions that are normally covered by the actual size of the dot in a MIL-DOT reticle, which reduces your view of the actual precision while the dots are really good for fast references. The round dot size on the Leupold MIL-DOT reticle is .20 mil, which means that at 100 yards, the dot actually covers a .72-inch circle of your target or a 3.6-inch circle at 500 and 7.2 inches at 1,000.

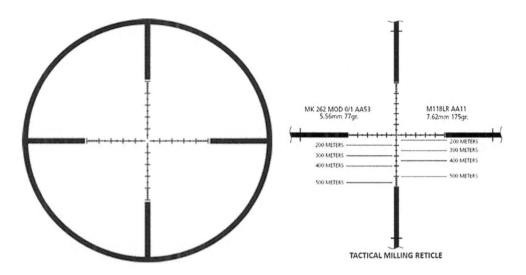

The TMR and its precision abilities. There are many manufacturers who vary in their specific designs. Know the Mill system used for your scope, or you'll get plenty of misses! Beware of metric turrets and reticles so that you do the proper calculations.

The TMR has hash marks (lines) instead of dots at each original MIL-DOT location, still being 3.6 inches center to center at 100 yards with the inclusion of shorter hash marks, marking the reticle in half-mil increments for even greater precision. Scope manufacturers offer scopes with various lines, patterns, or dots at graduated increments on the reticle, and although they can be used exactly the same way as the military, the manufacturer's own design, their purpose, or the distance between dots or hash marks must be known and not assumed to be similar to the MIL-DOT standard. ASK, but the salesman may have no idea, so if you want to buy it, have him get the information pamphlet out of the scope box and find out, or wait a day and call the manufacturer. Patience works wonders. A major point of concern while using a MIL-DOT scope is that the MIL-DOTs are calibrated on different focal planes by different manufacturers. Leupold MIL-DOT scopes like others are designed to be used on one specific magnification for MIL-DOT accuracy, so you have to crank up the scope to the highest power or recommended power, but usually in powers of 10 to assure of its properly calibrated accuracy, *but you need to check the specific scope's information spec sheet, no matter who makes it* to make sure of its proper calibration and requirements. If you have 2 scopes that differ in their methods or requirements, it would be advisable to attach a laminated card to the firearm for your own reference to avoid memory confusion, but the best policy would be to stick to a specific standard.

Scopes

One important thing to remember is that if you are shooting a gun that delivers excessive recoil and look for a proper scope, you need to make sure it is capable of standing up to such recoil due to shock waves, without getting knocked out of adjustment, or the second shot may never hit the target. Cheaply made variable-powered scopes may be more aggravating than you might want, so make sure you really need a variable other than a fixed power scope, which might not be as troublesome for short range shooting. Powerful rounds need tough scopes, and the tough scopes generally cost more, but no matter whether the salesman says that modern scopes will do most anything, make sure it will, or you lose your money. I won't buy *any* scope unless it's water-resistant, preferably waterproof and fogproof, and it generally costs a few extra bucks for one, but I learned early in life that when I had the shot and put the scope to my eye, my body heat immediately fogged the lens and killed the opportunity for the shot, so I will never make that mistake again. NOTE that water-resistant does not mean waterproof. A water-resistant scope if submerged under water will most likely fill with water because it is only resistant to water and weather resistance, but you can certainly buy waterproof scopes if you think you might need them, but again for more money. Remember that buying the scope is to fulfill your needs, not to waste your already spent money to find that you should have bought the other one that cost a few dollars more if it solves the problem. Without the proper knowledge of scopes, you may never know you might have a problem until the critical time for the shot. Some stores will not take a scope back once mounted, and even lifetime warranties might not be any good since the scope selection might have been improper (wrong scope for your needs). In addition, while firearms are capable of 1-MOA and so forth, make sure you know what your scope is also capable of! If you decide to use a scope such as a red dot scope, understand that the main reason for a red dot is for fast target acquisition in close quarters, but for military use, this would be the need for superior close-combat optics. When you normally focus on the front sight, you lose 20% of your peripheral vision, which endangers your life in close-quarter combat, so with some of these red dot sights, you are able to view the dot while maintaining more of your field of view to carry on the fight. There are several manufacturers who use different techniques for projecting the red dot to appear on target and dots claiming to be effective with assorted MOA availabilities. In these red-dot scopes, the MOA means its accuracy capability, where the horizontal crosshair is capable of adjusting in elevation to that particular amount or number of MOA, not the dot size *unless specified* for a given distance. While the military uses many makes of very good scopes, the US ARMY and the NAVY SEALs use aim point whose method of projecting the dot has been determined to be the most accurate with pinpoint accuracy, no matter where the dot appears in the objective since failure is not an option. The aim-point model CompM4 and CompM4S have a 2-MOA capable dot and are submersible to 150 feet. The US military adopted it as the M68CCO where the CCO stands for close-combat optic. Since longer range scopes have to have more MOA capability to be able to shoot the target at the desired longer distance, due to more bullet drop at a longer range, you can determine how far your old scopes are capable of by looking to see how many MOA adjustments they have, being specially aware of whether they are ⅛, ¼, or ½ MOA adjustments, where they may take either 8, 4, or 2 clicks to make 1 inch at 100 yards. While many of your red dot sights *are not magnified* scopes, their dot size capability is generally listed to a certain MOA dot but limited to YOUR vision capability, that is, how far YOU can see without magnification, and mostly used for close combat or building entry and sweeping while hopefully getting a hit anywhere within the dot, not necessarily centered in the dot. Know YOUR firearm and definitely know YOUR scope! Many new shooters at the shooting range have no idea that the rifle has its determined accuracy in MOA AND the scope has its own MOA capability, which might account for confused shooters wondering why they keep wandering all over the target downrange and their never-ending scope adjustments, which may never solve the problem. So you want firearms with less MOA for tighter groups and scopes with more MOA adjustments for refining the longer distance capability due to long-range bullet drop, but there's no need to overbuy, such as a scope with capabilities to shoot 500 to 1,000 yards when you're going to mount it on a hunting rifle that will never be shot beyond 200 yards. The cost is always factored on the scope capabilities. The MIL-DOT and the TMR scope reticles teach you to quickly estimate size, range, and your shot placement, especially at long range. The upper half of the reticle (like all scopes) is giving you sufficient FOV (field of view) and won't be any good for trying to use the reticle for shooting at an extended range based on your knowledge of the ballistic trajectory of the round being used. The impact point for further range requires raising the horizontal stadia possibly more than you can in your lower half of the reticle by aiming with what you can see, so to accomplish this with the same scope, you need adjustment of the dials or turrets on the scope to take advantage of the full view in the reticle, which doubles your otherwise lower half of your view. With some cheap scopes, you can actually see the horizontal stadia (crosshair) in whatever position in the reticle that it is adjusted for. In other words, quality scopes will have the same crosshair aiming-point *sight picture* when you look through the scope, no matter what the adjustment is set for, so you can consistently use that scope without any difficulty while some cheaper scopes will show the horizontal stadia raised into whatever position it is adjusted for; that is, maybe the stadia is ⅝ or ¾ of the reticle in height in the sight picture, which drastically reduces your field of view above the stadia to see your target. When I was looking through one such scope during adjustments, I immediately knew that any such scopes would never find a home on any of my guns, not even if they gave it to me, so if you have such a scope, you might want to give it to the kids for their BB gun.

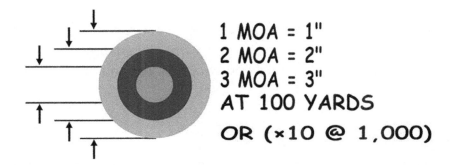

1 MOA = 1"
2 MOA = 2"
3 MOA = 3"
AT 100 YARDS
OR (×10 @ 1,000)

While 1-MOA is 1 inch, 2-MOA is 2 inches and 3-MOA is 3 inches at 100 yards, sub-MOA is less than an inch at 100 yards, so it also means less than 10 inches at 1,000 yards! This helps you understand quality, capabilities, and prices! MOA is always referred to at 100 yards as a standard!

Calibrating Your Scope

To take advantage of the full capability of the proper scopes abilities, the proper technique which is used by the US military is to zero your scope for 100 yards, which equals 1-MOA, and once the bullets hit the target in the intersection of the crosshairs called zeroed, then loosen the hex screws holding the scopes dial or turret in place, and for the elevation, rotate the dial to indicate number 1, that is, adjusted to 1-MOA at 100 yards, and then set the dial for the windage at ZERO, locking the screws to hold this setting. This way you know you're dead on at 100 yards and can easily adjust your range for further distance by dialing in the desired MOA on the scope and easily return it to 100 yards should you wish to do so. In other words, once calibrated, setting the elevation dial to number 2 would be setting the scope for 2-MOA without having to go out on a shooting range or even higher numbers corresponding to greater distance in 100s of yards (or meters).

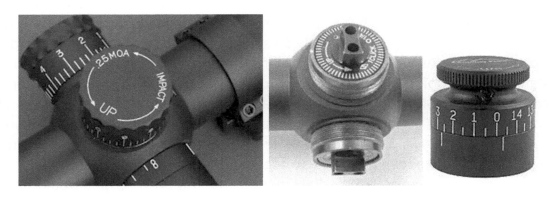

The turrets on the left are marked in ¼ MOA graduations, that is, 4 clicks to equal 1-MOA, while the turret on the right is marked in ½ MOA, being 2 clicks to equal 1-MOA. Notice how many graduations are there on the center scope. Some turret caps have to be removed to adjust them. Modern turrets say which way the bullet impact moves. Beware that some are marked in metrics or centimeters as well as in hundreds of yards. Know what you are buying! Beware of scope design and warranty! Make sure you can do this to your scope before you loosen any screws!

Scope makers will design a custom turret for your favorite cartridge for a few extra bucks, and it sure helps the estimating when you're on the trip of a lifetime! Notice the detail such as the caliber, bullet weight, type of bullet such as a hollow point boat tail, ballistic coefficient, velocity in feet per second, and even the temperature in the outside atmosphere.

Some scopes are marked on the turret in 100s instead of single digits, so if this is the case, then the zeroed calibration would be 100 instead of 1. Just remember to keep in mind the scopes, MOA click adjusting graduations being ⅛, ¼, or ½ MOA, whatever you might have, properly calibrated between the numbers if needed, depending on the type of scope you have, so once the 100 yard 1-MOA is zeroed and the dial is calibrated corresponding to number 1, you can dial in 4½ MOA in a few seconds, again not having to go out to a shooting range or adjusting any desired MOA your scope is capable of, while still using the crosshairs intersecting the aim point as you normally do. But always remember, the specific round you calibrate your scope for is going to perform differently from any other round you use, especially on the trajectory bullet drop, beyond the 100 yard setting, so to dial in your desired MOA for a 600-yard shot based on your estimated range may require a dialed-in setting of 6 plus whatever extra graduations that might be necessary like the 4½ MOA listed above, depending on what your particular click adjustments refer to. This way of calibrating your scope will always allow you to pick up your rifle and look at the setting and immediately know what it is set for, as well as anyone else knowledgeable, being able to pick it up and use it without question. Many people say most all scopes are ¼ MOA adjustable now, but that's simply NOT TRUE. Allow for only facts and tune your firearms as a professional. Know your scope! While it all sounds very complicated, studying the reticle that you have or buy based on your new knowledge can be quickly understood with a little practice on paper and a day at the range. The majority of scopes and reticles on hunting rifles are usually only good to the average hunter where many shots are within the first 200 yards, with most of the average shots being within 100 yards but may result in a missed shot if he doesn't really understand how to use the scope *or the reticle in the scope* or possibly both. Most scope reticles don't have any hash marks for ranges beyond the crosshair point of aim, so again it is best to understand your needs before you buy your preferred scope because the best scope in the world will still bag you no meat if you don't know how to use it, if you overbought too much scope, or if you underbought a scope not even being capable of doing what you need. Remember, a rifle capable of short-range accuracy doesn't do much good to fit it with an extremely expensive long-range scope, just as well as a rifle capable of long-range accuracy with a limited and short-range scope. Further, if you are setting up a particular rifle, a simple phone call to the scope manufacturer to tell them what caliber, bullet weight, and velocity of the round you're using can most likely get them to suggest a proper scope which just might be factory calibrated for you, for distance once you sight in at 100 yards (or according to their instructions), or they may even make you a special reticle for just a few dollars more. Scopes with a BDC means a bullet drop compensator, which may be etched into the reticle, adjustable on a turret, or they may even have an extra turret for focus or for reticle illumination. A word of caution: many people who buy scopes with adjustable bullet drop compensators on the turret never do seem to get them to work properly, but this is operator error because a lot of people don't figure out the proper way to use them, at least from my past experience and what I've seen. Using the military's calibration method of 1-MOA on the dial or turret at 100 yards will always be the most reliable and effective means of adjustment once you understand it, and then suddenly *all your rifles* will become so much easier to use while you quickly dial them in for a longer or a shorter range.

Gyroscopic Drift

There's also gyroscopic drift OR gyroscopic deflection OR spin drift, all the same thing, but people refer to it differently, which comes into play at extreme shooting distances, where a bullet with a right-hand twist deflects to the right and a left-hand twist deflects to the left due to the air resistance under the nose as it rotates. This is a natural deflection from its path due to the spin like a gyroscope and has nothing to do with crosswinds. There are books out there that say gyroscopic drift is completely negligible and of no concern, but for distance shooting, it is definitely a concern. Gyroscopic drift is variable, and it is not easy to distinguish any specific pattern. While referring to where the US military used Doppler radar to measure the gyroscopic drift of many bullets at 1,000 yards, a 5.56 caliber 55 grain bullet had a gyroscopic drift of 23 inches. Of four 7.62 bullet weights tested, a 173 grain drifted 11.5 inches, a 155 grain drifted 1.75 inches, a 190 grain drifted 3.0 inches, and a 220 grain drifted 7.75 inches. In addition, a (.338), 300 grain drifted 6.5 inches, a (.375), 350 grain drifted 0.87 inches, and a (.408), 419 grain drifted 1.90 inches. While those that were measured varied, it did show that the heavier bullet generally results in less gyroscopic drift. Longer projectiles and faster spin rates, distance, and time in flight or trajectory all increase the gyroscopic drift. If you become a serious or competitive shooter, make sure you know whether your firearm has a right—or left-hand twist barrel, so you will know which way the gyroscopic drift will be going. If the gyroscopic drift is *to the right* and the wind is coming *from the left*, then you need to add the two together, gyroscopic drift and wind deflection to get the total drift; however, if the wind is coming *from the left* and the gyroscopic drift is going *to the left*, you need to subtract the difference, shortening the effects of the drift.

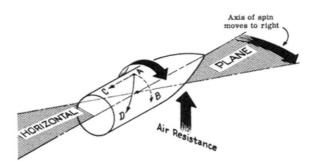

Firing a spinning projectile stabilizes it and gives it accuracy, while firing a projectile from a straight smooth bore causes it to tumble. Gyroscopic drift causes it to move in the direction of the rifling twist.

Ransom Rest Gun Vices for Testing

People who evaluate firearms and even write articles in popular magazines may sometimes refer to the fantastic and consistent shot group from a 3-inch barrel at 25 yards, but they fail to say that the gun was locked into a Ransom Rest, which is a gun vice designed to hold the firearm in place, allowing for the test-firing of each shot in such group. Then they usually report the best group of several. The Ransom Rest was first introduced in 1969 and has since been adopted by US manufacturers and also internationally for testing. Since that time, other manufacturers have developed similar firearm rests. When I read an article, I always look to see if the gun was locked in a rest, steadied on the bench, or fired offhand (the same as freehand), holding the firearm totally unsupported in the open air by hand. It, sort of, defeats the writing of any such article when they don't have the courtesy to say, so I really appreciate it when the author has such consideration and specifies the method of firing the groups so that I can determine how effective the firearm and/or the round may actually be. I usually shoot all three, rifles, handguns, and shotguns, offhand from unsupported positions, including with the proper use of a rifle sling, which many people fail to use *or even lack the knowledge of how*, and they just use it to carry their gun over the shoulder, while many think that's what it's for. I see shot after shot with loose hanging slings, or misused slings (misunderstood or unknowledgeable) while wasting the opportunity for a great shot, compared to a, maybe, shot. I keep *my sling properly adjusted for my arm length* and use the sling to steady my arm the way it's designed to be used so that I shoot the same way in the field when needed. To me, a sling is necessary in the field. Rifles with box magazines need to be practiced appropriately because extended magazines interfere with the use of some slings. So far, I have never used a support of any kind in the field to steady my shots, but I totally rely on my own skills with a suitable sling, which works very well most times. But I missed an extended shot on a giant mule deer once while later nailing a white-tailed that I quickly estimated at 220 yards uphill, but I guessed just a few yards short, although my rifle did its job. With the winter winds in the mountains, and the deer bolting, I hit the front leg bone of the white-tailed and grazed the chest and hit the other leg bone, blowing both front legs completely off with one shot from my 8mm Remington Magnum, using a 185-grain core-locked pointed soft point, which really does an excellent job. So it took a second shot to finish him off since the first shot took off both front legs when he bolted. The shooting sticks do seem to have their place.

I Banged My Scope and Lost My Zero in the Field

These Leupold scope mounting rings have holes for a broad view of your target if it is too close for the scope to be used or the scope is out of tune, and you need to see your iron sights. Many manufacturers make them in various designs. Beware! These rings will be of no benefit if you don't have iron sights installed on your rifle for backup.

Some people may prefer scope mounting rings that allow a clear view through holes beneath the scope to use the iron sights if needed. Once you understand the way it all works, it may even help you save the day during a once-in-a-lifetime hunting trip if you have to remove or re-sight a scope without the gear that you normally leave at home. A simple solution to sighting in a rifle without having the assistance of boresighting equipment available (bore sighting is aligning the center of the rifle bore with the impact point in the scope), such as in the field, the old way depending the type of scope you have is to remove the bolt from the rifle and support the rifle on a bench or suitable support while looking through the bore and pointing it at the bull's-eye on the makeshift target. Then adjust your sights or crosshairs to the same point on the target. The better way is to carry a small cartridge-sized laser boresight along since it will fit in a pocket. Within a few shots, you should be just about on the money or close enough to be able to avoid having lost the use of your much-needed rifle and save an expensive trip because sometimes it happens. I usually take a backup rifle along but once on foot, it isn't on the backpack and might not be available when needed.

Bore Sighting Firearms

Bore sighting is extremely accurate and necessary. Laser boresights are now the in-thing as compared to the older devices. From the left is a laser boresight for the following:

1. *A shotgun*
2. *A rifle*
3. *A sidearm or handgun. Align the laser dot with your stadia (crosshairs) or laser dot from your firearm laser sight. When the two dots meet, you're ready to go.*

Temperature Affects Trajectory

A word to the wise: when sighting in your rifle and the scope is zeroed, while we clearly make mention of the temperature affecting the velocity of the round fired, there are some important facts to study. Since we know that a heavier bullet is in the barrel longer, it could hit above the point of aim, while a lighter bullet being in the barrel less time could hit below the point of aim. These effects are caused due to the differences in the bullet weight and the velocity; however, we may experience such similar results with one certain specific round. If we normally use the firearm in summer months for target shooting or in winter months for hunting, or whatever the case may be, the temperature and gas pressures in the chamber of our rifle will be greater in warmer temperatures and lesser in colder temperatures. If you zeroed your rifle scope for the particular round, you will be using to impact dead center of the crosshair or stadia intersection (the point of aim) in the middle of August out on the range in 80-degree weather and then very confidently take it out for your annual deer-hunting expedition at the end of December in 30 degree or less weather, but you can't figure out what happened when you fired the kill shot and missed. There are a few things you need to consider. If you didn't touch any adjustments and take it back out in 80-degree weather again and hit dead center, you'd start getting somewhat confused. Although we all have bad days and some people blame the gun, the colder temperature reduces the chamber temperature and, therefore, reduces the gas expansion, which directly reduces the velocity of the round, or, in other words, 80 degrees versus 30 degrees is a 50-degree difference. This diminished velocity causes your round to impact at some point *lower* than it was originally sighted in for since it has less power. Since you may be shooting at an even greater distance than you sighted it for because you understand the trajectory of that round, you may be even further off target than you even would have been if you were shooting it at the same distance that you shot from when you sighted it in. Are you confused now? These very same phenomena also work in reverse, increasing the gas expansion and bullet velocity in warmer temperatures, which might cause the bullet to impact at a point *higher* than sighted in for since it's now traveling downrange with a much faster velocity. This is the very same round and equal in every aspect, weight included and maybe even from the same box, being fired in different temperatures. So what's wrong with the firearm? Nothing! Some of these impact differences may be small, but depending on the distance, *it could be* significant. If you're planning to use a firearm in extremely cold temperatures, then it would be in your best interest to zero the scope in similar temperatures or vice versa, or when the temperature gets to be 55 degrees, go out to the range and zero it, allowing for a 25-degree difference up to 80 or down to 30, splitting the 50-degree difference while understanding what happens so you can try to recover from any such situation if it happens to you. Remember that in the colder winter months, the winds are at an all-time high too, so the slower bullet is affected so much more by wind deflection now, and it even complicates the situation further. The 50- and 25-degree differences mentioned above were only for your reference for understanding. The US military considers 20 degrees or greater substantial, and they *require* their snipers to *re-zero* their rifle if the difference becomes substantial or at least 20 degrees in difference whether the temperature goes up or down, which will either speed up or slow down the bullet, causing the point of impact to be either higher or lower than initially sighted in for. Don't confuse this effect with rounds of different weight and powder charges, which will cause similar results in any temperature, but this effect is regarding the *very same round sighted in with* that will hit higher or lower due to the temperature differences.

Your Shooting Abilities

Some very experienced shooters may shoot extreme distances with handguns, but don't you even attempt it in a lethal encounter unless you've developed the necessary skills and proven yourself at the shooting range rather than becoming an additional danger to bystanders, that is, two of you shooting bullets may go to unintended victims. For handgun shots out to 25 yards with short barrels such as a 3-inch barrel shooting a heavy 230-grain .45 ACP round, it will take extra practice but very doable. The gun should be generally accurate and sighted in for 25 yards, giving you striking ability anywhere in between 0 to 25 yards. There was one gun that I've had to consistently visually raise and aim the top edge of the front sight blade about 1/16 inch above the top of the notched blade in the rear to compensate for bullet drop downrange, giving the same result as holdover, while still pointing it dead at the bull's-eye as compared to it normally being dead on accurate at 7 yards. This called for a shorter front sight blade for longer distance. Don't worry about reworking the sights on your particular gun if they need it because everything has to be a coordinated effort to make it all work the way it is intended to so that you can perform as close to perfect as you possibly can. Guns, sights, and eyes all vary; that is the reason why you need to practice and know your own particular gun. The gun cannot do anything that YOU cannot do (in *your* hands), so know YOUR limitations and learn how to properly handle the gun of your choice. While studying and learning, don't expect to buy your gun and be extremely proficient immediately without tuning and practice. You may be able to learn your way out of some of your inabilities as long as they aren't physical impairments. REMEMBER, once a bullet is fired, it cannot be called back.

While the FBI reported that most gunfights are within 21 feet (7 yards), most average indoor ranges seem to be 25 yards maximum unless you're in the military. I do have to admit that at 25 yards, the bull's-eye might be harder to see for some shooters being 75 feet away, but you should definitely *always* practice shooting *out to 21 feet at minimum*. For a man-sized target out to 25 yards, it will be easy enough to see as far as the height of the target, but the width might then pose a problem being narrow for some people to shoot at 25 yards away. When you feel the time is right, you should challenge yourself, and when you can, try shooting at greater distances all the way out to 25 yards. When you fire all the rounds and have an empty gun while wondering why there are no holes in the target, you will start to understand the reality of needing experience. Some firing ranges have a 7 yard or 21-foot marker as a line across the floor to help you learn to shoot within this specific distance, and in this 21 feet, it has also been established that a KILLER on the move can travel the full 21-foot distance in 1.5 seconds! A fact! Although it seems questionable, police put it to the test with an electronic timer, and while I watched the man running, he even simulated a knife wound on the victim by the time the timer reached 1.5 seconds! It's the very reason for needing reaction speed when it's time if you're physically capable, but the most important issue is to be able to get the gun out for your defense, and speed will come naturally, but only if you challenge yourself and practice. When confronted by a KILLER, you must NEVER divert your attention away from the KILLER or from the shooting you're currently involved in. Once you're skilled enough with your handgun, you might find yourself eventually shooting extreme distances, but also remember that shooting a KILLER at that range might make it hard to convince the prosecutor that they were still a threat, but *only you will know that*, and it just might save your life. NEVER trust a killer! ALWAYS shoot until the killer is out of the fight! If you shoot once, he might be partially out of the fight instead of completely out; shooting him again afterward could result in your getting charged in his shooting by the prosecutor who might claim that the killer was no longer a threat even if he might attempt to kill you after you allowed him to live. Shutting down the threat the first time could remove all other problems of justification. Confusion of the legal issues may cause hesitation on YOUR end of a 2-gun gunfight while the KILLER cares not and will shoot you down, so your mental skills and abilities are very important to develop and maintain the proper mental discipline and proficiency required to keep your confidence high.

Practicing your shooting skills 10 feet in front of you might be a good start. You might be thinking, who can't hit a target at 10 feet? I've had people say the same thing about hunting with a compound bow for 10 yards, but due to the unexpected circumstances, or maybe I should say unprepared circumstances, many of them missed their deer when it appeared much closer than they would ever practice for. I always practiced long and short shots, which can be two handicaps for the inexperienced with a gun or a bow, but too many people say that so close is so easy there's no need, and so far is too far, but if bullets are coming your way, you darned sure better have a way to deter them, being close or far, which will probably be by your ability to shoot back. There have been attacks on very skilled marksmen; one shot 7 rounds in a close confrontation within *a couple of feet* and scored 1 hit, and in another similar situation, the man scored 2 hits. There was an armed robbery in a convenience store where one of the customers had a concealed carry license and had his Glock on him at the time. Being under the stress of the armed robbery unfolding, he drew his Glock and fired everything he had in the high-capacity magazine and never hit the armed robber! Here are a few examples of shoot-outs in New York from 1990 through 2006. In 1990, there were 67 gunfights, firing 548 shots while getting 105 hits, which means that 443 bullets went somewhere else. In 2000, in 11 gunfights firing 185 shots, there were 16 hits, which means that 169 bullets went somewhere else. In 2005, during 16 gunfights firing 276 shots, there were 23 hits, which means 253 bullets went somewhere else. In 2006, during 13 gunfights firing 144 shots, there were 43 hits, which means that 101 bullets went somewhere else. So out of 1,153 shots, there were only 187 hits, which means that 966 bullets went somewhere else other than their intended target, or only a 16% hit ratio out of 100% in which an 84% (miss ratio) is extremely poor marksmanship with very little skill. So this also means that 966 innocent people could have died due to the lack of better training. Just be glad that *you* weren't in the area. Stress and being scared gets your heart racing, makes you nervous, and makes you quiver and shake, not to mention if you have to physically hang on to your gun that the thug (or thugs) might be trying to take away from you the way it was in two of the earlier examples just mentioned. We don't want to be shot with our own gun, or any gun. If you're going to carry a gun, then be responsible and train properly, so we don't fall victim to the anti-gunners who just might be justified if we missed 966 shots out of 1,153, sending those 966 bullets somewhere into houses and buildings in the neighborhood. Marksmanship is as important as knowing the operation of your gun, and it is not that hard to learn while practice is definitely always required to learn the much-needed skills and then to maintain them. Shooting a longer distance trains and steadies your hands sufficiently so that closer shots will be so much easier to achieve. Some people feel that once they can do it, they can put the gun in the drawer until they need it, but that's not the way it is because skills will degrade with time if not maintained. Of the many guns pulled on me, due to the various circumstances, they certainly were not expected when it happened, and while I used a gun grab for one that was close enough, I sure thought I was going to take a bullet in the chest that night. Remember, I'm alive now, and maybe dead in 30 seconds, but since you never know what day or what hour such an attack might happen, YOU are in control and have the ability to deter such aggression.

Rifling and Stabilizing the Bullet

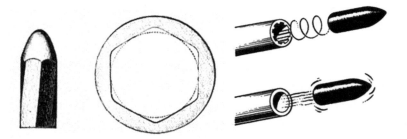

Polygonal-shaped bullets fit the barrel so well that they maximize the potential of the bullet for penetration due to the higher pressures it built with such a good seal. All rifling puts the spin on the bullet and causes it to fly more stable and accurate, compared to a wobbly projectile in flight. Different caliber and weight bullets call for a different rate of twist for rifling for the best stability and accuracy. Large diameter bullets provide more stability while long bullets are harder to stabilize. Too much twist rate per caliber will destabilize the bullet. The twist rate is determined for the specific caliber being used.

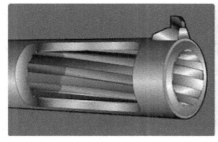 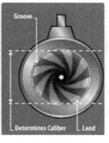 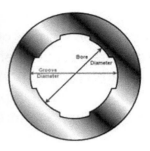

Rifling consists of lands and grooves. The lands are the smallest internal diameter to grip the bullet and put it into a spin.

While there have been numerous rifling designs over the years, modern firearms have either the following:

1. *Normal rifling which may vary in the number of lands and grooves or*
2. *Polygonal rifling which may also vary in the number of hills and valleys*

Of the many different barrel lengths available, longer barrels stabilize the bullet, in combination with what they call rifling and the twist rate. That is, rifling is a number of helical grooves cut through the length of a barrel. Lands on the inside of the barrel (raised surfaces between the grooves) apply pressure to the outside of the bullet by gripping it to put the bullet in a spiral to spin the bullet for more stability and accuracy. The rate of twist, that is, turns per inches (NOT per inch), is different in various guns due to bullet weights and calibers. Older firearms such as muzzle loaders that fire round balls may have a rate of twist of 1 in 60 inches, or 1-60", while modern-day muzzle loaders that fire a sabot containing the bullet may work very well with 1 in 28 twist, but different muzzle loaders will vary, especially with different calibers. Modern firearms generally have much more twist than the old round ball muzzle loaders, and different calibers will require different twist rates. My 1911 .45 has a rate of 1 in 16 inches left hand; that is, the bullet turns to the left at the rate of once in 16 inches, and regardless of the length of the barrel, the twist rate controls this. Once a bullet leaves the barrel, that applied force of twist combined with the velocity, which depends on the powder charge in the bullet cartridge, may actually cause the bullet to spin as many as a few hundred thousand revolutions per minute while in its trajectory downrange depending on its actual caliber and distance of travel. This might sound extreme. A 230 grain .45 ACP with 1 in 16-inch twist rate fired at a common 850 feet per second will result in 637.5 RPMs. So no matter how far it travels, it will hit the 25-yard target, achieving 56.25 revolutions in .088 seconds or the 100-yard target, reaching 225 revolutions in .35 seconds without regard to its ballistic coefficient (BC), which controls the bullet's ability to overcome air resistance in flight. Although the rate of twist is constant, the greater distance allows more revolutions to happen before impact. Too much twist combined with too much velocity may result in too much spin, therefore, increasing the air resistance in flight, depending on the bullet design, and may actually cause the bullet to disintegrate (never reaching its target), and this has happened to rifle rounds. As the bullet leaves the muzzle, it's already going to be hot enough to boil water, not including the additions of the air resistance. That means that various bullet designs and different bullet weights work better or best with specific rifling twist rates per caliber, which is necessary to put the bullet into the proper motion for the best or the desired results. A larger diameter bullet stabilizes more easily than a longer bullet, which becomes hard to spin-stabilize as the longer bullets tend to become back heavy. Barrel length can also affect the accuracy, which deteriorates due to excess vibration, so you will see certain rifles with shorter barrels that still perform very well. While six different rifling designs have been used over the years, one that was developed in the early to mid-1800s is called polygonal rifling, which was an older or earlier style of rifling but is far easier to make. And its supporters claim it has a much better gas seal because the bullet makes contact with hills and valleys which may be in actual hexagonal or octagonal design rifling in the barrel. A (CZ), Heckler and Koch, Glock, Kahr, and Desert Eagle among other handguns use polygonal rifling due to their claimed less deformation of the bullet and increased gas pressures as the bullet travels the length of the barrel, but this happens with other rifling too, slightly increasing the velocity and the accuracy. When polygonal rifling was first put to use, polygonal-shaped bullets were also tried in an attempt to get the best fit, seal, and pressure. In a test done in 1857 with a .45 caliber rifle with a 39-inch barrel and 1 in 20-inch rifling twist rate, the polygonal-shaped bullet fit the rifling so well that the increased amount of gas pressure building behind the bullet actually caused the bullet to penetrate 15 Elm planks, compared to the land and groove rifling firing a round bullet and penetrating only 6 planks, while both were using the very same amount of gunpowder. Smith and Wesson started using an electrochemical machining process (ECM) in 1993 to rifle most of their revolver barrels due to the increased speed averaging about a minute per barrel. But in discussions with those in the machining industry, they claim it to be much lower in quality than a broached barrel, although it's much faster and cheaper for production. Other manufacturers have also taken to this method of rifling, and although many say to bring the costs down, why do the prices still seem to be going up? They would do better to say to bring *their* costs down so *they* can make *more money*. I don't mind paying the few extra dollars for the higher quality firearms, but I certainly don't want to pay high prices for such *cheaply made* firearms.

An early original military M16 used in Vietnam had a rate of 1 in 14 right-hand twist for a 5.56 × 45 NATO round. The 5.56 with 1 in 14 twist would cause the bullet to tumble through flesh (yaw) on impact or usually upon reaching a depth of up to 7 inches of penetration, so that instead of passing directly through, it would generally travel in different directions inside a body, causing maximum trauma, but due to the complaints of it being inhumane, they eventually revised the round from the 5.56, 55 (grain) M193 Ball FMJ to the Belgian 5.56, 62 (grain) M855, SS109 design for standardization with several other twist rates, 1 in 9 and 1 in 7 in current military rifles. Yet there have been complaints that the improved stabilization and penetration of the round has less effective wounding ability. NATO, also called North Atlantic Alliance, is a worldwide intergovernmental military alliance, setting standards by signing a treaty in 1949 so that the small arms of participating countries around the world will have a method of standardization and interchangeability while all shooting the same bullet of that particular size with the NATO designation. The organization constitutes a system of collective defense whereby its member states (countries) agree to mutual defense in response to an attack by any external party. Beware, many people will tell you that standard ammunition and NATO ammunition are the same thing, and they clearly are NOT the same. We'll address these issues. There are 206 claimed countries in the world while some people argue about whether some are actually considered countries or not. They currently claim there are 193 *member* states around the world, including North America and Europe, while some other countries participate in NATO's Partnership for Peace. NATO's headquarters are in Brussels, Belgium, and it sets the required military standards for all its members, so while we are bound as a member of NATO to shoot certain FMJ ammunition at our enemies to be more humane in how we kill those who try to kill *us*, the non-NATO members are free to shoot at us with *anything they want* including high-velocity hollow point ammunition. Although the US even looked at the .30-06 Springfield round (7.62 × 63), following World War II, as maybe being a bit too much power for such close combat, some of NATO's reasoning for such ammo is that while the FMJ passes through creating a wound, it takes at least 2 additional troops (meaning, 2 men) to tend to getting him out of the field to safety, but they never do consider the fact that while they may shoot *us* with heavy high-velocity hollow points, a great deal of flesh and muscle may be blown out and it just may take 3 men to tend to *our* wounds, *if* we survive.

While we'll be addressing NATO spec ammunition from time to time, civilians are not bound to honor NATO's guidelines, so if we ever found a war on our own turf, and to those who live in denial, it's not impossible. The only way they can prevent us from shooting enemies with more destructive ammunition is to outlaw our guns in the US. I for one will shoot anybody who is going to *kill me* whether he's a criminal or an enemy (the same thing) with whatever I have available that will shut him down. Looking at handgun calibers and ammunition, there's 9mm NATO, which is often confused with the 9mm Luger or just 9 × 19. The 9mm NATO is also 9 × 19; however, it has its own designation and is loaded to military specs, 124 (grain) FMJ, and loaded similar or equivalent to the 9mm+P. The United States, however, has been rethinking the 9mm as compared to the earlier 45. NATO wanted the US to adopt the 9mm, and so we eventually did, allowing a soldier to carry much more ammo for the same weight ratio, but in Iraq and Afghanistan, it's taking on the average of 4 chest shots to stop the enemy (if it does) because they keep coming.

Cartridge Comparison

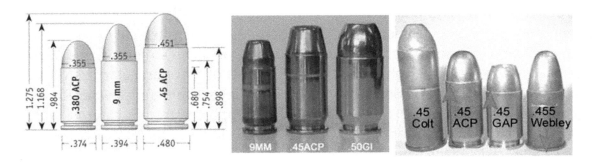

Since the .380 is a shortened 9mm, be careful and don't mix them up in your gun! The same goes for the .45 GAP, which is a shortened .45 ACP. Trying to mix any of these rounds in either of their guns will cause trouble, so don't try! In the picture on the right, the .45 Colt and the Webley are revolver rounds, which can be quickly identified by the cartridge rim on the base that is larger than the outer diameter of the cartridge. The extraction rim on the base of the .45 ACP and the GAP has the same diameter as the cartridge assembly, but the .50 GI has a smaller base, and all these rounds can be quickly identified as either a semiautomatic or revolver cartridge by the base design.

While the .45 dwarfs the 9mm, the .50 does the same to the .45 and is one bad hombre, one that has to make a thug think twice staring down your barrel compared to his. Most large caliber concealed carry sidearms are 9mm and .45 ACP.

It is Federal Hydra-Shock on the left, Mag-Tech in the center, and Gold Dot on the right, but many manufacturers make specific personal defense hollow point ammunition to work to the best advantage for self-defense based on research and development, specific design, and testing originally initiated for law enforcement purposes. In a test of 100 rounds, the 9mm Gold Dot expanded to twice its size, but there are many fine personal defense ammunition manufacturers. Recently a newly developed hollow point entered the market named R.I.P., or Rest In Peace, and is a very devastating round.

These are frangible rounds. They are available in handgun, rifle, or shotgun rounds. See how the frangible round splatters on impact and when hitting human flesh, they deliver all their energy on impact but cause somewhat limited damage as compared to a FMJ or a hollow point while they may or may not go deep. The Glaser Safety Slug is shown, which is a frangible round, and it has eithera blue tip ora silver tip. The damage depends on frangible round and the velocity.

In the picture above, a frangible round photographed disintegrating on impact.

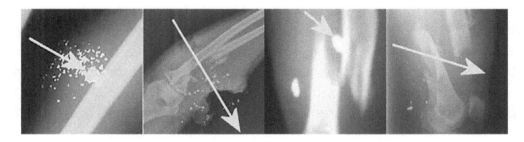

x-rays of frangible wounds and bullet wounds. The M16 round went right through the thigh on the far right and took the bone out while the frangible round took out the bone in the arm.

SIG 226   SIG 228

Although the Navy even uses the SIG-Sauer P226 in 9mm while claiming it to be effective, the SIG 226 and 228 have a double-stacked magazine and are chambered in calibers such as the .22 LR, 9mm Parabellum, .357 SIG, and .40 Smith and Wesson. While recent reports indicate the 9mm doesn't do the damage as compared to the .45, there's talk that the US is seriously considering leaning back toward the .45. While some US military groups do currently have use of the .45s including the Kimber 1911, there's no longer a standard military or NATO .45 ACP round. The 9mm that the military uses is also called ball ammunition, rather than being called FMJ. The permanent wound cavity of the 9mm is much smaller than the .45 where the .45 is obviously more effective. The effects of bullet diameter and permanent wound cavities will always hold true. Look at the caliber differences in the pictures below for a better understanding.

Caliber differences are shown for reference in the outer diameter of a bullet by the vertical row of circles, which represent the diameter of the bullet for an easy comparison. The2 cartridges with the rim at the base wider than the cartridge, the .44 and the .357, are revolver rounds while those with the extractor bevel and apparent rim looking base equal to the outer diameter of the cartridge are semiautomatic pistol rounds. They normally say semiautomatic rounds are rimless, but I'm showing you the facts of their appearance. One exception is the .22 rimfire round on the far right that fires in revolvers or semiautomatic pistols and rifles. Revolver rounds have a definite rim that extends outside the diameter of the cartridge case, but semiautomatic rounds have their base the same size as the cartridge diameter, and the bevel at the bottom of the case allows the extractor to remove the round. Notice the base of those that are semiautomatic and those that are for revolvers.

When people say stopping power, they get dozens of explanations. While there have been numerous tests and explanations on the subject, in 1935, the first attempt was made to assign values to specific calibers and evaluate their relative stopping power. The higher the value assigned to the round indicated, the round's greater ability to stop a lethal threat. The .22 LR had a value of 3.8, the 9mm Parabellum had a value of 29.4, the .38 Special had a value of 30.8, and the .45 ACP had a value of 60.0. While all these heavier bullets resulted in higher values, an index assembled by a computer modeled compiled data and showed that even the same calibers separated by differences in velocity resulted in greater incapacitation *by using faster bullets,* even though some were *lighter in weight*. Again, the higher the value results in, the greater the stopping ability due to this index. Here is an example: the .38 Special +P+ (125 grain JHP) at 1,108 fp/s showed a value of 25.5, compared to a .38 Special (125 grain JHP) at 911 fp/s, resulting in 7.0. The extra 200 feet per second upped the effectiveness of the round by an additional value of 18.5 above what it was. Similarly, a .45 ACP (185 grain) at 895 fp/s showed 21.1, compared to a .45 ACP (230 grain FMJ) at 740 fp/s, which resulted in a value of 6.5.

The 45-grain lighter bullet pumped up an additional 155 feet per second and upped the effectiveness of the round by an additional value of 14.6 above what it was. And a 9mm Parabellum (125 grain), at 1,058 fp/s, showed a 9.9 with no comparison. I'll give one more list where a police officer who compiled a list of gunshots over a 15-year span showed that velocity prevailed again. For 306 shootings with a (158 grain RNL) .38 Special at 704 fp/s, 160 were one- shot stops, compared to 183 shootings with a (158 grain JHP) .38 Special at 991 fp/s, where 126 were one-shot stops, indicating that the faster bullet upped the stopping ability by 16.57% in the same caliber. Since there was no mention of the shot placement and more modern bullets are becoming a science, compared to previous designs, if you are unsure of your self- defense round, then the largest diameter bullet, weighing the most and traveling at the highest velocity, is going to give the best results, according to research and experience. But if there's a comparable round with more kinetic energy at a faster speed, it just might be the wise choice. The heavier bullet has always been desired for maximum penetration, and although we select the heavy weight in a hollow point, it quickly loses velocity as it expands, but the heavier bullet weight helps to get it deep enough for more damage. If a smaller caliber is what you have to do, simple notes on a scratch pad can help you determine the smaller calibers that perform well with sufficient penetration, but there's additional information coming soon.

BASED ON RESEARCHES, TESTS, AND RESULTS, THE US ARMY HAS DECIDED THAT VELOCITY IS THE MOST CRITICAL FACTOR IN CREATING A WOUND. YOU CAN BELIEVE IT!

While this is the exact opposite of what so many already believe, these are the facts based on the research, tests, and results from the US Army.

We'll be addressing interchangeable bullets in some guns, so let's take a brief look at velocity and bullet diameter in military style and assault rifles first and *their* permanent wound cavities. Bullet gas pressures combined with barrel length create the bullet's velocity, and increased velocity gets greater penetration, depending on other factors such as bullet weight and design. This is the very reason bullet-resistant vests need armor plate inserts to prevent being shot *by faster rifle rounds*, which would easily pass through the vest as compared to the slower handgun calibers where the vests are otherwise designed to prevent penetration of most.

Velocity versus Weight

BULLET-RESISTANT VESTS: Here are a few examples of Class IV bullet-resistant vests. Notice the additional coverage for the groin and even the thighs. The weak point on all vests is, when an arm is raised, a shot can be taken under the arm and can even pass through the heart. If a killer doesn't respond to 2 chest shots, the head shot is immediately called for.

BULLET-RESISTANT STREET CLOTHES: On the left as well as the jacket on the right, the vest under the suit coat is bullet resistant. Leaving the jacket open in the front exposes center mass and may get you killed. There are many manufacturers and different styles of vest while they all fall into the Class of I, II, III, or IV. Class IV is the best, but high-velocity trauma plates, as well as many of the extensions are optional. Ask about back protection in the bullet-resistant clothing because killers will shoot you in the back.

Two identical bullets, one fired through a rifle at 3,000 feet per second and one fired through a handgun at 1,000 feet per second, will perform differently. Due to such a difference in velocity being an additional 2,000 feet per second, the faster bullet would normally give the greatest penetration, but the bullet design has to be structurally workable, or it may disintegrate on impact. The very reason why the small diameter of the 5.56 × .45 caliber in an armor-piercing round penetrates steel is due to the high velocity, or without the velocity, even the bullet construction won't help. The US military performed a test at Aberdeen Proving Grounds due to a belief that a slow heavy bullet was the best for penetrating heavy brush with less deflection from its flight path and found that the heavier *and faster* bullets performed successfully. Further, it should be understood that the very reason for bullet selection due to different needs is because lighter bullets run out of velocity much faster than heavier bullets and therefore lose their penetrating ability. The heavier bullet maintains velocity much better due to the weight in flight overcoming resistance by the elements and, therefore, maintains much of its punch or penetrating ability; that is the very reason why the military uses heavy rounds for long-range sniper shooting. Here is an example: a Navy SEAL reference chart shows a .224, 55 grain bullet fired at 2,900 feet per second with 1,027 foot pounds diminishes to 1,139 feet per second at 500 yards with only 158 foot pounds. Comparing it to the 7.62 × 51, 150-grain bullet fired at 2,800 feet per second with 2,611 foot pounds, it diminishes to 1,872 feet per second at 500 yards but still has 1,167 foot pounds available for more devastation, compared to the 158 of the .224 above. Since muscle and bone quickly absorb and reduce the remaining foot pounds being kinetic energy or the bullet's potential upon bullet impact and penetration, hunters shooting game at a longer distance obviously benefit from the larger round and bag their meat with a sure kill other than a slightly wounded animal wandering off and possibly dying without ever being recovered. This can also happen if you pursue your game after the shot without giving it sufficient time to bleed down first so that it has no energy left and cannot run off before it dies.

Velocity of every round fired is directly affected by the temperature of the outside environment. If you compare a round fired at 2,668 feet per second in 40°F, it will give 2,722 feet per second in 70 degrees or 2,827 feet per second in 100 degrees. It progressively increases with temperature rise just the same as it progressively decreases as the temperature drops. When Research Armament Industries in the US started the development of the .338 Lapua in 1983, it was initially designed under contract by the US Navy for long-range military sniper rifles, and its requirements were to be able to deliver its 250 (grain) round at 3,000 feet per second and penetrate 5 layers of military body armor and still make the kill at 1000 meters, which is 1,094 yards. While RAI couldn't solve their problems with the weak brass cartridge case, in 1984, they brought in the Lapua ammunition manufacturer of Finland who tried to solve this problem after RAI dropped out due to financial issues, hence the adoption of the name Lapua, but due to Lapua's inability to fulfill the Navy's velocity requirement, still due to weak brass, the Navy canceled their rifle contracts. The current Lapua round is a joint venture by Lapua and the British firearms manufacturer Accuracy International, and, in 1989, it finally became registered as a NATO round as 8.58 × 71 mm. A British Army sniper shot two Taliban machine gunners in Afghanistan with the Lapua round from a distance of 8,120 feet or 1.54 miles as measured by GPS equipment, resulting in immediate kills. The point is that high velocity *always* gets results, but high velocity combined with the weight of a heavier projectile always gets greater penetration and usually more devastation. This is the very reason why the US military uses the .50 BMG (Browning machine gun) for aircraft weaponry in addition to sniper rifles and much more. For bullets with less of a powder charge such as handgun bullets, which are fired from very short barrels compared to rifles, the heavier bullets are generally desired because handguns develop much less velocity than rifles. The heavier weight of the bullet gets deeper penetration than a comparable lightweight bullet *at the same velocity*, but lighter bullets in factory loads are generally faster. With factory ammo, lighter faster bullets of hollow point design may get more expansion with less penetration as compared to heavier and slower bullets of similar design, which may get less expansion with greater penetration. Under the right circumstances, a lighter faster round and a slower heavier round may meet in the same place. This helps you understand why wounds produced by projectiles of higher mass and/or higher velocity produce greater tissue disruption than projectiles of lower mass and/or velocity. Either round may completely pass through an assailant if the ogive (the curve of the bullet nose) is a FMJ or TMJ (full metal jacket or total metal jacket). This is the very reason why some handgun ammunition manufacturers mark their box of ammo with SB; that is, it was designed to perform with very short barrels. A US Navy SEAL did a penetration test using two standard NATO rounds, the 5.56 × 45 and the 7.62 × 51. He set up 16, 1-inch-thick acrylic blocks and fired the 5.56 × 45, which went through 2 inches of solid acrylic while the 7.62 × 51 went through 3-1/2 inches. These are good examples of a small round with sufficient velocity doing its job.

Interchangeability

If you were to buy a rifle of the .223 assault rifle design, it would be advantageous to buy a 5.56 × 45 mm NATO, which will develop about 3,110 feet per second. The 5.56 × 45 mm NATO will chamber and shoot a .223 Remington with possibly a little less accuracy due to the increased *leade* space (the space where the chamber meets the barrel without rifling) in the 5.56, but a .223 Remington won't safely shoot the 5.56 NATO.

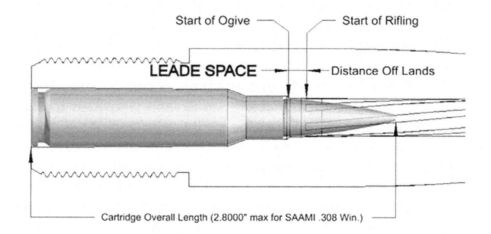

In the .308 Winchester illustration above, firearms have this typical chamber design. The leade space (also called free-bore) shows the area between the neck of the cartridge case and the point where the rifling starts. Although not identical, the 7.62 × 51 mm NATO and the commercial .308 Winchester cartridges are similar, and the Sporting Arms and Ammunition Manufacturers' Institute (SAAMI) considers it safe to fire the NATO round in weapons chambered for the commercial round. The people at Winchester told me since they are so very close to being identical, they can be interchanged and fired in either firearm.

If the 5.56 is put into the chamber of the .223, it will cause overpressure and may cause additional pressure problems with a blown primer or cartridge case—or whatever else may happen or even blow up. NOTE: DO NOT DISBELIEVE that firearms blow up, no matter what anybody tells you because they *may* or *may not*. I've seen quite a few that have! Many people (without the proper knowledge) think they have the ability to say *modern guns* won't blow apart, so I'm giving you proof! Modern has *nothing to do with it*; pressures and obstructions cause most of it. *Remember, I give you the facts and you do the deciding.*

I tried to show the differences in the chart below. It gives the differences in chamber dimensions for .223 versus 5.56 × 45. Though some people try, NEVER try to modify your own firearm chambers! It's a much faster way to the cemetery.

223 Rem vs 5.56 Nato

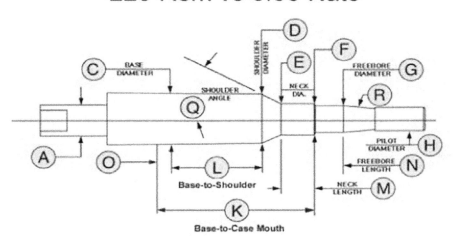

#	Item	223 Rem	5.56 Nato	Difference
A	Shank	0.4370	0.4370	0.0000
C	Base Diameter	0.3760	0.3780	0.0020
D	Shoulder Diameter	0.3553	0.3560	0.0007
E	Neck-2	0.2550	0.2550	0.0000
F	Neck-2/Case Mouth	0.2540	0.2550	0.0010
G	Freebore Diameter	0.2245	0.2270	0.0025
H	Pilot Diameter	0.2180	0.2180	0.0000
K	Base-to-Case Mouth	1.7720	1.7750	0.0030
L	Base-to-Shoulder	1.2340	1.2380	0.0040
M	Neck Length	0.2200	0.2180	-0.0020
N	Freebore Length	0.0250	0.0500	0.0250
O	Rim/Belt Thickness	0.2000	0.2000	0.0000
Q	Shoulder Angle (Degrees)	23.0	23.0	0.0
R	Throat Angle (Degrees)	3.1	2.5	-0.6

OVERPRESSURE: I've seen many blown-up firearms and I'm just showing certain ones for your reference. The AR-15 Law Enforcement Carbine on the left and the Glock on the right were overpressured.

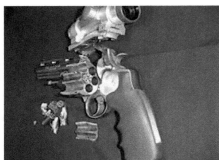

The revolver on the left had too much pressure while the pump shotgun barrel had an obstruction. Quite often, people find mud in the end of their barrels when walking along in the woods, not paying attention. The steel revolver is the strongest firearm shown here, but it blew apart just as easily as the Polymer Glock. Reloading by hand should be held to an exact science, and carelessness can get you killed instead of your assailant. Always know your gun's capability and never try ammunition you don't know for a fact is the right stuff!

These cartridges were overpressured. Overpressure results in guns blown apart similar to those above and even worse where people get wounded by the flying debris that becomes the same as shrapnel. Never experiment with hand loads! It takes a great deal of experience before you can alter loads, but you should always go by the factory recommendations.

The rounds above with the sealed and crimped ends are blank cartridges. Blanks only have gunpowder for the audio effects of having fired a round and are used for movies, ceremonies where they fire rifles and shotguns, and also for what they call starter pistols at the start of various events. Notice these shotgun blanks are short because they have no shot, just the powder charge, but there are also longer blank shells, so ALWAYS know what you have loaded!

I get quite involved with military protocol, funerals, and rifle details. One day one of the local VFW members fired a blank cartridge. A blank is a cartridge loaded with powder but crimped at the end with no bullet inserted, just for the effects of firing, but he fired it in an M1 Garand that malfunctioned and blew apart while seriously injuring him in the nose. Blank cartridges have less power than a fully assembled cartridge that contains a bullet, so remember that anything can happen in any firearm at any time, but it's less likely if we keep up on their maintenance and inspection. The 5.56 has stronger cartridges than the .223 and has crimped in primers and bullets and is sealed (watertight) on both ends. According to my discussions with Winchester, when it comes to the 7.62 × 51 mm NATO rifle round, a rifle chambered for the 7.62 × 51 NATO will properly shoot the .308 Winchester and a firearm chambered for the .308 Winchester will shoot the 7.62 NATO since they are so close to being nearly identical. Remember, sometimes I'll repeat something to make sure you remember it.

NATO rounds are marked with a head stamp, looking similar to vertical and horizontal crosshairs in a rifle scope reticle or circle, not like an X. The dent in the center of the primer next to the red arrow means it has already been fired. No dent means unfired.

The cartridge above left is a 5.56 military round, compared to a civilian .223 round. The two in the center are a 7.62 × 51 NATO compared to a 5.56 × 45 NATO, and on the right, the .338 Lapua Magnum, which is 8.58 × 70 and dwarfs the .308.

There are rifles currently produced with the chamber modified specifically—the Wylde chamber and the Armalite chamber. They are both designed to shoot the 5.56 NATO *and* the .223 Remington safely and accurately, but ask if you buy to make sure you have the right chamber other than a different one by the same manufacturer. While NATO rounds in calibers such as the 9mm are loaded to approximately 10% higher working pressures than their similar civilian counterparts, there's so much confusion about the 7.62 × 51 and its pressure. There are numerous Internet sites that claim that the 7.62 × 51 is greater than the .308 Winchester, and others claim stating the opposite, but I hate to burst their bubbles on both sides of the issue because the people at Winchester who make them both said that although the 7.62 NATO has thicker and stronger cartridge cases, crimped and sealed primers, and bullets, they are very much identical and about the same working pressures from either cartridge. In comparison, you figure the 7.62 × 51 will cause a greater permanent wound cavity than the .223, and even a round of a larger caliber with less velocity will do extreme damage due to the outer diameter of the bullet. Although the Communist government in Hanoi reported that 1,100,000 North Vietnamese Army and Viet Cong died in the war, captured documents later showed that the estimates originally reported by MACV (Military Assistance Command Vietnam) were somehow exaggerated and 50% less, but it still proves that the smaller bullet which tumbled on impact was quite effective *due to its velocity* and varied wound cavity, but the Vietnamese used weapons of Russian design, mainly the AK-47, which used a 7.62 × 39, so much shorter than the US M14's 7.62 × 51, but it was still a very effective round and we have 58,479 American soldiers, mariners, sailors, airmen, and coast guard who never returned from Vietnam alive, which proves its effectiveness and devastation. The AK-47, which was improved as the AKM, was later replaced with the AK-74, which used a smaller caliber of 5.45 × 39, which improved accuracy over the AK-47, which was not as accurate as the M16. Any bullet seeking you as the target is considered deadly, so NEVER underestimate *any* round whatsoever.

While nobody ever recommends a small caliber round for defense, the reason so many sidearms are passed over in the selection is due to the lack of power, ability, and effectiveness of the round, but personally I'd say the choice is yours, so with the proper facts, do whatever you feel is the way you should go (once you've learned how it all works). The FBI started using calibers such as the .32 back in 1934 when they started issuing guns to their agents, and since that time, they went through other calibers including the .38 Special, 9mm, .357 Magnum, 10 MM, .40 Smith and Wesson, and the full-sized .45 ACP round (not the shortened .45 GAP) through the past 77 years to find that their most successful round is the .40 S&W, although SWAT teams still use the .45 ACP.

Penetration Tests

The rifle round above illustrates the way the hollow point progressively expands as it penetrates from left to right, deeper and deeper. The more energy transferred, the more expansion. The energy is the impact potential of the combined velocity and weight. There are many bullet configurations, including armor piercing with carbide inserts harder than armor plate. While there are also specialty cartridges with 2 projectiles inside, being duplex one behind the other, and even triplex, all being fired at the same time as if they were one, I don't have any research data, so I would avoid using them to avoid accidents.

Winchester PDX1 is shown in the illustrations above—for handguns on the left and shotguns in four different configurations on the right. Winchester says the PDX1 offers critical penetration, compensates for aim error, is designed for 410 Gauge for close-range engagement, and designs for the 12 Gauge for long-range engagement. Notice the multiple projectiles in the shotgun rounds. The 410 BB and defensive discs and the 12 Gauge Buck and Slug are recommended by Winchester for home defense use. Observe the segmenting slug design on the right.

In a test at an FBI facility, the .40 S&W in a Winchester PDX1, which was manufactured for personal defense and available in .380 through .45 ACP including shotgun loads, was tested through sheet metal, plywood, wall board, vehicle glass, and heavy clothing attached to ballistic gel, which was cooled to 39 degrees to simulate *actual* results in flesh and muscle as compared to those performing tests in ballistic gel used at warmer temperatures which allow too much penetration and give false results. When tests are performed using ballistic gel, nobody ever specifies the distance from the muzzle, but it would be nice if they did. With the vehicle glass, 4 shots went directly through the angled windshield to their intended target without deviation. Many 45-degree angled windshield shots were tested, and they always easily penetrate through. The Winchester PDX1 Defender in .45 ACP consistently reaches a depth of 17 inches of penetration in *properly cooled* ballistic gelatin and *is currently used by the FBI*. In other tests, bullets took a slight downward angle upon passing through the angled windshield, but like everything else, you have to use proper ammo because frangible will disintegrate upon contact possibly with or without penetration of what they hit since they are designed to avoid overpenetration and ricochets. Some of the PDX1 rounds went through the windshield and out through the back window, some went through the windshield, target, headrest, and back seat, some stopped in the trunk, and some went through the trunk. Further, US Marine and Navy SEAL snipers jointly did testing on vehicle glass with rifle rounds fired from a distance and confirmed a downward deflection of the rounds that passed through the angled windshield, which was measured at 3 degrees (which is the opposite of the many Internet articles that say the spinning of the rounds in flight will cause it to deflect and ricochet off the glass without penetration) *by those who watch TV too much*. I couldn't believe my own eyes when I read a popular national gun magazine. An author said in an article that they couldn't put it on TV if it wasn't real. The misleading Hollywood ricochets and deflections you see in the movies are special effects, and *they ARE NOT real*, so they should be left at home for entertainment because anything can happen. Bullets punch through steel, metals, glass, wallboard, plywood, and many other materials, and they kill people on the other side. For those who unknowingly believe that bullets cannot penetrate cars, the TV show MythBusters set out to test a myth that bullets cannot penetrate cars lined (on the *inside*) with telephone books. So they lined the inside of the car and the doors with phone books for testing. In their tests, the rounds punched right through the vehicle body, but the phone books stopped the 9mm, the .357 Magnum, and the .45 ACP but failed to stop the more powerful shotgun slugs and rifle rounds, which both easily went through. Then the books were doubled, and the car was wrapped internally with 400 phone books, and the manikin-style dummies were wrapped in a shell of phone books, but all these phone books still failed to stop the shotgun slugs and the 7.62 × 51 rifle rounds, including the .50 caliber, which totally disabled the vehicle, and all the dummies were verifiably considered dead. My lifetime of troubleshooting and survival instincts says a lesson learned here is that if we would be a little creative and take the phone books with the largest front surface area and thickest phone books we have available and duct-tape all the edges shut in addition to duct- taping a large rope to hang the book around our neck, we have a makeshift emergency bullet- resistant vest that will increase the odds of our survival incredibly since it may stop the majority of handgun bullets being carried by criminals who invade homes and kill people. You can create one for each member of the family, but make the rope a different length for men, women, or children based on their heart-lung area-to-neck ratio so a little longer rope can be adjusted with growth or age. Wearing a snug T-shirt over the phone book vest will aid in preventing it from hanging outward or swinging sideways, exposing our otherwise protected vitals as we move into different positions, but remember to have the T-shirt *with the phone book emergency vest* so it can be used immediately without having to search one out. The addition of a 1/8 inch or greater *steel* plate (NOT aluminum) inserted in the back of the book would make it a bit heavier but much more effective against high-velocity rounds, but remember while this makeshift vest is great for an emergency, the real and proper gear is expensive, but it is always the best.

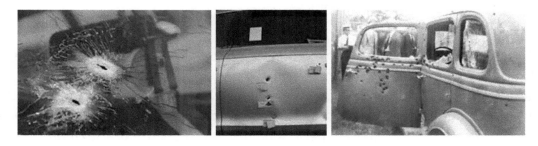

Even a small caliber round went through the vehicle glass and car door quite easily. Notice all the bullet holes after the shoot-out in the old car that had a metal body twice as strong as modern-day vehicles. Never underestimate any round because it could be the exception! Staying alive means tuning your thoughts to these facts. Every bullet fired may give a different result within reason, but the main priority here is to train yourself to the way firearms and ammunition work and the mechanics of materials so that you can use commonsense.

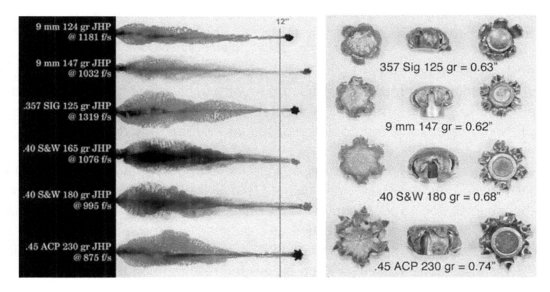

Note the assorted calibers in hollow point ammunition that made 12-inch penetration in ballistic gelatin. Note the lighter faster round had reached the same depth as the slower heavier round but had reached it first! Observe the temporary cavities.

Most people have some kind of phone books around the house. While they don't have bullet- resistant vests available for children, instead of discarding the phone books when the new ones arrive, you can use them for emergency protection for every member of your family in an emergency, but they have to be made into the emergency vest in advance of any attack so you have the time to fit one specifically to each person based on their neck, shoulder, and chest size and do it properly, but make sure they have each person's name on them for the exact fit, or they may be worthless if they don't cover the necessary vital areas. The real bullet-resistant vests are preferred and the best.

Back to finishing the information on the auto glass, the best shot through either building windows or automobile windows is always at a 90-degree angle, if at all possible, but we never know what will happen unexpectedly. According to Winchester's published information on the PDX1, it will perform when needed. I'd be especially happy to have *a gun chambered in any of these calibers* in an emergency, so if you must go smaller, make sure it works for you and that you develop the ability to use such a small gun.

Quit reading the Internet forums for actual technical performance and information and stop believing Hollywood, or you may find yourself hurt very badly or be found very dead! Most of these people writing such information online are searching for the right information too, and too many of them like to voice their opinion of the knowledge they don't have.

While the .357 Magnum revolver may have a five-round capacity and a bit too much recoil for some people, the .327 Federal Magnum is claimed to rival the .357 with less recoil and a 6-round capacity other than 5, due to its slightly smaller bullet diameter. Years ago, when our military determined the .38 was never quite effective as a defensive round for combat, they created a study where they actually shot corpses (donated for science) for evaluation and eventually went to the .45 ACP, which was quite satisfactory in their desired results. In another test, where a pig that was completely gutted was hung to observe internal damage as rounds for comparison passed through, they fired two .38 rounds that went completely through both sides, and they also fired one .45 ACP FMJ round that also went through both sides, but the .45 did far more damage with one round than the two .38s did combined. A .22 caliber short used to be called an assassin's bullet because if they shot someone in the head at close range, it was not strong enough to get back out but would actually bounce around inside the skull, causing extensive brain damage and probable death since it crossed both hemispheres of the brain. Some elderly who have obtained their concealed carry license and even for their home protection prefer to use a .22 caliber long rifle round. The round is very cheap and so easy to shoot that you'll probably barely realize it even fired if you're not listening and observing the target. Do not underestimate the power of the small .22 which will kill! According to a Winchester publication, the .22 rimfire has even killed coyotes and even big game, including, polar bear and elephant that have a very tough hide. *Hopefully*, the man who made this statement wasn't a space invader recovering from a night out, tripping out on drugs or alcohol. During a carjacking where a doctor and his wife were taken hostages, the doctor kept a .22 revolver in the pocket of his driver's car door. When the killer who was already facing the death penalty for so many murders let his guard down, because the doctor kept fussing to stop to empty his bladder, the killer made them all get out of the vehicle so the doctor decided to make his move and try to outgun the KILLER. The doctor drew his .22 revolver and pointed it at the KILLER *point blank*, and while he had the opportunity to place the shots in the KILLER'S head at point-blank range to shut down this KILLER, he fired 4 rounds into the center of his chest, but the carjacking KILLER became enraged and tried to fire his large caliber semiautomatic *stolen gun*, which didn't fire, so he took *their* gun away from them and beat the doctor and his wife up severely and drove away in their car by himself. After taking four .22 Long Rifle rounds in the chest, their assailant drove around the state all day with a bloody T-shirt, but when he stopped at a drug store and robbed them of bandages and supplies to treat his wounds, the clerk called and reported the robbery to the police who were already looking for this killer, which led to his capture. While the .22 will kill anyone who would intentionally try to use such a round for such big game or even for personal defense other than as a last resort if he is otherwise able to handle a bigger round, it is like someone representing himself in court and having a fool for an attorney or even a death wish. Even though the .22 will likely cause immediate incapacitation if it penetrated the central nervous system or the brain with proper shot placement, consideration for the suitability of the caliber, the ammunition, and the weapon must all be given. The .22 will be extremely cheap on ammunition for practice and has no recoil to mention or to worry about. The Walther P22, the Sig Sauer Mosquito, and the Ruger SR22P, all in .22 calibers, are pretty much the same in appearance, size, and weight and are used by many of the elderly and disabled, but you really need to see what's available before making a decision based on its size, what fits in your hand, dexterity, your ability to reach and work the trigger easily, and concealment factors. No matter what your gun of choice might be including the caliber, question any known problems with that particular gun in any way before you ever buy it, but you might research it because the salesman probably doesn't know. While they even have a muzzle brake available for the .22, I see absolutely no purpose in having one due to the small round and lack of recoil.

Muzzle Flash/Muzzle Brakes

The muzzle brake increases the muzzle flash into your view, so criminal encounters in the evening hours or darkness of night may somewhat blind you from your first shot, in comparison (like a camera flash does to your eyes), due to your increased muzzle flash directed upward toward and through your sights while you are trying to follow up with a second shot, especially in darkness with temporarily impaired vision, which just may get you killed! Some people might argue this, but are YOU willing to take the chance?

While the tiny flash from the .22 may be an exception, you cannot shoot effectively at your target with temporary blindness, as compared to those shooters using a muzzle brake for target shooting in normal daylight. Target shooting in daylight under normal conditions is very different from shooting for your life in low-light conditions under stress. If you have vision difficulties or eyeglasses, this may definitely momentarily worsen your vision. We want to create every advantage, not disadvantages! There are companies that cut vents in barrels in revolvers, semiautomatic pistols, rifles, and shotguns. They claim to have tested and found no significant loss in velocity, although they didn't give any figures for us to determine what *their definition* of *significant* means, and they claim up to 80% recoil reduction in some firearms and no night blindness, but again they didn't say what and in which gun and which rounds were used or didn't even offer any test results for our own evaluation. I can't understand their getting around the night flash in a revolver or a semiautomatic since the vent is cut in the barrel, which needs to vent upwards into the atmosphere to thrust properly, which exhausts portions of the muzzle blast right through the sights and through the line of sight. The cost is generally up to $250 or more, depending on what you want. Technically, if your eyes or even one eye experiences a flash, your body comes to the rescue, trying to protect the eyes, and the iris and pupils in both eyes will constrict, reducing the incoming light *and* your ability to see your KILLER, and although you already have to deal with losing 20% of your peripheral vision by focusing through the sites, this may cause an unintended but natural squint, which further reduces your already reduced vision and field of view even more. I personally wouldn't do it for my personal defense gun, *no matter who tells you it's negligible or OK*, while remembering the idea here is YOUR SURVIVAL, and in a shoot-out for YOUR LIFE, you get only ONE unrecoverable mistake, DEATH! Remember, I'm giving you the facts! You're the one who needs to make the decision!

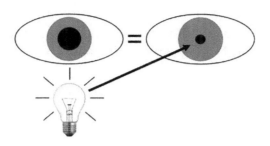

The eyes block out bright light as a defense to the eyes. Don't cause yourself to become a victim because you couldn't see. While gizmos and gadgets have their place, my self-defense is serious business! The eyes are normally dilated in low-light conditions, and a sudden bright light or flash will cause them both to constrict immediately, reducing your vision.

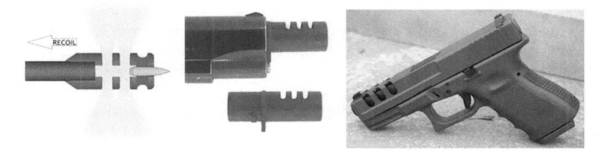

Above are three out of dozens of muzzle brake designs to vent pressure and reduce recoil!

Handgun Differences

The handgrips on a handgun are usually referred to as the two-side panels that attach to the main grip of the gun and are changeable on many guns to something of a better fit or other options. Many semiautomatics (mostly polymer frames) cannot be changed to a more preferable one like those on a 1911 or other models since the polymers are molded into the frame as one piece, but some of them currently come with the different interchangeable back straps to change the way it fits and feels in your hand, but you're still limited to what comes with them. There's even a rubber grip or sleeve, sometimes called a grip glove, that slides and stretches over the grip on many guns to increase the grip's size and gripping ability slightly. If you prefer a small caliber revolver as compared to a semiautomatic due to the revolver's simplicity in operation, Smith and Wesson makes the model 317 in .22 Long Rifle or .22 Magnum, which holds 8 rounds and weighs in at 11.9 ounces, or the 351 PD in .22 Winchester Magnum, which weighs only 10.8 ounces when it's empty and holds 7 rounds in the cylinder. Ruger makes the LCR-22, a compact polymer framed double-action (DA) revolver. Seven or eight rounds may certainly *fumble* a killer if he was counting and figured you used your 5 or 6 shots. Taurus offers the 941 Ultra-lite, and Charter Arms offers the Pathfinder, all three being small-framed lightweight double-action guns in .22 Magnum. They may also be fired in single action due to their hammer. Speer released a

.22 Magnum Rimfire 40-grain Gold Dot defense round for short barrels (SB). When fired from a rifle, it generates a velocity of 2,000 feet per second, and when fired from a 2-inch barrel revolver, it generates 1,050 feet per second, giving excellent penetration for such a small round due to its 40-grain projectile as compared to most .22s with a 36 grain. Winchester offers several .22 Rimfire rounds with some delivering up to 2,250 feet per second. Ruger specifically warns not to use .22 Stinger ammo in their 10/22 target rifles due to the Stinger's longer case length. In addition, some .22 cartridges may vary slightly in diameter so be sure not to use the wrong ammunition even if it looks identical other than using a micrometer to determine its length and diameter and be sure the pressures are loaded according to US firearm manufacturing standards. Using .22 semiautomatic pistols or rifles with low-velocity ammunition may cause malfunctions and failure to eject and chamber a new round. A simple replacement with high-velocity ammo cures many malfunctions. Since hands with different sizes fit guns quite differently, it's like wearing a pair of pants sized to fit your own waist and possibly leg shape and the way some guys might compliment on the way a woman looks as if she were poured into her stylish jeans. Anybody can use any gun that's available in an emergency as long as they understand how to use and operate it; granny proved this, but proper preparation means one specifically suited to you to maximize your potential ability to survive, so what works for one person might not work for another. It is similar to the way hunters have different guns for different purposes, as you're learning, or similar to your needing a prescription for your eyeglasses to work specifically for *you* and another person cannot use them. Sidearms work the same way; anyone with the basic skills to use one can use them, but a specially selected one that specifically fits our self and our own needs, including our hands with finely tuned parts, and select ammunition with our skills to use them will undoubtedly outperform the person with the basic skills using just any gun, but most importantly, be prepared in advance to outmaneuver a killer, beating him to firing the kill shot!

Calibers such as the .25 and .32 don't seem to be available as much, but the manufacturers are currently producing much more of everything to fill the gaps for concealed and pocket carry, including newer .25 and .32 pistols. In some rigorous tests between a couple of makes, the Walther USA PPK in .32 ACP outperformed the other in .32 ACP remarkably with immediate and fast follow-up shots, compared to the other's many double feeds and jams in this particular test, but even a duplicate of another gun may have none, or it might even have different problems, which is one reason why a gun known for its quality generally performs equally as well if you picked up any particular one out of 25, for example, as compared to those that may perform quite improperly on so many out of the 25. Just because it's a gun, or even a new gun, doesn't mean it will work properly. The .380 has been selling as if they are giving them away and so are the 9mm. Many of the law enforcement agencies are adopting the .40 Smith and Wesson, which was designed primarily to compete with the .45 ACP due to the .45's greater recoil and the .40's comparable energy and ability to perform as compared to many of their 9 MM. The .41 Magnum and the .44 Magnum used to be considered more of a hunting round while they are definitely a cartridge of choice for hunting, but newer handguns are appearing that might change that. Taurus makes a few versions of the Judge, including their shorter version called the public defender, which is a large revolver that chambers and shoots your choice of a .45 Long Colt or a .410 shotgun shell in the same gun and will even chamber both calibers in the five-round cylinder at the same time. It has a competitor called the Governor by Smith and Wesson that shoots the .45 Long Colt, the .410 shotgun shell, or the .45 ACP with the use of moon clips. The .45 GAP, otherwise known as the Glock Automatic Pistol, is actually a shortened .45 ACP (Cartridge) designed primarily to try to compete with the .40 Smith and Wesson and the .45 ACP, and it was introduced in 2003 as a joint effort by Glock and Speer. Speer is an ammunition manufacturer. The .40 S&W and the .45 GAP claim to have as much energy and satisfactory results all the way around as a normal .45 ACP with less recoil. Though I haven't put them to a real test between the two, I wasn't sure if the .45 GAP would actually stay around long enough, but it seems it may be here to stay since there have been so many guns sold, but I've bought expensive guns before and chambered for a popular round by a major manufacturer, and they *dropped* it from production because of insufficient sales. I use and prefer standard calibers so that commercial ammunition will always be available. For concealed carry, I would avoid nonstandard (caliber × length designation) bullets or even those that are sometimes called wildcats, which are generally devised on a reloading bench in someone's personal shop and later adopted by gun and ammunition manufacturers, because sometimes they get to be popular and seem to be catching on, but eventually they may prove to be a passing trend. If at least two gun manufacturers start chambering a few guns for a new wildcat cartridge along the way, it would be more of a consideration for owning one, in case one of the manufacturers quit making it, and they may even quit making ammo for it due to no sales. You end up with a gun that becomes an expensive paperweight, or else you need to set up and do your own reloading. Although *you can reload*, it's a science of its own, and although it always used to be much cheaper than commercially manufactured ammo, some of the recent higher prices on ammunition components may make it more of a serious consideration to justify unless you like shooting as a hobby or sport where you can fine-tune your loads for accuracy and always have the ability to obtain ammo for a gun when none of the manufacturers make it anymore. Once you learn who sells whatever components you might need for a reasonable price, it gets much easier. If you're shooting a .22 Rimfire caliber, or any rimfire for that matter, they cannot be reloaded, but it's so cheap to buy that there would be no reason to ever want to reload it. Various centerfire calibers in .22 *can* be reloaded because of the centerfire primer, so if it's not a center-fire, don't even ask. It's also very hard to sell a gun that has no commercially available ammo, so once you bought it, it might be yours forever and a possible candidate for a city buy-back program. Please don't confuse the term *wildcat* with the .22 caliber rimfire ammunition manufactured by Winchester that is actually *named* wildcat.

If you already own a handgun that you are used to or prefer, then decide if you can use it for concealed carry. Once you understand the way everything comes together for your defensive gun, then you might be able to rework it and tune it up if needed. Contrary to some gun schools that claim a large semiautomatic is best, and they even say this for the totally inexperienced, I normally suggest a revolver for a man or woman who has no, or very little, firearms experience because basically all you have to do is put the bullets in and shoot. As long as you don't have any uncrimped ammo loaded into it, and the gun is in good condition, there's nothing to jam other than snagging a hammer spur on clothing, but there are the bobbed hammer spurs (cutoff) to remedy this. In a previous study on 1800 felons that were arrested and incarcerated, it was found that they mostly preferred revolvers for their crime spree and other non-semiautomatic firearms due to their ease of use. Semiautomatic pistols require more experience to operate, and *even if you are experienced*, malfunctions can happen when you least expect it, so then you have to have reliable troubleshooting experience in a semiautomatic pistol in the hopes that there's sufficient time to correct the problem and still save yourself. Some who love certain guns or hate others make claims of certain guns malfunctioning or jamming, but the fact is that no matter what kind of gun you use, cheap or expensive, if it's a semiautomatic, anything can happen, and no matter what make the gun is, it can still jam! Some jams are self- induced! If students on the firing line experience jam and malfunction, since they are students and learning, I certainly wouldn't blame the gun and would possibly teach these individuals that they may have made a poor choice *depending on their needs*, but I would instruct them on learning to operate it more effectively *before* carrying it for life-saving purposes. If you do have one already, depending on what it is, it might not be worth investing too much money into it if it's not particularly suited, and selecting a better replacement may be the only way to go, but don't forget to question the option of trading your old one in at the gun shop for the new one which would be far better than trying to sell it to someone you don't know, IF there's even a market for it or a gun for the emergency bag in your trunk.

Ammunition Safe or Reliable

Other than gun malfunctions, sometimes the ammo is a problem. When I was on a shooting range and was being timed, after the beep, I reached for my .45 and drew it, quickly acquiring the target and firing what should have been a kill shot, but instead my gun went *click*. I had a *dud* round in the chamber, and it was commercially manufactured name-brand ammunition, not a hand load, so anything can happen but hopefully not in an emergency! Now you might understand more of a need for knowing what to do if the gun doesn't work. I'd much rather have a round fail to fire other than it being improperly loaded and getting stuck somewhere in the barrel. If it was just a dud, assuming I'm still alive, I could always quickly eject the defective round, recover from the malfunction fast, and get back into the gunfight before I get killed and become a statistic, that is, one more dead from another unexpected attack. Although I'm never one to buy name brands for such things as certain clothing, sunglasses, or similar accessories, I always use name-brand *guns*, especially *proven ammunition* for my carry load.

I hear people say very confidently that the cheap off-brands work OK in their gun, and although I test the different brands, if my life is on the line, I don't want any experiments going on. I want a bang and a hit each and every time! Someone might save $2 on a cheaper box of off-brand foreign ammo, but when confronted by an armed assailant and your ammo doesn't fire, I hope you have some toilet paper in your bag of tricks because you're going to need it. Even with the top of the line ammo, you could possibly get a dud once in a while; it happens. I actually had 2 in the last 3,150 rounds that I fired downrange, but they were in the first hundred or so rounds when I was testing a few different brands. Once is too many in a gunfight for your life. In a study of rounds that didn't fire, it was found that 93% of those that failed actually fired when struck again. Although *some* misfires can be attributed to operator error, IF your round doesn't fire the first time, you're taking a chance on your safety by trying to fire it again. Many guns have what they call re-strike capability that allows the firing pin to strike the failed round a second time just by pulling the trigger again. This could be beneficial as it is faster than trying to clear the failed round, but there is still the 7% that didn't work at all, which could spell disaster, but the odds are highly in your favor. If you select a semiautomatic, make sure you determine whether it has re-strike capability or not, or if you think you might need this capability.

Ammo Seals and Destructive Chemicals

  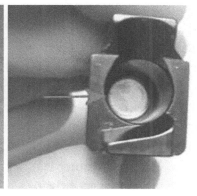

See the bullets stuck in these two barrels due to an inferior round that was under-pressured.

I read a supposedly knowledgeable person soaked his live ammo from different commercial manufacturers in water for so many hours and then tried to fire it to see if the water leaked in so he could see if it would actually fire to determine how dependable it was. All NATO military ammo is sealed at the primer and the bullet end to prevent any leakage into them. NEXT, I would NEVER soak my ammo in water. In addition, never put oil, penetrating oil, solvents, or ammonia on your ammunition because certain chemicals are designed to give maximum penetration, but ammonia is caustic and hazardous, and it will corrode the copper and brass, and will break down and weaken the brass cartridges. While anhydrous ammonia is commonly used as a household cleaner, it is even in simple cleaners such as Windex. Ammonia is compatible with carbon, steel, and iron, but it is not compatible with copper, brass, bronze, zinc, or mercury. Ammonia corrodes copper and brass into a blue-green salt, and if ammonia is mixed with anything containing bleach, it will produce toxic poisonous gas. For your ammo, avoid anything that has ammonia in it including not leaving residuals of chemical bore cleaning solvents that are designed to remove lead or copper fouling. The chemical must not be left in the bore after cleaning due to its destructive nature on the copper or the brass. When you read articles saying that they removed ammo from a handgun that hadn't been used for such a long time and the ammo was all corroded and green, it doesn't mean it's old; it might indicate they had cleaned the ammo with a destructive chemical. If I feel the need to clean my ammo, which is somewhat rare, I use simple alcohol available at the local drug store which cleans and immediately evaporates. If you really want to clean more aggressively, simply use a mild steel wool. Ammo does not have to be pretty but must be properly cleaned so it functions properly.

Ammo has a pressed fit, so hopefully leakage into the cartridge will never happen from the bullet or the primer end. The bullet is a tight fit in factory ammunition (certain hand-loading crimps) such as a roll crimp. An improper crimp, especially, may create an abnormal space between the outer diameter of the bullet and the inner diameter of the case neck that you may be able to notice it almost wiggle very slightly, but it's crimped improperly. This crimp is for reloaded revolver ammunition and is not used for semiautomatic pistols which use a taper crimp. Bullets should be tight in their respective cartridge cases. Although some powders will burn if wet, if there's even a trace of water (or any chemical) that somehow leaked into a cartridge, it would then be defective and could cause an interaction, a misfire, or what they call a hang fire, being a delayed firing. There might even be a combination of both some wet powder and a sufficient amount of dry powder inside the bullet cartridge to actually ignite but giving poor ignition—the same as a SQUIB. A SQUIB is insufficient pressure to launch the projectile. With insufficient pressure to propel the bullet through the barrel, it will result in a bullet getting lodged and stuck in the barrel! You may quickly recognize it when you hear that unusual pop but no kick or recoil! If you don't know what happened and you succeed in firing a second round, it could mean disaster or even death due to the pressure of the live round trying to suddenly expand when the bullet jams against the one stuck in the barrel, possibly or probably blowing the gun apart. It's a scary situation if there's an armed assailant with his gun pointed at you. If you *do* ever hear an insufficient bang and experience no recoil, DO NOT try to fire a second round until you've checked the gun, NOT EVEN FOR TEST-FIRING. This situation can happen in either a revolver *or* a semiautomatic pistol, including long guns, because it's caused by defective ammo. While the semiautomatic may not have achieved sufficient pressure to cycle the slide and chamber a new round, *it might actually chamber a new round* but the revolver *will allow* a new round to rotate into place to fire, SO BEWARE AND DON'T DO IT! If you succeed in firing the second round, following a defective round, it won't push the first bullet out that's stuck in the barrel, and if the gun doesn't blow apart, it will most likely create a bulge in the chamber or the barrel and make the gun very dangerous to try to use anymore unless you can get the cylinder, chamber, or barrel replaced by a qualified gunsmith, which might cost as much *or more* as replacing the gun, which is an expensive mistake. If you have such an occurrence and are not sure, unload the gun and check the inside of the barrel. If there's a bullet lodged in the barrel, a wooden dowel rod can be inserted, and tap the lodged bullet out, but if you do, then make a very good internal inspection of the barrel with sufficient light. If you see anything appearing to be a ring shape somewhere inside the barrel, you most likely have a bulged barrel and it needs to be replaced. I very highly recommend keeping your bullets dry. If you ever wanted to explore the inner components of a live round, I would suggest getting assistance from a friend with a bullet puller that's generally available with a serious hand loader's reloading equipment to properly remove the bullet from the cartridge case for internal examination other than trying to fire it, or you can get an inexpensive one for about $21 where they sell reloading supplies. Never try to fire *any* ammo that you suspect may be possibly inferior or damaged for whatever reason.

If you pull the trigger and nothing happens as far as the gun firing or you don't even hear a somewhat of a muffled bang, keep the muzzle pointed downrange for 30 seconds to make sure it's not a hang fire, that is, a delayed firing. If you still don't get a firing of the round 30 seconds later, then carefully remove it and DO NOT MIX IT WITH OTHER AMMO. Some shooting ranges will accept defective or undesirable ammo for disposal, and they disassemble it and recycle the components and burn off the powders.

In addition, if you build or buy a gun safe, get a dehumidifier which is small and inexpensive, and it's really a necessity. I won't even buy name-brand bullets with steel cartridge cases unless I know I'm going to fire them within a reasonable time because while in storage, humidity and sweat could cause them to rust, making them undesirable for proper functioning. While some shooters reported improper functioning in semiautomatics with steel cartridges, other users reported the same ammunition worked fine, but even though I've tested this ammo, I'm less likely to buy *any* ammo with cartridges that are made of steel or aluminum because they are not malleable, that is, not suitable for reloading, and have to be discarded, and I save my fired brass for reloading.

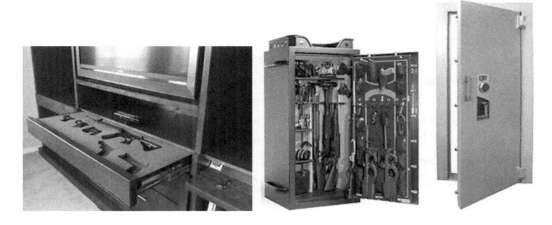

The guy who thought this drawer up was very creative, but I sure hope he has safety measures in place so they cannot open the drawer. Because it is one of the first places where crooks look for valuables. While the safe in the center is very large, there are dozens of safe sizes available for dozens of prices. Many gun safe companies make full-sized doors that will simply fit in and replace one of your interior house doors to conceal an entire room.

Some state laws regulate the storage of gunpowder and ammunition. Some people suggest homemade steel boxes. While it sounds great, a strong steel box is not necessarily a good thing for your explosives because without one panel designed to blow out before the pressure maxes out like the manufactured storage boxes do, the stronger box will hold together longer and build much greater pressures before it blows apart and gives similar results to a bomb going off with very destructive powers. There are so many powders and reactions that we cannot rely on assumed knowledge of any particular type, no matter what type of powder it is. Some ammunition is safely stored in gun safes, but you must comply with your state laws that may restrict storing the ammunition with your firearms. Those who supply reloading components should have plenty of gunpowder storage boxes available.

Evaluating Firearms

While considering your gun selection, you might borrow or rent a gun to try out a specific caliber or style of gun, but beware that some rental guns at ranges are not maintained properly and may jam or lock up due to lack of proper maintenance or low quality of manufacturing techniques or design. I knew a man who bought a new gun, a copy of the exact gun that I rented for an evaluation, but I asked him how he liked it without telling him about my own experience. His experience was about the same as mine, and he bought his brand-new firearm, so understand my desire for name brands in firearms, but even then you must study and evaluate it. If you borrow or rent a gun and you find you can handle the recoil from a gun you like and you can hit the target, *which you can learn to do*, then when you buy your own gun, you will feel much better because you already know you can shoot it, compared to just being advised from a friend. Then, if it doesn't function when it's needed, it will either be your fault for improper maintenance, lack of operating and troubleshooting knowledge, or because you had bought a bargain basement firearm without a thorough examination. Sometimes I've come across a handgun that was purchased brand-new for practically nothing, and they even gave a lifetime warranty. The lifetime warranty does no good if you fail in your attempt to stop a lethal threat because DEAD MEN no longer need their gun. And although some manufacturers cut corners and spend very little to develop their product, just because a gun might have a high price does not necessarily make it ideal. I've seen some that I would consider high-priced paperweights. Study the quality of manufacturing by checking the free play in the slide, making sure the magazine locks securely in place with no wiggle, removable sights, no sharp edges, or burrs on it, and make sure it functions smoothly. See if the finish is a special coating or blued or just plain spray-painted which on some guns will start to peel off in a short time even due to normal use, and I've personally seen this with cheap manufacturing in handguns while some have an underlying chemical to bond the paint on the finish to stay on, but some don't. I've read articles where the author has said cheap was just fine, but, remember, he won't be there when you're fighting for your life, and he'll be hiding when you come looking for him. Some fine guns are actually painted too, like many of the assault rifle styles that we used to spray paint over the past 40 years with flat black barbecue grille spray paint whenever they got scuffed up too much. It worked great, you couldn't tell, and it wouldn't come off. I have trouble remembering, but I think I learned this from a military M16 armorer's manual back in the seventies. A friend and military gun enthusiast told me that he uses flat black high-temperature paint available at the auto parts. At least in all these years, I haven't seen any come off so far, and, in all the guns I've worked on, nobody ever called me and had any complaints. I can preach cheap isn't necessarily good; one man asked me for advice in a gun shop, but he bought the cheapest and most inappropriate gun for concealed carry anyway, so I wish him luck if he's ever in a gunfight for his life. A gun is not all winning, and just because it's new doesn't mean anything as far as function or reliability is concerned. Regardless of the finish, it is a tool for saving your life IF you can use it properly and IF it works. When you ask for the right information and then grin and say, "Yeah, right," but buy the most inappropriate one because it's a cheapo, you figure you are making your best choice, NOT THE best choice. So if some thug takes your life in a robbery or shoot-out, you'll never have to worry about the comparison after the fact because most of our life we learn from our mistakes, but this is one you may never live to know. Remember the young thug who wondered why his $40 gun didn't work when he was caught?

After you've read everything in this book, you will be in a position to better understand what to look for and what to avoid that does not work mechanically or does not fit your needs. The American market is flooded with junk guns, and everyone who gets killed using one cannot blame anyone else! When you hear someone say accurate enough for concealed carry or good enough for your protection, personally, I wouldn't take any more advice from them. I have read so many times that a short snub nose is easier to carry and accuracy is irrelevant due to close encounters. This is completely wrong! You need to be as accurate as possible because other people, or even *me*, might be downrange of you when you're shooting and I *don't* want to get shot because the person sending bullets my way doesn't practice and develop his necessary skills to hit the right person, no matter what he's shooting. Someone getting killed in the crossfire will have their family filing charges for wrongful death against both of the shooters. If you're going to carry a gun for the protection of yourself and your family, you have to have the motivation, ambition, and desire to do this properly to be effective and succeed. Most importantly, you need to be accurate to hit your killer and stop the threat or you may die.

ALWAYS PRACTICE IN A CALM MANNER

USE COMMONSENSE AND BE SAFE

I knew a deputy who was playing quick draw with another deputy, but accidentally shot and killed him. They seem to have forgotten the part about unloading their guns to be safe. Never play with real guns or live ammo!

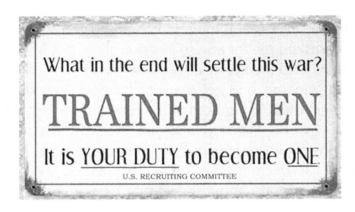

YOUR DUTY: I happened to come across this sign by recruiters to end the war, and it holds true that even in civilian life, the criminals are the enemy and we need to be trained to succeed in our own survival. Would YOU continue an attack on someone who pulls a gun and shoots back at you? They'll be moving out!

There are people who claim they prefer a high-capacity magazine so they can fire numerous smaller caliber rounds as compared to less larger caliber rounds and say they can *probably* get at least one hit or maybe get many more hits. In short, more bullets in the air mean more problems on the receiving end with YOU being responsible and liable for all of them! For those responsibly carrying a gun or those who carry a gun for a living who are far more likely to face a deadly encounter, high-capacity magazines will reduce reload downtime and increase the ability to continuously engage targets, resulting in less downtime and less target distraction in a firefight. If you think a high-capacity magazine is your answer and it's for your own personal use, then beware of the actual magazine capacity and your state laws because if the gun you love has a 16 round magazine and your state laws restrict it to 10, you may find it somewhat complicated if they don't specifically offer such a magazine limited to 10 rounds for the gun you want, and even by loading only 10 rounds into such a magazine, you may find yourself being charged with violating the gun laws since that magazine still has the option to load many more rounds. Contrary to some who will argue the situation, your carry gun should be given the same consideration you give your most important purchases in life, not necessarily higher priced, but very functional and effective because without it, you may lose your very life. If you're very knowledgeable in firearms, then you can be more selective in less costly guns. In a recent shoot-out between several thugs across town, they generally didn't care about skills; they just felt powerful by having a gun. Their inability to shoot accurately caused a young 13-year-old girl on the second floor of her home to take a bullet and die. A small error in sighting on one side of the street just may place your fired round upstairs into an unintended bedroom on the other side of the street. People who use such improper thinking by preferring a very short snub nose in unqualified hands and then think accuracy is not of concern are probably those same people who think they are in quite proper physical health because they wear a 34- or 36-inch waist size but overlook their 56-inch gut hanging over the belt. It's like the survival book that looked very impressive on the bargain table for half price. When I flipped to navigating my way without a compass, though I already knew how to do but thought maybe I could learn something new, the author said to bring an electronic GPS along, and then I realized why they didn't sell. So while many people think they have the answer, others who have more knowledge see their errors quite easily. Although snub-nosed revolvers are quite effective in the right hands and circumstances, don't cause yourself to become the victim because you couldn't use your gear at hand properly to stop the threat! If you read some of the articles that say they fired 1.6-inch 5 shot groups from a 1-7/8-inch barreled .38 caliber revolvers using rapid-fire at 25 yards offhand, it doesn't easily work that way. While many articles make such claims, some *real* experts *might* do this after many years of practice, but after you've fired the next 10,000 rounds of your own downrange, rethink my words here, but remember that nobody can do it without sufficient practice. Every time you miss your shot, it brings your assailant closer to possibly killing you! IN A BATTLE FOR YOUR LIFE, YOU LOSE ONLY ONCE!

Don't confuse this requirement for accuracy by choosing between a $1,000 fully capable gun as compared to a $4,000 to $7,000 + custom gun, which might get a half-inch smaller group *in the right hands* at 25 yards. If this becomes the question, then the $1,000 gun would probably qualify as accurate enough, providing it is a quality item and shot by a qualified shooter (hopefully meaning you). No matter how perfect the gun is, you have to be able to use it! No disrespect to those who make custom handguns because they are very finely assembled and tuned, but I look for need, effectiveness, and price, knowing that no matter what it is, I still have to have the skills to use it. If I were shooting in competition for a $100,000 prize, I'd opt for the $4 to $7,000 custom job where that extra ½" less in shot spread might bring home the money. Commonsense is required. Although many handguns are very expensive, from a few hundred to a few thousand dollars or much more quite easily, there are excellent handguns being sold for a fraction of what some heavily advertised custom handguns are sold for and almost equal in accuracy but again depending on the shooter's skill. If you ask a salesman at a gun shop, make sure you have someone knowledgeable with you so you don't buy what you don't want or need. Knowledgeable does not mean they own or shoot a gun. I've questioned employees in gun shops who said certain guns were very good, and one man even said it was the very best, but when renting that particular gun and putting it through a complete evaluation, I wouldn't even buy it for parts, and considering their reliability, they were very overpriced. What good is a gun that doesn't work? Would you put a flat tire ON your car because it was cheaper? Once settling the debate of controllability, a learned practice, unless you have a disability and cannot handle it, then remember you could put it in layaway for a few months to be able to more easily afford a quality *tool* that you will rely on to maintain your life if and when the time arises. You can study the laws while waiting to get your gun paid off, or you can study and get your concealed carry license and rent a gun for your range qualification since many schools will rent you one, but make sure of who is supposed to provide the ammo.

Once you have all the proper facts, guess whose fault it is if you get caught in this predicament?

Dominant Eye

While we want to use both eyes for personal handgun defense, long guns are different and usually scoped; however, some individuals may have difficulty aiming because of interference from their dominant eye, if this is not the eye used in the aiming process. This may require the shooter to fire from the other side of the weapon; right-handed shooter will fire left-handed. To determine which eye is dominant, hold an index finger 6 to 8 inches in front of your eyes. Close one eye at a time while looking at the finger; one eye will appear to make the finger move as far as a few inches and the other eye will not. The eye that *does not* appear to make the finger move is the dominant eye! If you don't seem to notice the finger position, alternate one eye open and one eye closed simultaneously, and one will make the finger appear a couple of inches to the side of where your other eye sees it. Everyone who shoots should know his dominant eye to sort out sighting differences.

The dominant eye cover that fits over either eye on your shooting glasses to help correct eye problems while training to shoot.

Sights

If you don't understand this information properly, you may shoot all day and never hit your target, but if you know what is happening, you can quickly compensate and start hitting the target somewhere within its boundaries and then adjust to sight in your firearm to impact at the bull's-eye. Fixed sights as in most handguns are made to properly shoot and hit your target within a certain range, generally *within* 25 yards, but depending on the particular style of firearm and caliber used, be sure of the distance your sights are set for when you buy it, and this doesn't mean a guess from the guy trying to sell it. The manufacturer may recommend a certain bullet and weight that the gun and sights were initially designed and adjusted for (various elevations in impact), so make sure you read the owner's manual, maybe even before you buy the gun. They are generally short. Once you buy it, they won't even take it back without labeling it as used, even if unused and unfired, and you can't use the excuse that the salesman said so! Ammunition manufacturers offer numerous self-defense loads to function in many guns that otherwise require certain and specific ammo such as round nose or FMJ, but you need to evaluate and try the personal defense ammo to make sure it functions in *your* gun. Handgun ammunition may vary in length 1/16" between round nose and hollow points and may or may not function in *your* handgun; that is, it could cause a JAM! Some hollow points have a round ball or other device to fill the difference in the nose length for proper feeding. Human error or inconsistencies including fear of recoil are responsible for most of the improper accuracy when the firearm is otherwise really very capable. Iron sights (the common term for non- scoped sights, no matter what they are made of) are usually cursed by new shooters as being defective or bent because they can't hit the target at all, let alone in the bull's-eye. When I see someone with a new gun and cursing it, I snicker to myself. First, make sure the sights are the real problem. Some people claim fixed sights, which are non-adjustable and in a fixed position, are worthless. I personally prefer fixed sights for my carry gun while I may opt for adjustable sights for target shooting because I may change what I do in different situations. Then if you are hitting low, you need to lower (shorten) the front sight to bring the bullet impact up or raise the rear sight, which gives the same results. If you need to move the impact to the left, then move the rear sight to the left, which angles the muzzle to the left and does the opposite to go the other way. Optical scopes have the crosshairs called stadia of various designs in the reticle for you to use as your line of sight guide when aiming at your target. The point where the crosshairs intersect in the reticle is the desired point of bullet impact when zeroed IF you do it properly. While the crosshairs are very thin across the center of your view, they become thick on each end of the stadia, which changes their name at that point to posts. When you buy a scope, you need to know the actual dimensions across the crosshairs between the posts at a 100-yard range for reference, and then you can further estimate the size of the target or the distance of your target. Be aware that different ammunition may print differently on target as much as a couple of inches, so if you're certain you have the sights configured properly, try a few different brands without sight adjustments and see what happens.

Factory and Optional Sights

I personally avoid guns that have no factory sights like some small pocket guns that leave you trying to sight down the slight channel, groove, or pyramid on top of the slide. When people tell me sights are not really that important because of close-range encounters, no matter what their credentials are, to me, they are one who isn't really as smart as he thinks *because you never know what you might need to do* and this is supposed to save your life. Many small pocket guns are generally assumed by many people to be used as a belly gun in CQB, close quarters battle. By telling someone something is good enough just to please them is doing them a serious injustice. Death comes around only once, and what would that person do after he told you this little cheapo is good enough and he found himself having to rely on YOU to save *his* life in a sudden robbery?

He might wish he wasn't trying to make his paycheck when he sold you el cheapo, compared to something a little more reliable and capable. While using your sights is not always an option in an emergency as you will see later, they should be there and you should know how to use them. While you learn how and get used to them, you'll become more instinctive. If you find a suitable defense gun but really dislike the sights, there are many high-quality optional sights available if you prefer something that you can see better or faster or even both, compared to what is installed on the gun you choose. Seeing what you shoot at makes you much more effective and also much safer for every reason (including your own survival). There are quite a few after-market sights in a variety of configurations, which just might be great as compared to blah, and we don't want to accept them as just good enough because fine-tuning means survival. Some three-dot sights have tiny dots but might be hard to see in daylight, let alone low-light conditions, so I personally like the larger dots. I would make sure that the factory-installed sights are removable for replacement, just in case I later determined that I preferred a different configuration as *I've done* in the past. I will never use sights that are glued on! Sometimes the currently installed sight might look very good at the time of purchase, but after using it at the range for a while, you might find problems and desire to look at optional installations. If they cannot be removed and replaced, you're stuck with what you bought. You need to be able to see that front sight blade clearly and quickly. While there have even been instructors who disregarded sights that illuminate in total darkness as not being necessary, I make them mandatory on my own gun since I've been attacked in daylight *and* in total darkness, so I take full responsibility for my own life. I'm addicted to living!

It's not their opinion that's important; it's your decision to live, that's important, and what YOU want, so once you know the facts, you have the necessary tools to make a life-saving decision. You need to SEE what you are going to shoot at.

Some Sight Picture Configurations

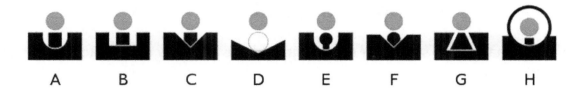

The gray dot over each set of iron sights represents the target. This sometimes is called a target hold or a six o'clock hold, that is, at the bottom center of the bull's-eye. For combat defensive shooting, where you normally see the sight pictures aligned across the top but centered at the six o'clock position, you want to place the point of aim in the center of that gray dot, not at the bottom. I don't shoot that way, but if I were shooting at the gray dots, I'd always shoot for dead center of the target, regardless of target shooting or combat to assure consistency. If the bull's-eye is a large area or circle, you want to keep your sights from wandering all over the entire area, so if you shoot a hole in the bull's-eye, then aiming for that first hole for each consecutive shot will give you a point of reference for aiming and help to improve your accuracy considerably. Look at the selection of open sights above and one aperture sight suitable for use with long eye relief:

A. U-notch and post
B. Patridge
C. V-notch and post
D. Express
E. U-notch and bead
F. V-notch and bead
G. Trapezoid
H. Ghost ring

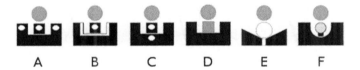

Notice the various methods of open sight contrast enhancement including the use of colors. Again, the gray dot is the target. From left to right:

A. Three dot
B. White outline
C. Straight-eight
D. Red insert
E. Dot and bar
F. Gold bead

Use what works best for your eyes!

The Correct Use of Iron Sights

All open sights, that is, non-scoped or non-magnified, are generally referred to as iron sights, no matter what they are actually made of, but I always avoid any inferior materials such as plastics glued on or magnetically attached. Beware of the era of plastics! Your LIFE is at stake!

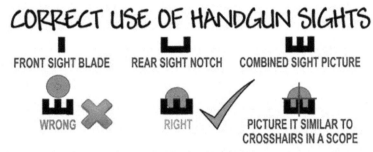

The front sight post should be centered on the smallest center dot in the target! The more you shoot small target reference points, the better you will become at shooting other than wandering around the bull's-eye.

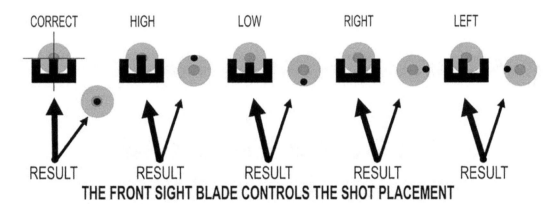

The top of your front sight blade should be exactly centered and exactly leveled across the top being equal in height with the two sides of the rear notch for a perfect shot. If your front sight blade is too far to the right, then your shot goes to the right and the same applies to the left, too high or too low! Even if the sights are perfectly aligned, the top of the front sight blade has to be located at your desired point of impact, and also, most handguns have the top of the sights approximately .8 inches above the centerline of the bore of the barrel or, say, from the center of the bullet. If your shots hit too low at your desired distance and everything is done right, you can raise the rear sight or shorten the front sight. I shoot my 3-inch 1911 in .45 ACP from 7 to 25 yards being realistic, while most encounters take place at 7 yards or 21 feet. Being able to shoot further out increases your chances of survival in addition to teaching yourself to steady your long shots sufficiently to hit home, which directly reduces error and makes your accuracy at shorter distances, say 7 yards, much easier to put them in the desired spot.

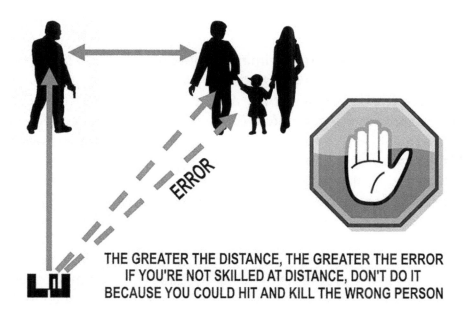

THE GREATER THE DISTANCE, THE GREATER THE ERROR
IF YOU'RE NOT SKILLED AT DISTANCE, DON'T DO IT
BECAUSE YOU COULD HIT AND KILL THE WRONG PERSON

Missing Your Shot Is Too Easy

While some of this line will be repeated elsewhere to make sure it's remembered, a small sighting error of about 1/10 of an inch at the muzzle will magnify downrange at a 25-yard target by about 15 inches or more if not a total miss, depending on your actual distance. You may see your killer in your sights, but if the front sight blade is too far to either side through the rear view in the sight notch, other than being exactly centered, then your bullet will go somewhere you didn't figure on. Imagine being a full-inch off target in a stressful encounter. An inch seems small or simple enough but could result in a miss by 150 inches! A sighting misalignment is magnified downrange at any distance, so say this one at 25 yards could result in 12½ feet! While 25 yards may sound extremely far, it's only 75 feet, which now sounds much closer.

Meprolight night sights are available in a fixed configuration on the left or adjustable on the right. They are available in dozens of configurations for assorted guns, sidearms, and long guns. The dots glow in the dark like small light bulbs and never need to be charged by any light source. Keep them in matched sets for accuracy.

Angular Shift Error

If the shooter does not observe correct aiming, maintaining the top surface of the centered front sight on a level with the top of the rear sight and equal light space on each side of the front sight blade, there will be very few if any accurate shots. Most often, he locates the front sight in a different position in the rear notch. This accounts for a greater dispersion of shots on the target since the bullets will deviate in the direction in which the front sight is positioned in the notch. This aiming error is known as angular shift error. Try shooting at your target at a 7-yard range of 21 feet, then try it at 25 yards of 75 feet, and see how easy it is to miss until you develop familiarity with *your specific gun* and the ability to shoot such distance *before* you ever attempt it in a deadly encounter. Saving ourselves and killing someone else didn't accomplish a life-saving response.

While far too many people use only large circles or BIG gray dots to simulate targets, they place the top of the sight blade at the bottom of the circle *without* explaining beyond that for precision shooting, you need to use a smaller target reference. Remember, you want to hit what you aim for, not just accepting a hit anywhere in the circle or target as successful because due to error in the path of the bullet, the further it flies, the greater the error becomes, not to mention you never learn the proper shooting techniques to be consistent in placing all your shots where they are actually intended to be. Always focus on the front sight blade and be very critical in the amount of precision in your alignment.

Now that you understand the correct way of sighting your firearm, go back up and look at the different sighting configurations again, and now maybe you'll find one you think you really like.

Buying Collectible Guns

Certain guns, such as commemorative or anniversary issues, bear very high-priced tags. This is because they usually have fancy custom engraving and even gold-plated parts on some, but for the most part, they are intended as collectors guns for increased value years later down the road, and, as collectors issues, they may be intended to be duplicates of the *very original* issue and may *even have the same internal working mechanisms and parts* as the original standard issue, not even the newer or the improved parts or conversions. Remember, the commemorative and anniversary model guns only hold their value if you don't ever fire a round in them. They also have *no* value if there's no collector interested in them. If the gun you consider has a higher price but has internal modifications for functionability without all the pretty cosmetic features, this is where you need to be looking. I don't buy guns to hang on the wall for people to admire; I buy only guns to shoot unless I win the lottery, but I stand a greater chance of getting shot than winning the cash. If I ever had such a collectors issue and my life was on the line, I'd never hesitate to fire that one round to save my life, and then maybe it would mean more to me when it was hanging on the wall.

Engraved and gold-plated firearms for collectors lose value when fired. The best bet here for a defense gun is the model 1911 on the far left. We want effective ones, compared to pretty ones. The ugly duckling might be a great lifesaver.

Gun Safety Mechanisms

I avoid guns that have no safety. Some are claimed to be safe but so were the sailor and the shotgun that blew my leg in two. *Accidents do happen!* I'm not beating up Glock, and maybe some of you will even go out and buy one after you learn so much. Who knows? I viewed photos of damage that occurred when a Glock discharged accidentally, but the cheap thin leather holster was actually determined to be the cause. The man was getting into the passenger side of his vehicle and his wife was in the driver's seat when suddenly there was a BANG, as he bent into the seat. They were startled, wondering what happened. In the photos, they put a wood dowel rod down through inside his waistband holster, out through his pants where the hole was blown through, through the car seat, and into the floor. He was very lucky. The mouth of the *cheap* soft leather holster bent into the form of a *V* alongside and into the trigger guard and pushed against the trigger as he bent into the seat, setting off a round. There have been a few more incidents where the drawstring on windbreakers pulled through the Glock trigger guard and discharged them. Again, quality is the name of the game with your gun *and* your holster! I wouldn't rub the holster down with leather softeners, especially on expensive holsters that are actually molded to the shape of the gun to maintain a tight grip, but manufacturers offer treatment oils that won't weaken the molded hold on your gun. If you're more worried about the pretty finish on your gun that may become somewhat worn due to inserting and drawing it from the tight holster so many times, especially in practice, then make sure you buy something that has a finish that won't do this or buy holster lubricant that manufacturers offer to get an easy withdrawal of your gun from a snug holster when needed, such as DRAW-EZ from Galco. A tiny bottle treats several holsters, and it really works great. No matter what finish is on my particular gun, my life and proficiency in using it is the most important consideration here. Pretty guns might be babied too much, and ugly guns just might save your life like the old ragged wrench in the mechanic's toolbox due to so much use since it worked the best. While some name-brand guns might be higher in price, they still might not be what you need.

The Glock advertises what they call a safe action, striker-fired pistol. Strikers are usually one— or two-piece spring-loaded striking mechanisms that do the same job as a hammer and firing pin. They have internal safety measures that they say protect it from going off. They have sold millions of them to so many people who obviously seem to like them. I personally dislike them because their claimed internal safety measures will still allow it to fire if the trigger is pulled intentionally or by accident, and I want my safety to prevent the trigger from being pulled like in my 1911. Some claim the 1911 may malfunction, but this isn't necessarily so; I've fired thousands of rounds in my 1911 without even a hiccup, but *every gun can malfunction*, even my 1911, so if you learn to use the gun properly, a quality manufactured gun, it usually works fine. Many individuals want a gun they can draw and fire without deactivating any kind of safety, but after my having been shot severely (by an improperly trained person), I won't do it to any innocent bystanders. When I draw my 1911 .45 from my holster, I thumb the safety off in the process as I always have and even practice the same way. Practice is always necessary. If you accidentally shoot the wrong person, wounding or killing them, you not only have to live with what you did, quite possibly in jail, but may be sued for everything your insurance company will pay in addition to everything you own. It might result in ending the same way if you cannot master self-control and wait until you are justified in the use of deadly force, especially if you draw a deadly weapon first, no matter how scared you might say you were (the first deadly weapon drawn is generally the aggressor in most jurisdictions!) Don't listen to those who make such ridiculous statements like, "Isn't so much practice or shooting so many rounds quite excessive?" You can only win in your attack and stay alive IF you defeat your assailant. Learning and preparing to save the lives of you and your family should be more important than your college degree and your weekly paycheck! LIFE always comes first! Some manufacturers, such as Smith and Wesson, are now offering some models such as their M&P (military and police) models, which are extensively used by the general public, *with or without* manual safeties. At least, they are making a safety available in the same model weapon *if you want one*. For this, I give the Smith and Wesson an A+.

A striker for a handgun is like a spring-loaded firing pin in a rifle. It pulls back against the spring and let it go to fire. This striker is from a Glock.

While some Glock enthusiasts brag about its being a plastic gun for weight comparison, to start, there's no such thing as an all-plastic gun. Many of the Glock internal parts are steel, especially the barrel. There's no plastic made that can stand up to firing a bullet, and sometimes the steel isn't sufficient when something goes wrong, and it even blows the steel to pieces in any gun made. There is also US Law, the Undetectable Firearms Act of 1988—Public Law 100-649; 18 USC 922. This 1988 legislation banned the production and sale of any guns that are undetectable by metal detectors and x-ray machines, that is, the mythical all-plastic guns. The NRA helped to rewrite this law so as to refine it and to exclude *detectable polymer-framed handguns* which are now in common use throughout America by police departments and civilians for concealed carry. The polymer handguns are *very* detectable, so don't let anyone convince you that they are not. If anyone ever tried to perfect an all-plastic gun, it would be totally ILLEGAL to own! If we're legal, we have *no reason to try to sneak it through* anything. Some people also boast on the smaller number of parts in various guns such as the Glock with 33 claimed parts, but even the 1911s that have 49 parts have quite a few of them as non- moving parts, including the grip panels, the grip screws, and bushings, which account for 10 parts right there. In a similar way, there are revolvers that may have twice as many parts as a semiautomatic pistol, but they are far easier to use. Claims of the polymers being field-stripped in seconds can also be matched by other guns including the 1911 and in the weight comparison; some 1911s are actually lighter than some polymers! Revolvers don't have to be field-stripped! Most semiautomatics don't need field-stripping either under concealed carry conditions. A little homework on your part can certainly go a long way. You did it in school while growing up, so spend a little time to stay alive. As far as safety is concerned, in comparison, the US Army says that the 1911 cannot be accidentally discharged by dropping it like the numerous Internet sites claim, but it can *only* be discharged by the hammer, striking the inertia firing pin, so if you have the thumb (hammer safety) disengaged when you happen to drop the 1911, then there has to be many conditions in the right order and at the same time to allow such a thing to happen because even the grip safety has to be made to allow the trigger or the hammer to function. And while anything *can* happen, it's very highly unlikely that the 1911 will ever go off if dropped, but there are designs with different internal functions. Even above and beyond all these 1911 safeties, there are many models *with a firing pin block* like the one I carry, and even cocked and locked, I have no fear but plenty of confidence. Remember one very important fact: certain guns such as the 1911 that I come to rescue all the time are made by many manufacturers including the ones in other countries, so if I say the 1911 is a very fine and safe gun, many 1911s are identical in the exterior appearance, but the inside parts are different in various models while some lock the firing pin. Your gun is always dependent upon who made it and the quality and perfection of the sidearm, while some are fantastic right out of the box! Semiautomatics and revolvers alike all fall into this questionable safety net due to the large number of imported *and* domestically manufactured arms.

Altering your thoughts to gain votes is not speaking a true belief but more like a con man selling his services to those willing to pay. If we had a politician who wasn't afraid to voice his belief in defensive arms to maintain the integrity of our future without his fear of losing half of his votes from the other side, it would certainly be nice to see a US Law written into the US Code, a firearms safety act, requiring certain safety measures *and having the development assisted by the NRA* so that any firearm, no matter whether it's polymer or steel, or any material, or future materials for that matter, has to be perfectly safe in its operational mechanics and its structural integrity to be not only made in this country, imported into this country, but to be sold and used in this country. This could immediately remove many of the so-called junk guns and Saturday night specials while showing concern for the lives of the innocent, law-abiding American people. Our politicians are always concerned with banning, other than regulating the safety of those sold here, which might have saved many lives in the past.

There are people who claim the firing pin blocks in some 1911 style handguns are additional unnecessary parts, and they say more parts may cause malfunctions. But to clear up some myths, I'd say in my disassembly and study of the firing pin mechanics and the blocking mechanism, it has an undercut that is interlocked with a mechanical block where the slotted block is automatically raised by the grip safety when you take a proper grip on the gun, but you still have to thumb the safety off. Many 1911 owners claim a titanium firing pin will assure safety because of its lightweight, so the firing pin won't bounce if the gun is dropped where it is claimed that it could accidentally discharge the gun. While I understand their issue, the mechanics are still the same, so I prefer the locking firing pin, which works extremely well, no matter what anybody who *doesn't carry one* might claim. Being into mechanical machinery and guns all my life, some of the machines had ten times as many parts and were 100% more reliable than the cheapos! Would you buy a little foreign car because it sells for $500 and has half the parts of the Cadillac or Lincoln where you might otherwise prefer quality? Gee, so many of you thought you'd rather ride your carcass around in comfort with a *reliable* vehicle! Guns are the same way, and LIFE comes FIRST, folks. Or you may never need that comfortable car. Even a criminal will steal the best before the worst, so why *try* to use the worst to save your life? Unless you're out in the middle of a combat zone where simple and easy is preferred due to limited ability to maintain, the only place you need things to be easier is in the operator accessible functions directly responsible for firing the firearm so that it can be kept in action. I'm giving you the facts, so you can study and make your own decisions, especially on items that have been proven time and time again!

There are several striker-fired pistols available now, not only from Glock, but from Smith and Wesson and others. Kimber just released a newly designed 9mm pistol, the Solo Carry, which is striker-fired and has a slide stop and a manual thumb safety similar in operation to the 1911. The Solo Carry is a very good choice if you want a 9MM because it's not too big or too small, and it's very light in weight with all metal construction. Ruger makes the LCP .380 and the new LC9 compact polymer 9mm, which seems to be back-ordered at the moment but is starting to show up in the stores. All major firearms manufacturers make a large assortment of very good firearms, including many other handguns. Different manufacturers seem to have their own preference for specific frame sizes, which make some guns large and cumbersome as compared to some that are more preferable and more easily handled. Obviously, very large calibers usually have large frames for structural strength, especially in revolvers due to the large calibers available, but if you find a revolver that you really like but the grip is too massive, many grips are easily replaced with a much smaller one or even a larger one, if needed, *if the frame design allows*, but question it before you buy! Revolvers with rounded buts on the grip won't snag clothing on the draw. Some guns come in a plastic carry case with a couple of extra back straps to change the feel and size of the grip, with the magazines, a magazine carrier, a holster, and so forth. So if the price is right, you can save a few bucks on all the extras you get, but just because they include a magazine carrier and a holster, that doesn't mean that it's the best one for you or that gun. You need to find the one that works the best for *you*. As much as these included accessories would cost separately, you might be better buying the sidearm by itself to save money and choosing the options separately.

Structural Strength

I have always preferred metal handguns as compared to polymers or plastics of any kind so far, but even though I'm old-school on structural strength, I'm studying some recent introductions in polymers on some guns including assault rifles. Knowing the history of plastics, they degrade and break down out in sunlight, being exposed to the UV rays or, as some knowledgeable people say, even in storage over time. Metal guns won't be affected by the sun and even if they are properly stored away for 100 years. Did you ever see a plastic item or a kid's toy that was left out in the yard for a while and have you wondered where the color went or why it became brittle? When I buy my metal guns, they'll be with me until the day that I die. It just may be what happens to some people if their polymer guns are pulled out some day to fend off intruders or an invasion if they don't keep up on proper maintenance, knowing their frame's integrity over time. By mass-marketing polymer guns throughout the country, one day those millions of firearms will become old and may develop cracks and no longer usable while many millions of Americans may then become automatically disarmed. But if you bought it, it's your responsibility to keep up on its condition and to maintain it; it's not the manufacturer's fault because *you* have the choice. It could be very advantageous for the manufacturer of polymer guns to include the expected safe, operating life span of their firearms due to differences in the chemical composition along with cautions as to what may be destructive to the polymer. They have the responsibility to maintain their own business in the same way as you have to maintain your life. I just want you to make sure you know what you want, but you may not be knowing of the structural strength and life span.

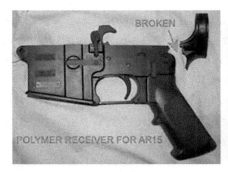

While we sometimes have exceptions to the rule, this isn't the first polymer firearm that broke. Some AR models broke at the front pivot pin, others at the rear pin, and others at the buffer thread, and cracked receivers, and handguns with broken grips, dust covers, and more. So study these broken firearms and decide what you want to buy. Gee, didn't they say it was such a technologically advanced firearm and a real bargain? I don't mind polymer grips and stocks, but I want my frame or receivers to be steel or aluminum in any sidearm, assault rifle, or shotgun. It's the part that takes all the abuse! Note: A policeman's grip cracked and fell off his polymer gun with the magazine still in it, and there are many complaints of drawers of broken polymer parts.

These are examples of an M16/AR-15 lower receiver aluminum forging on the left, and they are in the process of being machined on the right. It's the foundation that holds the entire firearm together, including the firing mechanism. You can count on this one being around for a very long time! The same applies for upper receivers and handguns. Plastics cannot compare to structural integrity.

The plastics industry was revolutionized in the 1930s with the announcement of polyamide (PA), far better known by its trade name nylon. It is very wear-resistant, and nylon is used for parts in many mechanical machines and gizmos alike. While many of the current polymer firearms such as new generation AR-15s are made of Carbon 15 composite, carbon fiber composites offer high specific strength and stiffness and provide alternative solutions with significant weight reduction compared to traditional metal and metal alloy parts. Many firearms have the polymers incorporated into them, including many handguns that are made out of a synthetic polymer known as nylon 6, among others. So many people claim that the polymer nylon 6 and other frames won't and can't melt, but despite their improper knowledge, everything melts with enough heat, including steel. The actual melting temperature for nylon 6 is 428°F, for carbon steel 2,800°F, stainless steel 2,750°F, and aluminum 1,220°F while the average temperature for molten steel in a steel mill is 3,200°F. This means that a steel gun will stand up to 7 times the heat. Even though there are many steel parts in a polymer gun, if the frame that holds the assembly together to make it work melts, then the rest is a pile of scrap. In the same way, there are now metal-framed guns that have plastic internal parts, which I won't buy. Even many military rifles, including the M16 and the M4, which is a revised version of the M16A2, have an all-metal functioning firearm, using plastics *only* for the forward hand guard, the pistol grip, and the shoulder stock ONLY to lighten the weight *while maintaining the integrity of the all- metal life-saving functions.* While the polymer guns are claimed to work quite well for so many people, I'm giving you the facts and you have to decide what to do with them! If you offer me a polymer-framed sidearm or a steel—or aluminum-framed sidearm to go into battle where wear and tear and unforeseen destructive situations happen without notice, I'd opt for the steel- aluminum combination, I assure you. Facts are *my* business, and the decisions are *yours*!

Stocks Affect Accuracy

Some people replace their stocks with much more expensive ones just because they're so pretty, but since I don't buy guns to hang on the wall to admire, I save hundreds of dollars per gun, but I really prefer synthetic stocks that resist warping. Expensive wooden stocks usually go along with fancy engraving, but these firearms are something you don't generally use extensively but more of a firearm to collect, but even then beware if you spend thousands of dollars on all your fancy modifications. It may only be worth all that money *to you alone*, and you might never be able to sell such a firearm for much more than it originally cost, if that, because they generally go for used gun prices, so make sure of what you do or your reasons why. Wooden stocks were always the standard, but wood stocks can warp, chip, and collect scratches and dents. So since the invention of synthetic stocks, I've been fond of the synthetic stocks on modern rifles for many years since I'd venture off into the wilderness in snow and extreme cold where *moisture affects the accuracy due to a wooden stock pressing against a rifle barrel*, which can change the point of impact, but the moisture won't affect synthetics to ruin the accuracy. Each material has its own advantages and disadvantages that gun owners should understand before making a firearm purchase; however, you need to make sure of what may harm the synthetic stock you might buy. Wood is a natural material designed by nature, and even when well varnished or oiled, it can take up moisture from the atmosphere and expand and then shrink again in dry conditions, and it can also permanently warp! Some people, unknowingly, might find themselves shooting in different places in different weather, so for wooden stocks, they do a *bedding process* and free-float the barrel so the barrel cannot make contact with the stock under varied or foul weather conditions. Synthetics don't! I used to set up my two-man backpack tent and intentionally leave my rifle outside in the cold to avoid warming the rifle inside the tent and then having moisture developing *inside the action* by taking it back out in the cold. This will, or *can*, freeze the internal components due to the internal ice, causing internally frozen actions *and* malfunctions, so remember that the cold can not only reduce the velocity and change the impact point, but it can freeze the action on your winter journey. For trophy hunters, this could cause the miss of a lifetime or maybe even death if confronted by a grizzly along the way and the firing mechanism was frozen and didn't fire. BELIEVE IT! Some people, with absolutely no knowledge of what they say, have a tendency to say modern materials these days won't have any such problems. I've heard it said, but don't you believe it! Temperature variations don't care what it's made from; I have a couple of patents to prove it, and the right circumstances will do it regardless. It's YOUR OWN RESPONSIBILITY to learn to stay alive!

Many modern rifle stocks have aluminum bedding inserts installed to assure clearance between the barrel and the stock so that the stock doesn't warp and touch the barrel, affecting the accuracy, which doesn't take much. The rife you buy may not have bedding in it, but while some do, bedding used to be a custom add-on at the gunsmith shop.

Polymers versus Metals in Weight

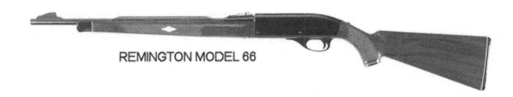

REMINGTON MODEL 66

Remington first introduced the Nylon model 66, .22 caliber rifle, in 1959. It actually became quite popular, and, needless to say, when we have soldiers carrying a 60-pound pack *and* their rifle, the military studies such new technologies. Later, the American M16 that was designed in 1957 and was deployed in South Vietnam in 1963 had the shoulder stock, the pistol grip, and the forward hand guard all made of plastics, which seemed to be very durable and lightweight where it again proved itself. I've pretty much put some assorted versions through somewhat of a torture test, and they always held up. The weight of the M1 Garand was about 9.8 pounds, and the M14 about 9.5 pounds give or take a few ounces, but the M16 weighed in at about 7.12 pounds or less, depending on the version—long or short barrel and stocks! This reduced the troops carry load by up to about 3 pounds. Heckler and Koch of Germany introduced polymer handguns such as the H&K USP, which used many functions of the 1911, but they claimed to have improved on the design and offered the USP (universal self-loading pistol) in many assorted calibers. Glock of Austria later adopted the polymers, making various calibers also available, but seemed to have out-marketed the H&K USP, which finally seems to be becoming more recognized. Another weapon that seems to always have fine reports of operation, handling, and accuracy is the Sig Sauer 229, which many police used, and quite a few of them were disappointed with the required replacement with a Glock. Sidearms are not necessarily always replaced because the newer model is better. But the few who were involved in the testing trials were impressed somehow, and they had the responsibility to save the department so much money per gun. So remember that you are the one making the choice for your own personal gun, nobody else. I would much rather spend a few dollars more than to die. While some polymer 9mm handguns boast of being only 27 ounces in weight, my steel and machined high-strength aluminum Kimber 1911 in .45 ACP weighs only 25 ounces when it's empty—being 2 ounces less than the polymer 9mm counterpart—so I have much more power in a smaller—and stronger-framed gun, with 2 ounces less weight than the polymer, and a faster trigger, so be sure to study the actual differences! Even the Trojan Horse looked great and made the people feel good until they learned the facts! Even a light gun can actually feel heavy until you're used to it, especially when you've never carried one before. Polymer guns may not necessarily be lighter, but the polymers seem to be holding the prices down to a somewhat reasonable amount. I'm even starting to see these prices rise now, so be sure to search out various gun stores. Some of the largest stores usually seem to sell for the lowest street price (meaning, what the local stores actually sell it for), despite the suggested manufacturer's price, but not always, so you have to do your homework. By looking around enough, you might find your desired gun for a couple of hundred dollars cheaper *or more* than the gun manufacturer's suggested retail price, making the actual purchase worth taking the time to look around. If you narrow the search down to 2 firearms for a carry weapon, then remember if you can rent one or arrange for a test-firing of a similar one and see how they both handle. You can better decide which one will actually be best suited to you. Gun ranges that rent guns only use so many to rent, so you might not be able to rent the exact model gun but maybe something close to it and at least in the desired calibers, with comparable barrel length, to see how you can handle them.

Physical Size of Your Carry Gun

Size matters! Remember one thing: selecting a large handgun like you see on a policeman's belt will stick out just about as far on you, although you will be using a different type of holster, so remember that he does not normally have to hide his, but you do. There are a variety of holsters designed specifically for women due to their difference in body shape and hips being so different from men, in addition to those who are overweight and find it a bit more difficult to wear a holster properly. Concealment will be easy while using the right equipment. We'll address quite a bit on holsters later, but there are small-sized guns that shoot big bullets and big guns that shoot small bullets. The gun must fit your grip comfortably, not too big or too small. If you cannot operate the gun due to its size (meaning, the size of gun and the frame, not the caliber), because of it being either too big or too small for your hands, then you won't be able to use it most efficiently. Remember your LIFE is at stake here, not the concern over $30 off on a particular model. If you cannot grip a small gun due to a small or short grip—where you need to be able to use at least two fingers on the grip and preferably three—some semiautomatic guns have a magazine extension that has a hooked end, making the grip longer for your little finger to assist in gripping the small gun. Some of these magazine extensions are optional, and some are included. I used to do this with an extended magazine 30 years ago, but someone decided to patent the process and cashed in on it. No matter how smart or knowledgeable we think we might be, there's always somebody who might know something we don't, so if anyone ever teaches you something new, confirm the facts before you believe it if your life depends on it!

Wrong Ammunition Fits in Some Guns

I had a big man show me his small .380 and complained that he couldn't get his large fingers into the trigger guard to fire, but he bought what was available without knowing what to look for as so many people do. I did explain some options and how to use his trigger finger, but there are small guns with larger trigger guards available that are intentionally made larger for using gloves, but these small guns will work very well for much larger fingers. The larger the bullet, generally the more the recoil, depending on the barrel length, cartridge length, and powder charge. For a comparison, let's look at the .45 ACP and its claimed competitor the .45 GAP introduced by Glock. They are both the same caliber and are shot out of comparable barrels, but the GAP has less claimed kick due to a shorter cartridge length, which holds less powder. There are other ways to help to counteract some of the recoil if you should decide to use it. As we were mentioning a while ago, some ammunition is interchangeable in some firearms but only in the right order. Don't try to put the shorter .45 GAP into a sidearm designed for .45 ACP, and don't try to put .45 ACP into a .45 GAP. A .357 Magnum revolver will also shoot .38 Special loads, which will have a little less recoil when fired due to being less potent than the .357. But a .38 Special revolver will not shoot a .357 Magnum due to the magnum's greater power. With all the current revolvers available today, including so many imports and no government safety restrictions because the ATF has no authority over any safety guidelines, except just the licensing, I'm not going to research each and every model, especially those imported, to see if the .357 will actually fit into any of the foreign revolver cylinders, even though it has a slightly increased length. But you need to know the facts, and don't ever try to chamber a more potent round than called for because the gun isn't made strong enough to fire a magnum. The same combination goes for a .44 Magnum and .44 Special like the old Clint Eastwood movie *Magnum Force*, where the police used that very combination of .44s. The .44 Magnum will safely shoot the .44 Special, but the .44 Special will not shoot the .44 Magnum. Magnums are more powerful rounds! Similar rounds will fit into other chambers, and people have accidentally put .41 Magnum rounds in a .44 Magnum and fired them, and others have done the same by putting the .44 Magnum round in a .45 Colt *but they were lucky*, so you really need to keep the ammunition separate, clearly marked or in color-coded boxes if you have several guns where the calibers are similar in size because your life depends on it! Don't ever try to insert ANY ROUND that's not the specific round called for, for your firearm. And never attempt to SHOOT ammunition that is not for the firearm!

Pressure-testing Ammunition

The ammunition called +P loads are physically and dimensionally exactly the same as their respective normally powered cartridge, but slightly more powerful than the standard load, approximately 10%. So remember this when buying bullets. In addition, +P loads are far lower in power than magnum rounds. Again, make sure you know your gun and the manufacturer specifications regarding safety, including if it's capable of firing +P loads. While there's also +P+, SAAMI has no current guidelines for this load. While the European countries have an organization equivalent to SAAMI, called CIP, or Commission Internationale Permanente, this organization has members consisting of 14 states (countries) that are mostly European. SAAMI interfaces with their European counterpart CIP to try and develop common, internationally recognized standards. CIP requires a proof test from member countries, which is a test wherein a deliberately overpressured round is fired from a firearm in order to verify that the firearm is not defective and will not explode on firing. The firearm is inspected after the test, and if it is found to be in sound condition, *then it is marked with a proof mark* to indicate that it has been proofed, but not proven. In many foreign jurisdictions, a proof test and valid proof mark are required for the sale of firearms. The standard proof test consists of firing two overloaded cartridges that produce 25% more chamber pressure than the CIP—specified maximum pressure limit for the same cartridge in its commercial version. The standard proof of pistol, revolver, and rimfire cartridges is performed with overloaded cartridges that produce 30% more chamber pressure than the CIP maximum pressure limit for the same cartridge in its commercial version. It's important to remember that SAAMI and CIP testing procedures are done differently, and pressure readings that are taken differently result in different pressure readings being obtained from the testing of the same round either by SAAMI or CIP standards, so it doesn't mean that a much higher pressure reading by CIP is a stronger gun than one that uses a lower reading taken by SAAMI. This really confuses a lot of people! In addition to SAAMI and CIP having their own testing procedures and guidelines, NATO also has *their own* methods of testing and guidelines, so now we have three sets of testing procedures that all result in different pressures, even by the same round. Know the firearm you buy and what it can or cannot shoot *before* you buy it! Don't confuse yourself by trying to study everybody's testing procedures and pressure requirements for a specific round just so you can select a proper handgun because you will be loaded down with a lot of unnecessary inquiries for many things that you will never need to know or ever have to use, not to mention that the people at the gun shops may actually have absolutely no idea what you're even talking about. It would certainly be nice to see a merging of SAAMI, CIP, and NATO pressure-testing standards to simplify our safety. Remember, that in the US, companies that are not members of SAAMI are not required to conform to SAAMI standards.

Semiautomatic Assault Rifles versus Fully Automatic Military Weapons: AR10, AR-15, M16, M16A1, M16A2, M16A3, M16A4, M4, M60, M110, BEOWULF .50 CALIBER

Millions of American households have assault rifles. I'm carefully selective in saying *assault rifles, not weapons,* as many anti-gunners and politicians are replacing the word *rifles* with the word *weapons* so that they can directly try to involve many other weapons in the same laws without having to readdress the issues. Be careful of the way things are worded when you vote! If in doubt, vote it out!

Before we address the assault rifles, let's look at safety. We can install a lock into the magazine well to prevent unauthorized loading of the firearm without a key to remove the lock. These and other items are available at http://www.gunvault.com.

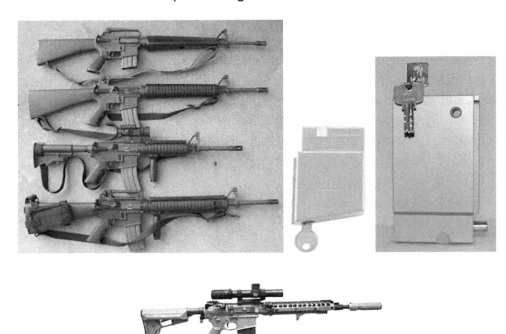

From top left to bottom: M16A1, M16A2, M4, M16A4 are in 5.56 NATO and the M110 Sniper Rifle at the bottom left is in 7.62 × 51 NATO, and the one below right is a .50 caliber Beowulf.

Above left: While the design style has proven effective and practical, the AR-15 may look identical on the outside, but the internal mechanics are different and they cannot do what their military cousins can do. Anti-gunners always use this ploy of claiming they are capable of the same thing

as the military weapons and spraying bullets when they cannot. Even the anti-gunners need to be educated. Federal laws prohibit replacing the internal parts with military parts to function in fully automatic or burst modes. Many assault rifles showing up are made from polymer or carbon plastics for receivers.

The left picture shows the comparison of the 5.56 × 45 NATO round on the right used by the M16 and the M4, alongside the .50 caliber Beowulf round on the left. The lower receiver fits either firearm while the upper receiver is where the differences are, in addition to the ammunition cartridge magazine. On the right, from left to right, are blank firing adapters for the AR-15, M16, and the M4 style rifles. They attach to the muzzle and seal the barrel, so the gas from firing the blank cycles the action. The Hollywood firearms are specially adapted for the movies and should be left in the theaters.

Above left is the Russian AK-47, while on the right is the AK-47-AKM. Notice the angled muzzle that allows the gas pressures to escape above the round being fired which helps to hold the muzzle down when fired. The downside to this is the unbalanced release of pressure at the crown of the barrel behind the bullet which affects accuracy.

This is here to clarify the many misconceptions in the general public. Many people believe that assault rifles are illegal to own, but at the time of this writing, they're not. While the government banned the sale of assault rifles and high-capacity magazines from 1994 to 2004, Congress allowed the law to expire in 2004 and failed to renew it, so the federal laws will allow you to possess, own, or sell them, but you have to study your own state laws because some states initiated their own assault rifle ban when the federal ban was allowed to expire. If you see them on the shelves in your local gun shop, then the state laws apparently permit them to be owned. The AR10 was developed in 1954 in 7.62 × .51 caliber and later transformed into an AR-15 version in 5.56 × 45, and in 1959, Arma-Lite sold its rights to the AR-15 to Colt, who eventually transformed it into an M16 in 5.56 × 45 and on through several improved versions of the M16 and now into the M4. All these rifles are based on the AR10 platform design with the exception of the M60. While the firing rate for those with full automatic capability is specified in rounds per minute, such as 650 to 950 rounds per minute for early M16s on through current M4A1s, these military rifles can only fire what's in the magazine, whether it's a 20, 30, or 40 round magazine, but the rate of fire is based on the weapon's ability to fire hundreds of rounds per minute if the magazine were able to supply the rifle at a nonstop rate continuously, and the barrel was able to function without the temperature getting too high (about 1,650 to 1,700 degrees) and the barrel warping and bursting at about 500 *continuous* rounds, but the necessity to provide a continuous supply of ammo prevents it from actually firing so many rounds in succession while the rounds per minute is ONLY used as a cycling speed capability reference. In army tests on the current standard M4, the barrel eroded and warped after 540 rounds were fired in 2 minutes and 48 seconds. In another test, the barrel bursts after 596 rounds were fired in 3 minutes and 39 seconds, according to weapons officials, but the heavier M4A1 barrel was able to shoot 930 rounds in 4 minutes 30 seconds, which was a rare situation. All these tests show that a 700 or greater rounds per minute reference are technical issues only and will never give such performance. In the M4A1 test, the heat shield melted, but the barrel *visually appeared* undamaged, but it's not very likely, even though it took 4½ times longer to fire against its *claimed* capabilities in FULL AUTO. One thing to note is that these tests are done by the military, being experts at what they do, while intentionally pushing these arms to the max for these tests, so the rounds actually fired by those with the most experience were still very far from what those unfamiliar with these weapons think they really do, not to mention that the firearms also become unusable at this point. Anti-gunners hear the firing rate per minute capability and assume that's how many rounds are actually being fired while they don't realize that in FULL AUTO, they don't even compare to the technical firing rate of the mechanical mechanism. The military owns these weapons, and the semiautomatic versions are only capable of what you can keep in supply by replacing the magazines. The anti-gun groups assume a person can run around all day, shooting such incredible numbers of rounds, so they always want to outlaw them, but they do not know that it's still limited to the majority of civilian allowances of *only* semiautomatic fire and the magazine capacity of say 20 or 30, which quickly empties and then needs to be replaced with a loaded one, regardless of how many magazines they have on hand. When the barrel reaches a certain temperature, even in the military, it all breaks down and comes to a halt, being UNUSABLE. I read an article written by anti-gunners where they say that the assault rifles are like their military counterparts capable sending a *spray* of bullets to the target *which is somewhat fraudulent*, which is probably why they don't sign their name to such claims. But too many people read something and just because it is in print, they figure it must be right. Another fact they don't seem to understand is that even though civilian assault rifles are semiautomatic, that is, it takes one pull of the trigger for each and every round fired, it again slows down the ability to fire so many rounds as compared to a fully automatic military weapon where some M16s and some M4s such as the M4A1 are capable of. Although the civilian assault rifle and the military twin look identical in appearance on the outside, their internal operating parts are different and regulated by US federal laws against the replacement of the internal semiautomatic parts with the full auto parts. These rifles are gas-operated by direct gas impingement, that is, a gas tube. Gas-operated means the expanding hot gasses from firing the cartridge are contained under pressure and are used to control the operation of the rifle. They are timed by the location of the gas block attached to the barrel at the front sight post with a gas tube, redirecting the expanding gas through the port to the upper receiver to unlock the bolt while there is still time left for the remaining pressure in the bore to drive the bolt carrier rearward, ejecting the spent round just as the bullet leaves the barrel and the recoil buffer spring drives the bolt carrier back in a forward direction, strips a new round from the magazine, and chambers the new round. If fired in full automatic, it quickly empties the magazine, but in these firearms, the actual rate of fire is faster for a shorter barrel than it is for the slower longer barrel. While the bullet is in the shorter barrel for a much shorter time than it is in the longer barrel, the shorter distance to the gas block which redirects the gas to ready a new round causes it to go through its function cycle earlier because the gas block is closer to the chamber on the shorter barrel, but further down the barrel on the longer gun. The downside of the shorter barrel, even though it has a faster rate of fire, is less accuracy at a longer distance. They each have their purpose whether it's for sweeping buildings (shorter barrel) or in the field where longer shots are normally expected (longer barrel). For the M60 machine gun, these problems are solved by loading ammunition link belts with hundreds of rounds usually in a 100-round belt length (a disintegrating belt) and replacement barrels when the barrel temperature gets too high for proper functioning, which could also cause cook-off, which is new unfired rounds going off due to the excessive built-up *heat*, making it dangerous. The upside to the M60 is more available firepower, but the downside is its weight and the need for assistance from other troops carrying extra barrels and ammunition belts, but due to the M60's size and weight ratio being 23.15 pounds, it was still considered an advantage, and the US Navy has used the M60 extensively onboard ships, PBRs (River Patrol Boats), and Swift Boats, which were very widely used during Vietnam, but the M60 is still used extensively by our military, including more modern patrol boats, including those used by the US Coast Guard.

While all versions of the M16 have been direct gas impingement including the newer M-4s, I've read test results where both versions, direct gas impingement and newer gas piston-operated designs (somewhat similar to the old M1 Garand and the M14), were put through extensive testing, including burying them, digging them up, and firing them immediately, where the direct gas impingement system outperformed the gas piston in reliability, but the US Army ordered thousands of piston-operated conversion kits for their own proper evaluations. While the army put many rifles to the test, they made mention that with the piston-operated designs, the barrels held up for 20,000 rounds as compared to the direct gas impingement by gas tube (old original style), where the barrels would make it for only 10,000 rounds. Since they both utilize the same cartridges and the internal functioning of the barrels remained the same, I had difficulty in understanding their claims since the only difference was the way the gas and piston operated as compared to the impingement gas tube where the bolt carrier would be driven back to eject the spent cartridge and chamber a new one. I've studied the situation and found that a claimed 100% increase in service life is to be expected, backing up the 20,000 versus 10,000 round barrel life, and it seems that the hot expanding gas under extreme pressures causes some erosion similar to the way high-pressure steam cuts and erodes steel in boilers, tubing, and valves.

The impingement gas tube also gets clogged as deposits build internally, seriously affecting reliability where the gas piston design doesn't have such a problem. The gas impingement tube design also vents the gas pressures into the upper receiver, which allows it to directly enter the lower receiver just as well, causing more carbon deposits to build up on the internal operating parts. This may cause improper functioning to occur sooner due to the increased friction and resistance of the bolt and carrier assembly, causing the firearm to need a proper cleaning so much sooner, especially the inside of the gas tube, while the short stroke gas piston operation vents much of its gas pressure to the outside of the receiver, avoiding so much fouling, and there are claims that these problems cause, in comparison, the impingement gas tube firearm to need about half an hour to clean it sufficiently to get it back into usable condition as compared to the short stroke gas piston having the ability to be cleaned sufficiently in 5 minutes to get it right back in action. Further, while the US Navy SEALs may be shown from time to time coming up out of water firing their weapons, don't ever try it with *any* civilian version of any assault rifle since this part is not just Hollywood, but the real SEALs have custom modifications to their own weapons for proper drainage to prevent catastrophes and their sudden blowing apart so they can very well come up shooting if they need to, and believe it that sometimes they may need to. An old safety tip that my buddies and I used to use is finger prophylactics, sometimes called finger cots or finger protectors (available at your local drugstore) over the muzzle of your weapon, no matter what type it is to prevent dirt and debris from getting into the bore. And if the need to fire the weapon arises, you simply shoot through it. In situations where they were a bit small for a particular need, plain old condoms may even be used. This could be a safety tip for teaching teenagers to hunt, without as much fear of their having mud in the bore as an obstruction which could blow apart the barrel and possibly kill someone.

While there are long and short after-market AR-15 barrels that locate the gas block in the same place on either the long or the short barrel and use the same *short* hand guard on either length barrel, don't confuse these with different timing on the rate of fire because long and short barrels alike will shoot at the same speed if the gas block is in the same location on either length but apparently slower due to the need for the rounds to be clear of the extended barrel length which makes no difference anyway since you have to pull the trigger for each and every round. If the gas block is located in the same place on both the long and short barrels, the cycling rate will be the same on both versions. Further, if the fully automatic rifles had shorter fatter cartridges, they could cycle the action even faster yet. Since the carrier assembly would have less distance to travel, shorter rounds would cycle the mechanical end faster. While there are different methods of cycling the action on other firearm designs such as blowback and recoil operated, shorter rounds offer the fastest cycling of rounds per minute such as in sub-machine guns. While machine guns normally fire higher powered rifle cartridges such as the 7.62 × 51 and above, all the M16 through the M4 versions that fire the 5.56 × 45 are considered light machine guns, while those that fire handgun cartridges are defined as sub-machine guns, due to their compact size and lightweight, and are used extensively by US Government organizations including the Secret Service for ease of use and concealment. While many assault rifles and light machine guns have the telescopic collapsing stock which has varied length adjustment stops, say 4 or 6, some offer a folding stock which folds to the side and up alongside the receiver opposite the shooter's cheek side if needed, but I've always been partial to the adjustable stock in preference of the side folding unit which I believe can get in the operator's way fast offering a somewhat thick receiver profile if he doesn't get familiar with this on the weapon pretty quick. Sub-machine guns offer similar alternatives.

The AR10 that started the offspring of so many weapons has finally come to US military use. In 2005, Knight's Armament Company won a military competition, and they were awarded a contract to provide the US military with an improved version of the AR10 and adopted it as the M110 and chambered it in 7.62 × 51 NATO as a semiautomatic sniper weapon.

There are also too many misconceptions of people improperly thinking their friends have real working M16s, which adds fuel to the anti-gun campaigns. So for those who don't know how to identify an AR-15 from an M16 at a glance without looking to see if the lower receiver is stamped for fire, burst or full auto, (or if it says property of the US Government) stamped into the side of the magazine well. When I was at a gun show and a man at the gun show (a dealer) tried to impress the customers with his real M16 as he claimed it to be, I challenged his claim from 3 feet away in front of the same customers, and he was concerned since he just lied to everyone. He said there was no way in the world to tell the difference, so I told him that I'd bet him the firearm he was holding. So on seeing his curiosity I pointed out that the M16 has an additional pin located above the firing-mode selector (and is clearly visible from 3 feet away) that holds the auto sear and allows it to function in full auto, and his did not, so it was an AR-15.

The pin for the auto sear is located directly above the selector in a real M16, where there is no such pin in an AR-15 as no auto-sear was installed. The auto sear allows the M16 to fire in full automatic and is viewed from the top, in the right picture.

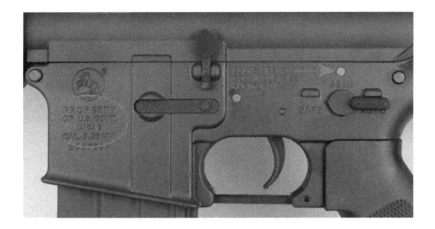

There are some AR-15s where some people use what they call a drop-in auto-sear IF the inside of the lower receiver was machined to allow a drop-in auto-sear, and all the internal parts have been replaced with actual M16 parts to allow the drop-in auto-sear to work in place of the proper auto-sear, but since it's controlled under federal and state laws, you can search it out elsewhere if you need to know. The point is, even some dealers lie, which makes things worse for gun enthusiasts when the wrong people hear such things. Don't get me wrong; there are many things I don't know, but I'm trying to provide you with the facts. Some dealers don't know everything they claim to know, which is fine, but one specifically argued with me over the firing pin of an AR-15 versus the firing pin of an M16. The dealer claimed that the firing pins were the very same pin with absolutely no difference, and I did have to *try* to educate this person because of my years of prior experience where the M16 firing pins were always tip-hardened for firing under fully automatic fire, where the AR-15 firing pin would rip a few rounds and flatten or break off the tip of the firing pin under full automatic fire, and many of the older M16 firing pins even had blue tips where they were hardened—the reason why M16 firing pins cost more. *And* I've personally installed them, so don't argue the issue, but beware and question everything you consider using or buying, including its legality, by federal or state law. Always make sure the firing pin for an M16 is verifiably full auto capable, or you may get a broken tip. I've read too many claims that the collar size and weight of the pin being titanium or steel are the only deciding factors between these pins, so if anyone bought AR-15 firing pins to fire in a full auto M16 because they looked the same OR because you were told there's no difference between the pins, you better correct it before you get caught dead! There are also differences between the pins fitting a fully shrouded or un-shrouded bolt carrier. A dealer is licensed to sell but not licensed in his knowledge of firearms or required to be truthful, so since they are willing to *argue the differences* other than to learn, they might be selling you the inferior part for the superior price, so if an M16 firing pin is really needed, you might opt for the actual manufacturer's sales site or a reputable supplier while paying the higher price for the actual M16 firing pin since now you know they differ. Many are made of superior materials these days but always confirm what you need is the proper part. Remember, saving two bucks on a box of foreign ammo might have called for the roll of toilet paper. Sometimes there's a reason for the price difference! Do your homework.

Laws from the BATF, Which is Now BATFE (Bureau of Alcohol, Tobacco, Firearms, and Explosives)

All the information you need regarding firearms, laws, and prohibitions can be found at www. atf. gov. Federal firearms laws restrict the ownership or the manufacture of fully automatic or burst capable firearms, so for any information, you might need to refer to or simply go to http://www. atf.gov/regulations-rulings/laws. There are hundreds of pages at this site that are downloadable as PDF files, so make sure you're legal.

1. Gun Control Act (18 USC Chapter 44)
2. National Firearms Act (26 USC Chapter 53)
3. Arms Export Control Act (22 USC Chapter 2778)
4. Importation, Manufacture, Distribution, and Storage of Explosive Materials (18 USC Chapter 40)

No matter which of the four items listed above you might want to review, they all come up under the same downloadable PDF, which is 243 pages in length but only takes a few seconds to load up and another few seconds to download on a home computer. For information related to the fully automatics mentioned above, you might also refer to § 478.36 Transfer or Possession of Machine Guns.

Revolver versus Semiautomatic Pistol

A 1911 semiautomatic pistol below a revolver

We're going to review a few guns, so you can pick up a handgun of various designs and operating differences such as a revolver and a semiautomatic pistol so you can understand their differences, but it's your responsibility to know what type of gun it is and what it does, before you buy it! For most handguns, the basics were generally all the same in operation, but now the single actions, the double actions, the "double-action-single-actions," and the double-action-only (DAO), in addition to the striker-fired, are changing everything. Even if the sidearm is striker-fired, it falls into the above categories.

First, when you consider comparing a revolver to a semiautomatic pistol, there are a few concerns. Men and women might have two different approaches to their handgun. While men have much larger hands than women, men are reported to have a grip approximately twice in strength than that of a woman. If either of them has a disabling hand problem, then this reduces their gripping ability or their dexterity. While any performance with your handgun will require a proper and firm grip or handhold on the gun grip, there are some semiautomatics that require not only a firm grip, but a proper grip, such as the 1911 with a grip safety that has to be made properly or it won't fire. In addition, the grip safety can malfunction if your hold is too loose, but if you fire several rounds consecutively, such as in double tap (two shots in succession) or rapid- fire, the loose hold on the gun's grip may cause the gun to bounce in your hands and again stop the weapon from firing due to the grip safety extending outward too far by bouncing in a loose hold, in and out of its non-firing position. Some 1911s have an extra deep grip safety to prevent this, or even what they call a speed bump, which is extended beyond the normal reach of the grip safety in case your hold on the grip loosens to keep the grip safety inserted deep enough into the gun's handgrip to maintain its firing ability. All semiautomatics require a proper hold to prevent self-induced malfunctions, not self-induced by the gun, but self-induced by you, compared to revolvers which will still fire even if you had a lighter hold on the grip if it were necessary because they are designed to operate quite differently.

There's the question of revolver versus semiautomatic pistol. First, many people improperly use the term *automatic* for a semiautomatic pistol, but the only thing it does automatically is eject a spent round and chamber a new round while it only fires a single round at a time. Some states that when they issue a concealed carry license, they imprint on your license whether you are qualified with and allowed to carry either a revolver (sometimes known as a wheelgun) or a semiautomatic pistol, whichever you are qualified with, and they don't allow you to carry the other. If this was the case, I would take both to the qualification range when applying. Some stipulate that if you qualify with a semiautomatic, you are obviously allowed to use a revolver since the semiautos require more experience. While revolvers are always compared to semiautomatic pistols, many people don't realize the difference in barrel length between the two. In a revolver, the barrel is measured from the edge of the forcing cone, where the barrel starts in front of the cylinder or barrel-cylinder gap, as compared to the barrel in the semiautomatic, which is measured from end to end, which also includes the integral chamber for the bullet as compared to the revolver having the cylinder behind the barrel where the revolver cylinder is actually the bullet chamber or a cylinder containing multiple chambers that rotate one round into alignment for firing with each pull of the trigger. The result is that if you buy both, a revolver and a semiautomatic pistol both having the same barrel length, you are actually getting about an inch more barrel in the revolver, including more rifling, than you are with the semiautomatic. Due to this barrel difference, the same exact round fired in each, a revolver and a semiautomatic pistol, both equal in barrel length, generated a higher velocity of about 150 feet per second from the revolver. Keep in mind though that as the bullet is fired and passes from the cylinder into the forcing cone of the revolver barrel—the slightly funnel-shaped entry portion of the barrel—the length of the actual bullet in movement transitioning from the cylinder (the revolver's chambers) creates somewhat of a momentary seal over the cylinder-barrel gap, allowing it to build higher pressure. A true comparison between revolvers and semiautomatics would be to measure the revolver from the back end of the cylinder near the hammer to the end of the barrel at the muzzle and to measure the semiautomatic barrel from the end of the bullet's integrated chamber to the end of the muzzle.

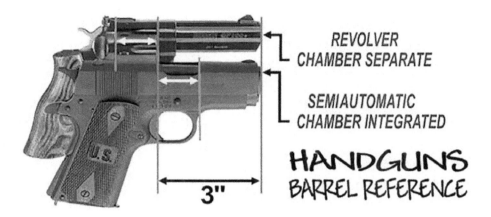

REVOLVER
CHAMBER SEPARATE

SEMIAUTOMATIC
CHAMBER INTEGRATED

HANDGUNS
BARREL REFERENCE

3"

While there are too many firing mechanisms and firing pins to mention, we'll cover some of those you are most likely to encounter. Modern revolvers usually have a built-in safety where a transfer bar interacts between the hammer and the firing pin. The transfer bars are basically of two designs that both require pulling the trigger to fire the round as compared to the older revolver designs where the hammer would strike the primer of the round to fire the gun, so before you buy a revolver, make sure of the type of safety it has built in to prevent it from accidentally discharging. While revolvers have no manual safety to disengage, and if compared to a semiautomatic, some people claim the revolver can be put into action faster than a semiautomatic pistol. This could hold true, unless the semiautomatic has no manual safety, like the many semis that are currently available today, but even then, my normal routine for my 1911 could definitely challenge this claim. Years ago, before revolver safety transfer bars were put into many guns, I was always taught the way to carry a revolver safely and was to let the hammer rest on an empty chamber in the cylinder, giving it the equivalence of a chambered round since the loaded cylinder rotates a new round into place each time you pull the trigger, no matter how it's fired. The revolver *cannot* go off if it is carried with the hammer resting on an *empty chamber*, but by simply pulling the trigger, the cylinder rotates to align the round with the barrel before the hammer strikes. If the hammer gets bumped, banged, or snagged, there is no live round under the hammer that can go off! Absolute safety! I even read an article in a popular magazine written by a writer without apparent revolver knowledge or experience, who said not to carry the hammer down on an empty chamber in a revolver because when you fire it in self-defense, there won't be any round in it, but his lack in experience with the way revolvers operate may cause the readers to learn the wrong information. Learning the wrong stuff can get *you* or somebody else *killed*. Other than the older style of revolvers, which still fire any round chambered in rotation, newer models have safety bars that interact between the hammer and an actual firing pin, so carrying a loaded cylinder is even much safer than it used to be. Even though some articles claimed that the transfer bar safety has been installed starting in the 1900s to replace all the others, this is only partly true. I bought new name-brand revolvers in the mid-1980s (85 years later) that were still made with the firing pin fixed and attached to the tip of the hammer, just the same as you probably find them today as well. Be careful in what you buy! In addition to so much contradiction of what and when certain parts and specific operation were designed and how it all works, with all the foreign handguns showing up, it's your responsibility to make sure you know the way it works *before* you buy one. If in doubt about the safety factor of a revolver you might own, simply rest the hammer on an empty chamber in the cylinder until you find out or just carry it that way, no matter what, and you'll know there's no way that it can ever go off unless you pull the trigger or cock the hammer first. If you rest the hammer on a loaded chamber in the cylinder, the concern is for safety while doing this to make sure if it's a design that the hammer can otherwise directly fire the round. With no safety interlocks or transfer bars, you have to make sure that the hammer cannot snag your clothing and get pulled partially back and pull free before locking back because when the hammer falls back in place, the impact may fire the round, if there's one in the cylinder and it's aligned with the barrel. It could be a very dangerous situation. Cutting off the hammer spur properly will eliminate this danger, but, first, make sure you know what you're doing or take it to the local gunsmith because it's a very easy fix.

While revolvers are generally slower in operation as compared to the faster semiautomatic pistols, *very experienced* shooters may easily challenge this with smooth and well-tuned actions; that is, the mechanical operating parts inside of the gun are machined, honed, or enhanced by a *qualified* and experienced gunsmith that currently does and has previously done this procedure. The work really needs to be done by someone experienced and knowledgeable; otherwise, you may get an unsafe gun.

While many may do well with shooting a revolver, if you need more than the usual 5 rounds, then when the need for reloading the revolver comes along, they will quickly fall behind due to many less rounds available per reload. If you were to try to reload a single-action-only revolver, you're limited to inserting one bullet at a time through a small loading gate, making it even more impractical for self-defense. Smoothing and tuning the action may be done to both, a revolver or a semiautomatic pistol of either single—or double-action designs, but there is no sense in trying to improve the way the hammer drops on a single-action revolver unless it's going to be used for precision shooting or hunting. Single-action revolvers generally take very little effort to drop the hammer and fire it already from the factory, but each person has his or her own preferences. Revolvers are generally wider than the semiautomatics' thin profile due to the revolver's cylinder diameter, but there are new developments with a flat-sided cylinder to reduce the width such as the Chiappa Rhino made by Chiappa firearms of Italy. While Chiappa seemed to have a good idea initially on the thinner cylinder with flat sides, they put the bullet path from the cylinder to the barrel lower than ordinary revolvers, shooting from the bottom of the cylinder as compared to normally happening at the top. They claim better control, but they somewhat fumbled their theory of easier carry due to their additions of very massive ribs above the barrel on their guns, adding additional weight and mass, especially for the longer barrel versions. Just because engineers designed it, doesn't mean it's the best or even suited for your needs! Engineers are human.

Note the single-action revolver on the left is the last choice of defense between these two due to slow reloading of one round at a time, compared to the double-action revolver on the right that can be loaded much faster since the cylinder swings out. Smaller calibers on the right fit more rounds into the same space as compared to the larger calibers, allowing for less capacity.

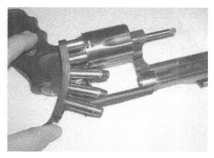

This speed loader holds 6 rounds for a fast reload into a revolver. You insert 6 rounds at one time and rotate the thumb knob to release them. On the right is a flexible speed strip that can be carried in a pocket instead of a magazine carrier, but I prefer loading them all at one time. They work very well.

As previously mentioned, the revolver has a separate chamber from the barrel which rotates (called the cylinder), but the semiautomatic pistol has the chamber as an integral part of the barrel. The bullet capacity of revolvers is usually from 5 to 10 rounds with the norm being about 5 depending on the caliber, since all the cartridges, no matter what their diameter is, have to fit into about the same-sized diameter cylinder, while semiautomatic pistols run generally from 6 to 20. The larger capacity revolvers usually mean smaller calibers, and some are not exactly desirable for defensive carry due to the larger size of the gun, but I've seen real hawgs, that is very big guns, under some jackets. There are a few exceptions to round capacity of the semiautomatic magazines, where a magazine is actually the cartridge clip that holds the bullets. Some magazines are generally available for certain guns that hold many additional rounds. While these extended magazines might not be much good for concealment while carrying, they might be exceptionally fine for a higher capacity reload where concealment is no longer necessary. Beware, your state laws may regulate and restrict your allowable magazine capacity, which may differ from state to state. Although, years ago, they have always made all handguns in steel and advanced into stainless steels, today there are various types of steel and alloys even in combination. Currently, they make revolvers and semiautomatic pistols *both* of polymers with steel inserts for barrels and metal frame reinforcements. The polymers reduce the weight considerably while manufacturers compete by using different combinations of materials to make an equally light and very strong gun for carry. Parts *machined* out of high-strength metals, especially the frame of the gun, are much stronger than those that have been cast in molds, but now some manufacturers are using a metal-injecting process. The new practices and technologies are claiming to challenge the argument of a material's structural strength and precision for guns today. I still prefer a machined frame and parts as compared to any casting or molded process if at all possible. According to past history and my knowledge of steel, castings were always easily broken due to inferior material strength and after spending hundreds of dollars, not to mention entrusting your life to the gun. You want to make sure it's reliable when needed—the only reason for having it! But again, I'm not aware of any newer production models experiencing such difficulty, but even if there are a few, we may not even hear about them.

Back to single-action guns, I mentioned a single-action revolver is not hardly suited for personal defense but mainly due to having to cock the hammer back for each and every shot, (unless you're in a home and its quickly available for an emergency), (and loaded), yet a single-action semiautomatic pistol is ideal since you cock it only once, (making sure there's a loaded magazine inserted and a round in the chamber), and the hammer is cocked back, which initially happens together when you rack the slide, and when fired, it continues to re-cock itself and will fire with each pull of the trigger until empty. Once the ammo has been used up, the bullet follower in the empty ammo magazine pushes the slide stop in the gun up, and the slide generally locks back in the open position depending on the gun, and then it requires reloading and re-cocking, but the gun is already cocked if you insert a freshly loaded magazine and release the slide to return to battery position. Some guns are designed not to fire if the magazine is removed and called a magazine disconnect safety, even if there's a live round in the chamber! While some people claim this is a safety advantage, it would certainly be doomsday if your magazine got accidentally released or dropped in a scuffle while having a fully functional LIVE round in the chamber that becomes worthless. I've read articles that said in an emergency you could *intentionally* eject your magazine and then the thug cannot use your gun against you, but this way of thinking defeats the purpose of having your gun, and I much rather prefer stopping this assailant because I really don't intend on allowing him the option of having my gun or my life. If I have a perfectly fine gun that won't fire, it gives my killer an advantage over *me*, so the only time to ever consider a reload unless you're empty is if you're absolutely sure it's safe to do, which may not be possible in a shoot-out for your OWN life! Magazines could get *accidentally* released with a stressful incident unfolding, and if this were to happen, I would be much more confident in my being able to fire that one available round left in the chamber for my own survival and stop this threat despite no magazine being inserted. If you have such a gun that prevents it from firing if the magazine is ejected, it could really be a nightmare in the middle of an emergency or tactical reload because the assailant might be within reach, or even worse, he, or they, might shoot you while you're delayed in your attempted reloading because you can't fire back. We could *theorize* improper scenarios all day long that might never even happen, but instead of trumping up stories, let's get down to learning to defend ourselves quite effectively in the few seconds we might have to survive. That's all it takes for the average shoot-out in seconds. You will have to weigh the advantages compared to the disadvantages and decide which way you prefer to go for your own self-defense, but you will have to know whether you want a semiautomatic that will or will not fire that last available round if the magazine is removed. I prefer to fight until I have no available means, which means I want to be able to fire that last bullet since a killer may be viewing you in the process of attempting a reload, where he knows you're suddenly vulnerable to attack, so I want the ability to fire that last chambered round, OR I MIGHT DIE! I want every single advantage and every single fraction of a second that I can have to gain *my* advantage, not contributing to his. If you're an elderly person with disabilities or a weakness where you're unable to fight off the perpetrator and he gets a hold of you, then you might consider such a thing as to be able to eject the magazine to prevent being shot with your own gun, but if the assailant gets your gun and replaces the magazine, he just might shoot you anyway, so YOU have to decide on that. While some of this might confuse you, don't be rushed, but take your time and think it through. Take notes in a notebook and, if you need to, discuss it with someone knowledgeable to further assist you in reasoning it out. Hopefully, you'll never have to get down to the last round that's in the chamber, but I somehow seem to walk into and experience the unusual or extreme situations every now and then.

Easy Semiautomatics

These Taurus semiautomatic pistols have pop-up barrels.

For people with disabilities and difficulty using their hands or those who are just plain inexperienced in handguns but like the semiautomatic pistol, there are a few calibers available such as .22 LR, .25 ACP, and .32 ACP in a semiautomatic pocket-sized pistol that is the easiest semiautomatic to use with no experience. Several manufacturers such as Beretta, Phoenix Arms, and Taurus make quite a few of them. While they have double-action-only, many function as a normal double-action-single-action. You insert a (six, seven, or eight round) magazine of bullets like you normally would, but if you're not capable of racking the slide very well, the barrel actually tips up so you can drop a round into the chamber at the end of the barrel and flip it back down again. These guns give you the option of racking the slide or tipping the barrel, so they work both ways in the same gun. Then, know whether you have to cock the hammer back or just pull the trigger. Some are double action on the first shot but then act as single action and fire every round in the gun by pulling the trigger once for each round you want to fire. Unfortunately, these small calibers are not something to write home about because of their lack in sufficient power for self-defense, but if I had no gun, then it would be considered a fantastic weapon. The .22 LR gives fair penetration due to it being scaled proportionate to a larger round (meaning, length, diameter, and charge), but due to its 36 to 40 grain bullet, it's usually 36.

Unless it's a .22 Magnum, it has insufficient mass and energy to be considered a good choice for serious defense. The 50-grain round nose of the .25 ACP has very little penetration due to its small caliber being fired from a short barrel. The 71-grain .32 ACP is still short of a proper defense round. If an assailant fails to get the drop on you and you do manage to present your gun, remember that even the criminals don't want to be shot by *anything*, regardless of the caliber, and hopefully they won't feel the need to outdo you in any way and just flee the scene unless they're on drugs and decide to have a standoff. These small pocket guns are more suited as a means to escape deadly danger, but they are not *gunfight guns*. A counterattack breaks the confidence in quite a few of these thugs, and if you're willing and able to defend yourself, they might wonder what else you might be capable of—the very thing we never allow them to know—until it's time, that is, when it's too late for them. While these guns are certainly capable of killing an assailant, if you place a proper shot, they are not as likely to kill your KILLER, compared to more effective calibers, but they are very inexpensive as compared to most others, so if you buy one, make sure you inquire about its proper functioning sequences and even have the salesman demonstrate it properly. Due to the lack in proper defensive capabilities, you might think the manufacturers would drop them from production, but they don't drop because so many people buy them regardless of what they are told but mostly because of them being so cheap.

There are double-action revolvers which would be the revolver of choice for personal defense. This means that after you load the cylinder, you simply pull the trigger back which will self-cock the hammer and then you keep pulling the trigger to fire, but even if fired in double action, you have to *continue the trigger pull all the way to the back* while the cylinder rotates for each and every shot. The downside that leads to poor accuracy with every firearm is the strength it takes from you to pull or press the trigger all the way until it trips the hammer and fires. The trigger pull is measured in pounds; that is, if the trigger pull is 4.5 pounds, that's how much force it takes to pull it all the way to fire, and there are handguns with trigger pulls that vary, let's say in the 14-pound range, so be alert to this when shopping. Some trigger pulls require greater travel than others, and expensive trigger jobs in custom shops usually refine this for a price, if it's a sidearm that *is capable of being modified*, but by selecting something after studying carefully, even if it takes weeks or a couple of months to find what you feel will be your proper carry gun, you just might find a high-quality handgun with a proper trigger pull for an out-of-the-box price, requiring either no or very little custom work. Due to the polymer used in so many current handguns, custom work might be very limited if even possible on some models due to the comparison of metals that can be machined to very close tolerances in thousandths of an inch—millionths of an inch if need be by honing or lapping. But, so far, thousandths has always been the norm, as compared to plastics that may not even be revised or machined due to their structural make-up. Internal metal inserts and steel parts might be enhanced in a plastic or polymer gun, but it seems drop-in replacement parts are the only thing I've seen offered for them, but if you do this, save the removed parts, in case you decide to put them back in. I had a friend bring me his new .45 with a polymer frame with the box that it came in to see if he should send it back to the factory because of all the free play in the slide and the way the magazines locked in, but I told him that this was their manufacturing tolerance standards for this gun and that they won't be able to do anything about it other than to send it back to him. This is the very reason you need to study what you like *before you buy* and then decide if you want more or less quality at this time, but why settle for less when you can put it in layaway for a couple of months so you can get a quality firearm other than just good enough for half the cost. Additionally, for striker-fired designs (some striker-fired designs are different), to reduce the trigger pull, you need to replace the spring, which also reduces the striking power of the firing striker. Companies offer after-market drop-in replacement parts to improve the internal mechanics of striker-fired guns for a hundred dollars or two, but beware of proper functioning. Qualified people should install them. Personally, I like companies that are offering many of these preferred options that used to be considered custom and previously charged extra as a part of their normal manufacturing process, and more of them are starting to come into line with offering something much more suitable for your money, which not only gets the company the sale but saves you some cash. Sig Sauer now offers a model 1911 with all the options for a very reasonable price, including laser grips and a beveled magazine well, and it's very similar to the Kimber. It's pretty much the equivalent of buying a functional gun and having proper modifications already done to it, so it's actually putting a better handgun in the hands of those who are otherwise unknowing, right out of the box! Before I'd get upwards of $1,000 invested in a polymer handgun with its enhancements, I'd buy another metal gun with most of the modifications already built into them for a couple of hundred more, if that, right out of the box! This is why I chose my last three carry guns from Kimber for everyday carry! Lighter trigger pull and smoother trigger actions make all guns, including rifles and shotguns, much easier to handle and shoot much more accurately because they fire smoothly, as compared to jerking the trigger and missing the shot.

RACKING THE SLIDE

GRASP THE SLIDE FIRMLY
PUSH THE FRAME AND SLIDE
IN OPPOSITE DIRECTIONS
"ALL THE WAY"

THIS COCKS THE GUN AND CHAMBERS A ROUND

There's information on racking the slide further down, and you'll get instructions on just how to do it!

There are also double-action semiautomatic pistols that are designed a few different ways, but if you pull the slide all the way back and let it go (called racking the slide), it will chamber a round, but the hammer that actually hits the firing pin and fires the bullet remains un-cocked until you pull the trigger all the way back until it cocks and trips the hammer and fires, in which, at this point, will automatically chamber a new round. There is also what they call double-action, single-action guns which operate similar to the double action on the first round but cock the hammer and chamber a new round every time they are fired like the normal single action. To sort it all out, look at a few and ask the person in the gun shop to clearly explain its operation while demonstrating it for you prior to your decision and purchase. Para-Ordnance makes double-action semiautomatic pistols with either single-stack or double-stack magazines, in addition to their making single-action semiautomatic pistols.

One consideration is that if you get a polymer handgun or a lightweight gun, depending on the caliber, it may flip the muzzle (the opening at the end of the barrel) upwards due to the recoil and the lightweight of the gun. Short barrels will do this. Some people get this backward. If you were not aware of how to control the gun and started to fire it repeatedly in a fast sequence, while the muzzle is rising, each bullet hole would be higher than the previous one, which necessitates the ability to recover to the original firing position before firing each shot so that they are all headed downrange to the same aim point on the target as the very first shot. Don't compare the handgun to rifles because rifle cartridges are greater in length, pack much more powder, shoot longer bullets, and have very long barrels that allow the various powders burning at different rates to build extreme pressures before the projectile exits the barrel, and you get thumped on the shoulder. The previously mentioned muzzle brakes and vents allow for high-pressure gas to escape just before the bullet leaves the barrel so that it somewhat reduces the thump on the shoulder *or* the hands if it's a handgun. Although assault rifles such as the fully automatic M16s or semiautomatic AR-15s have buffer springs that absorb the recoil, with others you can learn proper control, but you must not be afraid of what you are doing. You're selecting a tool and tuning it to suit YOU, not to suit your brother or sister or the man behind the counter. YOU will be the one using this to save YOUR life, so that brings up the fact that you need something of proper quality, spending what is necessary for that quality, which will avoid possible miscellaneous malfunctions, although anything can happen, but less likely to malfunction at your much-needed time or emergency. A major fact you need to know is that a revolver in proper working condition *generally* has nothing to malfunction, but the hammer can get caught on clothing in the top edge of a pants pocket getting stuck and not coming out or whatever, but remember, they make what they call a *bobbed* hammer where the hammer spur is cut off, which also prevents you from being able to cock the hammer back on a double-action revolver to fire it in a single-action mode. They also make an enclosed frame where there is an internal hammer, which might not be visible, or a bobbed and recessed hammer, but they will fire every time you pull the trigger until it's empty.

Double-action handguns generally take much more strength to fire due to tighter trigger spring tension and the length of the trigger pull, but then some semiautomatics have tough recoil springs in the slide and some people might have difficulty racking the slide in a large caliber semiautomatic pistol due to tough springs, but they may have equally as much trouble or more, trying to rack the slide in a very small pocket-sized semiautomatic since the slide is only half the height and length and it has very little to grab. While some guns have multiple springs, some have replacement springs available to safely reduce the trigger tension for firing by many pounds in both semiautomatics and revolvers. The military currently requires a minimum of 5 and a maximum of 8.5 pounds on the trigger pull required to fire an M16, but military sniper rifles are even lower. Trigger pull should be light enough to develop proper accuracy when firing but not so light as to be too easily or accidentally discharged, so you have to learn your own specific gun because they do vary, and if the gun was previously owned, you can't be sure what's inside until you've properly checked it out.

Semiautomatic pistols have many things that can go wrong even if it's a perfectly tuned firearm. If you fire it with a limp wrist, the slide and frame may not reach their proper required distance in opposite directions to eject the spent round and chamber a new one. If you take a firm grip on the frame when you fire, although your fingers will be alongside the slide, don't press them against or touch the slide because it may not retract all the way, may not come back all the way, or may not chamber a new round properly if at all, while you may not even be aware that *you are causing the problem*. After the slide has retracted and the extractor has pulled out the spent cartridge and the ejector has ejected the spent round through the ejection port on the slide, then chambering a new round and the slide fully closed forward being loaded and ready to fire is called battery. If you pull the slide back and don't let it go to freely return by itself, by using your hand to carefully return the slide to its closed position, it may not chamber a new round or it may otherwise cause the new round to misfeed and jam. It needs a specified amount of torque and speed to strip a new round from the magazine and make the angle of the feed ramp into the chamber in the barrel correctly while closing. Remember, some gun manufacturers will caution you not to use any ammunition other than FMJ because the round nose of the FMJ will ride the feed ramp and chamber quite easily as compared to other bullet designs including hollow points. Remember, the ammunition manufacturers come to our rescue though by even designing hollow points with sufficient ogive, the shape of the bullet nose, including plastic inserts to feed and chamber properly in place of the round nose, but even then you have to shoot a number of your desired defensive rounds downrange to make sure they really work. Some might not work. It might be just a bit expensive to test the special defensive rounds you'll be carrying, but just because someone says they will work, doesn't mean they will, not to mention you need to know their accuracy potential with YOU shooting. Some may feed a few OK but then misfeed a few, so make sure they feed properly. Again, I say *most of them* because perfect ammunition sometimes misfeeding in semiautomatics, where even a round nose or FMJ can drive its nose into the feed ramp at the chamber transition and stop the feed process cold as the bullet abruptly stops and you have an unanticipated jam. Even if such misfeeds happen only once in 500 rounds or greater, we want quality, tuning, and experience in using our own gun so we can learn to properly identify unusual things that may happen, even if they happen only once in a while, and then we can work to correct it.

Remember, if you look at semiautomatic pistols, check to make sure the magazine (cartridge clip that holds bullets) locks in place properly and securely and, when locked in place, the magazine has no slack or slop being loose or wiggle. Someone showed me his bargain basement .380 semiautomatic pistol that he even paid too much for at a gun show for a personal carry gun, but it jammed constantly, and it was really a poor piece of craftsmanship as far as I was concerned. When I tried the magazines in it and locked them in, they wiggled and jiggled up and down, which was most probably the very cause of all the jams, but then even if you go buy new magazines (you shouldn't have to with a new gun) and if a few magazines (other than those that came with it) do the same thing, then it is most probably the gun, and there's no way to ever count on that gun for protection, or anything else for that matter, unless the problems are corrected. If it's a junk gun, then don't even bother trying to spend money on improving it. Sometimes the garbage can is the better deal, or back to the emergency automobile trunk bag just in case. If you find a gun that you feel is a very good deal and you're getting everything you need for a fair price, then after studying this book and knowing what you have to rely on, then make the best decision you can, but don't jump on what some people might say is a real steal or deal. Have you ever heard the sayings that if it's too good to be true, it probably is? But, sometimes, real deals do come along. Make sure you can rely on it for your life, or you might end up wasting half of the cost of what could have been a properly designed high quality and very reliable gun while later finding that you cannot even sell the one that was such a steal, especially if you have to explain why you're selling it. It might otherwise be another gun to save for one of the local city government buyback programs, where they offer the residents of the city money for their gun to get them off the street. Unbeknown to the city managers, a lot of those sold back are usually old, dangerous, and undesired weapons anyway but were quickly replaced with brand-new fine guns with all the money the city gave them for the old one, other than it becoming a few hundred-dollar paperweight! I did see a few fine firearms though that really makes you sad to see somebody turn these in. The honest people are being disarmed, so the thugs may choose their crime. You might even look in gun shops that sell used guns or come across someone that has one for sale, but beware that by buying a used gun, especially from someone you don't know! It might not work properly either, or it might get you locked up if it later turns out to be a murder weapon. Sometimes there's an exception, though, like a policeman who retired and sold his service gun, a Glock, several boxes of ammo, several holsters, and all the other accessories for $300. I'd have even bought that one that was really somewhat of a giveaway. Retiring shouldn't mean submitting yourself to becoming a potential victim of the criminals.

There are many manufacturers now who currently make quite a few handguns very suitable for concealed carry, especially with the growing number of concealed carry licenses being issued. Of the nine million concealed carriers nationwide so far, last year, in Ohio, there were 60,000 concealed carry licenses issued, and in the first quarter of this year, there were 13,204 issued. The numbers are growing. In Ohio, the term of the license before needing renewal is currently 5 years while there were 265,083 issued at the end of 2011. For carry guns, the striker-firing mechanism is catching on design-wise and more are being manufactured, but with different internal working mechanisms. Some striker-firing designs remain in half-cocked firing positions while other striker-firing designs are not cocked at all. Concealed carry is stimulating a great assortment of very effective guns, and companies are really competing for the business and offering very improved designs and warranties. By the government and the states allowing the personal carry of our firearms, it's forcing the firearms manufacturers to compete and to put their thinking caps on! Know what the gun does, or does NOT do, before you buy it! Some manufacturers are stating that they have no physical safeties on the outside of the gun, but, say, they made the trigger pull tough to avoid accidents. Remember, a hard trigger pull disrupts accuracy as you have to pull so hard that it pulls the gun off target by the time it actually fires. For those who might want to have an action or trigger job done to reduce the trigger pull for better accuracy, it might not be possible with guns that have the trigger pull made tough intentionally as a safety measure, or it might affect the mechanical workings of the striker-firing mechanism. You must be the one to make your choice, and remember that *if* you ever fire your handgun in a self-defense situation, they will definitely study your gun, and a district attorney might even try to use such designs against you if they don't think it's safe, no matter whether it was legal to buy it or not! A district attorney may use anything he can if he thinks you might be at fault. I have a friend who used to be the county prosecutor for 21 years; hopefully, he'll read this book.

So many people, when they buy a new gun for concealed carry, immediately buy new magazines from other custom gun makers, and people who are claiming to be knowledgeable suggest buying the extra magazines right away, but I have had the best operation in my Kimber with the Kimber factory magazines, absolutely flawless. They come with 2 removable base plates and 2 different thicknesses in base bumper pads for positive locking into the gun while reloading. The bumper pads are a real necessity for positively locking the magazine into the gun if you have a beveled magazine well so that you get sufficient depth into the grip of the gun which varies; that's an add-on, which makes the magazine too short for a positive tap with the palm of your hand to lock it in. In other words, for deeper bevels, you use thicker pads. I'd use a bumper pad even if I didn't have a beveled magazine well because it allows for that additional length to tap the magazine securely into place. I have no problem with using a magazine with *no* bumper pad on it as my first carry load that resides in the gun at all times because this keeps the *printing*-through-clothes profile down. I later purchased a few different magazines that come very highly recommended, but, in comparison, some custom magazines had the floor plate welded in, and I actually preferred the original Kimber magazines of which I happen to have so many due to their excellent reliability and very high quality. The same might not apply to your own selected gun though due to manufacturing quality and functionability, so when you finally buy your gun, you have to shoot a few boxes of ammo through it to break it in, get the feel, and get used to it while learning its proper operation. You must also know how to load and reload it—a major concern. We'll address these and other issues in learning to shoot, but don't get annoyed if something is repeated as I tend to do it intentionally because they need to be remembered.

High-capacity Magazines

There seems to be a lot of hype on large-capacity magazines all the time. I've had people tell me their gun has a magazine capacity of, say, 15 or 20 rounds or so. I saw some Glock 30 round magazines in a gun shop today. A high-capacity magazine is generally called a double-stacked magazine because it holds two rows of bullets as compared to a single-stacked magazine, which holds only one row. I intentionally carry a single-stacked firearm which holds 7 in the magazine and 1 in the chamber for a total of 8. Although the reality of an assailant on the move is very different as compared to stationary targets, I practice regularly at the shooting range, which is necessary to be effective in an emergency. I also shoot (double tap) quite frequently, that is, two simultaneous shots timed very close together and sometimes more in practice so that I will be able to do it effectively at the proper time. Double tap is two quickly *aimed* shots, not just bang-bang. While double tap is suggested for any shot to a killer because we may not be sure of hitting him, if he still doesn't stop, then two similar quickly fired shots to the pelvis should break the supporting bones and bring him down. If I cannot hit and stop my target with the first 8 rounds—hopefully the first two rounds—I'm most likely going to be dead. If I survive long enough to reload, the perpetrator is probably no longer a threat, but I carry a double-magazine carrier anyway with two extra 10 round single-stacked magazines for backup just in case and a few more in my vehicle which I'll address later. Even though we have statistics for reference which might say only a few shots may be needed in a confrontation, you might experience the exception, which generally happens when you're not prepared for it. An extra magazine or two are well worth the money just in case but only if they're accessible!

These are single-stacked magazines for a .45 caliber 1911. They all lock into the gun with the notch on the right side, so though the length below the notch is irrelevant, providing the magazine is longer or a higher capacity than the one required. In other words, if you have a 6-round magazine, then anything greater will fit properly, but if you have anything 7 rounds or greater, then the 6 won't be long enough to fit nor function. These are all single-stacked 1911 magazines. From the left to right:

1. *A 7 round single-stacked Kimber magazine with a thick bumper pad.*
2. *An 8-round Kimber magazine with a thin bumper pad.*

3. A 10-round Chip McCormick Custom Power Mag, which is an extended single-stacked magazine.

4. Kimber bumper pads that come in thick or thin, but no matter what make of magazine and bumper pads you buy, your magazine has to have threaded holes for the screws to attach the pads.

5. The magazine at the far right has a hooked bumper pad installed from the factory and is available for small pocket guns to assure of getting that extra finger on the grip. No matter which magazine you have in the gun, you still have the option for one more round in the chamber. Some companies sell the bumper pads in different colors, which is handy for loading different magazines for different purposes.

Note the beveled magazine wells for inserting a magazine in a hurry to assist in guiding the magazine into the gun faster without missing the gun in an emergency. With beveled magazine well, the bumper pads are necessary to assure of inserting the magazine deep enough until it locks in. On the right, the lower slide release is a standard length while the stainless one above it is an extended release, which makes one-handed operation of the slide possible for faster reloads. They are made for various guns but should be fitted by a qualified gunsmith to prevent accidentally bouncing due to recoil and locking the slide open prematurely.

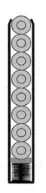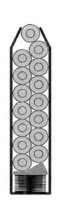

On the left is a single-stacked magazine, a single row of bullet cartridges, as compared to the double-stacked magazine on the right, a double row of bullets. The single-stacked allows for thinner grips for those with smaller hands or for concealing better.

On the left, the 7-round flush magazine with no bumper pad inserted in the Kimber 3inch .45 1911 for a lower profile for concealed carry, and on the right, the 10-round Chip McCormick extended Power Magazine for a reload since concealment is no longer an issue but more rounds are needed.

According to FBI statistics, most police shooting encounters average from 4 to 6 shots being fired, but it is important to always practice reloading so you will be able to do it properly while in a hurry when necessary. A single-stacked magazine conceals much better than a double- stacked due to its thinner profile as compared to an extra thick grip, which is harder to hide for concealment. When selecting a carry gun, if you're looking for a semiautomatic pistol, then the option of it having a beveled magazine well opening (where the magazine is inserted into the gun) is beneficial when trying to reload and insert a new loaded magazine quickly. Some add-on beveled magazine wells are larger, deeper, and wider than a standard internally beveled well opening in the frame where the magazine enters but are more useful for competition shooting as compared to concealed carry, so remember, if you use an extended beveled magazine well, you have to use the right magazine base bumper pad to make sure you get the magazine locked deep enough into place. If it's *not* locked in, you're going to be in deep trouble when you try to fire your sidearm, and the magazine drops out or slides down partially out of place. It happens! While some people are always concerned with an extra round in their magazine capacity, there are actual base pads for bumping the magazine into a locked-in position, which are hollow internally and allow for an extra 2, 3, or 4 extra rounds to be inserted into the same magazine, depending on the caliber and whether it's a single—or double-stacked magazine. A word of caution! Some of them are polymers, that is, nylon and plastics, and some are machined out of aluminum, but many replace the removable base plate in the magazine. The extended magazines with only surface pads, such as Chip McCormick Power Mags, would be more reliable because the actual magazine is extended. Some come as assemblies consisting of the extension, spring, and follower and some by themselves, while you can even buy longer magazines with them already installed. Using the original magazine, spring and follower with just the addition of the extension for a bumper pad, may cause a malfunction due to the factory spring requirements and tension, not to mention that the molded plastics that some are made of won't work for me due to the possibility of breakage, especially at the most inopportune time. The primary magazine that is always in the gun when carried MUST function! The need for tuning your specific gun means confidence in everything, being functional and reliable, especially for that first shot or two. We don't want excessive numbers of bullets flying through the air because each bullet you fire has an attorney's calling card written on it, and we do not want to accidentally take an innocent life of any person, which could even be that of a child. I lost a daughter when she was a child to open-heart surgery, so I certainly don't want anyone losing their child because not only is it really tough, but I couldn't imagine my child *or any family member* being shot by an irresponsible gun owner just because he wanted to be macho or doesn't think he needs to learn to use his equipment and practice sufficiently, so just be careful and be very responsible. It could have definitely created a different situation for me if I had someone to blame. Accidentally shooting the wrong person, especially one of your family members coming into the house unexpectedly, can create very traumatic emotional wounds that may linger on through the rest of your life with no way to heal. I want you to *remember* and understand all these differences when we address them, and while there are many fine handguns out there, I'm explaining possible difficulties and why they might happen. I'm providing a great deal of facts; you decide what to do with them!

Glock

While so many people love and swear by the Glock, I was always somewhat hesitant to like the Glock. The Glock is a striker-fired pistol that was introduced in 1980, and one of my main concerns was their claiming that there were not any safeties to have to disengage to fire this pistol and that it was absolutely safe. I really didn't like the plastic polymer compared to the all-metal construction of my 1911s, and, for years, since I'm a die-hard 1911 fan, I'm a bit hard to interest in the Glock. While I saw a couple of Glocks that malfunctioned and accidentally discharged, I was obviously somewhat confident in my not purchasing one, when a relative tried to get me to buy one, but I was quite proud of my new Kimber 1911 in .45 ACP. While everybody talked about the Glock being the safest pistol ever created, I realized that every type of gun ever made has an occasional malfunction once in a while, so I decided to give the Glock a fair evaluation and compare it to my 1911 with complete honesty, just the facts, win or lose, so that I don't give any one gun in particular a bad rap if it's not deserving of it.

Glock Safe Action System: One of the things that makes Glock pistols some of the safest in existence is their unique safe action system. This is comprised of a trigger safety, a firing pin safety, and a drop safety. The trigger safety prevents accidental discharge caused by lateral force on the trigger. The main portion of the trigger cannot be pulled without the trigger safety first being pulled. Some people refer to the trigger safety as a second trigger or the *trigger's trigger*. The firing pin safety is a little metal button on the bottom of the slide itself that blocks the firing pin channel, rendering the ability of the firing pin to strike the primer of a round impossible. The firing pin safety is pushed upward and out of the way only when the trigger is pulled. Releasing the trigger automatically re-engages the firing pin safety.

The Glock Drop Safety: Last, but in no way least, the drop safety prevents accidental discharge of a Glock pistol by hard impact, such as dropping it on the floor. All three Glock pistol safeties must be disengaged in order for the gun to fire. All three safeties are disengaged when the shooter places his finger on the trigger. The safeties are re-engaged when the shooter takes his finger off the trigger. There is a reason why these three safeties operate from the trigger. The use of a defensive firearm exposes users to tremendous psychological strain. With Glock pistols, there is only one rule to remember about the safeties: finger off the trigger, safety on; finger on the trigger, safety off.

Kimber

One of the things that makes the Kimber 1911 pistols some of the safest in existence is their equally safe 3-point system in their series II designations (3-point system is *my* definition!) This is comprised of a firing pin safety, a grip safety, and a thumb safety. The trigger cannot be pulled unless the grip safety is engaged and the thumb safety is lowered. The grip safety is automatically engaged when you take a firm grip on the gun, which presses the grip safety in. When the grip safety is pressed in, it raises the firing pin block to allow the firing pin to strike the primer if the hammer hits the firing pin, and the grip safety also unlocks the trigger, so it can be pulled *if* the thumb safety is disengaged.

The hammer cannot fall, no matter what you do to the gun because the thumb safety locks the hammer while at the same time locking the slide. The trigger still cannot be pulled unless you disengage the thumb safety to allow the hammer to drop if the trigger is now pulled; at the same time, the slide is unlocked and free to cycle. So if you dropped this 1911, it cannot discharge because it takes all these safeties to be released at the same time, which cannot happen since the grip safety cannot be made and cannot release the hammer locking thumb safety, and the firing pin block is still locked because the grip safety has to be held in to allow for all the gun's functions to work. While some people complain that they still have to release the thumb safety, I prefer it that way, and it's the *only* safety that you have to disengage because the natural hold on the grip automatically releases the other functions. Although all manufacturers warn against carrying their guns loaded due to their reasons of liability, I feel this 1911 can be carried cocked and locked with *no worry* about any kind of discharge whatsoever with this gun in proper working condition, but you must make your own decisions. It's the perfect sidearm in .45 ACP, and the laser grips by Crimson Trace really improve its effectiveness. For the Glock, you have to make a hundred dollars or more in modifications to lighten the trigger pull while the Kimber is good to go out of the box. All guns can possibly be improved, but make sure it's by a *qualified* gunsmith.

Sighting in Your Handgun

Sighting in your gun is another science! Depending on your age and as to whether you wear eyeglasses or not changes the way we see things. If you pull your gun on anyone, you definitely have to be able to clearly and properly *see* what you're going to shoot. Let's address the sight radius of any gun you plan to buy. The further apart the sights, that is, from the front sight to the back sight, is the actual sight radius, so if the sights are 5 inches apart, you have a 5-inch sight radius. The greater the sight radius, the more accurate you should be at hitting your target generally unless you are very well experienced and can shoot well with a short barrel, but it still takes a lot of practice after you're certain of clearly and properly seeing the target. One reason police opt for a rifle or shotgun other than a handgun if possible is long-range accuracy and power. When I first purchased my carry gun, it had three dot sights on it, which I really liked, but in shooting the first thousand rounds through it, I figured I must be getting old because I just could not see that dot on the front sight blade because it appeared darker than the two dots on the rear. It shot an excellent group, but I wasn't pleased with the group, so I started wondering why I couldn't seem to get the group tight enough. The gun was certainly capable, and they are generally more capable than the shooter. I started reviewing other sights including the sight paint that they sell to color the dots in whatever color you wish or in combination, while some sights even come that way. Then there are the sights made of an acrylic fiber optic rod, which absorbs light, and during bright daylight, it seems like it could be very handy, but I wanted to be able to see in any light condition since my life is at stake here. Finally, I seemed to settle on the Mepro-Light sights which have assorted configurations. The design I chose a three-dot combat-style system with tritium gas ampules the size of a large dot inserted. While Mepro- Light publicly claims to be 20% brighter than any others, the sights I picked had thin white rings around the outer diameter of the dot for daylight visibility, and, in total darkness, they glow brilliantly like little light bulbs, but, in total darkness, they appear very well. When I picked up the gun with its new sights installed, I went out to the range with a hundred rounds to try it out, and it immediately tightened the group with many of the shots touching in different groups and at different distances. Now I was pleased. After using the new sights for a while, I shot holes touching and actually enlarging the first hole with each next shot offhand.

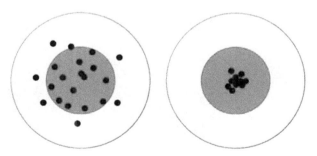

Being able to see what you're shooting at certainly makes a difference in the final results. Practicing the proper shooting techniques will help develop the necessary skills for proper shot placement. Just trying to hit the target isn't what you're trying to do, but controlling your gun and getting a tighter group is! Remember, a small error at the muzzle is many feet or yards downrange!

A very good investment of another hundred bucks, the sights are guaranteed for twelve years. I realized it wasn't just my age creeping up on my shooting but my ability to clearly see the sight placement on the target under varied lighting conditions. Later, a firearm's instructor (with his own opinion which was insufficient knowledge) said there's never any need for such glowing dots in total darkness because you couldn't see the killer, but in my tests in total darkness, the sights are miraculous, and I studied them carefully while observing many silhouettes and configurations of an attack, so my comment regarding those who say such glowing dots aren't an advantage is, I wanted them due to my own preferences since I'm addicted to living, and if you and I ever get attacked by killers and we're involved in a shoot-out for our lives, requiring proper sighting in low-to-no-light conditions, leave a copy of your will with me, and I'll give it to your family. If you're caught in the dark, especially if your eyes are adapted to the dark situation at hand, the Mepro-Light sights will really make you glad you have them. If you sit in your house at night in total darkness, in about 30 minutes, your eyes will eventually adapt to the lighting, and even though your vision will be very limited, by looking through these sights while your eyes are adapted to the dark, they work incredibly well, and in my tests, I was able to take specific aim on many points that were not prearranged or set up so that it simulates the real situation. If I didn't have these sights on my gun, I definitely wouldn't have been able to sight in on anything in such low-light conditions including on a killer, so I'd be subject to dying. I'll never be caught without such sights on a self-defense gun. Remember, know your target!

When sighting your new handgun, be sure to use both eyes open for the sights! Study this when reviewing guns at the store. If you had magnified optics, it would be different; however, you need to be able to see what's going on everywhere around you while reacting to a threat and you need both eyes open for depth perception in a gun fight, so you will certainly do your best ONLY if both eyes are open while sighting in on the front sight blade or sight post of your gun and acquiring your target. Once practiced this way, you will quickly adjust. I always see people closing one eye and then squinting with the other, a sure recipe for disaster, especially since we already lose 20% of our peripheral vision while aiming and sighting because our eyes are preoccupied with what's ahead. One eye shut and the other eye squinting or half shut just may get you shot, stabbed, and killed!

Picatinny Rail

Note the three versions of a Picatinny rail above. From the left:

1. *A basic Picatinny*
2. *A forward grip quad Picatinny*

3. *An AR-15/M16 handle Picatinny for easy on and easy off with the thumb nut underneath. The quad Picatinny may be too much rail. Too many gadgets can be terribly distracting to the average person, and the extra rails on all four sides cost a great deal more. You must decide!*

First, do you need laser sights? Let's see if you think so. Out of all the laser sights I've studied, I love the Crimson Trace laser grips. I prefer having these laser sights for a few good reasons. In studying a variety of laser sights, you have to draw your gun and turn some of the laser sights on, but they seem to have differences in their means of switching on the power to do this, probably due to the patent infringement laws. On a semiautomatic, many lasers mount in front of the trigger guard or in a Picatinny rail below the muzzle, otherwise known as a rail gun. On revolvers, the lasers generally mount on the side of the frame, but laser grips are becoming quite popular on the revolvers too, but don't misunderstand and don't ever buy any part of your firearm or sights due to being told that it's popular because sometimes everybody buys what's supposed to be the hottest and most popular thing whether it's good for you or not due to their *not knowing* and their truly understanding the part or even its operating procedures and options. A Picatinny rail is a slotted rail mounting system devised in 1995 by the US Army's Picatinny Arsenal in New Jersey for mounting optics, but its use immediately took off and was quickly adopted by manufacturers and offered to the public for mounting other items such as lights, lasers, accessories, and just about everything. Some of these handguns (rail guns) have two horizontally indented grooves above the Picatinny under the muzzle to assist in mounting other systems and devices. Even NATO is adopting the Picatinny with suggested revisions but maintaining backward compatibility. Keep in mind that the Picatinny rail is generally expensive on some guns like rifles where they line the top and sometimes the forward grip on 4 sides in Picatinny rails, but all this rail might unnecessarily raise the cost of the firearm by $200 or so, so beware of so many rails on firearms and try to decide beforehand whether you need all these rails or not, and if you do, how much rail do you really need? Too many gadgets are extra bulk and weight, which might also take some of your thinking away from your response time to deal with a deadly threat while subconsciously wanting to make sure all your gadgets are working while Mr. Simple who has nothing to do but shoot puts a bullet in you. Every single thought you have to process takes time! Professionals in the military and SWAT teams may have many rails on their weapons for specific reasons, which might not be what *we* will ever be doing, so remember we're NOT trying to be COOL or buying such accessories just because they have them, especially on military and police weapons, but we're trying to be effective at saving our lives. Just because they make all these gizmos and we know people who have all this hardware mounted on their defensive guns, it doesn't mean *we* need to do it and follow suit, but we do need to be unique in our own situation. Be sure of what *suits you* and what you need *before* you buy!

Laser Sights

Laser sights? Most people don't know what a laser is, so we'll look at them briefly. *LASER* is the acronym of *light amplification by stimulated emission of radiation*. The laser is defined by the way it produces light by *stimulated emission*. Its beam can be focused in a very tiny beam sometimes called a pencil beam, and although there are numerous types of lasers with different colored light beams that are used for many different tasks, a very simple laser design is used for firearms sights due to the accuracy and the intensity of the light beam and is offered in either a red or green light beam configuration. The green is known for its ability to be visible in brighter light conditions such as sunlight and also at a much further distance than the red beam while these two colors are both offered for firearms, usually red for handguns and green for rifles or shotguns. But the green is catching on for the handguns too while we remember that we use the handgun for defense within a reasonable distance, and the laser doesn't mean the bullet will impact at that specific point if it's not zeroed for that spot, so while the laser beam is perfectly straight, extending out from the muzzle of your gun, remember that the bullet drops and will only hit the right spot when zeroed there. Currently, the technology has progressed to the point of being able to produce a laser of sufficient capability into a very small laser diode powered by batteries. The whole laser sight assembly probably only weighs a few ounces. No matter what type or power level of a laser you might have, *never* intentionally allow the beam to illuminate on anyone's eyes since lasers can do damage. NOTE that this does not mean to worry about a KILLER you're responding to; *your only concern is stopping him,* and by being armed with a laser or laser grips, they know where your bullet is headed, and if he's still alive at that point, he just might change his mind and disappear into the darkness of night.

My laser grips replace the actual grips on the gun, and a small extension on the top of the grip contains the tiny electronic laser diode, which uses very little energy. If turned on, when you take a firm grip on the gun, the laser activates its light beam automatically. The laser turns the beam off if you release your grip due to the momentary contact switch being attached across the front strap of the laser grip, with some momentary contacts being mounted on the back strap of the grip other than the front according to the model gun you have. I find it very advantageous to keep the power switch for my laser grips turned on all the time, 24 hours a day, so that if I ever draw my gun, it will automatically turn its laser light beam on, and if I'm in a somewhat close encounter where I cannot reach and extend my arms out to sight my gun on the assailant due to such a close quarters confrontation, the laser beam immediately turns its light beam on as I'm drawing from the holster. It shows me where I'm pointing while sweeping the muzzle of my gun up at the target's center mass so that if I don't have the time or space to sight in on the killer, I can quickly put an effective shot into my would-be killer as close to my intended spot as possible by viewing the red dot sweeping up onto him, as compared to not otherwise knowing where the gun is even pointed in such a close encounter and maybe being in a scuffle and without the laser grips getting no shot at all. This gives me a great advantage here, but there's more to that later. I'm only mentioning so much of each to help you in your selection, so you know what you want *and understand why*. If you purchase your gun with a laser or laser grips installed already from the factory, you will save quite a few dollars here too, and the Crimson Trace laser grips if installed when you buy your gun are already sighted in at the factory for 50 feet, but you get a hex key wrench to adjust them in ¼ turn increments alternating windage and elevation between adjustments for proper accuracy. As much as I like the Crimson Trace Laser Grips, I readjust the sights to *my own* point of impact at my own desired distance, especially to make sure of a positive aim point if I'm going to use it to save my life, so always check them to be sure they didn't get out of adjustment in transit. My removable laser bore sight works extremely well for this purpose, bringing the two dots together at your desired range. On the laser sights, windage is your bullet impact from side to side and elevation is vertically up and down—the same as the sights normally are on a firearm or a scope.

Another way to adjust your point of impact for any distance *other than for a specific range* is to have an observer with you, then tape a paper up at point-blank range, put the muzzle up close to the paper, then activate *both* the laser boresight and the laser grips, and mark the two dots on the paper. So if I'm using one of my .45 1911s, then say the dots are about 5/8-inch apart. Drawing a crosshair in each dot, then tape the same paper up as a long-range target but within easy view and activate both lasers again while adjusting the laser grips just a hair at a time so both lasers meet the point of impact already previously marked on paper, and check it at a few distances whether it's close or far so that the laser from the grips and the point of impact (centerline of the bore) are both parallel to the bore at any distance. No matter how far you are from the target, always remember your point of impact is about 5/8-inch to the left of the laser dot, so your laser is now sighted for *any distance*, or the furthest distance you can still see the laser because it's parallel to the bore other than originally angled diagonally for a specific range, but don't forget to keep the elevation in check.

Otherwise, when the laser from the grips is normally angled and adjusted to meet and merge at the desired point of impact at a specific distance, say 50 feet, once the lasers meet at the point of impact at 50 feet, it continues beyond the desired distance. Since the laser beam is mounted about 5/8 inch to the right side of the bore in the laser grips on a 1911, when the laser is adjusted to meet diagonally at 50 feet, once it passes the 50 feet, the laser will still return to the 5/8-inch distance from the bore but on the left side of the point of impact at 100 feet due to the angled laser beam. Since this 100-foot distance would now shift the point of impact 5/8 inch to the right side of the laser, we could simply use the red dot from the laser as a direct aiming reference anywhere within the 100-foot range and be within 11/4 inch, either 5/8 inch right or 5/8 inch left. The batteries on Crimson Trace laser grips are good for 4 hours of continuous use, that is, a constant red laser beam, so an occasional blink here and there will go for a very long time before a battery change is required, but I keep a spare set of batteries on hand all the time just in case. When I was on the phone with Crimson Trace, they said they will replace the batteries free of charge while they have an option on their Web site for enrollment into FREE batteries for life! Another major advantage of the Crimson Trace laser grips is that by replacing the original grips with the laser grips, you have no additional bulk or odd shapes added on your gun to worry about when trying to buy a proper holster like you would if you had another object or laser on the outside of your gun that can get in the way and snag, similar to some other laser designs. Although you need to practice regularly, I spend most of my practice time with the laser sight turned off, so I don't become dependent on it. When it's time to practice with the laser sight turned on, you'll definitely see how much your hands do shake and quiver when you otherwise think it's very steady while the beam will shake and wander at the slightest movement whatsoever, all over the target further downrange. The further you are away from the target, the further across the target the light beam moves with the slightest amount of movement at the gun's location or from the vertical axis of the handgun's grip due to the angle being magnified greater with distance. A small sighting error of about 1/10 of an inch at the muzzle will magnify downrange at a 25-yard target by about 15 inches or more if not a total miss, depending on your actual distance. Imagine being a full-inch off target while in a stressful encounter, which seems simple enough but could result in a miss by 150 inches! Do you remember what we said about shooting the wrong guy? We certainly don't want to aim at the assailant (or think we are), and when we fire, we hit the man 12½ feet to either side of him. Without practicing to know your specific gun, it can very well happen. While not making fun of any shooter because these things take time to learn every specific gun and make any necessary adjustments, I've watched people shoot rifles with 20 and up to 26-inch barrels and open sights at 50 yards, but even though it was in a completely relaxed situation as compared to being under stress, they completely missed the 18-inch square target numerous times. Compare these 20 and 26-inch barrels to your probable 3-inch barrel. Do you see how easy it is to miss your target? The further away your KILLER is, the more skill you need to stop him! But you need these skills regardless of the distance! The laser grips are excellent for simulated fire in dry practice where you can draw your gun from the holster while bringing your point of impact toward your intended target immediately, and they will really help you in learning point-and-flash shooting, but while using the laser, remember you will be able to see how steady you're not, and you can learn to move your hands much less. Think about it now. With different laser designs, do you really think you can draw your gun and stop to turn it on? It's like stopping to chamber a round when there's a gun pointed at you. You only have a few seconds or less to respond, so the laser grips are the cat's meow as far as I'm concerned, and I take my choice in personal defense AND SURVIVAL very seriously! Victory and success loves preparation, and if you get caught unprepared, you may certainly be caught dead. While assembling a proper defensive handgun, you don't want to be found dead just because you had to stop to turn on your laser sight; otherwise, you might be better off without one. An automatic laser response just by taking the firm grip on the gun eliminates one more thought and action that otherwise has to be processed. Just remember that you need to be qualified with open sights!

These are sets of Crimson Trace Laser Grips mounted on a revolver on the left and on a 1911 semiautomatic pistol on the right. They replace the natural factory grips exactly and don't add

additional bulk and weight like other types of lasers. The black rubber below the trigger guard on the front strap of the grip is a momentary contact switch that automatically turns on the red laser beam when you grab the gun and have a natural grip, which compresses the switch. By turning the laser on automatically when you grip the gun, it saves one step in the process of drawing and presenting your gun during an attack that could otherwise get you killed by the delay and distraction because you have to turn on some laser models. Draw, aim, and fire! YOU have an advantage! Crimson Trace also has other models to choose from even if it's for a rifle or a shotgun!

There are also laser guards, as shown above left, that mount on the trigger guard, and rail gun mounted lasers, as shown above right, under the dust cover. Don't buy without taking your gun into the shop to make sure they fit the gun you have.

What's Your Answer to How Much Is Your Life Worth?

I, for one, never pay attention to those who say they buy a small caliber handgun because the ammo is cheaper, but I do go for reliability, accuracy, and the intention of knocking down and eliminating the threat as quickly as possible. A delay, any delay, can result in you being KILLED. There are also those who downplay the question, how much is your life worth? Not disrespecting instructors, I'd say some of those who ridicule such questions regarding the value of your life are even instructors who feel they can downplay the situation, but just because they are an instructor does not mean that they are so wise. It means they passed the necessary qualifications to instruct you; that's all. Some are very qualified, and some are just qualified enough. They won't take on the responsibility of your death, not to mention; we don't want to deny our own responsibility to survive. I personally believe that any instructor should never try to influence you to just settle for whatever may be available since it may also be inferior. To me, your instructor should give you all the facts, explain whats and whys, and allow you to make an informed decision. Remember, failure is NOT an option. I believe it's his duty as an instructor to keep you in the most positive state of mind with the best mental preparation and skills, so an instructor should never say such things or downplay any such comments on the value of your life but maybe tell you to research the issues and make your decision. Back to the guns, you can always buy a .22 for target practice for very cheap practice and still have your desired and effective caliber for defensive measures. While I prefer the 1911 in .45 ACP for defense, I like the 1911 style gun in .22 caliber for practice because it's the same operating system as my carry gun but in a different caliber so that I'll always maintain my ability to continue practicing with the very same (instinctively, *learned*) operating system and that I'll be forced to use if my life is threatened. While I have no problem with owning and using other guns, by my using a 1911 for defense and a 1911 for practice, this will reduce the possibility of my messing up my sequence of moves in a real emergency because all my actions will remain exactly the same through thousands of repetitions including the safeties. No matter what you shoot, you still have to shoot a minimum of the carry caliber and your specific defensive carry round downrange to maintain your ability to properly control your gun and know how the ammo performs, but you can shoot cheaper *comparable* ammo, but use quality ammunition for practice and personal protection ammo for concealed carry.

Green Ammo/Contamination

In 1999, the US Army started looking to replace lead bullets to reduce the possibility of contamination in the ground from millions of rounds being fired downrange due to so much military practice; they finally settled on what they call green ammo (not to be confused with green tips or green cartridge cases). The term *green ammo* is ammo made of tungsten composite or nylon with the same copper covering (jacket). Researchers studied different combinations of metal to design a slug that would perform the same as the old one and have the same density, ballistic quality, and so on, and planned to have the replacement fully in effect by 2005. If they didn't use it up, you might be able to pick up some of the old military ammo for some really good prices just for practice. I used to buy it in crates by the thousands of rounds very reasonably priced, but times change, so always be on alert for a deal pricewise.

Bullet Weight and Velocity—Which Gun Do I Use?

Some of the biggest questions all the time are what gun can I use for home defense, what caliber can I use for which particular game, and what bullet weight can I use. To start out, by now in your reading this information, you should have a very good idea on which way to go in general, but I'm going to cover it briefly to make sure you're on track. Heavier bullets will almost always get the job done, but many of those experienced in shooting claim they can hit the animal and do just fine with their .223 versus a .308. While there is much to this, there are also downfalls to this. If you were hunting a small animal out to 200 yards or so, it might be taken just fine with the .223, but if you were using the same round for a hog of, say, a couple or a few hundred pounds or even much more, then even that very round might take the game down within 100 yards. When the round gets out to 200 yards, your velocity diminishes with the lighter round much faster than it would with a heavier bullet, which also means that the kinetic energy (energy applied to the wound channel) upon impact, which is terminal ballistics, is far less than it would be closer or at a shorter distance. The further the distance, the lesser the power you have. If we compared the .224 to the .308 in rifle cartridges, the 55-grain FMJ

.224 with a muzzle velocity (velocity of the round while leaving the muzzle of the barrel) of 2,900 feet per second diminishes to 2,187 feet per second at 200 yards with 584 foot pounds or 1,139 feet per second at 500 yards but with only 158-foot pounds left. The 150-grain FMJ .308 with a muzzle velocity of 2,800 feet per second, when it gets out to 200 yards, diminishes to 2,404 feet per second with 1,924-foot pounds, or, at 500 yards, it diminishes to 1,872 feet per second with 1,167-foot pounds, so while the .308 started out with 100 feet per second less muzzle velocity, it still retained enough energy due to its weight in flight to equal 1,009-foot pounds more or 7.38 times the power than the .224 both measured at 500 yards. But it is 95 grains heavier while being proportionate from the muzzle to the specified distance. So this means that the rifle shooting the lighter round may be capable of hitting the target or your hunted game out to very good distances but offers very little wound damage, compared to the rifle shooting the heavier round and offering 7.38 times the wounding effect. If you find yourself having to shoot at a distance much further than anticipated, the heavier .308 round will certainly outperform the lighter .224. In a study of 81 hunters who each shot a deer, the majority of these deer were taken within 100 yards. Many were taken with the .223 in states that allow this round for deer hunting while many don't believe in such a small caliber for deer due to the great possibility of injuring and losing the animal. For these hunters, 31 deer were shot at 50 yards, 27 deer at 75 yards, 16 deer at 100 yards, 3 deer at 150 yards, 3 deer at 200 yards, and 1 deer at 250 yards. Remembering the tests showing that it takes 170 feet per second to penetrate human tissue with a ¼ inch spherical projectile, the tests didn't stipulate the weight of the projectile, but the weight and the velocity are used to calculate the kinetic energy while shot placement of a lighter and less capable round is very critical. A target which has bone will interfere with penetration may deflect a bullet or bring it to a halt much easier and faster than anticipated, resulting in a wounded animal and quite possibly a very poor wound channel, which immediately calls for the heavier round to be used to avoid the lighter round from being deflected too easily to get proper penetration and more energy transfer on impact. While referencing handgun projectiles, you can see a 200-grain .45 ACP cartridge within CQB (close quarters battle) range, such as most close confrontations in a gunfight, may give 1,080 feet per second with 518-foot pounds as compared to a .224 rifle round at 200 yards, giving 584-foot pounds of energy. Study your needs BEFORE you buy! Suddenly, the .308 becomes more of a choice if the distance is going to be unknown or the game animal may be larger than anticipated. Velocity pumped up on a lighter round will increase the applied energy in foot pounds, but a heavier round with higher velocity is certainly the winner. Small calibers and lighter bullet weights have their place while larger calibers with heavier bullets also do the same. A hunter taking a very long shot with a caliber that has no power left when the bullet gets downrange may only wound an animal, allowing it to run off, compared to one that drops the animal in its tracks. Your needs should be matched to your choice of calibers and the available cartridges while remembering that shooting different cartridges or bullet weights in the same firearm also gets different results. The laws of physics rule the outcome of every round fired in every gun made, so it's very important to first understand that the atmospheric conditions with air and wind resistance work against the bullet in flight from the moment it's fired, and the lighter bullet slows down much faster over distance than the heavy round does, thereby reducing its velocity, which directly effects and reduces the kinetic energy of the round on impact, which is absorbed by the medium of the target to determine the degree of damage and/or wound channel produced with that particular round and bullet weight. Bullets are designed for specific amounts of energy transfer (kinetic energy) to do specific damage upon impact and won't do their job if they run out of velocity and kinetic energy before they reach their target, and you can do all the troubleshooting in the world, trying to figure out why the round didn't do what the ballistic tests and pictures may illustrate on a chart, but it's very important to know where the transition is, such as what range in yards does the velocity and its impact potential diminish to a level below what is actually needed for the round to perform as it was intended, and it is a major part of the kill or wound criteria. While everyone publishes charts for ballistic measurements, especially bullet drop at a specific distance so you can compensate by adjusting your sights, being able to hit the intended target in the kill zone, pay attention to the velocity and the kinetic energy of your specific hunting round at your increments of 200 and 300 yards and so on to determine where the round becomes ineffective so you know that your animal must be within these parameters out to this distance. But remember that your bullet may very well be capable of reaching out much further and still has the ability to accurately hit the target but maybe not enough power left to do its job the way you might have hoped for. You may also discover that you want to bring a box of heavier rounds along to reach out beyond, but remember that you need to be able to have your specific hunting round sighted in for that particular firearm, or you will need to understand the reticle in your scope so you can holdover to compensate for the heavier round. To further simplify the issue, you might want to use the heavier round in the first place since you know that it will reach out and bag your dinner at every distance out to your zero point reference and at every point between the muzzle and zero. Different calibers, bullet weights, and designs for expansion are the reason we need different firearms for different purposes. While you may have an exceptionally accurate rifle round at long range, if it has no kinetic energy left for power absorption while creating a wound, it becomes very ineffective for a clean kill, compared to punching a hole through paper. So different cartridge capabilities must be known and established with specific barrel lengths, resulting in the need for several firearms for different purposes.

While understanding velocity in combination with bullet weight equals kinetic energy, many people automatically remove a rifle from consideration for home defense due to the velocity and kinetic energy of the round at such close range to avoid overpenetration through walls and beyond out into other houses. But certain configurations may qualify as a home defense rifle with capabilities to reach out and strike where the handgun may fail. Shotguns are also a very strong defense firearm but also have great capabilities above and beyond the handguns. I like an AR-15 assault rifle configuration with a short-barrel making maneuverability easier while reducing the velocity of the round, and having it loaded with personal defense ammunition for immediate expansion, you have the option of frangible rounds. All the above come together to assist in avoiding overpenetration while getting the job done when longer-range accuracy and power are needed. You must make such decisions based on your own knowledge, your living quarters, and your specific circumstances after you've scoped out the area in advance of any attacks upon you or your family and paying special attention to entry and escape routes while checking their actual distance and possibly altering their actual means of criminal access so that YOU will be the one most familiar with the surroundings, not them, giving you the definite advantage. Remember one important item: even if you set up a home defense rifle, if it might possibly be called for, remember how the larger caliber rifle, shooting a heavier round, tends to hold velocity and deliver much more kinetic energy than the smaller caliber rifle shooting the lightweight bullet. Two rifles may appear exactly identical in appearance but may be capable of delivering two completely different sets of results, so develop a plan according to your own specific needs. What works for one may be totally inappropriate for another. For hunting purposes, remember to select the right bullet design so that if you're shooting at a great distance, the projectile is capable and structurally designed and constructed to hold together for the distance needed, as compared to the one that may disintegrate even partially before it reaches the target.

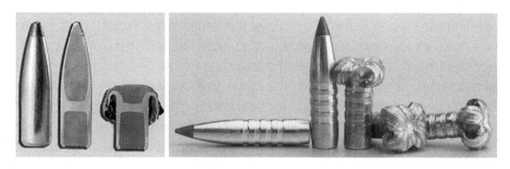

There are a variety of rifle bullet designs, so make sure you have one that will hold together for the velocity, distance, and size of the game you are hunting! The explosive effect of the bullet due to high rifle velocity puts a much larger hole than that of the expanded projectile.

Shotguns

(Also Called Trench Guns, Riotguns, Scatterguns, and Coach Guns)

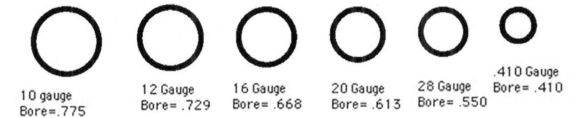

10 gauge
Bore=.775

12 Gauge
Bore= .729

16 Gauge
Bore= .668

20 Gauge
Bore= .613

28 Gauge
Bore= .550

.410 Gauge
Bore= .410

To start out, many people teach that the first thing you should reach for is your personal carry sidearm even if you're in the house due to the ease of maneuverability. Sometimes things happen in such a way that may actually call for the need for a shotgun, so I'm going to give all the facts and let you decide what you think you should do. Modern shotguns come in various sizes, in .410, 28, 20, 16, 12, and 10 gauges, and have been given many nicknames over the years. And while the police always have a shotgun readily available, they've been called riot guns since it was always used to prevent riots. And due to the way the shot spreads, they're sometimes called scatterguns. Since the military has always used shotguns since their invention, the first military shotguns designed for combat were called trench guns or trench shotguns. Modern double-barrel shotguns with one barrel above the other are called over and under, while double-barrel models (having side-by-side barrels) like those that were carried on a stage coach years ago had come to be known as coach guns. While the handgun is the most widely used due to its ability to be carried and readily available, since we cannot carry rifles or shotguns around all the time, handguns, rifles, and shotguns all have their place for defensive purposes. Remember, law enforcement officers always look for the long guns whether they are rifles or shotguns due to their ability to reach distant targets with powerful loads and accuracy. So many people believe the shotgun is the all-powerful problem solver, but the fact is that it can be depending on the shotgun and the actual situation where it's needed. While limited in range, compared to a rifle, the multiple projectiles typically used in a shotgun shell provide increased hit (probability) unmatched by other small arms. For our home defense, there are several things we need to consider: functionability, effectiveness, maneuverability, the type of sights it has, the size of the round, and the number of rounds it holds. The majority of shotguns over the years were chambered to shoot a 2¾-inch shotgun shell but were later revised to shoot either a 2¾-inch shell or a 3-inch magnum shell. Current shotguns may even be chambered for a 3½-inch shotgun shell, but no matter what type of shotgun you ever buy, you need to make sure of what size shells it is capable of chambering. If it is only chambered for a 2¾-inch shell, you cannot put longer shells into it. In the same way, if it might be chambered for a 3-inch shell, you cannot put a 3½-inch shell in it, but remember that there are quite a few that are chambered to take either the 2¾ or the 3-inch shell in the same barrel. The shotgun barrel is imprinted with the size of the shell that it is capable of shooting. While there are many barrels that are interchangeable on some shotguns, some people try to alter barrels that are not designed for their shotgun to try to make them work, but this is a very dangerous move! You also have to remember that a barrel that will chamber a 3½-inch shell cannot be used on a shotgun that was originally designed for a 2¾-inch or a 3-inch shell because the internal mechanical operations won't work since they cannot handle the longer round. Use only the proper parts and ammunition! Wouldn't the thug be happy if you blew *yourself* up?

Now study what I'm saying because your life depends on YOU. Many people claim that the short-barreled single or double-barrel shotgun that offers either one or two shots is all you'll ever need, and when you break open the action, you actually have to pluck out the rounds on the many shotguns that don't eject shells that have already been fired, and then you have to insert new rounds to be on the ready once again. This is a lot of work for only two rounds at a time, and it *might* work sufficiently if you have only one assailant trying to KILL you, and hopefully he's taking his time, but I have studied the many shotguns currently available to see what might be new and their current capability to save my life if I need to use one. While there are pump action and semiautomatic shotguns that the military has used for years throughout every war since their being invented, the pump shotguns like the Winchester model 97 pump was discontinued in 1957, and the model 12 pump was discontinued in 1963, but the Winchester Super-X Defender is relatively inexpensive. The Winchester model 1300 series shotguns are also known as the Speed Pump because of the very fast-cycling pump action while the model 1300 Defender is designed for self-defense and security, especially with the availability of relatively short-barreled models with long magazine tubes. The Remington 870 pump was very widely used by the military and civilians alike and was responsible for blowing my leg in two. On April 13, 2009, the ten millionth model 870 was produced, and the 870 holds the record for best-selling shotgun in the history of the world. The Mossberg model 500s are a series of shotguns. Model numbers included in the 500 series are the 500, 505, 510, 535, and 590 pumps, which are very good, but the current-day semiautomatic shotguns are also there. Mossberg claims the Model 500 is the only shotgun to pass the US Army's Mil-Spec 3443E test, "a brutal and unforgiving torture test with 3,000 rounds of full-power 12 gauge buckshot." While the Marines officially switched to the semiautomatic Benelli M1014 Combat Shotgun in 1999, various branches of the US military are still acquiring pump shotguns. The Navy acquired several thousand Mossberg 590A1 shotguns in 2004, and the US Army placed an order in 2005 for 14,818 units. In 1963, Remington introduced the model 1100 auto-loading shotgun. The model 1100 holds the record for the most shells fired out of an auto-loading shotgun without any malfunction, cleaning, or parts breakage with a record of over 24,000 rounds. After my cannibalizing a Remington 1100 years ago to convert it to a tactical style shotgun, where the new customizing trend was going at the time, I studied the new semiauto shotguns and bought one for *my* home defense due to its options from the factory right out of the box, which years ago used to cost you more just for the conversions than the actual selling price of the entire tactical shotgun today. Although there are many fine shotguns on the market, I took a liking to the Mossberg model 930 SPX semiautomatic 12 gauge tactical shotgun with an 18½-inch barrel, an extended magazine tube under the barrel offering an 8-shot capacity if using 2¾-inch shells, by loading 7 + 1. Although it will chamber six 3-inch magnum shells also, once you chamber a round, you can simply insert another 3-inch magnum, increasing your capacity from 6 to 7 by adding that 1 additional round. The Mossberg model 930 has winged fiber optic front rifle sights with an LPA ghost-ring rear sight. LPA is the manufacturer's name, and I chose it with a shoulder stock other than a pistol grip. The model 930 SPX weighs 7.5 pounds, which is about average for a combat firearm, and is designed to vent excess gas that's not needed to cycle the action which reduces the recoil of this auto-loader. Despite some claims of no provisions for the sling mounts, mine had the provisions to mount on the forward grip and to the stock, so I found a perfect nonslip sling and put it on while making sure I had the perfect adjustment for my arm to use the off-hand sling if need be, but I also passed on purchasing a sling that holds numerous shotgun shells due to their interference in the time of an emergency, so I bought a bandolier and a couple of belts to load up with all the spare shells in the various types that I prefer. There are similar tactical shotguns for 5 times the price, so study and research what you want.

The Mossberg model 930 SPX semiautomatic tactical combat shotgun with a rifle stock. I found this to be an excellent choice and bought one for my home defense.

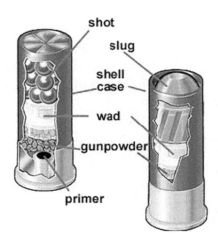

Thugs are afraid of getting hit with shotguns due to the firepower and number of projectiles coming their way all at once. Although there's a limited example around the dime, there's so much more available for shotguns for protection!

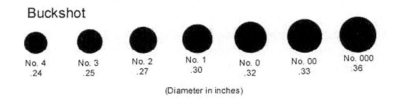

The decimal given below each buckshot of different size indicates the caliber of the projectile. The thought of 15, .33 caliber projectiles coming their way all at the same time should make anyone change their mind.

Shotgun shells come in a wide variety of shot loaded inside, many more than shown here. Some people think the flats on the projectiles get that way from being fired, but they are made that way according to design.

The US military uses many shotgun shells, some loaded with steel flechettes, small steel darts 1 inch in length. The shotgun is a feared firearm by many thugs due to its ability to deliver multiple projectiles at the same time, including multiple sizes in the same round. If you have a shotgun pointed at your vitals, you have very little chance of survival.

While searching for the semiautomatic shotguns, I was quite surprised to find quite a few new entries in the market for tactical shotguns, even with detachable magazines, and one in an AK-47 configuration and another in an AR-15 configuration with gas piston operation. I do get tempted to buy another one, but I figure I'll wait until I get a few other guns that I'm studying, so remember that if you do your homework, you'll find certain firearms that you never realized are even in the market. With the detachable box magazine AR-15-style shotguns, it would certainly be hard to beat them while they'll reload much faster than a fixed magazine tube under the barrel which should otherwise be plenty of rounds based on the average situations, but I always prepare for the unusual and the unexpected one that will otherwise kill me if I'm not prepared to take it on. Another shotgun, the SPAS-12, was designed in 1979 by the Italian company Luigi Franchi Spa as a special-purpose military and police close combat weapon and was manufactured until 2001, and if you can find one, it could be a great shotgun to add to your collection. It featured a selective action for greater versatility and can be used as a gas-operated semiautomatic repeater or as a manually operated pump action shotgun. The SPAS-12 can be switched between gas-operated self-loading mode and manually operated pump mode by pressing and holding a button at the bottom of the forearm and pulling the forearm slightly forward for AUTOMATIC mode or backward for PUMP or MANUAL mode, but while it even has folding stock variants, it's a bit heavy at 8.75 pounds. Having the necessary equipment and never needing it is far better than not having it when YOU ARE ABOUT TO LOSE YOUR LIFE!

The Franchi SPAS 12 is shown above!

There are those who believe that a couple of shotgun rounds are sufficient, and they say the need for 8 rounds with a shotgun is not necessary, but when I had a gang of 25 to 30 in a confrontation of their own out in front of my house one day, when the bullets started flying, I had to consider their attempting to harm anyone in their path if they so desired, and if they chose to come through my door in force, the 8-round capacity will look pretty good and maybe even a bit short in supply, where my .45 1911 would have to take over due to shortage of time to reload the shotgun with so many gang members, even though I have belts and bandoliers of extra shells ready to go if needed. So many people believe that all you have to do is to just point the shotgun in the direction of the trouble and the trouble will come to a halt. They are *very wrong* because the shotgun can very easily MISS your intended target. The shot group fired from a shotgun is terribly misunderstood by many people who watch Hollywood too much, so some of them pretty much figure that the whole wall will come down if you point a shotgun toward it and shoot. While the shotgun is a mighty weapon for defense, different barrels and different loads will perform and pattern quite differently on your target, so no matter how many shotguns you've used, if you buy a new one, you have to shoot it to know what it will do for you when you need it. Years ago, the hype was on rubber slugs and rubber buckshot to stop your assailants. At that time, I slipped on my own knowledge of criminals and what's needed to stay alive, so I tried this rubber ammo for a few weeks in one of my shotguns, which really bothered me (rubber versus lead). While I had my dozens of shells in rubber slug and rubber buckshot configurations, the thugs kept pulling guns with real bullets on me, so I finally got frustrated and trashed all the rubber ammo! I'm glad I never felt confident in any of this rubber ammo and never responded to a threat with that particular shotgun in the short time it was loaded that way. I didn't even try to give or sell the rubber ammo to anyone because I wouldn't want to be responsible for their getting shot with the real stuff, once I realized my thinking surely slipped a bit. So I loaded that shotgun up again with real live ammo just like I used to do because that's all the criminals will do—they use real bullets or none. As our agents were restricted to use firearms and our border patrol agents along the Mexican border were required to shoot the criminals with bean bags—no bullets were allowed—the thugs that got shot at with bean bags returned fire with live ammo and killed a border patrol agent who otherwise might have been alive if he had live bullets, so bean bags were clearly in the best interest of the criminals who have very high confidence in committing their crime now due to the ban on live ammo. Hopefully, they use live ammo again. Once I was at a gun show where a fellow thought he had the miracle of answers and tried to sell me rubber ammunition, but I clearly told him that since the killers would be shooting real live bullets at *me*, I would prefer to *stop them* as compared to my dying while I let them survive with a slight bruise after KILLING me. All the anti-gun hype by too many across the country is to shoot back at criminals with toys (bean bags and rubber bullets) while the criminals are shooting at us with live ammo; the idea of using rubber ammo and bean bag needs to be trashed if you want to stay alive. Those poor criminals know they are subject to die if they pull their own gun on an innocent person, so if they pull their gun, it's their own fault if they happen to get shot and die like they want me to do because I'm not going to *throw away my life* just to satisfy some group who has never had to use a gun or any weapon to save themselves. So they can make people think they made a difference. They may be just about as guilty as the criminals in their own desire for what they might think is some kind of glory; otherwise, why argue the situation? The *only* difference they might make is getting innocent people killed. WHY would we want to fire rubber slugs at this person who's trying to KILL us? To save his poor ignorant life with rubber bullets while we get shot in the very same confrontation and die from our wounds? NOPE! You shoot live ammo at me, I shoot live ammo back! I've yet to see a criminal with his gun loaded with rubber bullets. Those who claim they can cycle the action of a pump as fast as I can use my semiautomatic combat tactical shotgun, with a lot of experience using the pump action, may get quite a few rounds off, but while their pump action is cycling, due to all the body movement they have to do, the barrel is wandering from side to side and up and down, and their particular target might not be the one that actually gets shot or maybe even the wrong one. While they might be good with their pump, with my semiautomatic shotgun, I can acquire a new target for each pull of the trigger with speed and dead-on accuracy. I know I can put out more rounds in the target with deadly accuracy than the pump can in the same amount of time; try me! Even though semiautomatics may malfunction, so can the pump if you short-stroke the action, leaving it inoperable momentarily while you TRY to correct YOUR error, while possibly being under attack. Any delay or malfunction right in the middle of a gunfight can mean your immediate death. I personally prefer the shoulder-fired stock without a pistol grip that everyone seems to think you need, and if several assailants are coming at me at once—overlapping of their bodies while coming through my house or in any way to try to kill me—I can quite easily aim between their overlapping bodies between the two killers at elbow-to-shoulder level and fire one round of double 00 or triple 000 buckshot with 9 to 15 pellets per shot, disabling the arms and shoulders or much more of the two killers simultaneously, with one single shot, taking two of them out of the fight for now unless one has his gun trained on me. And I cannot afford to risk the possibility of not stopping him at that very instant, so I may have to take better aim specifically on his vitals. Those who really prefer a pistol grip shotgun, and there are some that I like, have shoulder stocks that fold to the side or over the top of the receiver and won't interfere with any necessary operation other than the sights that you may not be using in this way, that is, a very close encounter. A major concern is to remember that shouldering a stock may cause it to catch in a shirt or jacket chest pocket when trying to remove it from your shoulder, so if trouble is anticipated beforehand, make sure you remedy this problem before it can happen. The two-shot shotgun method of shoot and load, and shoot and load is fine for those who believe it's the way to go, but while the fight is on, I'll be loading anyway at any available opportunity if one appears (a tactical reload), but I certainly prefer my tubular magazine extension, and I'm seriously considering a detachable magazine model that can be changed out quickly, no matter what anyone else says about not needing it because like I said before, I'm addicted to living and surviving. I take no improper advice from anyone when my life is on the line. If you're not sure about something, research it! A DEAD macho man or one that lives in *denial* is proof he screwed up when he had the opportunity to overcome his ego, or accept what can happen and properly prepare for the situation before it ever happened. But, unfortunately, you get only one such mistake, and you may never be around after the fight to know you even made it. Understanding that a shotgun may be the weapon of choice for a certain encounter is the first step, but then by denying the possibility of needing additional rounds, it seriously reduces your ability, including your mental mindset, to survive at all costs. The ammunition is the one that does the damage, and the shotgun is only a tool needed to fire that ammo, so while Hollywood takes a few shots and throws the gun away and grabs another one, we are facing real-life combat here where we need to be able to feed the shotgun as effectively as our handguns, considering whether it is actually needed or not and if it at least has the option for that extra round or two. YOU must decide!

Just because you have a shotgun doesn't mean you're ready to take the killers on if need be. You have to know your own specific gun even if it's a duplicate of your buddy's. You have to shoot the rounds that you are using for your defense, preferably at least out to 100 yards to know your gun, while the shotgun can quite easily double or triple that distance. YES, it can! Remember, the further the target, the less effective the shot, and the effectiveness and actual penetration depend on the barrel you have, the type of ammunition you have, and your ability to put it where it belongs in the target, which again brings us to your being familiar with *your* particular shotgun, since duplicate guns may give different results. While I probably wouldn't use a shotgun beyond 100 yards for very much of anything other than to practice and develop skills, many people mistakenly believe that a shotgun is only a close-range weapon. If someone doubts the shotgun's range, tell him to stand at 200 yards while you'll first shoot at a target that you offer to post at 300 yards, and then if he still wants to stand at 200, when he sees the holes in the 300 yard target, tell him you'll be happy to send a few rounds his way to prove the shotgun's ability to reach out. The shotgun is exceptional at close range due to its ability to send so much firepower downrange, but always remember that it will certainly reach out beyond what many people expect. The bead front sight is fine for up close, but I say use the rifle sights as a rule, for me anyway, and stay in tune to them for fast target acquisition close or far. Your sights may need adjusting to get your pattern in the target. If you cannot get your pattern in the center of the target and have a barrel clamp sling mount up front, not the magazine tube cap mount, the clamp might be too tight, causing the barrel to print the pattern one way or the other. In the same way, when a stock is pressing against a rifle barrel, it may cause a flyer or two out of the consistent pattern, or maybe the whole group might be off, so if the shotgun barrel has tension, forcing it in any direction, the shotgun round may go either right or left or even up or down, depending on the device clamped on the barrel, but you need to make sure you know where the projectiles are going before you use this firearm for defense. Remember, a round that MISSED is the same as NO ROUND FIRED and also that FAILURE IS NOT AN OPTION, and DEAD IS DEAD, not to mention that if the whole shotgun round was missed, then where did it go or whom did you shoot? Proper ammo selection is really necessary for your own select purposes and you have to fire some of everything you plan to use for defense, so you know what's going to happen under fire.

Many people don't understand how a shotgun shell actually propels the shot. In a normal handgun or rifle round, they may understand that the pressure builds behind the bullet and creates a gas seal, thereby pushing it down the barrel. The shotgun has assorted shot in different shells, so some people wonder why the gas pressure doesn't blow through the shot since the barrel of the shotgun is so large. The shotgun shell round has what they call a wadding inserted against the powder charge, which may even be a 3-piece assembly, but it creates the gas seal and holds the shot until it's launched from the barrel. Modern smokeless powders are so powerful that they allow for a substantial amount of shot, which is usually loaded by a different size in each particular round, sized from birdshot all the way up through assorted sizes of buckshot and further up to slugs, which are like a giant bullet for comparison. While ammunition manufacturers make personal defense ammo, remember that Winchester makes their personal defense round for all ammunition from handguns to shotguns, by name of PDX1, but in the shotgun shell, they load 3 pieces of 00 buck and even numerous slugs, depending on which shell and what gauge shotgun it's made for.

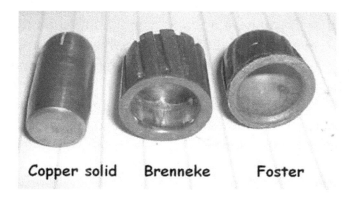

Copper solid   Brenneke   Foster

Shotgun slugs may be referred to by the few names of their inventors such as the Brenneke slug, the Foster slugs, or the saboted slugs. The Brenneke slug was developed by the German gun and ammunition designer Wilhelm Brenneke (1865-1951) in 1898. The original Brenneke slug is a solid lead slug with fins cast onto the outside, appearing to be much like a rifled Foster slug. The fins impart little or no spin to the projectile, where the actual purpose of the fins is to decrease the bearing surface of the slug to the barrel and therefore reduce friction and increase velocity. A Foster slug, invented by Karl Foster in 1931, is a type of shotgun slug designed to be fired through a smoothbore shotgun barrel. The standard American domestic shotgun slug is sometimes referred to as American slug to differentiate them from the standard European slug design popularized by Brenneke. Sabot slugs are lead-cored, full copper-jacketed, or solid copper projectiles supported by a plastic sabot, which is designed to engage the rifling in a rifled shotgun barrel and impart a ballistic spin onto the projectile. This differentiates them from traditional slugs, which are not designed to benefit from a rifled barrel, though neither does the other any damage. They can take the usual variety of shapes, but for maximum accuracy are typically aerodynamic ogives. The slugs are generally significantly smaller than the bore diameter, increasing the ballistic coefficient, and use the sabot to seal the bore and keep the slug centered in the bore while it rotates with the rifling. Saboted slugs, when fired out of a rifled barrel, are generally far more accurate than non-jacketed slugs out of a smoothbore, with accuracy of 300 meters (330 yd), approaching that of low-velocity rifle calibers. By 1984, Ballistic Research Industries was producing a 440-grain .50 caliber sabot slug of a new design. The projectile was wasp-waisted, hourglass-shaped and made of a hard lead alloy. This sabot slug was not designed for rifled barrels; the self-stabilizing shape allowed it to be used with bore cylinder or improved cylinder barrels. There are even French manufacturers who make slugs containing an all-steel slug, which will give excellent penetration, and they will certainly shut down an automobile if the need arises.

When we look at 00 buckshot like so many always refer to, the majority of people use this reference because they are familiar with it or familiar with those who use such a round for deer hunting. In reality, there are many shot sizes even in buckshot. The larger the size of the shot, the less pellets are able to fit into the round unless you use a longer shell. Let's say the normal 12-gauge shotgun shell is 2¾ inches in length, but your shotgun is also capable of shooting 3-inch rounds or 3-inch magnums. The longer hull allows for an increased amount of powder and/or a few extra pellets, so if you have a round with 00 buckshot, depending on whether it's a 2¾ inch or a 3-inch shell, even though it's 00, one may have a few more pellets than the other one. I like the Winchester 3-inch shells with 00 buckshot, having 15 pellets per round at 1,760 feet per second, while there are many faster ones loaded in different velocities, so again, what might appear to be the same thing might be quite different in shot or velocity. Here is a simple reminder: no matter what size the round, bullet, pellet, or slug is, those capable of more velocity will usually give the greatest penetration.

One 3-inch 00 buck 12-gauge shell delivering 15 pellets is sending the equivalent of 15, .33 caliber bullets, weighing 54 grains each at your target. No matter how far your target is, the shotgun does not give the dramatics that Hollywood does, but some spread very little and some may spread much more, as far as 25 inches in 25 yards, but shells vary by manufacturer and so do barrels and chokes. Chokes are the shape of barrel opening while some have inserts to change the pattern. So they give much different results in their pattern spread and even different results in different barrels. Shooting at would-be KILLERS coming into your home in force makes people think they just need to point in the general direction and shoot—and I always hear people say this—but since some of the patterns will be spread very little at these close distances, you need to aim your shots *at any distance* just like you do with your rifle or handgun. Or when your shot misses them, they'll be certain to have the edge and quite possibly KILL YOU *before* you get off the next shot. Getting off a shot under such circumstances is already in your favor, but if you blow it on that first shot, you may not live to tell the story. You have the option to go for being macho, ego, ignorance, or your LIFE.

Many accessories are available for shotguns to convert them into tactical combat-style weapons, but I chose to study the availability of some of the most effective combat-style shotguns already assembled from the factory, which saves hundreds of dollars. Many people differ in their preferences and tactics, so they may wish to choose a collapsible stock or a pistol grip for their shotgun, but, first, make sure it's really what you want, and if it is, then make sure you practice with it, which includes firing it the very way you anticipate, to confirm its supposed effectiveness and make sure the thoughts and reality both give the same results where they often do not. A good used shotgun might be good for a rebuild or maybe even your old one in the back of your gun safe.

Shotgun Laws in the United States

Rifled balls for shotguns are an unusual legal issue in the United States of America. Firearms with rifled barrels are designed to fire single projectiles, and a firearm that is designed to fire a single projectile with a diameter greater than .50 caliber (12.7 mm) is considered a destructive device and as such is severely restricted. However, the ATF has ruled that as long as the gun was designed to fire-shot and modified (by the user or the manufacturer) to fire single projectiles with the addition of a rifled barrel, then the firearm is still considered a shotgun and not a destructive device. In some areas, rifles are prohibited for hunting animals such as deer. This is generally due to range concerns for safety. Shotgun slugs have a far shorter maximum range than most rifle cartridges and are safer for use near populated areas. In other areas, there are special shotgun-only seasons for hunting deer. A modern slug shotgun with a rifled barrel and high performance saboted slugs is the top choice for hunters who must hunt with a shotgun as it provides rifle-like power and accuracy at ranges over 150 yards (140 m).

Adjust the sling so that with your arm, it is a perfectly tight fit as in the picture on the left in A while the dashed line B represents the sling behind the arm. While sling designs vary and firearms are of different lengths, whatever design you might have, keep it tight to keep it steady.

Sling on a Rifle or a Shotgun

Remember my mentioning, so many people are losing the knowledge and the ability to use a sling to steady the weapon while aiming it offhand, that is, freehand in open air. But the fact is that I strongly believe in the sling which has always carried me through tough shots with rock- steady aiming at my target at lightning speeds, being fast enough to prepare, aim, and shoot on a target that suddenly presents itself in the blink of an eye while claiming a sure kill. Those who have become accustomed to using a shooting bench, tripods, bipods, and shooting sticks, although they are all great if you expect such circumstances to present themselves, will lack the ability to hold a steady aim if they need one, and they never practiced. Practicing both methods is acceptable, but we don't want those new to shooting to never gain the knowledge or the skill for offhand shooting with a sling. I never expected any target or animal to just stand still while I get a careful and proper aim with my shooting pod or stick. I always practiced a sequence: discover your target, wrap sling, and aim while simultaneously guesstimating the distance and snapping off a shot, NOT jerking off the shot by jerking the trigger. This way people won't assume the target will stand still for them to get ready; that is, they *are not ready* to take a sudden shot unless you're a sniper and set up for such a particular situation. IF you always practice from a prepared steady rest of some sort, when the NEED arises, then you will have little or no skill at trying to take the target down in an instant, so you may never get to shoot or you may just never hit your target. Remember, a major thing to know is that rifles or shotguns with detachable bottom-fed magazines may not work as easily when you're trying to use the sling due to the magazine interfering with your forearm position if you tension the arm with the sling. In these situations, you may want to use a forward vertical broom-handle grip attached to the lower side of your forward hand guard, to even grip the magazine where it meets the firearm, or have the right sling combination and use it to steady your aim, but this has to be done beforehand so you know how to aim, fire, and shoot with any particular firearm you own. Short magazines may not be a problem for you like the 30 rounders, but *you* need to know how it works long before you're in the field.

Remember, while the handgun is easier to maneuver, it can only fire one bullet per squeeze of the trigger while the 12-gauge shotgun can send 15 projectiles (or more) in the direction toward a killer with one pull of the trigger and usually at a much higher velocity than average handgun bullets. But depending on what kind of penetration is needed, the round will certainly be effective at normal handgun range but may only be effective for penetrating tissue while the slug will always give superior penetration through much stronger materials over buckshot, especially at long range while it again retains superior velocity and kinetic energy due to its weight. Now you might understand why the police always opt for the long guns, that is, rifles and shotguns when they get down to the nitty-gritty. While the rifle will penetrate so many materials, including body armor, the shotgun has the ability to help even the odds or become the greater advantage in many situations. Everyone serious about home defense should add a shotgun to their plans.

Body Armor

While the assailant has always been at an advantage and will continue to be by his selection of which people will become his or their next victim, the decision to defend yourself, especially with concealed carry, will turn the tables. Once you're properly qualified, an attacker won't know you are prepared to fight him off, and he will very confidently figure he's at an advantage until he attacks! Since we're now turning the tables on the criminal's success of such an incident if it should happen—*and it will happen to somebody*—let's take it even a step further. There are currently various items that will help to prevent you from being shot and killed. Since the thug *always* cheats, in the defense of your own life, there is no such thing as cheating! When we were growing up, the local thugs would call us cheaters if we overpowered them or found some kind of weapon to use to fight them off in our defense, but to save ourselves, there is no such thing as cheating! As a responsible adult, it is pure SURVIVAL! Survive or DIE! We must have the attitude of surviving at all cost, which will become more instinctive and be learned with proper practice and mental conditioning, which works similar to a typist who instinctively works the keyboard once the skills are achieved. So we can even buy body armor too, providing your state law doesn't prevent it. While they have bullet-resistant vests available, if you should decide to buy one, remember that there are differences. They are defined as Class I, Class II, Class III, and Class IV. Remember that even if you have a bullet-resistant vest, a shot under the armpit may penetrate the heart, and they won't help prevent a head shot. If you buy one, you also have to question back protection from behind, so you don't get shot in the back! The military has bullet-resistant masks, but we cannot walk around going about our daily life wearing such a thing. A proper vest will protect your vitals, and some even have lower abdominal and groin protection as shown earlier, providing that the projectile is not from a more powerful handgun round with sufficient velocity and penetrating ability—maybe a custom hand load—or a rifle round sufficient to penetrate a specific vest quite easily. But then there are vests offering greater protection for more money, the usual way of the world. Remember, they also have the trauma plates that can be inserted to prevent high-powered penetration, so you might want to make sure it's an option for a vest before you might buy the one you like. The higher the class rating, the more protection they provide, but the prices rise accordingly. There are also casual wear jackets that are actually made to try to stop a bullet, providing you don't have the front open as most people do when wearing jackets, which gives a clear shot at the center mass. Think of everything you do!

The point of mentioning this that YOU will pay particular attention to YOUR acquiring the proper shot the first time if possible and an immediate second (aimed) follow-up shot if the threat still persists. It's generally taught to make two shots minimum or three if you think you need to. If a KILLER attacks us, we would like to have the ability to go for one shot one kill, but Murphy's Law says that anything that CAN happen WILL happen, so we want to try to get the shot at the center mass. One important thing for you to know is that many people who ride motorcycles buy what they call ballistic jackets for riding, which may even say that they were constructed with Kevlar, on the tags. But the word *ballistic* may have the Kevlar being used in the jacket construction like they use for bullet-resistant vests; don't misunderstand their construction! The motorcycle jackets are not bullet-resistant, not unless they specifically say so! They use Kevlar in making the jacket or pants because it resists abrasion incredibly well the way it resists bullet penetration, IF the Kevlar is woven into the fabric properly. The Kevlar jacket for riding is in the event of an accident, so if the rider falls to the ground at any given speed, the jacket holds together much better than non-Kevlar jackets and helps protect the skin from being ripped and torn. Kevlar is 5 times stronger than steel, ounce per ounce, and modern military bullet-resistant vests are closer to being bulletproof other than bullet-resistant due to *34 layers of Kevlar*. In US Army tests on Kevlar bullet-resistant vests, numerous .45 ACP rounds at somewhat close range were fired at the vest, and the rounds actually penetrated 5 layers of Kevlar while there were still 29 more layers undamaged. With the ballistic plate inserts put into the vest, the Army tests showed that the plates actually stopped the 7.62 × 51 NATO round and the Russian 7.62 × 39 fired from an AK-47, where the rounds were stopped cold. If you *ever* buy a jacket made with Kevlar but *your* purpose is to help resist bullet penetration, you need to know from the manufacturer if it is made to resist bullets, *before you buy it*. It certainly wouldn't be your day if you bought a riding jacket because it said, "Kevlar" or "Ballistic material." Even though it is made with Kevlar, in a lethal encounter, you wouldn't have as much fear and will find bullets ripping through your body because of your ERROR in ASSUMPTION. Some vests may even have metal threads woven in to prevent knife penetration but, again, only if they say so. When your life is on the line, no assumptions are allowed! Only the facts!

Obviously, we all want to live, but you have to be very determined and have the will to fight. Remember, survive at all cost! No matter how big and intimidating the assailant might be, if I'm attacked, I'm going to fight back with whatever means I have available. If I'm unarmed, I'll use any previously learned and acquired combative hand skills and even reach for anything that can inflict harm upon the KILLER, no matter what. If you should ever find yourself in a close quarters combative situation where the assailant is within arm's reach and you don't really have any hand-to-hand skills, remember that the nose area and up between the eyes is very sensitive to trauma. A striking blow to the nose and eyes may help give you sufficient time to draw (called presenting) your carry gun. I knocked out a very big assailant with one striking blow up into the nose between the eyes, and the blood shot out of both nostrils like a ruptured balloon, but I love the element of surprise. If you're ever in a life-and-death situation and the assailant has a gun fixed on you, you still have to survive at all cost instinctive mental capabilities. It all depends on everything YOU put together as your personal self-defense plan and how knowledgeable and familiar you are at the time of any shooting incident.

What If You Get Shot?

If involved in a shooting confrontation and you get struck by a bullet—while it's easy to say not to—don't panic at the thought that it just happened and become overrun in fear for immediate medical attention. If you don't stop the threat *before* you remove yourself from the fight, unless you're able to get away from it, you stand a greater chance of getting killed. While you obviously need immediate medical attention, if the assailant knows you're hit, he may become much more aggressive and advance on you, thinking you are less capable, incapacitated, or out of the fight, which again increases his chance of killing you. Many bullet wounds are survivable, but don't panic at the sight of blood if it happens. While many people say not to fall down if you're hit, there's some truth to this, providing you're able to continue the gunfight. People who say many of these things have never been shot before, and they have no idea what it's really like, so they downplay the situation in comparison to a Hollywood movie where they further state that everyone who gets shot *thinks* he must fall down. There are so many situations that *may* happen, and there's no way to know what the situation will be until it suddenly appears. Some people watch too much TV and think running around with bullets in you is so easy, but it's not! The resulting wounding effects will depend on what you got shot with. Your body goes into SHOCK, which alters your body's functions and reactions. If you give up the fight in any way whatsoever and the threat is still mobile, you increase your chance of losing your life. The main factor is, do not panic, even if you've been hit. It's easy to say, but I've been there, and it is hard to keep it all together with a portion of your body blown apart. This is where YOUR survive-at-all-cost mindset comes into play, but you have to use commonsense in what's happening.

When I was shot by a 12-gauge shotgun from 5 feet away, I took the full blast dead center in my right thigh. A 3½-inch hole was blown most of the way through, which destroyed muscle, blood vessels, bone, and nerves. I immediately went face down in the dirt while my leg folded beneath me, but I didn't go flying across the field like Hollywood puts it in the movies. I went into shock, but I was determined to survive. There were 6 of us in the field, but nobody took the initiative to try to save me until my survival training kicked in, and I managed to scream at them. They were alarmed at what happened, and they were as unprepared as I was, and their mind was drawing a blank.

I tried to move, but my body was partially paralyzed. I was able to yell at them to tie me up with a tourniquet, while my buddy wasted too many very important seconds at hand to argue that the tourniquet was no longer used in this manner the way we were taught to survive, but I quickly argued that it was definitely required and needed because I was losing all my blood, so he finally managed to put one on me. I tried to move my leg, but the only thing that moved was a nub of bone attached to the ball joint at the hip, which wiggled up and down with nothing attached, so I knew it was really broken up. As the tourniquet was applied, I was in tremendous pain. Some of my thigh was numb, some super sensitive, a varied mix of sensitivities all mixed up. While my mind was in survival mode, I was having trouble in maintaining consciousness due to the loss of so much blood, but I made sure they periodically loosened and retightened the tourniquet to avoid gangrene, even though that was also disagreed on. My life was draining from me, but I was going out, fighting to survive. No matter what practice they changed or currently teach in the military, I immediately redirected my thoughts to what I was taught in an effort to save my own life, at least until we were out of the field and into a hospital for medical assistance. Fortunately, even though they said I shouldn't be alive due to the loss of so much blood, the tourniquet worked, and this was the very beginning of a very long year ahead of me in military hospitals. It also shows that all gunshot wounds are not the same. Some will incapacitate you faster than others—the very thing we want to do to our assailant. If your leg bones are not broken, you need to get to any available cover quickly, and such cover means preferably something that a bullet cannot penetrate.

  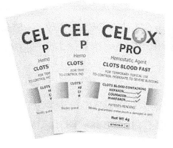 

Just in case you get shot, it would be wise to have a couple of QuickClot trauma packs or Celox on hand with a few other medical essentials to stop the bleeding. You can get a medic bag at the Army Navy store for a few bucks and keep it in your vehicle in case somebody else comes to your rescue so they can see what it is. Study the QuickClot or Celox instructions before you pack it in the bag so you know what to do because there won't be any time when seconds and minutes count to save your life, but keep the instructions in the bag just in case someone else has to treat you. It could also be helpful to take an emergency medical course for penetrating trauma, which covers punctures, stabbings, and gunshot wounds.

While television always shows the bullets bouncing off all the cars, remember back to the old days when the bullet riddled cars with dozens or even hundreds of holes in and through them where the steel was twice the thickness in the old car bodies, yet probably every round fired went through. Reality is quite different, and if we're wounded badly and feel the threat is gone, even those friends or bystanders around you need to be capable of assisting you if you're shot down, even if you're the only one who can direct their actions to save your own life. This will require additional studying for proper first aid and even having some QuickClot Trauma Packs available in the event you do take a round or two, to try to stop severe bleeding and stay alive either until medical attention arrives or until you get to an emergency treatment facility. Studying the instructions on how to use such things as QuickClot is required in advance of any lethal encounter, NOT while lying on the ground bleeding. Emergency medical services provide an important role in the care of trauma, so you will need to get to them as soon as possible or you stand a chance of dying. Even among trauma centers, there are different levels of expertise and capabilities, so make sure you know in advance the most qualified in penetrating trauma (bullet or knife wounds), in your area close by, to increase your chance of survival. If you're shot and down, don't consider yourself out of the fight or play dead, or your assailant may approach and put a round or two in your head to finish you off. Never put your weapon down if you are unsure of his or her whereabouts, but if you have the opportunity to reload your gun back to maximum capacity (a tactical reload), then it would be advantageous in the event your KILLER surfaces once again. Since most people will hide behind such cover as cars, the safest place to use for cover on a vehicle is alongside the engine, which is in the front of most cars, so the engine will stop the bullets. Despite arguments that bullets won't penetrate car doors or any area of a car, sometimes the bullet won't penetrate all the way through the door, depending on the caliber and what it hits inside the door, but this isn't fantasy land; it's reality! If it misses all the hardware inside a car door, you stand a very good chance of getting shot if you use it for cover, especially if the caliber is a much more powerful round, but you have no way to know what the killer might be using, so the best way to stay alive is not to listen to anything that could mean death! That's why I'm giving you the facts, not opinions or assumptions, which both may get you killed.

Some criminals are spaced out on drugs, and maybe they feel no pain when shot or maybe you might get hit by a bullet that passes on through soft tissue or muscle without doing any physical damage to your vitals or major blood vessels, and you only feel numbness, but if it hits bone, you're much more likely to be in pain if not knocked to the ground. I know, moving with shattered bones hurts like hell. You can learn to ignore the pain under such circumstances because if you don't, you may die as your killer moves in. Bullet's type and velocity, depending on where you're hit, will determine what happens and what you feel. Generally, the bullet impact is the equivalents of the recoil of the round, so you may be able to tell immediately when you're hit, but as stories go, they are all different, but I will always remain in the fight until I know it's over—that is, I'm safe—because this is truly the life-and-death moment YOU prepared and practiced for, TO STAY ALIVE. Some KILLERS may flee once they get shot at—something they don't normally expect to happen. And although they do not want to get shot, with anything, if they are under the influence of drugs, there's no way to determine what response they will have.

Get medical attention as quickly as possible once your particular situation permits. If you shoot your assailant and fail to stop him, even though center mass is a valuable shot, then it might be to your advantage if you could shoot him in the hip or crease of the leg joint to shatter the pelvis and put him down. Don't try to hit an arm or leg because the target is far too thin and will most likely waste a valuable round and miss, especially on a moving target. While a full-width body is a hard enough to hit target, a side shot gives an average of about 12 inches, more or less which is only about half the frontal view, if that, depending on their physique. Don't WASTE your ammo if the shot is likely to be missed unless it's do or die, which also means you better make your *best* shot!

Assailants get very close for many lethal encounters. Remember, FBI statistics on real police shootings reveal 70% of all police shootings over the last 40 years are between 5 to 10 feet. Therefore, there is no need for a barrel delivering a great deal of extended range. Since many 1911s being carried have a 5-inch barrel, that's very sufficient if not a bit lengthy for a fast draw. Do you remember the man carrying the 5-inch-barreled 1911 and effectively drawing it faster than me? Some people make the draw twice as fast as people carrying assorted others with shorter 3-inch barrels. YOU are the only deciding factor! Study, select, train, and practice! After buying all the necessary items for defending and saving your life, they are NOT MAGIC, and if you don't learn to use them once acquired, you stand a high chance of losing the battle.

Since you're going to carry a concealed weapon or a concealed handgun, yes, there are differences such as knives and more, but we're going to learn how to use your gun, especially the sights. True gun control means knowing the operation of your gun and hitting what you shoot at. So many people think they already know how to shoot, and maybe they do, but even though I'm currently 60 years old, I always observe everything because *I still learn things* on occasion. Practically everyone can learn to shoot effectively at a stationary target under ideal conditions out at the local range, but these very same people may fail completely under the stress of an attack and may even fire several rounds at the killer who is on the move, while not even hitting him, which could spell disaster for you, depending on where your bullets go, not to mention the pending disaster for you, because they didn't go where they were supposed to go, allowing the assailant to continue his attack and still, try to or, succeed in KILLING you. Also be aware of any prescription drugs you might take on a steady basis because some of them might slow your reflex reactions.

Non-powder Guns

You might be asking what these are. Most people ask, "What is a non-powder gun?" Many assume they are another gun design without questioning the issue. These are simply BB, air, or pellet guns that kids and teenagers use. While the anti-gun crowd in the US seeks an eventual total gun ban in America, they use the term *non-powder guns* to get laws enacted against these simple sporting arms, claiming that children and teens get hurt by them, so they should be illegal. They even use this adopted definition of non-powder gun while looking for leverage because how many people in this country will know what a non-powder gun is when they see a bill on the ballot to vote against these so-called very dangerous arms? And believe it or not, many states have already enacted such laws against, or even banning, them. Before you ever vote for any gun issue, make sure you know what this issue is *exactly* because not only do politicians or anti-gun groups call things by terms unknown to most people, there's usually a reason which is generally to get those unknowing to cast their vote, assuming they are doing such a good deed. This is somewhat like voting yes to mean no, and no to mean yes.

Blank Gun or Non Gun

There was one guy who carried a blank gun like those they regularly advertise in magazines. In some articles, they even claim carrying such a blank gun will scare the daylights out of a would-be attacker. This one fellow was very overconfident in having this blank gun and had pulled it a few times on others. In his routine, he was pointing it into the air and firing several warning shots and then aiming it at what he felt to be potential assailants. While there are people who try to teach you to do this by using blank guns, THIS IS LIKE BUYING A WINNING TICKET TO YOUR OWN FUNERAL! If you ever draw a fake gun that can only shoot blanks and another person, possibly your KILLER or the person who thinks *you're the killer* because of your premature gun presentation, by lack of your self-control, if he pulls out a real gun and returns fire, you're obviously the loser and most probably dead. If you ever draw your gun, it better be real and very capable of firing real bullets as compared to blanks, BBs, or otherwise. Many of these guns look just like the real thing, and some criminals have modified them to fire live ammunition and killed people with them. Some even think they're cute and try to use *cigarette lighter pistols*. In an emergency, nobody is going to be able to try to take the time to see if you're playing with them or what. A lethal threat is what you prepare for, so don't unnecessarily cause yourself to become the *dead* victim.

Lock Your Gun Up Away from Children

Heat-shrink tubing from RadioShack color codes your locks and keys for fast and easy access to what's locked. Match the key ring color band to the lock color band.

Toy Guns versus Real Guns

There are so many toy guns that look just like the real gun, and, even from a short distance, many can be mistakenly taken for real. There are federal laws that prohibit the selling of a toy gun without a safety orange ring at the muzzle to identify it as a toy; however, the law is not enforced and many toy manufacturers don't bother to put the orange ring on the end. Never buy your children or grandchildren a toy firearm without the safety orange ring on the muzzle in an attempt to keep the children safe. If I found toy guns without it, I'd complain to the store manager and to the manufacturer. A bank robber used a very real-looking toy gun with no orange on it to indicate it was only a toy, and while he was holding a teller at gunpoint, a bank employee with a concealed carry permit drew a .357 magnum revolver and shot the robber who was threatening to shoot her.

Assorted Color Firearms

Currently, manufacturers have decided to make cute and pretty firearms in assorted colors such as pink rifles, pink handguns, and blue guns and in orange, green, gray, red, and a rainbow of color options. This complicates things for children because if someone is holding a colored firearm on you, demanding your money or he'll shoot you, you face the problem of guessing if it is a toy or a real gun. Unfortunately, you cannot afford the chance of not defending yourself because if he pulls the trigger and a bullet or two rip through your body, it will be a very costly mistake. Pretty and colorful guns for adults are complicating fun for children and endangering peoples lives.

Which Guns Are Real?

In the middle of an open-air gathering of motorcycle riders and enthusiasts, which I was attending with friends, there was a fellow who must have felt clever because he was wearing a large belt buckle, the kind that takes a real functioning derringer and snaps it into the belt buckle. There was a derringer snapped in place and ready to go, and while so many people see it as a novelty, it was very real, and it's as dangerous as any other if he were up to no good. Since I always study what I see, I immediately knew what it was and eventually involved the man in conversation, which didn't take long to confirm my suspicions. You never know!

The guns in these belt buckles are real .22 caliber revolvers, but the one I referred to where the man was wearing the buckle had a larger caliber derringer in it. They can be loaded and ready to go and detach for use in seconds.

In the picture above left, the top pistol is a water gun while the bottom pistol is a real functioning Beretta capable of killing you. I'm making it a special point to make you aware of so many guns, toys, replicas, blank guns, dummy practice guns, BB guns, and so forth being identical in many, if not most, features other than a small orange ring on some, but those few are a very small percentage. Since most of them are currently made in an assortment of colors including REAL guns, many people may use many of them for various purposes including the committing of crime. If you are being attacked, robbed, or mugged with a colored gun, it just may be the real McCoy, and resisting while thinking it's a kid's toy or a fighting practice gun just may get a few bullets ripping through your chest. A firearm drawn on you in any attempted crime calls for emergency action and lifesaving procedures. Be familiar with the assorted varieties of unusual colored guns to help

you further make your immediate decision to shoot or not to shoot. Mistaking a REAL gun for a practice dummy gun can cost you your life.

In the picture on the right, the gun on the left is a toy and the gun on the right is real. Be informed that you need to pay attention to what you buy the kids.

Dummy Practice Guns: These are just a few of all the rubber practice guns. They are especially good for practicing gun grabs.

Toy Guns: Which one of the following guns is the real one? None, they are all toys! Some have the orange displayed while some don't. When a teenager stepped out in front of a policeman one day with a toy laser gun and took a stance while aiming and firing the toy gun at the cop, the red laser flashed and the police officer who was startled and scared at the sudden appearance of the gun and the laser flash quickly drew his weapon and fired killing the teenager. It was unfortunate for the teen, but it was determined to be a completely justified accidental shooting. From a given distance, they may be assumed to be real weapons, so when you buy toy guns for kids, please make sure of how much safety orange they have. The kids will be just as happy with them regardless of their safety orange!

Replica and Blank Firing Guns: Which one is the real gun? None, but some of them are capable of firing blanks.

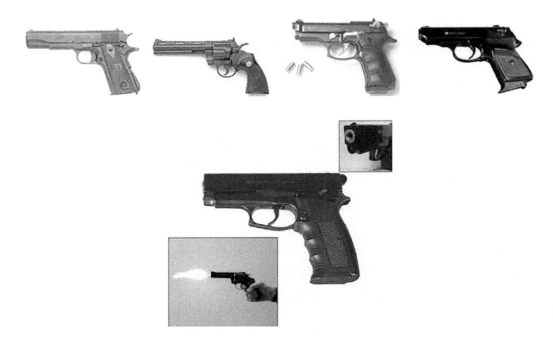

Although this semiautomatic pistol above looks very real, it's not, and neither is the revolver in the picture given below it, showing the muzzle flash, but by firing a blank round, (a blank is a dummy round with gunpowder but no bullet), they all give the exact impression of being very real, especially with their muzzle flash, and everyone trying to survive is naturally going to pull their real gun and put a few very real rounds into this man. You willingly risk your own life!

CO2, Air, BB, and Pellet Guns: These are not toys and not real, but they look real enough.

Real Guns: While many are colored and look like toys, they are all very real and deadly! You can't tell some guns apart, whether they are toys, for blanks, or real guns.

The Facts: While there are many more dozens of guns and color combinations, including camouflage in every one of these categories, the point of these illustrations showing some guns that are available in assorted color schemes is to show you that they look alike and they look like the real thing. Remember one important fact: if any gun is pulled and pointed at you, you're the only one who can decide what to do, which is basically DO or DIE! If you carry a replica, a blank firing, or a toy gun, while thinking you're going to scare away the killer, you may be reserving your space in the cemetery, so it's your choice!

Color Camouflage Weapons

My carry sidearm will *never* be camouflage! Murphy's Law says that if anything can happen, it will, so the idea of preparation is to prevent undesired events. Any attack in low light or darkness will be difficult enough, but if you drop your camouflaged weapon in daylight or darkness of night, especially in a scuffle, the gun may not be found fast enough to save yourself if it blends into the surroundings. Don't be cool; be ALIVE!

Firearms Record Keeping

It is very important to keep a log book entering every firearm that you buy, sell, or give away to show ownership if you ever lose them in a fire or by theft, especially to prove you're no longer owning any particular firearm if it should ever turn up in the hands of criminals or even become a murder weapon. The log will be especially helpful since records will be intermingled and dates and information will be entered in their proper place to show such transfers before any such crime occurring. Insurance companies, as well as law enforcement agencies, will greatly appreciate this, not to mention it could keep you out of jail for something you didn't do. The ATF makes such a booklet available, called a personal firearms record, in a PDF download as a convenience for everyone involved, at: http://www.atf.gov/publications/firearms.

Study the Crime Scene to Help Find Your Assailant

National Integrated Ballistic Information Network, otherwise known as NIBIN. In order to discover links between crimes not known to be connected, firearms examiners have long maintained *open case files* of physical evidence. Now, advanced technology creates the possibility of an open case file with many thousands of exhibits, searchable in minutes instead of the lifetimes that would be required for an entirely manual search. To use NIBIN, examiners or technicians enter bullet and casing evidence into the Integrated Ballistic Identification System (IBIS) unit. Then the new images are correlated against earlier entries. It is possible to search against evidence from the same jurisdictions, neighboring jurisdictions, and other jurisdictions across the country. Search results alert firearms examiners to possible matches. Firearms examiners then compare the original evidence to confirm a *hit*. This investigative lead helps investigators connect two crimes or connect a crime to a recovered firearm. Investigators can take this lead and use it with other case information to help solve the crime. If you get shot or shot at, you can help by picking up cartridge casings at the crime scene and submitting them for imaging. Consistent evidence entry helps agencies get hits by giving the maximum amount of crime gun evidence for comparison.

NIBIN is deployed nationwide; most State Bureaus of Investigation (or equivalent) are connected to NIBIN, as are many other counties and city laboratories. If you need assistance in finding a NIBIN site in your area, you may contact your local police department and question their contacting the NIBIN coordinator in your ATF field division or call the ATF NIBIN Branch at 202-927-5660. It may be sufficient to just put your evidence into a clean zip-lock bag and turn it over to the local police. ATF's partnership with State and Local Law Enforcement through ATF's NIBIN Program and state and local agencies receive technology that they could likely not afford on their own, as well as the capability to exchange investigative information with other jurisdictions. The NIBIN program is currently in the final stages of deployment nationwide. There will be 235 sites nationwide. NIBIN will be available in every state and in most major metropolitan areas. In addition to its support of the NIBIN program, ATF provides comprehensive support to state and local NIBIN partners. They have access to a variety of resources such as the expertise in ATF Laboratory Services, assistance with firearms tracing and crime gun analysis, and industry resources. Side-by-side images allow initial comparison onscreen. Firearms examiners confirm *hits* by comparing original evidence. Even damaged bullets can be entered into IBIS successfully.

The recovery of one handgun and its imaging into IBIS revealed links to a recovered gun, showing that it was involved in 15 shooting incidents where 10 people had been injured that took place in 4 jurisdictions across 2 states. In another incident, sheriff's deputies responded to a drive-by shooting, recovered cartridge casings, and submitted them for NIBIN entry. Two weeks later, a child was killed in a drive-by shooting. The local police department recovered the bullets and casings and entered them into NIBIN. NIBIN revealed a link between the incidents, and an investigation was opened into gang activity, resulting in several high-ranking members of a gang being found guilty of various federal offenses. Deputies investigated an armed robbery in which one person was shot and the casing recovered was entered into NIBIN. Later, deputies arrested a wanted felon who brandished a .45 caliber pistol. His weapon was seized and test-fired. When the test-fire casing was entered into NIBIN, the armed robbery was linked to the armed felon. The suspect is currently serving ten-year imprisonment. For more information about the NIBIN program, you can visit http://www.nibin.gov.

A word to the wise might be to save half dozen empty cartridges that have been fired from each of your guns, especially from your handguns, and put them in closed containers, marking them and putting them away in the event that somebody steals them. Then you can send them to the nearest NIBIN office with a letter of explanation, and they might enter them into their database.

Stay Alive

When deadly force is justified, you want to, YOU HAVE TO, stop the threat as soon as possible, and *losing is not an option*. I do hope you're not tired of hearing this because I want you to know it! Center mass, *dead center of chest between the nipples*, is always the first intended target since the head is much narrower, but if you're within arm's length, you might choose the head, but a head shot being a narrower target may result in a miss under the stress of the encounter.

A survey on police shootings proves accurate head shots effectively stop the threat 100% of the time, even though they do not always cause death. Center mass is always the first shot in an attempt to incapacitate the assailant because you can fire more rounds accurately as compared to firing fewer rounds that need more precise aiming in the same amount of time, mere seconds, and very few killers are going to stand still for a more precisely aimed shot. The heart, heart-lung blood vessel connection, heart-body blood vessel connection are all configured in the center area of the chest and attached to the heart. If you damage the heart, the blood supply necessary for the body to function becomes altered or stopped, thereby shutting down the attack.

If you damage the heart or the blood vessels inadequately, or the projectile goes through the assailant by slipping between these critical vitals without sufficiently or without even doing much damage to them, there is still hope of the round hitting the backbone that is housing the spinal cord, which is still located in the center of your intended shot. In other words, even if you're not a competition shooter, by placing your shots in this area, you stand a very good chance of incapacitating your KILLER. FBI studies on real police shootings proved the only way to *consistently* stop a threat as soon as possible is to severely damage or sever the central nervous system. While head shots are much more difficult to do, especially with a moving target as compared to a stationary target at the local range, you can see why center mass is usually always the first choice. A person usually walks at a speed of 3 miles per hour and walks fast from 3 to 4 miles per hour, and adults run at 8.5 miles per hour as long as he's not running a marathon, so he can be moving at a rate of anywhere between 3 and 8.5 mph. The estimated speed of those running past the Marine snipers in Iraq and Afghanistan is 8.5 mph, according to their successful kill shots, so we'll assume it's the same speed in an attack on the street. If two shots at the center mass appear to do nothing to stop your assailant, the head shot might be an immediate consideration. Beware, the attacker might be wearing body armor. While we are living our daily lives in suburbia, we are not generally prepared for *combat*, and we are not usually walking around wearing body armor, but the assailant KNOWS he's going to attack and KILL, which means that he *will be prepared*.

Preparing Your Gun

If you've made your gun selection, which already has proper sights installed, no matter what you have, and if they don't allow you to acquire a fast sight picture, that is, the sights being properly aligned on target, giving you maximum visibility very quickly, and ready for a kill shot to the bull's-eye or KILLER, you might need to tune them up, depending on what kind you have. Some are very visible in daylight; however, many attacks are in the low-light hours of evening and even the darkness of night. Many attacks are by two to four assailants, making the necessity of your proper skills even more important.

Although there are people who prefer their adjustable sights similar to those on a target pistol, remember, I prefer *fixed sights* on my concealed carry gun. While they say, "Beware of the man who owns only one gun because he probably knows how to use it," the same goes for your sights. Once I become adjusted after learning to shoot with them properly, I know they will always be in proper adjustment and ready for an emergency. They cannot get *out of adjustment*. If they are not adjustable in any way, that's a major part of my sidearm that I know will always be reliable, providing they are not damaged. By shooting with these sights, I learn to shoot close and far by proper sight alignment as compared to adjusting them for various distances. If you have adjustable sights, I recommend keeping the rear-notched blade centered until you've shot enough rounds for practice because it will take a while to become accustomed to the sights. If you start readjusting them too soon, you may be wandering all around the target until you finally get all the basics in order. Remember, make sure you *really need to readjust* the sights before you start doing it. Familiarity and skill are needed, not moving the sight all around while claiming it just won't hit the target. If the rear sight is adjustable, measure the distance from side to side to assure it is centered. Learn to shoot at 21 feet, *more than at any other distance*, because that's the most common distance for assaults, but remember those that are far too close and very scary.

While making sure you can operate your gun properly and perfectly, no matter what, learn to reload and practice reloading by gradually picking up the pace as you become coordinated in responding to a death threat. After you can shoot fairly well, start practicing shoot, recover, and aim again, and shoot the second shot. This is double tap, but it will sound like bang-pause-bang as compared to a competition shooter who can squeeze them off as bang-bang and hit the target both times. It proves you can do it, but don't push the speed until your coordination and shooting skills are coming together.

Make any necessary cosmetic adjustments, acquiring the proper desired sights—dots, shapes, lines, and circles, whatever floats your boat but *works with YOUR eyes*. Refer to the proper sight alignments including a proper sight picture. While most semiautomatics have a three-part appearance, a single front sight post centered in the notch in the rear sight blade, some sight pictures do vary. If you have a handgun that has a groove the entire length down the center of the slide, this is the manufacturer's intended sight for shooting—usually very small calibers or some revolvers—but it leaves a lot to be desired in many ways when considering visibility and accuracy. These guns are usually intended for very close encounters. I will avoid such a gun due to errors from shadows and misinterpretations while sighting down the length of the channel. Those knowledgeable will tell you that you can place your index finger along the side of the slide and point your finger and gun in the direction of the target *naturally* by keeping the pointed finger in alignment with the bone in your forearm and even firing it with the next finger. To me, the natural alignment is OK, but using the next finger to fire is like learning to be unorganized and uncoordinated in an emergency, but if you were facing a criminal and that was all you had, that is, you were probably unprepared, or your trigger finger was out of action, this might help at the right distance. By trying to do it, it's, sort of, like trying to drive a perfectly manageable car backward on the highway when it will drive forward perfectly if you just put it in drive. I'd much rather help you to learn to be properly prepared with the right equipment and be ready, avoiding accidents caused by shooting somewhat blind in addition to more. No matter what anyone tells you, never shoot at *anything* at all that you cannot identify as a lethal threat, and always be confident in what you do. Confidence, proper equipment, and practice are necessary to bring you to success and survival. I was in a discussion with a woman who had a drug-dealing boyfriend at a young age, and when he left the apartment, he told her, if anyone came to the door, to shoot through the door with the gun he had handed her. Shortly after he left, there was a loud banging on the door to open up, and she quickly raised the gun pointing it at the door but couldn't bring herself to shoot. Moments later, just as she lowered the gun, the door was broken open, and it was the police! If she would have fired, they would have returned fire and killed her. Know your target!

While there are currently so many sight designs available, remember, you need to be able to use them in bright or low-light conditions. If you have a revolver, the sights are usually different. They still have the front sight blade, which not only may be taller, but many of them have a colored insert in it. The revolvers generally don't come with three-dot systems, which I like, but it would definitely be an asset to have as many options available that would help many people if they did. Many revolvers have a groove along the top of the frame in the rear, which aligns with the front sight blade, and some have a rear-notched blade similar to that of the semiautomatic pistols. You want to acquire the proper sight alignment with the revolver, the same as you did with the semiautomatic pistol and the same sight pictures as well. Despite whichever type of gun you prefer, a semiautomatic pistol or a revolver, the sights all work the same. Sights are made in sets of front blade and rear blade and are not normally meant to be mixed between styles due to their vertical height and calibrations as a matched set. Some front sight blades, sometimes called posts, are made in different heights for shooters more experienced in their use. Although the front factory blade is sized for correct accuracy normally at close range, for more distance, you can reduce the height of the front blade or increase the height of the rear notch, which will give the equivalent of holdover to compensate for bullet drop downrange at the further distance. In addition, your sights should be glare-free for easy sighting, and both the front and rear sight should be rounded on the edges and snag-free for fast effective presentation of your gun, drawing your gun, with no interference such as snagging on a shirt or jacket.

Shorter Trigger Pull May Speed Up Your Response

Assorted guns have assorted trigger pulls, not necessarily in pounds of force to initiate the firing of the gun, but in the distance the trigger has to be pulled to fire the gun. Some triggers have to travel the full distance of the trigger guard to fire the sidearm while others may only have to travel 1/16". Then after the gun fires, the trigger needs to reset to fire the next round, but some triggers need much more room than others to reset, just the way they need more room to fire due to their mechanical design. Double-action triggers need much more room to fire than single-action triggers. The gun with the shortest trigger travel to fire and reset the trigger is going to function that much faster than those with longer travel requirements to function. These differences could mean more to you than you think when it comes to life and death. Some guns can fire twice as many rounds in the same amount of time due to the distance required for the trigger to travel to fire each round. Many people have trigger jobs to improve their trigger, but even then, you can only do so much, depending on the firearm model and design. Some firearms come with a finely tuned trigger from the factory while most do not. Study before you buy. Measure the distances the triggers have to travel to trip the firing pin or hammer and the distance for the trigger to reset, that is, re-engage the firing position for the firing mechanism. Trigger jobs are usually done to lighten the trigger pull in pounds of force it takes to fire the gun to improve accuracy, allowing the gun to fire more easily on the bull's-eye other than having to apply much more pressure, which might pull you off target before it fires. Know YOUR gun!

The shortest trigger pull is on the left and the longest is in the center.

Targets

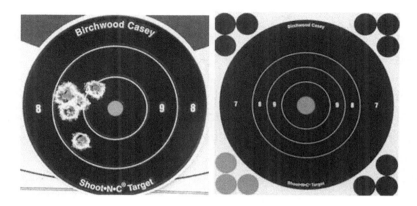

While very small targets make you a better shot, for a beginner or those who are beginning to shoot out to 25 yards might want a rifle target, which is larger, and as you learn to shoot, you can downsize the target. Targets called Shoot-N-C by Birchwood Casey are self-stick and fantastic but usually cheaper at a shooting range than sporting goods stores due to their volume sales of targets. Everywhere the bullet hits the target, it shows a splatter ring around each hole, which makes the holes extremely visible from a great distance. The small spots in the corners are for patching the holes, so you can shoot it again!

While Birchwood Casey has dozens of targets available, they have target spots. I found that the local office supply has Avery color coding labels in ¾ inch while target spots are available that work very well for shooting out to 21 feet or more if you can see them. More precise aiming makes you a better shot! The Avery spots can be used for patching holes.

An excellent backing for shooting targets is corrugated plastic available in craft or building supply stores for a few bucks for a two-foot square, and it will withstand thousands of rounds; it's incredible.

Learning to Shoot

Read the Operators Manual First: Now, if you bought a carry gun or even if you've had a gun for a while, I want you to read the owner's manual for the handgun that you will be carrying, even if you've read it before, just to familiarize yourself with anything that you might have forgotten and be sure to read it from cover to cover. Pay special attention to loading and unloading your gun because it's something you're going to be doing all the time now, and you have to be safe each and every time. Be aware of the way the safeties work. Don't skip this part for later; stop and do it now because it will help you learn as you read and study.

Assuming that you made yourself familiar with your carry gun, I assume you know how to load it and unload it safely while being fully knowledgeable in the way the safeties work. Make sure you don't have any ammunition available or even near you, and it would be advisable to place the ammo in another room or lock it up, but continue to read just the same. Double—and triple-check the chamber, magazine, or cylinder of your gun, making sure it is empty and unloaded. It is advisable to triple-check it every time you unload it or every time you hand it to another person, and even have the other person you hand the gun to verify that it is unloaded the same way that YOU should if someone hands a gun to you as absolute safety precautions. You're developing good habits that will become easier soon.

Unloading Your Gun: Since you will be carrying your sidearm all the time now, you will preferably want a designated spot to load and unload your weapon, keeping it in an area away from others and especially children. Since this is going to be an everyday part of your life, it would be advisable to get a small bucket and fill it with sand, placing it in a corner in a room, your basement, garage, or other area you designate for loading and unloading. Be sure you are pointing your gun into the bucket of sand while loading or unloading just in case something goes wrong and you accidentally discharge your gun. An accidental discharge could get your carry license revoked, so be careful.

While I was in firearm classes, the instructor actually used his Kevlar bullet-resistant vest in place of a bucket of sand—great idea—pointing the gun into the vest during loading and unloading. Like I said, I still learn, but with the vest sitting on a hard wooden table, the round just may compress the vest against the hard wood and ma penetrate the vest since the vest is designed to compress against the cushioning effect of the body. Maybe a pad behind the vest might be better. While the bullets may travel through walls and into other rooms or houses, they will actually be stopped by the depth of the sand or by the vest, preventing injury to anyone. Beware of magnum loads such as .357 or larger including exceptional loads due to the possibility of certain powerful rounds going through Kevlar vests, especially certain high velocity rounds or rifle rounds. Remember that even a bullet-resistant vest, if against something hard, might allow the bullet to penetrate other than the vest normally being compressed as it would be if worn on the body.

Semiautomatic: While inserting a loaded magazine and racking the slide, if the magazine is out of the gun before you rack the slide-and it has to be if you're unloading the weapon- then the round that is currently in the chamber, if any, will be removed by the extractor and ejected without chambering a new round. remember, racking means to pull the slide all the way back and release it to return under its own power which will properly strip a live round from the magazine, which also chambers the live round. Remember that *if* the loaded magazine is inserted, then a new live round will be chambered when you rack the slide. Always empty the chamber, even if you think it's already empty.

Racking the Slide: The recommended way is to grip the slide with your weak (support) hand by grabbing it with your thumb and your index finger, first finger next to your thumb, while your weak palm is face down against the slide, holding the slide firmly, pushing the frame forward with the strong hand, and, after you run out of travel, releasing the slide. Don't use your hand to slowly or carefully return the slide to the forward closed position like many people try to do because due to the slower speed and difference in applied torque, this will cause a probable jamming problem due to it being out of sync since it is designed for a self-functioning return.

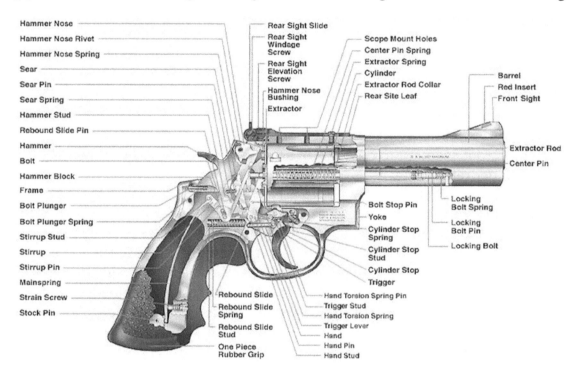

The Revolver

A revolver is a repeating firearm that has a cylinder containing multiple chambers and at least one barrel for firing. There are three types of revolvers: a single-action, a double-action, and a double-action-only. The original name was a revolving gun, but the short-form revolver is universally used. As the user cocks the hammer, the cylinder revolves to align the next chamber and round with the hammer and barrel, which gives this type of firearm its actual name. Different brand-name revolvers may rotate the cylinder either to the right or to the left. In modern revolvers, the revolving cylinder has all the individual chambers in it, one chamber for each round, typically and most commonly chambers five or six rounds, but some models hold as many as 10 rounds or more. Those that hold more rounds are of a smaller caliber because they still have to fit in approximately the same cylinder diameter. Each chamber has to be reloaded manually, which makes reloading a revolver a much slower procedure than reloading a semiautomatic pistol. Their lower ammunition capacities and relatively longer reload times compared to auto-loading pistols make them much less desirable for those who have to carry a gun for a living such as police and the military. Revolvers also have no mechanical safeties. Revolvers are also ambidextrous. While there are a few different claims of what ambidextrous actually means, most say that it's for either right—or left-handed users, but this is only half right! True ambidextrous isn't just for right—or left-handed users, but *its real purpose is to be usable by either your right OR your left hand at the very same time* so that in a confrontation, in the event that you might get wounded and one hand is taken out of the fight, then the other hand can operate the gun to increase your chances of surviving. While any revolver can be fired ambidextrous, the revolvers that have their cylinder release on the top other than the side are more easily used as a true ambidextrous handgun. Some people who carry a gun for a living, even if using a semiautomatic pistol, prefer to carry a small revolver, generally in the .38 caliber range, for a backup in the thoughts of it being faster to access this second gun other than trying to reload their primary weapon, which could easily be challenged by many since they have to re-holster the primary weapon and then draw their secondary. If this is the way they believe in doing it, then sufficient practice should help them, but I prefer the reload, which keeps me pretty much on target seeming to be more of an advantage and provides me with many more rounds available per reload.

Single-action Revolver: A single-action revolver requires the hammer to be pulled back by hand before each shot, which also rotates the cylinder. This leaves the trigger with just one single action left to perform—releasing the hammer to fire the shot—so the force and distance required to pull the trigger can be minimal. Each chamber has to be reloaded manually, one single round at a time through a small loading gate which makes reloading a single-action revolver a much slower procedure than reloading a double-action revolver.

Double-action Revolver: A double-action revolver is a self-cocking revolver where one long squeeze of the trigger pulls back the hammer and revolves the cylinder and then finally fires the shot. This generally increases the weight of the trigger pull considerably in the double action due to having to operate all the extra parts for both, the single—and the double-action sequences. But even if you have a double-action revolver, you can fire it in a single-action mode by pulling the hammer back. Releasing the hammer to fire while it's in the single-action mode takes very little effort due to it skipping the double-action sequence, which would otherwise be first to cock the hammer and rotate the cylinder. Double-action firearms, being either pistols or revolvers, will have a stronger trigger pull in the first portion of the trigger pull travel and lightens up to far less in the second sequence required to trip the hammer, so if you pre-cock the hammer in the double-action revolver, it will fire very easily with very little effort. They can generally be fired faster than a single-action, but at the cost of reduced accuracy in the hands of many shooters. Most modern revolvers are traditional double-action, which means they are able to operate either in single-action or double-action mode. The accepted meaning of double-action has come to be known as self-cocking, so modern revolvers that cannot be pre-cocked by pulling the hammer back are called double-action-only. The reason these revolvers cannot be pre-cocked is because their hammers have either had the thumb spur cutoff to prevent snagging and accidental discharge or an internal firing mechanism that does the job of a hammer or firing pin, so the only way to fire this revolver is to pull the trigger all the way back until it fires, so it's called double-action-only. The double-action-only revolver design is intended primarily for concealed carry due to its safe hammer design, compared to a traditional hammer. In a double-action revolver, each chamber has to be reloaded manually, but since the cylinder swings out on what's called the crane, giving access to the entire cylinder and all the chambers at once for reloading, there are speed loaders available to drop in a full load of the exact number of rounds needed to load the revolver's entire cylinder all at one time, which makes reloading a double-action revolver a much faster procedure than reloading a single-action revolver but still far slower than loading a semiautomatic pistol, which allows any number of rounds to be loaded up to the semiautomatic's magazine capacity. While some semiautomatics can use extended magazines, it makes these magazines ideal for backup reloads. The double-action revolver has a cylinder release either on the side or on the top that allows the crane to swing out to gain access to the cylinder, and the crane has an ejector rod that will eject all the empty cartridge cases at once when pushed all the way in.

Revolver Notes: Though there are differences in the revolver operations and differences in their design and their firing and safety mechanisms by manufacturers, such as Ruger, Smith, and Wesson, I'm not going to address all the differences. If you buy any revolver, you will get an operator's manual with it that will give you the entire set of manufacturer's guidelines and information regarding the operation and the safety of using your revolver. This will avoid a lot of confusion. I want you to be able to remember what you read here, rather than trying to teach you the operations of a half dozen guns that you might never use.

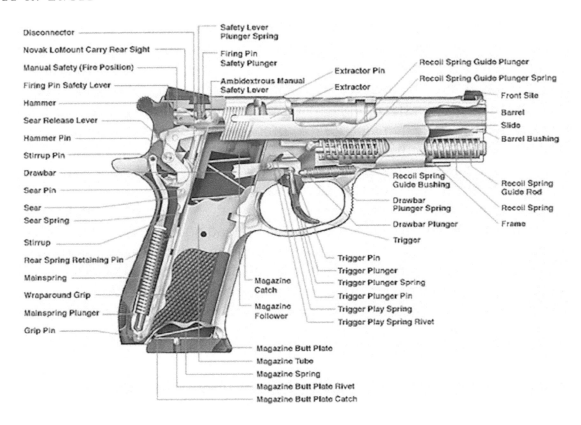

Labels (clockwise / by region):

Disconnector — Safety Lever Plunger Spring — Firing Pin Safety Plunger — Ambidextrous Manual Safety Lever — Extractor Pin — Extractor — Recoil Spring Guide Plunger — Recoil Spring Guide Plunger Spring — Front Site — Barrel — Slide — Barrel Bushing

Novak LoMount Carry Rear Sight — Manual Safety (Fire Position) — Firing Pin Safety Lever — Hammer — Sear Release Lever — Hammer Pin — Stirrup Pin — Drawbar — Sear Pin — Sear — Sear Spring — Stirrup — Rear Spring Retaining Pin — Mainspring — Wraparound Grip — Mainspring Plunger — Grip Pin

Recoil Spring Guide Bushing — Drawbar Plunger Spring — Drawbar Plunger — Trigger — Recoil Spring Guide Rod — Recoil Spring — Frame

Trigger Pin — Trigger Plunger — Trigger Plunger Spring — Trigger Plunger Pin — Trigger Play Spring — Trigger Play Spring Rivet

Magazine Catch — Magazine Follower

Magazine Butt Plate — Magazine Tube — Magazine Spring — Magazine Butt Plate Rivet — Magazine Butt Plate Catch

Semiautomatic Pistol

A semiautomatic pistol is often referred to as an automatic pistol, self-loading pistol, auto pistol, and auto-loading pistol. It is a type of handgun which uses a single chamber and barrel, which are integrated into one piece, with a mechanism powered by the previous shot to load a fresh cartridge into the chamber. One round is fired each time the trigger of a semiautomatic pistol is pulled. A semiautomatic pistol harnesses the energy of one shot to reload the chamber for the next, typically via recoil operation, blowback, or gas operation. After a round is fired, the spent casing is ejected and a new round is stripped from the magazine and is loaded into the chamber, allowing another shot to be fired as soon as the trigger is pulled again. Most types of semiautomatic pistols rely on a removable magazine to store ammunition before it is fired, usually inserted inside the grip. This mode of operation generally allows for faster reloading and storing a larger number of cartridges than a revolver, although semiautomatic pistols are potentially more prone to malfunctions than revolvers due to their more complex design and mechanism.

Single-action Semiautomatic Pistol: A single-action semiautomatic pistol must be cocked by first operating the slide or bolt or, if a round is already chambered, by cocking the hammer manually. The famed Colt M1911 is an example of this style of action. All single-action semiautomatic pistols exhibit this feature and automatically cock the hammer when the slide is first *racked* to chamber a round. A round can also be manually inserted in the chamber with the slide locked back. Then the safety can be applied. The normal mode of carrying a single-action semiautomatic pistol is Condition 1, popularly known as cocked and locked. *Condition 1* (a term popularized by Colonel Jeff Cooper) refers to having the magazine full, a round chambered, the hammer fully cocked, and the thumb safety engaged or on, at least for right-handed users. For many single-action semiautomatic pistols, this procedure works well only for right-handed users as the thumb safety is located on the left side of the pistol and is easily accessible only for those who are holding the pistol in the right hand. On many single-action semiautomatic pistols, there is also a hammer position known as half-cocked. Squeezing the trigger will not fire the gun when it is in the half-cocked position, and neither will dropping the gun in this state cause an accidental discharge. So they claim! The half-cock was revised by Colt in 1970s and subsequently by other manufacturers, so the hammer will fall from half-cock if the trigger is pulled on most newer 1911-type guns. In general, single-action semiautomatic pistols should never be carried uncocked with the safety off because the hammer will be resting over the firing pin on a live round, although many newer single-action pistols have modified actions that lock the firing pin, and it allows the hammer to exert pressure against the firing pin *only* when the trigger is pulled. Many modern single-action semiautomatic pistols have had their safety mechanisms redesigned to provide a thumb safety on both sides of the pistol (ambidextrous), thereby meeting the needs of left-handed as well as right-handed users. Remember, ambidextrous means usable by both, either right—or left-handed users without disassembly or switching any parts from one side to the other. I've heard a salesman tell people at the gun counter that a certain firearm was ambidextrous because they could take the parts out and reinstall them on the other side. This is false information! Others say ambidextrous is for either a right—or a left-handed user, which is only half right. True ambidextrous isn't just for right—or left-handed users, but its real purpose is to be usable by either your right or your left hand at the very same time so that in a confrontation, in the event that you might get wounded and one hand is taken out of the fight, then the other hand can operate the gun to increase your chances of surviving.

Double-action Semiautomatic Pistol: Many modern semiautomatic pistols are usually double action, also sometimes known as double-action-single-action (DA/SA). In this design, the hammer or striker may be either thumb-cocked or activated by pulling the trigger when firing the first shot. The hammer or striker is re-cocked automatically during each firing cycle. In double-action pistols, the first pull of the trigger requires roughly twice as much pressure as subsequent firings, since the first pull of the trigger also cocks the hammer (if not already cocked by hand). A common mode of carry for double-action semiautomatic pistols is with the magazine full, a round chambered, and the gun holstered and uncocked with the external safety unengaged or off.

Double-action-only Semiautomatic Pistol: Some modern semiautomatic pistols are double-action-only; that is, once a round is chambered, each trigger pull will cock the hammer, striker, or firing pin and will additionally release the same to fire a cartridge in one continuous motion. Each pull of the trigger on a double-action-only semiautomatic pistol requires the same amount of pressure. Double-action-only semiautomatic pistols are most generally recommended only in the smaller, self-defense, and concealable pistols, rather than in target or hunting pistols.

The picture shown above is the striker-fired semiautomatic pistol. There's no hammer to get fumbled or caught in anything.

Striker-fired Semiautomatic Pistol: Firearms use triggers to initiate the firing of a cartridge in the firing chamber of the weapon. This is accomplished by actuating a striking device through a combination of spring and kinetic energy operating through a firing pin to strike and ignite the primer. There are two primary types of striking mechanisms: hammers and strikers. Hammers are spring-tensioned masses of metal that pivot on a pin when released and strike a firing pin to discharge a cartridge while some hammers actually have a pin attached to the striking surface. Strikers are, essentially, spring-loaded firing pins that travel on an axis in line with the cartridge, eliminating the need for a separate hammer. Although some rifles have hammers, the majority of rifles operate similar to the handguns with the striker where the spring-loaded firing pin is in the center of the bolt and strikes the primer. The connection between the trigger and the hammer is generally referred to as the sear surface. Variable mechanisms will have this surface directly on the trigger and hammer or have separate sears or other connecting parts.

Strikers are basically spring-loaded firing pins, generally of a one—or two-piece construction. In the one-piece striker, the striker is turned on a lathe out of a round bar of metal, much larger in diameter than a firing pin, to provide the mass required to detonate the primer. Two-piece strikers generally consist of a firing pin attached to a heavier rear section such as a hammer or a slide hammer attached to the base of a firing pin. Two—piece strikers are commonly found on bolt-action rifles, while single-piece strikers are found on pistols.

Holstering Your Gun

If you considered open carry (worn in plain view visually) but are undecided, personally *I would forget* open carry because you become an immediate target for a thug who might shoot YOU first or advance on YOU to get YOUR gun, not to mention unnecessarily scaring someone who does not understand because they don't have any firearms or are unfamiliar and inexperienced with them, so they may assume you're a criminal and even call the police. Once the police are called for a man having a gun, they will obviously investigate the matter. I was watching a man at the beach who had an open carry gun on his right hip, which had his shirt bunched up above it, so he might not have been aware or he might have done that purposely for clear access. While it seems that nobody pays much attention, when someone actually realizes what it is, it suddenly gets a lot of attention. There have been numerous incidents nationwide where police officers have detained legally licensed concealed carry citizens for hours, claiming reasonable suspicion and assorted other charges because they claim that if you are carrying a gun, it's not a normal thing to be doing. Currently, while not being popular with some lawmakers and anti-gunners alike, it's a very normal thing to be doing to save your life. While some people being detained have been let go a few hours later, there have been charges filed by district attorneys, claiming reckless endangerment among other things, so be cautious and be smart about what you do. Don't challenge the system! The individual policemen are not always as familiar with the open carry and the concealed carry laws as you would think, especially when the state laws change periodically. I listened to a taped incident where the Philadelphia police detained a resident for open carry, and the policeman who detained the man was holding the man *at gunpoint* and said it was absolutely *illegal* to open carry in Pennsylvania, but after calling in for backup units and contacting the station, he eventually learned that it was perfectly legal; however, the man was still detained for hours, and later the district attorney filed charges against him anyway. In studying the circumstances, I felt that the young guy was purposely testing the system for whatever reason; otherwise, why was the recorder in his pocket and it just happened to get turned on, recording the entirety of the situation? More policemen are learning to keep up with their state laws (which are constantly changing), regarding the personal carry of a firearm. It's your responsibility to be careful and to know the law.

Now you need to determine how and where I will carry my gun for protection. While there are numerous places that people place their handguns for defense, in locked boxes, in glove compartments, in gun boxes and range bags, and in so many others, no matter how fine and expensive your gun is, and even with all its options, it won't do you any good in an *emergency* if you don't have it immediately available for defense if someone suddenly points a gun at you. You must decide as to whether your gun is going to be *on you* or off you but nearby. Once a gun is drawn on you, if you make an obvious attempt at drawing a carry gun that is apparently going to be very visible while trying to gain access to a gun holstered somewhere on you during the draw, you might get shot at the sudden sight of the gun appearing while you're trying to get it out. You need to have it available in an instant, which generally means on your person and in a safe and effective holster, even if you have to wait for an opportunity to draw it, depending on your particular situation. The element of surprise wins most battles!

While considering how you are going to carry it, for women, a purse seems to be so common, yet it's the *last* place you might want to carry your defense gun unless you're a police woman because they always snatch your purse, which now gives them your gun too. Carrying a purse with the strap over your shoulder and your elbow bent with your hand grasping the strap half way down will give you the advantage over a grab and run crook. If you're out of town or in an area you are not sure of, it might pay to have a second purse, something cheap and inexpensive with hardly anything in it and a cheap $5 wallet with only a few dollars in it. So if you are confronted, they get away with your purse and wallet. While their confidence is high, they will run far before checking their take, but the joke is on *them*. I carry my wallet in a front-side pocket and a cheap $5 wallet with $5 bucks in it where most men normally carry their real wallet so that if I get robbed, possibly at gunpoint, I can reach to that particular spot for the wallet the thug is demanding and, depending on the circumstances, either pull the wallet or draw my gun. It's not worth dying or having to shoot someone for $5, but then you might have no option than to draw your carry gun and maybe even fire in the defense of your life, depending on the situation.

In the movies and unfortunately in real-life situations, there are people who want to carry their handgun in their waistband without a holster, which is sometimes defined as Mexican carry. First, it might be against the law in your state to carry without a holster, and, second, it is not safe carrying your gun in the waistband since there are people who have died from their gun falling out of their pants or through the waist and down a pant leg to the ground while accidentally discharging which killed them. Then there was a man who carried his handgun, a revolver in his back pocket, but it accidentally discharged one day, shooting him through the behind. And then there was another man who carried in his right front pants pocket *un- holstered*, and it accidentally discharged, shooting him through the leg. One day, I saw a man wearing shorts from a sweat suit coming into a restaurant, and I just had to observe this because he had what appeared to be a very heavy un-holstered revolver in his pocket printing through the material, which pulled his pocket into such a severe sagging position in this light material that it looked as if his shorts were going to come down at any moment. These stories could go on for hours and in a variety of situations, but I'm sure you get the point. There are pocket holsters, not only for your own safety but which hold a pocket gun in the ready position and the holster stays in the pocket when you draw your sidearm.

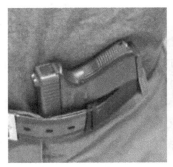

The two examples are inside the waistband (IWB) with no holster. They can easily fall out and possibly kill you or an innocent bystander who doesn't deserve getting killed because the gun owner is negligent. The one on the right has a lanyard (a cord) attached to the lanyard eye on the back strap of the gun frame, but even so, lanyards have their place and could still allow the sidearm to fall through the waistband without a holster. Avoid taking risks and be safe.

Are there unsafe holsters? Well, the answer to that question is obviously yes. There are devices people use that I would not recommend. I see holsters of assorted designs that are made cheaply and sold for just a few dollars, but you get what you pay for. Some leather holsters are made out of such thin leather that it scares me out of ever using them while thinking of it is actually tearing and becoming dangerous. Normal and proper holsters are made of thick leather and stitched very well. There are also leather and/or Kydex holsters of assorted designs that are custom-made other than factory holsters, but since some are made in somebody's home shop, they might not have the desired retention to grip your gun like those made at the factory, but then some of the custom holster makers that do a one-on-one actually do a perfect fitting to suit your desires. Kydex are generally ugly to begin with, but we're not trying to win a beauty contest here; we're trying to be effective! Then there are the grips that attach to your gun and actually replace the original grip. The grip has a hook designed on the top of one of the grip panels, and there are also other hooks to do the same that attach to your gun so that they can be hung on your pants or belt without the use of a holster. In my opinion, I see these devices as a potential hazard while there are so many various holsters available, but we'll address specific options and problems so you can make a better choice.

Choosing the proper size and weight of a gun is very important concern for everyone who carries. Remember that you will be carrying your gun all the time now and *preferably* in a holster sufficient in strength to carry the weight of your new sidearm around the clock. The weight of the gun may not be much of a problem if it's in a hip holster on your strong side, which might be easier for you. If you're right-handed, right is your strong side, or left, if left-handed. If you try out a holster with your gun, you may notice a sore spot after about a week or so of wearing it every day, feeling like a big bruise, but it will go away. Just take the holster off for a couple of days to let the spot feeling bruised recover and then put it back on, and you will get used to it. After you selected your gun and decided on a specific holster, you will benefit from wearing the holstered gun around the house for about a week or two while making sure the gun is not loaded. Make sure the gun is cocked and locked and safety's on and ready to draw and fire but there is no ammunition in it. This will help you see while it is so close to you against your body, the safety (if you have one) does not get deactivated or accidentally bumped off or de-cocked from possible friction and resistance caused by brushing against your body. The more you wear it, the more you will become accustomed to it, and you can even start practicing drawing, (presenting) your gun, and acquiring a target. Practice when you're alone and nobody can get scared or hurt. When you feel comfortable enough with your gun, including wearing it and operating it, which also includes shooting it, then you can advance to wearing a loaded gun with the magazine only, and then you can eventually move on to a round in the chamber if that's your choice of carry while I caution you to the safety factors. Eventually, you'll be ready to respond to an attacker who may have a gun on you or is attempting to. You have to develop the ability to always be ready to respond to a threat! You have to develop these skills!

Remember, I'll mention certain things a time or two along the way throughout the book to assure you remember them. If you're right-handed, then your right hand is your strong hand or strong side, and if left-handed, then your left hand is your strong hand or strong side, where your opposite hand is your support hand. While many experienced gun professionals have their preference, your strong side outside the waistband (OWB) belt holster is the most effective for immediate reach, proper grip, and draw where again the draw is called gun presentation. But then you also have to wear something like a windbreaker or jacket to cover it so nobody knows you have it on. I also wear the OWB a lot using my Galco holster, mostly at the range. I try keeping my IWB positioned more toward my kidney or positioned at 4:30 with 12:00 being straight ahead, which helps make it more invisible from any obvious frontal view, and it allows me the freedom to reach into my pants pocket so many times a day without my hand or forearm being obstructed by the holster that's holding my .45-1911 with a 3- or 4-inch barrel. It's a short holster riding high and making it very difficult for others to tell it's there at all.

Here's a major concern. When wearing your holstered gun, if it's on your strong side at 3:00, it's at a very proper location—the immediate access point where police wear them. If you have an assailant or multiple assailants such as in a gang who normally make many of their approaches from the rear, then reaching to your kidney or the small of your back for your gun may be very difficult to do since they will see it happening from behind you, and if they are close enough, they just might go ahead and grab it from behind you. Remember that a sudden step into a doorway and drawing your gun while stepping in and turning to face the would-be assailants may give you the precious seconds needed, but then remember, you have to be sure of their actual intentions before you let them know you have a gun and will shoot them. The confined space of the doorway will prevent any of them from getting behind you since one of their tactics is getting spread out and around you so that they will have the greatest advantage. Prevent this if you can.

Even though I've mentioned my wilderness adventures with bears, remember that I purposely holstered my .44 Magnum across my chest due to the hunters and even rangers who have been killed by the bears. Holstering mine across my chest was after some serious thought so that I could reach between my chest and the bear and draw my .44 Magnum and fire a few rounds with the first being up the nostril, which is a pathway to the brain. Doing your homework and proper preparation in advance is always the best way to achieve success. Plan for your survival!

Where normal day-to-day pocket access for your hand is a concern, an IWB (inside the waistband) holster prevents this *external* pocket access problem. Although my IWB and OWB give me just about the same access capability, the IWB gives you more concealability. When learning your preferred carry position for your holster of either kind, remove your shirt and adjust it in the mirror while carefully observing the angle and location of the grip. If your holster is on the radius of your kidney, the grip may protrude into view with a raised bump or shape from beneath your clothes, seriously affecting your secrecy, so you might need to make some adjustments. So there are no points or corners of the grip protruding, which will do the same thing to your shirt, making it obvious that something is under it. Proper adjustment of just an inch or so can usually solve this problem. There are guns that have the grip angled or rounded on the back corner (usually called melting, which takes all the sharp edges and corners off the gun, smoothing them out) to prevent a sharp edge or point from printing while printing is showing observers something is underneath your shirt, but the melt option makes it easier to handle, so you don't have any edges that can injure you. If someone realizes and asks what that bump is under your shirt, I'd simply say that sometimes I have to wear equipment to keep me alive, which may be assumed to be medically involved, but, with practice, nobody will know.

With my kidney carry position, access is very good as my time on the clock for being alerted to a threat—reaching, properly gripping, drawing, quickly aiming, and acquiring my target while placing a kill shot on the target—is 2 seconds, which seems so slow compared to some, but I've seen many at 4½ seconds. At my age, my reflexes may be a bit slower, so maybe I need to continue my practice drills a little more these days. A kill shot means after it was fired, that's what it actually would have been; otherwise, the timer will continue while you attempt to place a follow-up shot, trying to get that kill shot, which will stop the timer. In my practice drills for dry-fire practice (at home indoors), it takes much less time from the draw to the fire, but in actual live fire, you have to become alert to the threat, take aim on a particular silhouette or given target that you are not necessarily used to at whatever given distance, and make the shot. Reality always works a bit different and especially when you're under stress and may even triple your access time, but remember that time in seconds is a matter of your life or your death, so believe me that timing is important, but don't let that disillusion you because getting the gun drawn to stop the threat is very important in itself, *the most important*. Do you remember the policeman I mentioned earlier who unexpectedly walked into a robbery in progress and had no idea that within the next few seconds or minute, he'd be dead? It happens.

While there are many options available for holsters, one main advantage is a holster that is anchored to your body or belt sufficiently for proper stability while drawing. For this very reason, you want to make sure you use a very sturdy belt to maintain the weight being placed on it all day and not a cheap and flimsy one so that the rigid belt will keep your holster in the same place all day without stretching and sagging or sliding around, which happens when you walk or sit down if not properly secured. There's a definite difference between a normal belt and a *rigid* gun belt, believe me! The proper belt prevents you from pulling up your gun all day. Belt loops on a holster spaced far apart are preferred and work very well as compared to loops being very close together, which does actually work well on a short radius of your kidney, unless you take a holster such as my IWB Galco Summer Comfort, and take the two straps that are only separated by one-strap width, and place one on each side of the belt loop, which keeps it anchored in that same spot, no matter what you do. It wouldn't be very good if you reached for your gun in an emergency and it was somewhere else on your waist. Remember, failure in preparation is NOT an option because the outcome may be a disaster.

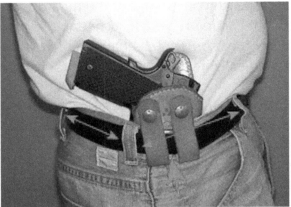

A single belt loop on your pants located between the two belt loops on the holster will secure it in place so that it cannot slide to either side and will be right where you reach for it rather than to slide away by a few inches and not be where you expect it in an emergency. Kidney carry is ideal with this arrangement. A loose shirt, windbreaker, or jacket will conceal this firearm very well since it's on the radius of the kidney and can be pulled from this location very quickly. Beware some holster belt loops may not be spaced far enough apart to place a pants belt loop between them!

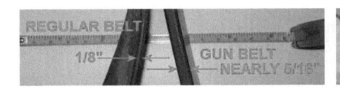

Look at the comparison of belt thickness. While many people use normal everyday belts for carrying their sidearms, the sturdy belt keeps the weight off the hips and you live in comfort. Good gun supporting belts are available in heavy thicknesses, and you will get used to wearing it. You will be happy for the investment of a few dollars.

Remember how much of an advantage it is when your holster cannot slide to the right or to the left because the belt loop between the straps or holster loops keeps it there. Some holsters have a single loop, but when I tried them to see what they'll do, the gun continued to lean over forward by gravity, making it a bit unreliable because you have to worry about if the gun might fall out, and while trying to get a proper grip on a leaning gun, it's very difficult to draw your gun from a single-loop holster, especially with the grip leaning over. Due to all my experiments with holsters, I would very strongly suggest *never* using a holster with less than two straps or belt loops.

Even if your holster has two belt loops, straps, or clips, if you make any attempt to use a bathroom somewhere, you have to remove the handgun from the holster first and place it firmly out of view while pointing into a solid bullet stop for safety such as into a corner.

If you unbuckle your belt with your gun still holstered, the weight of the gun will allow it to flop over upside down while the belt is loose, and the muzzle may be pointing directly at your midsection and the gun will probably even fall out, so remember the importance of removing the gun first. This also applies to magazine carriers. The same thing can happen when you're undressing, so make sure you always remove the gun, just the same as reversing the procedures when dressing and putting your holster on, which works best if you keep the belt unbuckled until you put the holster's belt loops in place and snap or clip them in, but then snug and buckle the belt *before* you put the gun into the holster. Absolute control of your gun at all times is necessary, and it's very important to develop the proper habits while tending to personal issues because you have to deal with them on a daily basis.

The Galco Summer Comfort IWB holster in the first and third pictures are very small and compact while maintaining full stability from leaning over forward due to gravity. They come according to the barrel length of the gun you have. The brown Galco OWB holsters are the second and fourth pictures on the right, one with and one without a thumb break strap to retain the gun from falling or being pulled out. Either one works for concealed carry under different circumstances. The Summer Comfort makes an ideal kidney carry while the outside-the-waistband holster can be positioned on the hip (ideal) or in a variety of positions, but you have to make sure the chosen position allows the gun to be accessed with the forward cant, that is, angled forward. Notice the thick leather and the double stitching in both. The Kimber 3" .45 1911 is shown holstered in both left holsters. The forward cant makes it easy to obtain a proper grip quickly. The Kimber Solo Carry in 9mm third from the left also works well in the Summer Comfort holster.

Holsters that are made with the pocket angled so that the grip is at an angle for easy grasp is called a cant or the FBI cant since the FBI made it popular, which may vary by a few degrees in different holsters and some may be adjustable. No matter what type of holster you decide to use, make sure it is either right-handed or a left-handed to suit your needs for your strong hand. The holster is not ambidextrous, that is, the right and the left. It fits whatever gun you need, but one holster is designed to fit your left side for a left-hand draw and one is designed to fit your right side for a right-hand draw. Some are considered universal or ambidextrous, a single right—or left-handed holster, but I avoid these in favor of a well-designed holster for a specific side. If using an IWB holster, make sure to experiment with adjusting your belt tension after the gun is holstered. If the belt is too tight, the gun may not draw easily, and, in an emergency, it could spell disaster. It would be advisable to wear a belt in the same color as the holster belt loops or clips that attach to your belt, which will otherwise be visible if the colors are different but will easily blend in if the color matches. Most people won't have enough time to view your belt to focus and question what the clips might be.

Some holsters that *clip* into your pants or onto your belt have disadvantages to them, depending on their design. In a special holstering class, while a person was being instructed on proper drawing techniques from his holster, and just as the very discussion of such an incident happening came up, it actually happened at that very instant where the man who drew his carry gun had the cheap clip-in holster come out with his gun, and while he tried to take aim, he realized the holster was still on his gun. A dead man in a true emergency, and this event was not staged, which proves that it can happen at any time. If you buy a clip-in holster, make sure it is a quality and proven design.

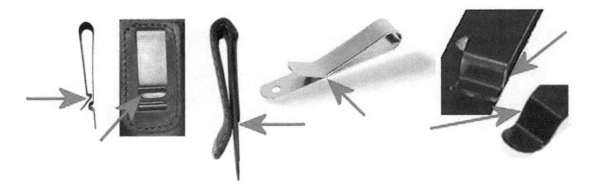

Notice the design on all these holster clips above where they allow for easy opening and removal. We don't want easy removal! Good quality holster clips are easy enough to remove while retaining your holster and gun when you need it, so either it doesn't fall out or when you draw your sidearm, you don't want the holster to pull out while having the holster still attached to the gun. The clip above left has an angled end, but very little of it to supposedly prevent it from coming out, but believe me they come out. You need a stout clip similar to those shown below to keep everything functioning properly.

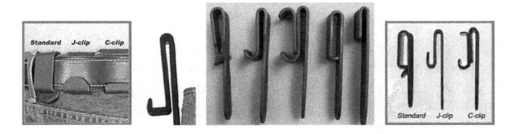

While there are 3 clips on the right, the one that says standard is actually a high-quality version of standard. You want proper holster hooks with an effective mechanical means of preventing the undesired removal. Notice the width of the J-hook at the bottom. Even though manufacturers make quality hooks, some are better. The length of the lip on the J-hooks varies, but the longer one is preferable.

Since you're trying to save your life, study the holsters and the clips they have on them, but some high-quality holsters may have additional interchangeable clips. In the picture, note the bottom of the standard clip loop where it is bent into a very distinct flat at the bottom to prevent sliding over the belt when the gun is being pulled from the holster. Further, even if it looks satisfactory, the strength of the materials mean a lot, so if the hook is very flexible, or *too flexible*, then the chances of failure are very high as compared to a more rigid hook that won't slip over the belt when the gun is drawn in a hurry. Now that you know, when you find one you like, then TEST and TEST and TEST what you're going to buy, but preferably BEFORE you buy it! LIVE or DIE! This same rule applies to a magazine carrier, pouch, or holster that uses clips!

Some people buy $5 holsters generally speaking, just like their bargain basement guns, that is, cheap and possibly not mechanically sound and functional. You may only get one chance to save your life. If we all avoid this inferior and dangerous stuff, maybe the manufacturers of such items will quit making them and make more of the higher quality items. But with all the imported *junk*, it probably won't change anything, so YOU are responsible for your own proper learning, selection, and training that is required to maintain your life! You are your own survival school! I'm only providing the facts! If I had no other holster available and just had to use such an inferior item even once, and it came out with my gun, I'd certainly hope there was a way to fire the gun through the holster since there would be no other option. If you have very little money available and think the cheaper clip-in holster might at least get you carrying, then I suggest saving a few bucks and giving up a few other items that people normally spend disposable income on until you buy a proper holster, but you can always buy another more preferred design later. Your life isn't negotiable, but the other things are.

There are holsters that have belt loops that actually snap around your belt for easy on and off and are pretty good for those working in offices and need to remove it sometimes, and then there are those that you have to remove your belt and pass the belt through the provided slots. For OWB, I prefer to remove my belt and put it through the slots, which are generally much stronger, but *my* needs are different from *yours*. While I was watching a movie one day, a cop had an OWB that snapped onto his belt, and in an intense struggle for his life, he reached for his gun and the snaps had apparently come open and the *gun and holster* were both gone when he needed the gun. If the slots don't align for your desired holster position due to the location of your pants belt loops, alternate your belt through the holster slot, then the pants belt loop, and then the holster slot again, which generally makes the alignment of your desired position work very close or within a couple of inches. Some holsters may have two sets of slots or at least 3 individual slots to change the angle of your gun, which is again called the CANT, depending on your preference for reach. While I love the cant, I avoid holsters that have a cartridge magazine carrier built into the holster *unless it's in a waist pack* or such similar device, or if it's a cross-draw holster, because if my gun is drawn, my shooting hand is occupied and it would be hard to avoid fumbling to access the spare magazine properly by using my support hand (the hand opposite your strong hand) while trying to reach across.

Always try to keep your shooting hand free of holding anything if you ever suspect a possible need to draw your sidearm because it will slow you down to change the items in your hand to the other hand, and the best option would be to drop anything in the shooting hand to the ground while you reach! Learn and always think!

At the same time, in reference to the magazine carriers that will clip onto your belt, I will AVOID them completely unless they also have belt slots through them. I was trying out a new double-magazine carrier by a name-brand company. While being out in a public building one day, I had to sit and wait for a while. When I sat down, my clip-on double-magazine carrier started slowly sliding off, and when I stood up and started walking down the hall, it fell out from under my jacket onto the floor fully loaded with 2, .45 ACP magazines, where two people looked down at it, but I just stooped down, picking it up and shoving it into a cargo pocket, and continued walking, avoiding attention, and I said nothing. It's worse than the cell phone cases you have piled up in the drawer. You buy one that they guarantee won't come off, and although I've paid twice the price for some that even look very secure, they still fall off. It's not a good feeling when you reach for something important (to save your life) and you discover it's not there. I AVOID clip-on holsters, no matter how good it might look! It has to be a proven item!

For the best concealment when you want to remove your windbreaker or jacket to avoid sweating in warm weather, you might opt for the IWB holster, but there are different styles available. An IWB like my Galco Summer Comfort is small and has two 1¾-inch belt loops with snaps somewhat close together but puts the gun inside the waist of your pants from just forward of the grip down to the muzzle, which helps hide it while the grip extends above the waist. Even if you're wearing a short jacket and stoop or bend over, this would otherwise *reveal your OWB gun holster* at times. The Galco Stinger belt holster is nearly identical to the Summer Comfort but has only one belt loop. If you wear an IWB holster that is *tuckable*, it has provisions so that you may also cover the grips of your holstered gun with a shirt and *tuck the shirt between the pants and the gun* that is in the holster, completely hiding your gun. This may be very handy during the summer months or living in warmer climates.

This holster is tuckable; that is, you can tuck your shirt between the long clips and the holster holding your gun so that it's completely concealed—even the grips are hidden—but you have to remember to practice drawing your gun while pulling the shirt from the holster clips. These clips are adjustable to allow for a deeper concealment if desired. Notice the yellow line that shows the waistline of your pants while the red arrow shows the depth of the shirt which can be adjusted all the way down to the blue arrow. There are concealed carry shirts that have Velcro breakaway slots that assist in getting to a fully concealed sidearm.

Galco also makes a single polymer J-hook tuckable holster, Tuck-n-go IWB, which catches the lower part of your belt to prevent the holster from coming out with your gun. While tuckable holsters have the metal or polymer clips that may show on your belt, if you're knowledgeable in holsters and you see it this way on somebody, you will most probably know what it is; however, some tuckable holsters have special or optional C clips that have the top and bottom of the C, over and under the edge of your belt, so your holster stays put if you draw your gun. Most people will probably never see the C-hooks even if looking very hard, giving you excellent concealment. They're small hooks but effective, and while some of the current C-hooks available seem too small for wider belts, Galco makes its C-hooks for its King Tuck IWB holster for up to 1¼-inch belts, which would be more appropriate for a dress belt as compared to casual while they make the C-hooks for their V-Hawk up to 1¾ inches. So maybe a phone call to the manufacturer might get them delivered quickly to meet your needs. In today's world of concealed carry, if I were the manufacturer, I'd make every hook for every holster available up to 2 inches.

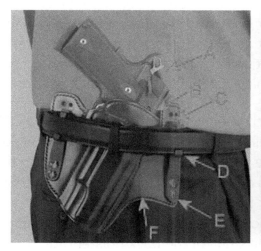 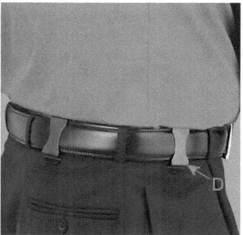

In the picture above left, the holster you see is normally invisible as shown in the picture on the right.

The Galco V-Hawk holster is illustrated above:

   A. *High leather to keep the cold gun from irritating you while assisting in a smooth draw against your body*
   B. *A double reinforced leather mouth so the holster doesn't collapse at the most inappropriate times*

C. *Tuckable holster clips so your shirt can be tucked between the gun holster and your pants for concealment*

D. *C-clips in the left picture make the knowledge of you wearing a holster less obvious if at all*

E. *Interchangeable clips, an obviously high-quality holster*

F. *Thick high quality and very durable leather with very strong stitching. In the picture on the right, (D) shows the metal clips which are totally obvious to anyone knowledgeable, compared to the 4 tiny hooks being visible on the edge of the belt with the C-hooks, which most people will be totally unaware.*

Crossbreed makes a super-tuck holster made of a combination of leather and Kydex, with a leather extension above and between the grip of your gun and your body to prevent sweating on your gun due to the temperature variations while being against your body, and the leather above the holster also helps prevent clothing from snagging under parts on the gun. There's also a cross-draw holster that attaches on the opposite side of your strong hand, so you have to reach with your strong hand across to the other side, and they have angles (CANTS) on them to make gripping the gun easy, but design varies according to the manufacturer. These cross-draw holsters are very easy to access while driving as compared to some that might otherwise be more difficult to draw your gun when seated in a vehicle. They do make holsters with metal clips that attach them under your steering column or on the lower edge of your dashboard, making them easily and immediately accessible to the driver, but you have to check your state laws regarding the way your gun needs to be carried within a vehicle. One thing that I find advantageous in wearing a holster such as the Summer Comfort on the kidney is by lifting your jacket up and tucking the jacket between your body and the grip of the gun while seated in a vehicle. It gives you very good and somewhat immediate access to the gun even in a seated position, while not having to mess with the seat belt or fumbling to try to get into or under your jacket. Just remember, when you leave the vehicle, to pull the jacket back over the gun.

There's also the small of the back holster, which also has the gun angled with a CANT, so that access for the strong hand is easier. This makes it very easy to conceal if covered, but bending over quite a bit might put it in view. While some people like this option of locating the holster at the small of the back, many are afraid to try this method due to complaints from those *including policemen* who have been knocked onto their backs, which pushed the gun into the small of the back, causing a spinal injury, but then we do what we think works for us effectively because we might never be knocked onto our backs. The small of the back holster requires an extended rearward reach, so before you spend your money, make sure you can do it easily and you might even ask to try it out at the gun shop. So when holster-shopping, you bring your gun along to make sure of what will and what will not work the way you might want.

The ankle holster is on the left, the small of back holster in the middle, and a Kydex paddle holster on the right. Whatever your preferences are, I'm sure there's a way to accommodate you; however, beware that you need to be very effective in drawing your gun for an emergency, and hopefully it will be in the holster when you reach for it. Some Kydex paddle holsters have an adjustable cant.

There are dozens of ammo magazine carriers available in either single—or double-magazine capacity. Study before you buy, but you'll probably end up with a couple at minimum if you're not sure before you get it.

There's the ankle holster which works well for some people who don't mind the weight of their gun on the ankle and even the ankle-model holsters that lace into your boots. I've seen short-barreled .45 ACPs in them. There's also the ankle magazine holster, which can hold as many as two spare magazines or a magazine and a knife! You might also consider using a large pocketknife holster to carry a spare magazine, depending on the caliber, and while it would look normal on your belt, you would have a spare for a reload. These might be handy if you have a tuckable holster, but you won't want to be carrying a visible spare magazine around due to deep concealment or carrying it in your pocket. Galco makes a tuckable magazine carrier too with a J-hook that will fit a 1¼-inch belt. The only difficulty sometimes is not only getting into your shirt for your gun, but also getting back into it to retrieve the spare magazine, but you will have to decide, depending on your own particular needs. Wear a normal-length shirt for tuckable holsters to avoid too much material bunched up between you and the gun. I never wear a belt smaller than 1½ inches, so it does seem that Galco only offers certain items for those wearing clothes with a thinner belt, other than casual wear with a wider belt, which is a sure loss of many sales to them because I'd buy some of those items if they were available.

While we're on ankle-mounted devices, there's even an ankle wallet that could really be handy if away from home. No matter what holster you decide on, if it's leather, make sure it has a reinforced mouth—the opening where the gun goes in—so that you can re-holster it with one hand, without looking, after sufficient practice. This will also prevent the mouth from bending into a V such as the one I mentioned earlier that accidentally discharged the Glock. Some of the very soft holsters might appear to be comfortable and cheap, but they might also be too unsafe for your needs. Some of the nylon holsters fold-shut when the gun is drawn, and re-holstering your gun will be rather difficult if not impossible without the use of both hands. Some somewhat generic holsters might fit *assorted guns*, but I would also avoid these for concealed carry, which requires everything to be in its proper place and properly tuned for a smooth gun presentation if needed. A word of wisdom while you study various ways to carry your sidearm concealed is to remember that while we want our gun hidden from view, we have to consider the circumstances for different days and events. A gun having the grip covered over with a shirt in a tuckable holster will be much more difficult and slower to present from such deep concealment than one worn inside the waistband with the grip exposed for quick access under your windbreaker or one worn in an OWB holster under your jacket or loose un-tucked shirt. Shoulder holsters are fast to access too, depending on your preferences. Sometimes we need to conceal differently, but we must always consider our ability to respond to a deadly threat quickly. The speed of deadly encounters is only mere seconds!

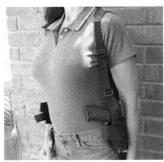

See where some shoulders attach to your belt for extra retention. They are available for either revolvers or semiautomatic pistols.

Some gun and magazine holsters both have a tension control screw that allows you to tighten the holding ability of the holster against your magazine or your gun, assuring they *should* be there when you reach for them; however, there are also gun retention straps, otherwise called thumb breaks, which reach over the back of your gun or across the hammer and the slide, depending on which gun you have, preventing the hammer from accidentally dropping on the firing pin or helping to hold your gun in place if you might be in an active situation, or you just plain want it safe in case someone tries to make a grab for it. The tension screws are not necessarily set from the factory and have to be checked for proper gripping ability each time you use the holster, but some manufacturers recommend using a drop of nail polish on the screw threads while you can even use mild Loctite thread locker available at a hardware store to maintain proper adjustment, but avoid using Loctite strong set on the adjustment screws. Many of these holsters are available in several assorted styles.

There are also the properly designed Kydex holsters, like a sturdy polymer or plastic, that are made by Blackhawk and many others. Some of their designs will lock your gun in by compression over the trigger guard, or you need to unlock your gun while pulling it from the holster, depending on your preferences. It works for many, but I don't use it because I already thumb off my safety in my drawing routine, and if I ever decide to use one personally, I'll have to make sure I have extensive practice with it before using it for concealed carry. For someone new to carry it would work just fine because you're developing your technique, but some have a paddle that you need to depress with your finger, which is half way down the holster alongside the trigger guard, making it impossible for IWB carry.

A young guy was recently running his video camera while going through his gun-drawing procedures from a holster that locked in his 1911 Kimber .45. In his normal routine to draw, he thumbs the safety off before drawing the gun. While the camera was running, he went through his entire routine. He thumbed the safety off while he gripped the gun and tried to pull it from the holster, but his finger missed the release on the locking mechanism, holding the gun in the holster, so his gun wouldn't come out, but since he had a grip on the gun, which was still securely locked into the holster, as he was pulling his hand up initially, it caused his grip to start to loosen and the finger that missed the locking mechanism was pulled into the trigger guard while he was still in the process of the draw, and it discharged the .45. He accidentally shot himself through the holster into the top of his right thigh and out just above the knee. He was very lucky that was all that happened. It goes to show you that while he had the camera running, he was under pressure to do it fast and smooth, probably to show his buddies, but instead he fumbled the whole process, which *can* easily happen if under the stress of an attack. It has confused me a bit in seeing people use a gun that has no external safety because they don't want to turn one off, but they have that very same gun in a holster with such a locking mechanism. No matter what kind of a holster you think will work for you, you might go to the gun shop and ask to try your gun in several style holsters that you are considering, to see how well it might work for you. Even though holsters are available for just a few dollars, I would expect to pay anywhere from about $80 to $125 quite easily and possibly more for a proper, strong, and secure holster. Prices are usually more for larger guns than they are for smaller ones. This includes off-the-shelf holsters or specially designed custom holsters and shoulder holsters. No matter how good the holster is, your developed skills are what's going to save you. Practice!

For ladies' handbags that have internal holsters, you can pay anywhere upwards all the way to several hundred dollars. Remember it's your life! Back in the 1980s, I met a man who owned a security company and also invented the ladies' carry purse with an internal hidden pocket and a holster that snapped into it, so I had him make one for my wife for her snub-nosed Smith and Wesson .357 magnum. It had a Velcro seal along the edge, and if you yanked the edge open, the gun was immediately available. From viewing the purse from its normal opening on the top, you viewed two separate compartments, not knowing that the divider inside was actually a secret pocket accessible from the end. It was extremely high quality and, at that time, cost me only $85 compared to current pricing of hundreds. His original intention was for policewomen to use, but it really caught on since then. While shoulder holsters vary in design and style, they mount a gun horizontally so you can grab the grip easily, and some hold the gun vertically with the grip high under the armpit and attach to the belt at the bottom end of the holster. Many of the horizontal mounts seem too loose and floppy for me, although I've used them for my Ruger GP100 .357 magnums. I've seen people open their jacket and have BIG guns with long barrels in vertical shoulder holsters, so I'm sure glad they're not the bad guys. Everyone thinks differently, and each one of us has our own life's circumstances, such as my own where I cannot run from anyone if I ever had to because of my old gunshot wounds, so I have to make a stand and either win or lose if something comes down, and I most assuredly prefer to be on the winning edge here.

There are dozens of concealed gun purses in the market in assorted designs and colors to choose from. They have a special access pocket for fast retrieval.

There are also holsters that you can wear under your pants, which consist of a band around the waist with a pocket that rests inside your pants in the front, center groin area, which might be especially helpful for someone who sits in a wheelchair. People wear them while they are out and with their carry gun in that very center pocket, but your belt must be loose enough to allow you to reach inside the waistband and get a grip on your gun, which I'm sure will take considerable practice, as is normally the case. Surprisingly, people even carry full-size 1911 .45s in there. When selecting a pocket holster for inside-the-pocket carry, the main idea here is not only to protect the trigger from causing accidental discharge but to also keep the shape of the gun from printing (appearing as a gun shape) through your pants, shirt, or jacket, so nobody can see an image appearing to be that of a gun showing through your clothes. An important thing to remember is that when using a pocket holster, every time you sit down, your gun is pointed along your thigh wherever your knee is pointed. For many people, pocket carry isn't as efficient and fast as carrying in a holster on your belt, so you have to decide what's for YOU. For the illusion of carrying and pulling a wallet, they have a pocket wallet-holster combination that actually covers and holds your small gun but is designed in the shape of a leather wallet with a finger access hole to be able to fire after pulling it out. These are available for small pocket guns from .25 through .380 calibers. Never carry a revolver in a pocket carry holster unless it has the hammer spur removed to prevent snags, or else carry a revolver that has an internal hammer or firing pin with a closed frame such as a double-action-only revolver. Accidental discharges do happen in a pocket without a pocket holster, and you never know where it's pointed while accidental discharges even happen to police officers!

These are pocket holsters. The one on the left is a wallet holster designed to fire while drawing the wallet without trying to remove the gun from it.

There are various waist packs available that have a holster attached on the inside, and some have quick-pull opening devices. These come in assorted sizes being small, medium, or large, according to your gun size. When someone experienced with firearms (such as a thug) sees a waist pack appearing to be similar in design to many that are known for having such internal holsters, they might normally assume that you have a gun inside, just the same as a policeman who will also assume you could have a gun. If you must use a waist or shoulder pack, try to be careful and always be on guard in case of trouble because you might be the first victim. Many of the waist packs designed for concealed carry look similar in design and very square in appearance, making them somewhat easy to determine or to assume what they might be, but there are some that look angled on the ends, being very close to the appearance of a regular fanny pack, so it might pay to shop before you buy even if it takes another trip or two, or dollar or two. If you pick one, it could be to your advantage if it has an additional pocket for normal use to give the appearance of an everyday pack as you go in and out of it for whatever you might need, which may also take any serious observations off you since you're already reaching in and out of it. I saw one particular fanny pack designed for carrying your gun, which was a pretty good design, where they had a full-size .45 1911 inside, but the length of the 5-inch barrel actually extended internally down into the angled extension of the pack.

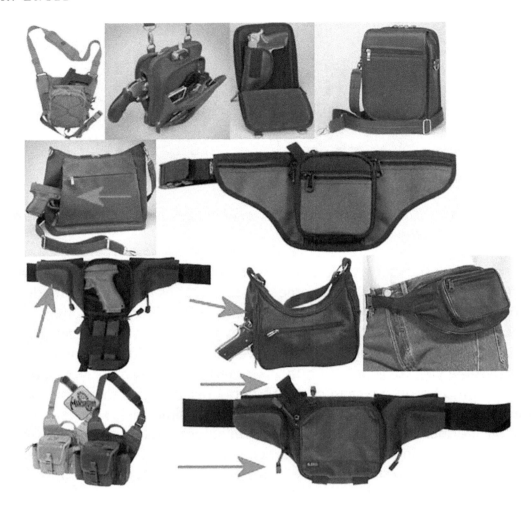

For some unknown reason, all the manufacturers make their gun bags, totes, and waist packs for concealed carry. No matter who the maker is, they all seem to think we need a square bag, but we don't. It's so very easy to assume most of these are concealing guns because they all have the same square appearance. Watch when you see them in the streets, and then you'll start to understand how easy they are to pick out, even in a crowd. Notice the waist pack on the left that has the gun with the muzzle shoved into the angled side, thereby reducing the thought of it concealing a carry gun. Some even have the quick pull tabs and releases to open the compartments. Be cautious in what you do. We want to have the element of surprise on them, not having them surprise us. If you buy any such device, look for the unobvious and the very different. The purses here provide the best chance of not being discovered, but even then only the ones that have normal-appearing hardware and rings on them, not those that look as if they are ready for combat gear to be attached and clipped on.

I find it very convenient to use many items not normally designed for carrying a handgun, like being zipped in a small Bible case, maybe with a happy face on it and a church bulletin sticking out of the pocket. Or maybe a very small ladies' purse with a cell phone pocket attached. You can put a small gun in the purse and a spare magazine in the cell phone pocket. These can be on the passenger seat beside you, and nobody would be the wiser as compared to someone having a plastic gun case on the seat with his gun in it, or a range bag, or something similar, indicating it has shooting accessories in it. Be creative, but make sure it's legally within your state law. Some artificial books that are hollowed out internally look too fake on the binding, but you can make one from a real book without too much difficulty or glue a real book cover over one of the fake-looking books. While the NRA sells these books in sets of 2, being two different sizes, if the criminal knows anything about guns (and he probably does), when he sees the books sold by the NRA, they have the insight to put different titles on the binding, but then they blew it by putting the year the NRA was founded in big bold numbers on the binding too, so the minute you see the book that says 1871 in big numbers, you already know there's something inside. If you have to leave the vehicle for any reason and cannot have your gun in a holster on your body that particular day due to carry prohibitions in your state, you don't want someone looking through a window and seeing any gun accessories, especially a range bag or gun case, and knocking out your window while committing a smash and grab while grabbing and running off with your weapon.

They will never expect the little Bible case above to be carrying a 4"-barreled .45 with a spare 10 round magazine! Be creative! It looks NOTHING like a normal gun case!

Would YOU expect two spare .45 caliber 10 round magazines to be in the Juicy Fruit box? It might even be on a car seat beside you for easy access! Be aware of state laws on carrying your gun in your vehicle!

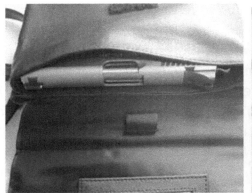

This small women's purse A with the built-in cell phone pouch B on the outside would never be expected to carry a 4" barreled .45 with a spare magazine in the cell phone pouch! I bought it for $5 at a flea market! Be creative!

For that very reason, even though I'm a LIFE member of the National Rifle Association, I don't put any kind of logo or sticker on my vehicle, indicating that I favor or use firearms, so they won't break into it at any time while I'm not in it, regardless as to whether there's actually a gun in it or not. The bad guys look for indicators of guns, especially in cars and pickups parked outside of places where you're prohibited from carrying, because they very well know that where the law says you cannot carry your gun, they would normally assume there *could* be some guns left behind in the vehicle if they see such a gun or gun organization membership signs on your vehicle. If you have no such item on your vehicle, they may just move over a space or two and hit the vehicle that's advertising the owner's love for guns. It's like the thugs who frequent the local convenient store parking lots, looking for a vehicle that's running while the driver is in the store—I see it occasionally—and then they drive away with your car. It's *your fault.* Sad to say a police officer did this one day while I watched. He left his car running. So if I was watching what he did, then anyone desiring an unmarked police car with all the police equipment, computer, and guns could have easily stolen it. Everybody always thinks well; I'll just do it this time! Once is too many just like one confrontation resulting in your KILLER and yourself shooting it out because somebody is probably going to die, which again happens only once!

Once you start carrying, you always have to think gun and be aware of your actions, like never leaving a gun in any kind of case in plain view if at all possible when you are not in the vehicle. In reference to bumper stickers, signs, and the like that say such things like "If you are found here at night, you will be found here in the morning," or "Survivors will be shot again," or "Protected by Smith and Wesson," and so forth, if you are ever forced to fire in self-defense, the perpetrator's attorney and/ or the prosecutor may very well use those signs or stickers against you in trying to make their case. Advertising your guns and your willingness to shoot isn't going to scare away the thug, but instead let's assume it may always work against you. By the guns being prohibited from carry in various places when you have legally obtained a license to carry, they are actually making situations more unsafe due to having to put the gun in and out of its concealed holster so many times, thereby handling a handgun so many more times per day than you would normally have to. This is subjecting you to the possibility of accidents many more times, or others discovering your sidearm, so you really have to think gun all the time as a responsible and safe concealed carry license holder.

There are also T-shirts and underwear available with built-in pockets on the sides for deep concealment. Some have the same style pocket on both sides, and your gun slides in vertically very nicely and your shirt covers it easily, one being made by 5.11 tactical that makes a great deal of accessories. There are other shirts that have a Velcro strap across the back of the gun to hold it in securely and horizontally on one side and a magazine pocket on the other side; however, I prefer the one without the Velcro and the identical pockets on both sides by 5.11. This gives you the option of using either side; it's tough enough to have to get inside your shirt to retrieve your gun in a hurry, but you have to worry about coordinating the horizontal gun, the Velcro, and gripping the gun with the same hand; it may not work as well as the 5.11. For your convenience, removing the inside of a pocket from a jacket or windbreaker allows you to reach inside and go for the gun in the holster, rather than having to open a Velcro pocket seal and then try to reach inside. Use creativity and commonsense when developing your plans.

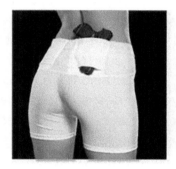 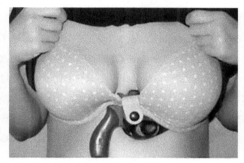 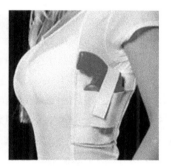

Wearing your gun at the back of your waist or kidney area works very good on windy days because if you have a holster outside the waistband on your strong side hip or an IWB holster with the grip of the gun showing above the belt, then when the windblown shirt, windbreaker, or jacket flies off to either side, flopping in the breeze, it doesn't expose your concealed sidearm. The gun in the bra may be another good tactic, but whatever you do, make sure you practice retrieving your gun in many practice runs, or you'll certainly fumble the issue in an emergency.

There are what they call belly-band holsters too. It wraps around your belly and has a pocket in the front, so you can raise your shirt or sweatshirt and grasp your gun, and they even hold a spare magazine. They have different manufacturers, and some are lightweight and some heavyweight, but I've heard complaints that the heavier one makes you sweat, but if this is something you think might be good, especially if you're a walker or jogger, the lightweight might be good for a smaller gun and the heavier band for the heavier gun. They sell a jogger's holster, which looks like a square pouch on your chest with straps over your shoulders, holding it on your chest, but it's advertised wearing it over a sweatshirt. This certainly alerts the bad guys, and they most probably know what's inside the pouch, so beware and try to always be conscious of what's going on around you, and *don't advertise* that you are carrying a gun. Instead of scaring off an attack, it could get you killed, making it much easier for the thug rather than you're popping the element of surprise on him, and personally, I love it when the assailant gets the surprise sprung on them! Use commonsense!

While many manufacturers sell some of the very same holster designs, you might check out some of the differences like thicker and stronger leather, reinforced mouth openings, and double stitching as compared to single stitching, but tight-molded shapes to your own gun are advantageous, and concealability options are great due to holsters being tuckable.

If you're really in need of having some kind of gun with you, but with your activities for the day ruling out a holster of any kind, depending on what you're doing, they have baseball caps of various styles that have Velcro closures on internal secret pockets, called pocket caps. My buddy bought me a pocket cap that says "Navy Retired" on the front, but if you look inside, there's a tab on the internal headband, and if you pull the tab opening the invisible Velcro seal, a large internal pocket opens up. I had the perfect use for this! I went into one of the local gun shops, took a small micro-sized .22 single-action revolver-style gun made by North American Arms, put it in the pocket, closed the Velcro, and put it back on my head. To my surprise, it worked! This could be good for absolute emergencies. Someone could search you thoroughly, and if they don't take your cap off and open the Velcro seal on the normally invisible pocket, they won't see the small bulge, which is only visible on the inside of your cap due to the micro-sized .22 caliber gun, and they would assume you had nothing on you, but you also have the option to hide anything there, including your money, a knife, or whatever you desire. The element of surprise usually wins many battles, like the thug I struck between the eyes and knocked him out, when he didn't expect it, after his continuous attempts made on me when he was actually ready to fight, so always expect something, especially in a bad neighborhood. Never give any indication of having anything on you *until it's too late* for the thug, making sure you don't miss the opportunity to counter or prevent an attack. There are several styles of pocket caps available too, so you might have to actually put a snap or Velcro on those that come without one, or call the seller to see what else they might have with a Velcro closure.

Other things you might do is, put one of these micro revolvers in a cell phone case or a handheld GPS case and attach it to your belt; who'd know? But to use such a small handgun in an emergency, you have to be able to put the bullet in the right place, like that of a real pro. If you're holding or wearing binoculars around your neck, you can conceal a handgun in the binocular case over your shoulder. You can place a small gun in a work glove held in your hand or in a pocket on a potholder or hot glove kept on the counter in the kitchen, if no children frequent the house, or in just about anything, being sure not to put your gun in any kind of container that a thief might otherwise want because of what it says on the cover. A visit to the local locksmith shop might pay off because they tend to have items with secret compartments such as various aerosol spray cans with assorted labels that you would normally see on the shelf in the stores with real products in them, but the locksmith shops sell them revamped into a secret container with a bottom that unscrews and gives you room for a couple of spare magazines, a small micro-sized gun, speed loaders, or just about anything including emergency money. Just make sure the label is appropriate for wherever it's stored, such as your house or your vehicle such as WD-40, engine degreaser or furniture wax, or whatever they may have on hand. You can always read the outside of the package and check out the manufacturer's Web site for more available options.

When you're carrying with your preferred holster, if you need a shirt to cover your gun, there are such shirts offered for this purpose being a few inches longer or having Velcro or magnetic closures for slits along both sides of the shirt for quick opening and access, but there's another way to save probably hundreds of dollars. If you choose your size in a particular shirt and you're somewhat average in size, you can buy it for a TALL person for just the cost of a dollar or two more, saving you more bucks where such shirts might be selling for $60 to $85 each as compared to $10 to $30, depending on as to whether it's a T-shirt or casual or dress shirt, but you have to decide on IWB, tuckable, or OWB, whatever the situation is going to be. It would be advisable to have something for each type of holster, depending on the weather. You can have a holster OWB or IWB and tie a shirt or sweatshirt around your waist to cover everything. You see people with shirts tied in this fashion all the time while taking a walk through the park or around the block a few times. There's also concealed carry vests designed with numerous pockets, inside pockets and outside pockets, but if walking around wearing just a concealed carry vest, many people know what these are. The vests are slightly different in length and sell for as much as $45 to $100 or even more quite easily, and they vary a little in their design. You can always pick the one you like and load everything in it that you want on you, making sure it's short enough, and put it on under a jacket. And when you return home, just remove it, and it's ready for the next trip. During winter, the easiest time of year to carry concealed, it is most difficult to draw from winter clothing due to the thickness and stiffness of the clothing. They sell assorted winter jackets for concealed carry but, depending on how and where you want to carry, change what you might prefer in design. Make sure of what you really want to carry your sidearm in because when people are new to having this new ability, they tend to think this would be good, and that would be good, but then after you accumulate a handful of such accessories, you realize, by actually doing, that many of these are not what you really prefer to do. So save your money until you've given it extensive thought on its practicality so you don't pile them in the never-ending accessory drawer that already has that pile of cell phone cases that every salesman has promised that it wouldn't fall off, so you have to wear them to find out that they all fall off anyway. Understanding that all these cell phone cases fall off, think of the weight of a gun attached by a similar attaching device, and most of us have already cursed many of the cell phone cases due to our experience. A foolproof anchoring system or method increases your chances of survival!

The high leather tab on the back of Winthrop's holster, as shown in the center, prevents your clothing from sliding up into and under the parts on the side of your sidearm. In my many practice runs, a few times, my shirt got caught as it slid under the slide release during my daily activities. It's certainly not a good feeling to have the shirt hung in the firearm when you try to pull it out for an emergency. The high leather would certainly be a good choice for a semiautomatic (http:// www. winthropholsters.com). You can even get *custom* holsters made from Winthrop Holsters. Winthrop takes great pride in their holsters because they know how much you depend on them. They use heavy leather with extensive stitching and are incredibly reasonably priced. Study holsters before you buy and, by all means, ask the manufacturer if you have any questions because they know more about holsters than anybody because it's their business. Be creative, and most of all be safe, and hopefully we'll all live a long life.

For those confined to the use of a wheelchair, there are a variety of wheelchair holsters.

Shooting from Cover

If you're involved in a defensive shooting incident, timing is important. Taking advantage of the best cover you can find in an emergency might help, but don't take your eyes off your assailant. If you're right-handed, shoot around the right edges of cover because if you go to the left, you have to expose the width of your body to get your right hand out to fire. This also works the opposite where left-handed shooters shoot around the left edge. Don't reach through windows with your sidearm or any gun for that matter, but shoot from behind the window to prevent exposing your body and preventing any gun grabs. While it's been established that so many rounds will go through multiple panels in an automobile, remember, the safest place in using your car for cover is behind the engine, NOT the car doors, or you may end up dead. I watched a test of many calibers, and they all went through car doors, so be careful. Remember to try to prevent the thugs from getting behind you, and never run between them. Bullets go through walls, doors, furniture, and so many other things that you really need to study to know and understand.

Sound Suppressors (Silencers)

You see silencers on firearms in the movies, and they really don't function the way Hollywood does it. Bullets that fly at supersonic speeds break the sound barrier, so you hear the loud bang associated with the firing of a firearm. Silencers use what they call subsonic ammunition, which is loaded with propellants to fly slower at subsonic speeds, below the speed of sound to first take the initial bang away from breaking the sound barrier. Then the silencer is designed with a series of internal baffles and wipers and other porous materials, filling additional space. The baffles create small individual chambers and the wipers seal between the chambers to trap the escaping gas from the subsonic round, and the sound diminishes as it filters out to the atmosphere through these baffled chambers and through the porous filter. The bang of an already subsonic round is further reduced and muffled through the silencer to a small pop so it doesn't sound like gunfire. Revolvers cannot be silenced due to the barrel/cylinder gap where the flash and sound escapes despite Hollywood using them all the time. Many claim the silencer reduces the power of the round fired, but a Navy SEAL put it to the test and found the difference negligible. Never trust Hollywood in technical firearms issues!

Notice the muzzle flash escaping from between the cylinder/barrel gap where the sound also comes through.

The semiautomatic pistol above has a sound suppressor/silencer screwed to the barrel to muffle the crack of the subsonic round to a pop so it doesn't sound like gunfire.

Silencers are a consideration for shooting indoors like you will be doing during a home invasion to keep the sound that is enclosed indoors from being overbearing, but it takes a special application and fee to the BATFE (Bureau of Alcohol, Tobacco, Firearms, and Explosives) to own one.

Properties of the Human Eye Relevant to Sight Alignment The Eye in General

The principal difficulties which confront the shooter during aiming are determined by the inherent characteristics of the organ of vision, the eye, and its work as an optical apparatus during the aiming process. It is well known that the aiming process makes very exacting demands upon the vision; consistency and degree of accuracy are directly dependent upon the sharpness of vision and the conditions determining them. Therefore, it is necessary for the shooter to have knowledge of certain optical properties of the eye. The optical imperfections of the eye also include nearsightedness, farsightedness, and astigmatism, the existence of which also hinders the correct focusing of the optical system of the eye and the obtaining of sharp images of objects upon the retina.

Normal Eye: If the eye is constructed in such a way that rays of light entering it in a parallel beam are focused exactly on the retina without any effort at accommodation, we say that the eye is a normal one.

Nearsighted Eye: The eye is nearsighted if the rays entering it in a parallel beam are focused in front of the retina. Nearsightedness is caused either by the fact that the eyeball is excessively long from front to back or by the fact that the eye has great refracting force or by a combination of both factors. Nearsightedness can be corrected comparatively easily by means of eyeglasses. Many pistol shooters suffer from nearsightedness, but this defect of vision, after being corrected by the proper choice of eyeglasses; does not prevent them from achieving record- making competitive results.

Farsighted Eye: The eye is farsighted if the rays entering it are focused in back of the retina. This can occur either as a result of the eye having a weak refracting force or due to the fact that the eye is too short from front to back or by a combination of both factors. In such an instance, in order for the rays to focus upon the retina, they must enter the eye in a converging beam, and, therefore, a farsighted eye sees near objects worst of all. This type of eye is harder to correct, but eyeglasses help it overcome the difficulty. Shooter's suffering from farsightedness will see the sights very poorly. The characteristic complaint of farsighted persons is that the rear notch seems to fuse with the front sight.

Motion-induced Blindness: Now this is something that came to my attention that was somewhat difficult for many people to believe, but since it is a true phenomenon, I felt the necessity to include this due to the possibility of having a lethal encounter with numerous assailants while on the move. According to Professor Michael Bach PhD, "Steady fixation favors disappearance, blinks or gaze shifts induce reappearance. All in all reminiscent of the Troxler effect but stronger and more resistant to residual eye movements."

Go to this Web site and study what you see: http://www.msf-usa.org/motion.html

The page above is provided by Prof. Michael Bach PhD, Ophthalmology, University of Freiburg, Germany, from his collection of optical Illusions and visual phenomena.

Poor Visibility Firing: Poor visibility firing with any weapon is difficult since shadows can be misleading to the shooter. This is mainly true—a half hour before dark and a half hour before dawn—where there is insufficient light to see the sights effectively and insufficient darkness for night sights to illuminate. Even though the weapon is a short-range weapon, the hours of darkness and poor visibility further decrease its effect. To compensate, the shooter must use the following three principles of night vision.

1. Dark Adaptation: This process conditions the eyes to see during poor visibility conditions. The eyes usually need about 30 minutes to become 98-percent dark- adapted in a totally darkened area.
2. **Off-center Vision:** When looking at an object in daylight, a person looks directly at it. However, at night, he would see the object only for a few seconds. To see an object in darkness, he must concentrate on it while looking at 6° to 10° away from it.
3. Scanning: This is the short, abrupt, irregular movement of the shooter's eyes around an object or area every 4 to 10 seconds. When artificial illumination is used, the shooter uses night fire techniques to engage targets, since targets seem to shift without moving.

Effects of Lighting Conditions in Your Sights

Many new or inexperienced shooters do not realize that light conditions can affect your shooting accuracy. A change in the light conditions can cause a shooter to aim at the incorrect aiming point since we shoot at what we see. What appears to be the aiming point of center mass on the target or killer may actually be several inches higher or lower or left or right.

No matter how the target appears, maintaining a center-mass hold ensures the best chances for an effective shot. He must know the degree and the conditions under which the optical imperfections of the eye can affect the accuracy of aiming.

Mirage: Mirage can be explained a couple of different ways:

1. Mirage can be blamed for shooting groups in a target very close, but they look like they are one hole and make it difficult to see and focus on the point of impact. Then it starts to appear distorted, and you may get a stray or flier outside the group.
2. Mirage can be heat waves viewed by the eyes similar to what you see on the road while driving in warm weather, where it looks like the heat is radiating from the pavement up into the air while sometimes appearing to be a wet spot on a dry road but distorts the target. Mirage can be seen in various circumstances including through your sights when trying to achieve a proper sight picture. At high temperatures, ground mirage can cause a target to appear indistinct and drift from side to side while the mirage can distort the shape or appearance of the target. Mirage such as heat waves may also be seen radiating up from the heated barrel of the firearm, causing the shooter difficulty in seeing the sights clearly. This may also give the appearance of a distorted front sight post or blade. Some sight designs might help you improve, but the problem will always be there.

Bright Light: Bright light conditions exist under a clear blue sky with no fog or haze present to filter the sunlight. Bright light can make the target appear smaller and further away, and, as a result, it's easy to overestimate the range. Bright light shining from above makes the front sight post appear shorter, and bright light from the side makes the front sight post appear narrower. This affects aiming because the shooter will aim at the center mass using the perceived tip of the front sight post, which is altered due to the effects of light.

Haze: Haze exists when smog, fog, dust, smoke, or humidity is present. Haze is not bright, but it can be uncomfortable to the eyes. Haze can make a target appear indistinct, making it difficult to establish the sight picture.

Overcast: Overcast conditions exist when a solid layer of clouds blocks the sun. The amount of light changes as the cloud cover thickens. Overcast conditions make a target appear larger and closer. As a result, it is easy to underestimate range.

Light Overcast: Light overcast conditions exist when no blue sky is visible and a thin layer of clouds is present. In light overcast, both the target and the sights appear very distinct. Light overcast is comfortable on the eyes with no glare present, making PROBABLY THE BEST LIGHT CONDITION FOR SHOOTING.

Dark Heavy Overcast: Dark heavy overcast conditions exist when the sky is completely overcast with most of the light blotted out by the clouds. As the overcast thickens, it becomes difficult to identify the target from the surroundings.

Scattered Clouds: Scattered cloud conditions exist when the clouds are broken up into small patches with the sun appearing at times between the clouds. A shooter's eyes may have problems adjusting between a target that is brightly lit and one that is shadowed.

Moving Clouds: Moving clouds exist when scattered clouds move across the sky rapidly, making the sun appear periodically. Rapidly moving clouds can fatigue the eyes due to the rapid changes from bright light to shadows. This condition is probably the most difficult to contend with because the light changes rapidly. If the situation permits, this condition can be compensated by selecting one of the two light conditions (bright light or shadow) to fire. The best results are obtained if each shot is fired under the same light condition.

Sunglasses, Eyeglasses, and Shooting Glasses

The colored glasses on the left are shooting glasses, and those on the right are sunglasses, a major difference in chemical makeup.

Before we get into the sights, let's address those who try to wear their sunglasses all the time because it really may be more of a disadvantage if their life were threatened than they ever realize. Crisp vision and clarity are important for shooting! If you ever suspect a possible encounter approaching, unless you're sure the sunglasses will be advantageous, it would be very advisable to remove the sunglasses and secure them elsewhere because while they may seriously interfere with your vision, you may miss your shot or even hit someone else in the vicinity, which can be a double whammy because even if you hit or miss an innocent bystander, the round you fired has missed the guy shooting at you, so you may get KILLED. On TV, the guy looks cool with his sunglasses while he shoots everybody, but, in reality, he wouldn't be seeing very well. Your sight pictures should be observed with no glasses other than prescription glasses, but if your prescription lenses are transition lenses, there may be disadvantages. Transition lenses always keep a slight tint, even in low-light conditions, which is not enough to be a problem, even at night. If you have poor night vision or are frequently in dimly lit conditions, you may prefer the slightly higher light output of clear lenses. Transition lenses do not change right away, and when you go from a light location to a dark one or from dark to light location, it can take two to three minutes for the lenses to fully change. For a casual day-to-day wear, this is not a problem since lighting conditions usually change very slowly, but where you need to see clearly in rapidly changing lighting, transition lenses may not be the best choice. Transition lenses don't respond to visible light, but, instead, they react to changes in ultraviolet (UV) light. If you are outside, they work well to protect your eyes in UV-saturated sunlight. Car windows, however, block most of the UV light. As a result, your progressive lenses will not work in your car. In some cases, this may be an advantage, since the glasses won't darken unpredictably in response to headlights. You have to be able to see the sight picture very clearly. Later, and after you have your gun and are heading out to the shooting range, there are shooting glasses that will improve your vision by improving the contrast, but there are different colors that different people may prefer to improve their vision under different lighting conditions. At last count, there were over 35 different brands of shooting glasses on the market today, and each one has quite a few different models to choose from. While you need a pair of clear safety glasses to keep the ejected brass from hitting you in the eye, they make frames with interchangeable lenses of assorted colors, which might be a good choice, so you can study the colors under the various lighting conditions and get familiar with what works. While some of the manufacturers will make you a pair of prescription shooting glasses, the glass lenses are not impact resistant. The preferred lens is made from a polycarbonate lens material, but it's so expensive; most prescription shooting glasses get made from CR-39 plastic. There's one easy option to cut down on expenses until you decide what you'd like to do. Some manufacturers make what they call over the glasses shooting glasses, where the actual shooting glasses easily fit right over your prescription eyeglasses completely, and allow you to see differently while not affecting your prescription.

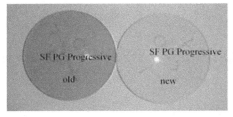 

Above left are transition lenses, and on the right are shooting glasses over eyeglasses.

Yellow Hues: Yellow is one of the most popular colors of shooting lenses because it helps with contrast by blocking blue light and enhances depth perception for contrast and haze. Many target shooters like yellow lenses because the yellow tint helps bring out the orange color of the targets. Orange, amber, and amber-brown lenses also block blue light and work well on cloudy days. A good rule to follow is that the lower the light, the brighter the yellow for the lens color. I love the yellow!

Purple and Red Hues: Purple isn't a common cosmetic tint but works well for shooting, especially mixed with a neutral gray color. Vermilion-gray mix is a common shade used for shooting glasses because it brings out the orange in a target, especially when there is background contrast like foliage or trees. By itself, vermilion also highlights and contrasts. It is helpful to test the different versions of purples and reds to see which works best for your needs.

Additional Colors and Considerations: Plain gray works well under some conditions, especially bright sunlight. Gray tint is often used in sunglasses because gray is a neutral color that helps you to see colors without distorting them. Gray also helps to reduce glare but won't improve contrast. Polarization is not a color, but polarized lenses help reduce glare. The lenses cut down reflected light off water and flat surfaces outdoors and enhance vision. Polarized lenses are available in any color.

Shooting Techniques You'll Need

While there are various techniques in shooting, find those that work well for you, and practice, practice, and practice!

Sight Alignment: Sight alignment is the most important contribution to firing an accurate shot. In order for the bullet to hit the center of the target, the shooter must aim the pistol and give the barrel a definite direction relative to the target. In theory, accurate aiming is achieved when the shooter places in exact alignment the rear sight with the top and sides of the front sight and holds them in alignment in the aiming area. A requisite for correct aiming is the ability to maintain the relationship between the front and rear sights. When aiming, the front sight is positioned in the middle of the rear-sight notch with an equal light space on each side. The horizontal top surface of the front sight is on the same level as the top horizontal surface of the rear sight notch.

Relationship of Sights: It is necessary to be acutely aware of the relationship of the rear sight to the clearly defined front sight. Normal vision is such that the rear sight of the pistol will be as nearly in focus as the front sight. Some shooters may be able to see only the notch of the rear sight in sharp focus; the outer extremities may become slightly blurred.

Point of Focus: Correct sight alignment must be thoroughly understood and practiced. It appears on the surface as a simple thing, this lining up of two objects, front and rear sights. The problem lies in the difficulty in maintaining these two sights in precise alignment while the shooter is maintaining a minimum arc of movement and pressing the trigger to cause the hammer to fall without disturbing sight alignment. The solution is partly in focusing the eye on the front sight during the delivery of the shot.

Improper: It is improper if the control of your sight alignment is not precise. Distinct focus on target renders sight indistinct. Error incorporated here is not as readily apparent.

Proper: It is proper if control of your sight alignment is precise. Focus is limited to front sight only and renders the sights distinct and target indistinct, and sight relationship can be controlled constantly. It is imperative to maintain front sight point of focus throughout the sighting and aiming of the pistol. The shooter must concentrate on maintaining the correct relationship between front and rear sight, and the point of focus must be on the front sight during the short period required to deliver the shot. If the focus is displaced forward, and the target is momentarily in clear focus, the ability of shooter to achieve correct sight alignment is jeopardized for that moment. Frequently, this is the moment when the pistol fires. A controlled, accurate shot is impossible under these conditions. When the eye is focused on the target, the relatively small movement of the arm appears magnified. However, when the eye correctly focuses on the front sight, this movement appears to have been reduced.

Concentration: If the sights are incorrectly aligned, the net result is an inaccurate shot. Carelessness in obtaining correct sight alignment can usually be traced to the shooter's failure to realize its importance. Many shooters will, in the initial phase of holding, line up the sights in a perfect manner. However, as the firing progresses and the shooter is concentrating on delivering the shot, he often loses correct sight alignment which he attained in the initial phase of his hold. Usually, when the shooter is unable to maintain a pinpoint hold, his concentration on sight alignment wavers. An accurate shot is lost because the shooter is thinking of his arc of movement and not the perfection of sight alignment.

Another factor which contributes to the deterioration of sight alignment is the feeling of anxiety, which arises over the apparently stationary pressure on the trigger when attempting to fire. An impulse is generated to get more pressure on the trigger so that the shot will be delivered. When the shooter thinks about increasing the trigger pressure, a degree of the intense concentration required to maintain correct sight alignment is lost. Even if trigger control and the hold are good, the net result will be a poor shot. Sight alignment must remain uppermost in the shooter's mind throughout the firing of the shot. Positive trigger pressure must be applied involuntarily. Consistently accurate shots are produced when the shooter maintains intense concentration on sight alignment during the application of trigger pressure while experiencing a minimum arc of movement. Control of the shot is lessened in direct proportion to the loss of concentration on sight alignment.

The average, advanced shooter is probably limited in sustained concentration to a period of 3 to 6 seconds. This short space of time is the optimum period in which a controlled shot can be delivered. This concentration interval should be attained simultaneously with acquiring a minimum arc of movement, a point of focus, satisfactory sight alignment, and the involuntary starting of positive trigger pressure. If exact sight alignment is maintained, and the trigger pressure remains positive, the shot will break during the limited time the shooter is able to control his uninterrupted concentration. Result: a dead center hit on the target.

Extensive information regarding breath control follows due to the significance of breathing and holding your breath while shooting!

Breath Control: The firer must learn to hold his breath properly at any time during the breathing cycle if he wishes to attain accuracy that will serve him in defensive combat. This must be done while aiming and squeezing the trigger. While the procedure is simple, it requires explanation, demonstration, and supervised practice. To hold the breath properly, the firer takes a breath, lets it out, then inhales normally, lets a little out until comfortable, holds, and then fires. It is difficult to maintain a steady position, keeping the front sight at a precise aiming point while breathing, rather than wandering around the target. Therefore, the firer should be taught to inhale, then exhale normally, and hold his breath at the moment of the natural respiratory pause. The shot must then be fired before he feels any discomfort from not breathing. When multiple targets are presented, the firer must learn to hold his breath at any part of the breathing cycle. Breath control must be practiced during dry-fire exercises until it becomes a natural part of the firing process. The object of proper breath control is to enable the pistol shooter to hold his breath with a comfortable feeling long enough to fire one-shot slow fire, five shots in 20-second timed fire, or five shots in ten-second rapid-fire without loss of the ability to hold still or concentrate on sight alignment. To be effective, breath control must be employed systematically and uniformly; the ability to concentrate and maintain rhythm is aided.

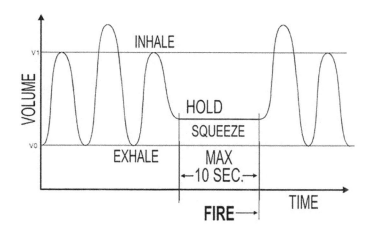

In your breathing cycle, when you breathe, it causes your steady hold on your firearm to move as you inhale and exhale. When you learn to hold your breath and fire, it causes a great deal more accuracy. Practice this, and it will become a routine part of your shooting activities.

Promote a Steady Hold: It is generally known that one must not breathe during aiming. Breathing is accompanied by the rhythmical movement of the chest, abdomen, and shoulders. This causes the pistol to move about excessively, making it almost impossible to produce an accurate shot. Therefore, one must not simultaneously breathe and try to fire a shot but must try to hold the breath for a short period of time.

The Physiological Processes (Body's Natural Processes) Involved in Breathing: The shooter, however, must not view the breathing process solely from the movement of the chest and the gun. He must not forget that the process of breathing, which consists of a combination of processes which occur constantly in the human body, determines in general the condition of the human being. Therefore, proper breathing is of great importance during shooting exercises, which may last several hours. Incorrect breathing technique has an adverse effect upon shooting, especially if the concentration is disturbed by sensing of the need to breathe. During the process of breathing, there is an alternating increase and decrease in the volume of the chest; as a result, the person inhales and exhales. A person inhales when the dimensions of the chest increase. Once inside the lungs, the air provides oxygen to the blood, and, in turn, it absorbs carbon dioxide and aqueous vapors. Exhalation occurs when all the muscles relax, the diaphragm presses upward, and, under the action of the weight of the chest and the elasticity of the lungs, air is forced out of the body. Exhaling does not require muscular effort; it occurs as the result of the resiliency of the ribs and the muscular tissues and the elasticity of the lungs. When breathing calmly, a person produces an average of 12 to 13 respiratory cycles a minute. Consequently, one respiratory cycle lasts 4 to 5 seconds. If one traces the respiratory cycle, it is not difficult to note that the strained position of inhalation is replaced very quickly by exhalation. The very next inhalation begins after a respiratory pause of 2 to 3 seconds, during which time the carbon dioxide accumulates in the lungs. The duration of the respiratory pause is determined by the ratio of oxygen and carbon dioxide in the air remaining in the lungs. The respiratory pause and the problems of the ventilation of the lungs are of great importance to the shooter. It is obvious that during aiming and applying pressure on the trigger, the breath must be held only after the shooter has exhaled, timing it so that the breath is held at the moment of the natural respiratory pause. During that time, the muscles are not strained and are in a relaxed state. A person can prolong by several seconds this respiratory pause, that is, hold his breath comfortably for 15 to 20 seconds, without any special labor and without experiencing unpleasant sensations. This time is more than adequate to produce a shot or shots. Experienced shooters usually take a deep breath before firing and then, exhaling slowly, hold their breath gradually, relax, and concentrate their entire attention upon sight alignment and the smooth application of pressure on the trigger.

Recommended Method Prior to Fire Commands: You might want to use a coach to help you learn to shoot. When expelling the air from the lungs before aiming, no effort whatever must be exerted. The exhaling must be natural and free as in ordinary breathing. The air must not be held in the lungs; incomplete exhaling before aiming leads to straining and to stimulation of the nerve centers, regulating the breathing, and the shooter's concentration on aiming is distracted. In order to make sure that during prolonged firing, the interruption of the rhythm of breathing does not have an influence upon the shooter, the breath must not be held for an excessive period when trying to fire a slow-fire shot. If the shooter does not produce a shot in 8 to 10 seconds, he must stop aiming and take another breath. Before holding his breath for the next shot, he must empty his lungs well, taking several deep breaths. The same should be done between shots and strings of shots throughout the firing. This facilitates the lengthening of the respiratory pause before aiming and provides for regular rest between shots and strings. The oxygen level in the blood is slightly increased. As a result, the shooter is relaxed and comfortable during all shooting without excessive and premature fatigue.

Stance: The stance is the way you stand while shooting to maximize the effectiveness and accuracy. There are two common stances widely used, the Weaver stance and the isosceles stance, but when you develop your own skills, experiment and develop your own unique differences in the stance to make it work best for you, but these are the way to go for now.

Weaver Stance: How to do the Weaver stance? Stand with feet about shoulder-width apart and knees locked. Keep the foot on the side of your gun arm back from your other foot.

Step 1: Extend the hand holding the pistol out in front of you until your arm is almost fully extended. Keep a slight bend in the elbow. Hold your gun at shoulder level.

Step 2: Grip your gun hand with your other hand. Keep the elbow of that arm bent, held close to your body, and pointed toward the floor. When firing, push forward with your gun arm and pull back with the other arm.

Step 3: Turn your body at a 45-degree angle to your target. Bend your head slightly to align the gun sight.

Arms should be fairly close together when employing the Weaver shooting stance. Do not allow your elbows to flare out from the body.

Control the recoil and improve shooting accuracy by remembering the push/pull action when firing in the Weaver stance. Straighten out your gun arm fully to employ the modified Weaver shooting stance that is becoming more popular today. Shooting accuracy may be lost when using the Weaver stance because the gun arm may overpower the support arm; thus, a right-handed shooter may pull shots to the right, and a left-handed shooter may to the left.

Isosceles Stance: Standing *square to the target*, the shooter grasps the gun with two hands, extending the arms straight out fully toward the target with the two arms locked, with both the arms and the shoulders forming an isosceles triangle. Lean your upper body toward your target. Your shoulders should be tipped toward the target, closer than your hips, and your hips should be tipped farther forward than your knees.

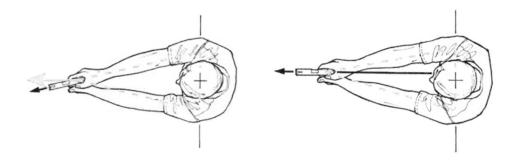

In the two drawings, the isosceles stance shows the axis of your hips and shoulders, where the image on the left is incorrect and the image on the right is correct! Pay attention to the vertical and horizontal crossed lines in the illustration. Sometimes it takes a while to determine a straight line in front of you.

During the Fire Commands: Take a deeper than normal breath at the command "Ready on the right," take another at "Ready on the left," extend your pistol, and take the final breath and exhale to the point of comfort at "Ready on the firing line." As the shooter gains experience in proper breath control, he will find that he will hold his breath, or extend his normal respiratory pause, without being too conscious of the action, and allow intense concentration on sight alignment and trigger pressure. DURING ACTUAL FIRING, the shooter should not be conscious of the need to breathe. If, during practice, a shooter finds that he cannot hold his breath the 20 seconds necessary to fire a timed-fire string, he should make a practice of firing his timed-fire strings in less than 20 seconds. However, if during a timed—or rapid-fire string, the shooter feels compelled to breathe, he should take a short breath quickly and continue to fire. This causes a lapse of concentration on sight alignment and should not be the normal technique used.

Marksmanship

Phases of Training: Marksmanship training is divided into two phases: preparatory marksmanship training and range firing. Each phase may be divided into separate instructional steps. All marksmanship training must be progressive. Combat marksmanship techniques should be practiced *after the basics have been mastered*, or you will be practicing and learning to use improper skills and techniques.

Fundamentals: The main use of our carry pistol or revolver is to engage an attacker *at close range* with quick, accurate fire. Accurate shooting results from knowing and correctly applying the elements of marksmanship. The elements of combat pistol or revolver marksmanship are the following:

1. Grip
2. Aiming
3. Breath control
4. Trigger squeeze
5. Target engagement
6. Positions

Grip: The weapon must become an extension of the hand and arm (do you remember this?). It should *replace* the finger in pointing at an object. A firm, uniform grip must be applied to the weapon. A proper grip is one of the most important fundamentals of quick fire. With enough practice, you'll instinctively do this automatically when needed.

One-hand Grip: Hold the weapon in the non-firing hand and form a *V* with the thumb and forefinger of the strong hand (firing hand). Place the weapon in the *V* with the front and rear sights in line with the firing arm. Wrap the lower three fingers around the pistol grip, putting equal pressure with all three fingers to the rear. Allow the thumb of the firing hand to rest alongside the weapon without pressure. Grip the weapon tightly until the hand begins to tremble and relax until the trembling stops.

At this point, the necessary pressure for a proper grip has been applied. Place the trigger finger on the trigger between the tip and second joint so that it can be squeezed to the rear. The trigger finger must work independently of the remaining fingers. Note that if any of the three fingers on the grip is relaxed, the grip must be reapplied. If your gun is small and does not have sufficient room on the grip for 3 fingers, you might opt for a magazine extension that extends the gripping ability of your weapon. These are not available for all guns, so do your research before you buy.

Two-hand Grip: The two-hand grip allows the firer to steady the firing hand and provide maximum support during firing. The non-firing hand becomes a support mechanism for the firing hand by wrapping the fingers of the non-firing hand around the firing hand. Two-hand grips are recommended for all pistol and revolver firing.

One on the left is a left-handed shooter and on the right, a right-handed shooter. Remember the finger goes into the trigger guard only when you've decided you're ready to fire.

DON'T PINCH YOUR HAND!

A). SLIDE DIRECTION
B). PINCH POINT!
C). GUARD
C). GUARDS YOUR HANDS!

WARNING! If the non-firing thumb is placed in the rear of the weapon behind the slide or any portion of either hand or web of the hand getting in the path of the slide at point A, the recoil from the weapon retracting the slide could result in personal injury. Point B might bruise your hand, while point C is the beavertail grip on this particular gun, but it's also a guard for your hands! If you get caught or hurt, it would be your own fault, not the gun's!

This might cause someone not to understand that it is actually *their own fault* and not the gun's. They could then easily become scared of using the weapon and think it is inferior, but practicing the proper techniques can eliminate this problem.

Fist Grip: Grip the weapon as described in the paragraph above. Firmly close the fingers of the non-firing hand over the fingers of the firing hand, ensuring that the index finger from the non-firing hand is between the middle finger of the firing hand and the trigger guard. Place the non-firing thumb alongside the firing thumb.

Note: Depending upon the individual shooter, he may choose to place his index finger of the non-firing hand on the front of the trigger guard of some pistols since these weapons have a recurved trigger guard designed for this purpose. While some manufacturers say to do so, I have watched instructors correct students not to place this finger on the trigger guard that was designed for it, but everyone is not always aware of everything, the very reason to study and determine what works best for you. The majority of shooters collect the data from professional shooters who do so well with their techniques, and then their techniques are generally adopted due to their success such as the Weaver grip and stance.

Palm-supported Grip: While this technique is no longer recommended for use, I'm educating you to what it is in the event when you come across someone who says he knows a better way (which happens). You will know and won't undo your learning more advanced methods. This grip is commonly called the cup-and-saucer grip. Grip the firing hand as described in the paragraph above. Place the non-firing hand under the firing hand, wrapping the non-firing fingers around the back of the firing hand. Place the non-firing thumb over the middle finger of the firing hand.

These are two examples of what SHOULD NOT be used! Remember what the manufacturers said about the curved trigger guard on the right, but professional shooters don't do it since they have very successful techniques. Don't put any pressure on the slide, or you may get a self-induced malfunction!

Weaver Grip: Apply this grip the same as the fist grip. The only exception is that the non-firing thumb is wrapped over the firing thumb.

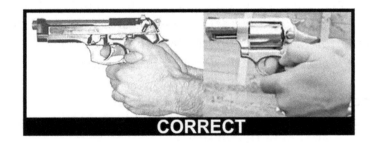

The two illustrations above show the Weaver grip on both a semiautomatic pistol and a revolver.

Isometric Tension: The firer raises his arms to a firing position and applies isometric tension. This is commonly known as the push-pull method for maintaining weapon stability. Isometric tension is when the firer applies forward pressure with the firing hand and pulls rearward with the non-firing hand with equal pressure. This creates an isometric force but never so much to cause the firer to tremble. This steadies the weapon and reduces barrel rise from recoil. The supporting arm is bent with the elbow pulled downward. The firing arm is fully extended with the elbow and wrist locked. The firer must experiment to find the right amount of isometric tension to apply. Note that the firing hand should exert the same pressure as the non-firing hand. If it does not, a missed target could result.

Natural Point of Aim: The firer should check his grip for use of his natural point of aim. He grips the weapon and sights properly on a distant target. While maintaining his grip and stance, he closes his eyes for 3 to 5 seconds. He then opens his eyes and checks for proper sight picture. If the point of aim is disturbed, the firer adjusts his stance to compensate. If the sight alignment is disturbed, the firer adjusts his grip to compensate by removing the weapon from his hand and reapplying the grip. The firer repeats this process until the sight alignment and sight placement remain almost the same when he opens his eyes. This enables the firer to determine and use his natural point of aim once he has sufficiently practiced. This is the most relaxed position for holding and firing the weapon.

Aiming: Aiming is sight alignment and sight placement. Sight alignment is the centering of the front blade in the rear-sight notch. The top of the front sight is leveled with the top of the rear sight and is in correct alignment with the eye. For correct sight alignment, the shooter must center the front sight in the rear sight. He raises or lowers the top of the front sight, so it is leveled with the top of the rear sight.

Sight placement is the positioning of the weapon's sights in relation to the target as seen by the shooter when he aims the weapon. A correct sight picture consists of correct sight alignment with the front sight placed at the center mass of the target. The eye can focus on only one object at a time at different distances. Therefore, the last focus of the eye is always on the front sight. When the front sight is seen clearly, the rear sight and target will appear hazy. Correct sight alignment can only be maintained through focusing on the front sight. The shooter's bullet will hit the target even if the sight picture is slightly off center but still remains on the target. Therefore, sight alignment is more important than sight placement. Since it is impossible to hold the weapon completely still, the shooter must apply trigger squeeze and maintain correct sight alignment while the weapon is moving in and around the center of the target. This natural movement of the weapon is referred to as wobble area. The shooter must strive to control the limits of the wobble area through proper breath control, trigger squeeze, positioning, and grip. Sight alignment is essential for accuracy because of the short-sight radius of the pistols and revolvers. For example, if a 1/10-inch error is made in aligning the front sight in the rear sight, the shooter's bullet will miss the point of aim by about 15 inches at a range of 25 yards. The

1/10-inch error in sight alignment magnifies as the range increases, so at 25 yards, it is magnified 150 times, equaling 15 inches. Sloppy shots at close range become total misses at any given distance, but good shots at any distant target become much more accurate at close range since any movement is not magnified much if any up close. Learning to achieve good long shots teaches you to steady your hands so that when you attempt close shots, you're very accurate.

Focusing on the front sight while applying proper trigger squeeze will help the shooter resist the urge to jerk the trigger and anticipate the actual moment the weapon will fire. Mastery of trigger squeeze and sight alignment requires practice. Trainers should use concurrent training stations or have firing ranges to enhance proficiency of marksmanship skills. No matter how hard you try, your shooting can never be more exact than your aiming!

Trigger Squeeze: Improper trigger squeeze causes more misses than any other step of preparatory marksmanship. Poor shooting is caused by the aim being disturbed before the bullet leaves the barrel of the weapon. This is usually the result of the firer jerking the trigger or flinching. A slight off-center pressure of the trigger finger on the trigger can cause the weapon to move and disturb the firer's sight alignment. Flinching is an automatic human reflex caused by anticipating the recoil of the weapon. Jerking is an effort to fire the weapon at the precise time the sights align with the target's preferred point of impact.

Trigger squeeze is the independent movement of the trigger finger in applying increasing pressure on the trigger straight to the rear, without disturbing the sight alignment until the weapon fires. The trigger slack, or free play, is taken up first, and the squeeze is continued steadily until the hammer falls. If the trigger is squeezed properly, the firer will not know exactly when the hammer will fall; thus, he does not tend to flinch or heel, resulting in a bad shot. Novice firers must be trained to overcome the urge to anticipate recoil. Proper application of the fundamentals will lower this tendency. To apply correct trigger squeeze, the trigger finger should contact the trigger between the tip of the finger and the second joint, without touching the weapon anywhere else. Where the contact is made depends on the length of the firer's trigger finger. If pressure from the trigger finger is applied to the right side of the trigger or weapon, the strike of the bullet will be to the left. This is due to the normal hinge action of the fingers. When the fingers on the right hand are closed, as in gripping, they hinge or pivot to the left, thereby applying pressure to the left. With left-handed firers, this action is to the right. The firer must not apply pressure left or right but increase finger pressure straight to only the rear; the trigger finger must perform this action. Dry-fire training improves a firer's ability to move the trigger finger straight to the rear without cramping or increasing pressure on the handgrip.

The shooter who is a good shot holds the sights of the weapon as nearly on the target center as possible and continues to squeeze the trigger with increasing pressure until the weapon fires. The shooter who is a bad shot tries to *catch his target* as his sight alignment moves past the target and fires the weapon at that instant. This is called ambushing, which causes the trigger jerk. Follow- through is the continued effort of the shooter to maintain sight alignment before, during, and after the round has fired. The shooter must continue the rearward movement of the finger even after the round has been fired *while holding the trigger back through the recoil*. Releasing the trigger too soon after the round has been fired results in an uncontrolled shot, causing a missed target.

Target Engagement: To engage a single target, the shooter applies the best method he knows, but when multiple targets are engaged, things change. You must track your target so that as you shift your eyes, you track with your muzzle, which is already aligned with the line of sight from your eye to the threat. The closest and most dangerous of multiple targets in combat is engaged first and should be fired at with two rounds. This is commonly referred to as a double tap. The shooter then traverses (moves) and acquires the next target, aligns the sights in the center of mass, focuses on the front sight, applies trigger squeeze, and fires. The shooter ensures his firing arm elbow and wrist are locked during all engagements. If the shooter has missed the first target and has fired upon the second target, he shifts back to the first and engages him again. If you have multiple targets, you need to be aware of available cover for you if at all possible while you quickly determine which target is from the *most dangerous* to the least dangerous, which can change quite easily as the gunfight progresses. If you see the closest target which is generally assumed to be the most dangerous, be especially aware of those on the outer edges, say, either to your right or your left. Even though they may be a bit further away, they may have an angled shot, say, at about 40-45 degrees from either side, which just may reach behind your cover due to the angle and kill you, so it's important to be aware of this.

Recoil Anticipation: When a shooter first learns to shoot, he may begin to anticipate recoil. This reaction may cause him to tighten his muscles during or just before the hammer falls. He may fight the recoil by pushing the weapon downward in anticipating or reacting to its firing. In either case, the rounds will not hit the point of aim. A good method to show the shooter that he is anticipating the recoil is to have an observer stand to the side of the shooter while the shooter is firing. The observer loads the magazines or the cylinder for the shooter by placing snap caps, which are dummy rounds in between the live rounds, and watches the shooter who has no idea as to the dummies being in place so that when he shoots, assuming everything is normal, if there is no live round, the shooter may flinch and jerk, assuming there is a live round going off and will be required to become more skillful. The observer may do this at random and in any particular magazine or cylinder load that the shooter is not aware of in an effort to resolve the anticipation of recoil problem.

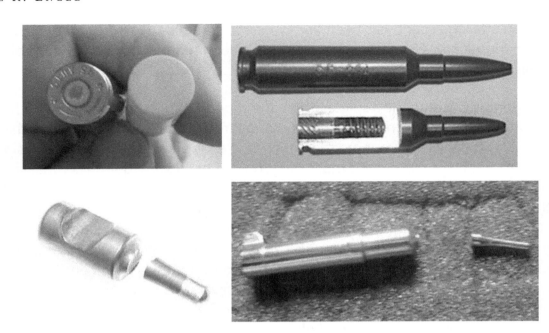

Proper snap caps have a spring-loaded compression device in the center for the firing pin as compared to a solid plastic one (solid), where the firing pin crashes into a solid object. The compression device is the one you want. We don't want any broken firing pins. This is an example of a few bucks or a few cents, but the seeming bargain could damage your gun. Snap caps are available in all calibers, including shotguns. Dry firing on a spring-loaded snap cap is safer than firing empty and stressing the firing pin.

Trigger Jerk: Trigger jerk occurs when the shooter sees that he has acquired a good sight picture at the center mass and snaps off a round before the good sight picture is lost. This may become a problem, especially when the shooter is learning to use a flash sight picture. To help cure this problem, use the same technique as described above with mixed live and dummy rounds while learning to use the proper trigger pull.

Heeling: Heeling is caused by a firer tightening the large muscle in the heel of the hand to keep from jerking the trigger. A shooter who has had problems with jerking the trigger tries to correct the fault by tightening the bottom of the hand, which results in a heeled shot. Heeling causes the strike of the bullet to hit high on the firing hand side of the target. The firer can correct shooting errors by knowing and applying correct trigger squeeze.

Positions: The qualification course is fired from a standing, kneeling, or crouch position. All the firing positions described below must be practiced so they become natural movements during qualification and combat firing. Though these positions seem natural, practice sessions must be conducted to ensure the habitual attainment of correct firing positions. Assuming correct firing positions ensures that shooters can quickly assume these positions without a conscious effort. Pistol marksmanship requires a shooter to rapidly apply all the fundamentals at dangerously close targets while under stress. Assuming a proper position to allow for a steady aim is critical to survival. If you have a disability that prevents you from assuming any normal position, then make necessary adjustments to make the best accurate shots that you can, and once the issue is resolved, then practice the corrected positions the same as you would do any of the normal ones.

Pistol-ready Position: In the pistol-ready position, hold the weapon in the one-hand grip. Hold the upper arm close to the body and the forearm at about a 45° angle. Point the weapon toward target center as you move forward.

Standing Position without Support: Face the target. Place feet a comfortable distance apart, about shoulder width. Extend the firing arm and attain a two-hand grip. The wrist and elbow of the firing arm are locked and pointed toward target center. Keep the body straight with the shoulders slightly forward of the buttocks. Sometimes it is advantageous to put the foot opposite your shooting hand forward, but many use the other foot and the opposite back—whatever works to balance and stabilize you the best.

Note: During defensive combat, there may not be time for a shooter to assume a position that will allow him to establish his natural point of aim. Firing from a covered position may require the shooter to adapt his shooting stance to available cover. Those with the greatest ability to adapt to the surroundings are the most likely to succeed.

Kneeling Position: In the kneeling position, ground only the firing side knee as the main support. Vertically place the foot used as the main support, under the buttocks. Rest the body weight on the heel and toes. Rest the non-firing arm just above the elbow on the knee not used as the main body support. Use the two-handed grip for firing. Extend the firing arm and lock the firing arm elbow and wrist to ensure solid arm control.

Crouch Position: Use the crouch position when surprise targets are engaged at close range. Place the body in a forward crouch (boxer's stance) with the knees bent slightly and trunk bent forward from the hips to give faster recovery from recoil. Place the feet naturally in a position that allows another step toward the target. Extend the weapon straight toward the target and lock the wrist and elbow of the firing arm. It is important to consistently train with this position, since the body will automatically crouch under conditions of stress such as combat. It is also a faster position to change direction of fire.

Prone Position: Lie flat on the ground, facing the target. Extend arms in front with the firing arm locked. The arms may have to be slightly unlocked for firing at high targets. Do not rest the butt of the weapon on the ground, although some people say to do so (for single, well-aimed shots) unless you have no choice because they will most likely veer off target and possibly miss. Wrap the non-firing hand (fingers) around the fingers of the firing hand. Face forward. Keep the head down between arms as much as possible and behind the weapon.

Standing Position with Support: Use available cover for support, for example, a tree or wall to stand behind. Stand behind a barricade with the firing side in line with the edge of the barricade. Place the knuckles of the non-firing fist at eye level against the edge of the barricade. Lock the elbow and wrist of the firing arm. Move the foot on the non-firing side forward until the toe of the boot touches the bottom of the barricade.

Kneeling Supported Position: Use available cover for support; for example, use a low wall, rocks, or vehicle. Place the firing-side knee on the ground. Bend the other knee and place the foot (non-firing side) flat on the ground, pointing toward the target. Extend arms alongside and brace them against available cover. Lock the wrist and elbow of the firing arm. Place the non-firing hand around the fist to support the firing arm. Rest the non-firing arm just above the elbow on the non-firing-side knee.

Combat Marksmanship: After a shooter becomes proficient in the fundamentals of marksmanship, he progresses to advanced techniques of combat marksmanship. The main use of the pistol or revolver is to engage the KILLER at close range with *quick, accurate fire*. In shooting encounters, it is not the first round fired that wins the engagement, but the first *accurately* fired round. The shooter should use his sights when engaging the killer; the only exception is, if this would place the weapon within arm's reach of the killer.

Hand-and-eye Coordination: Hand-and-eye coordination is not a natural, instinctive ability for all shooters. It is usually a learned skill obtained by practicing the use of a flash sight picture. The more a shooter practices, raising the weapon to eye level and obtaining a flash sight picture, the more natural the relationship between the shooter, sights, and target becomes. Eventually, proficiency elevates to a point that the shooter can accurately engage targets in the dark. Each shooter must be aware of this trait and learn how to use it best. Poorly coordinated shooters can achieve proficiency by being closely supervised. Everyone has the ability to point at an object.

Since pointing the forefinger at an object and extending the weapon toward a target are much the same, the combination of the two is natural. Making the shooter aware of this ability and teaching him how to apply it when firing result in success when engaging deadly targets in combat.

The eyes focus instinctively on the center of any object observed. After the object is sighted, the shooter aligns his sights at the center of mass, focuses on the front sight, and applies proper trigger squeeze. Most crippling or killing hits result from maintaining the focus on the center of mass. The eyes must remain fixed on some part of the target throughout firing.

When a shooter points, he instinctively points at the feature on the object on which his eyes are focused. An impulse from the brain causes the arm and hand to stop when the finger reaches the proper position. When the eyes are shifted to a new object or feature, the finger, hand, and arm also shift to this point. It is this inherent trait that can be used by the shooter to rapidly and accurately engage targets. This instinct is called hand-and-eye coordination.

Flash Sight Picture: Usually when engaging a killer at pistol/revolver ranges, the shooter has little time to ensure a correct sight picture. The quick-kill (or natural point of aim) method does not always ensure a first-round hit. A compromise between a correct sight picture and the quick-kill method is known as a flash sight picture. As the shooter raises the weapon to eye level, his point of focus switches from the enemy to the front sight, ensuring that the front and rear sights are in proper alignment, left and right, but not necessarily up and down. Pressure is applied to the trigger as the front sight is being acquired, and the hammer falls as the flash sight picture is confirmed. Initially, this method should be practiced slowly, gaining speed as proficiency increases.

Quick-fire Point Shooting: This is for engaging an enemy at less than 5 yards. It is also useful for night firing. The weapon should be held in a two-hand grip. It is brought up close to the body until it reaches chin level and is then thrust forward until both arms are straight. The arms and body form a triangle, which can be aimed as a unit. In thrusting the weapon forward, the shooter can imagine that there is a box between him and the killer, and he is thrusting the weapon into the box. The trigger is smoothly squeezed to the rear as the elbows straighten out. This could be a situation for assisted sighting by laser for speed and accuracy in stopping the threat before he makes physical contact with you.

Quick-fire Sighting: This is used when engaging an enemy at 5 to 10 yards away. It is used only when there is no time available to get a full picture. The firing position is the same as the quick-fire point shooting. The sights are aligned left and right to save time, but not up and down. The shooter must determine in practice what the sight picture will look like and where the front sight must be aimed to hit the killer in the chest. This could be a situation for assisted sighting by laser for speed and accuracy in stopping the threat before he makes physical contact with you.

Target Engagement: In close combat, there is seldom time to precisely apply all the fundamentals of marksmanship. When a shooter fires a round at the killer, many times, he will not know if he has hit his target. Therefore, two rounds should be fired at the target. This is called a double tap. If the KILLER continues to attack, two more shots should be placed in the pelvic area to break the body's support structure, causing the killer to fall. This could be a situation for assisted sighting by laser for speed and accuracy in stopping the threat before he makes physical contact with you.

Traversing (TRAVERSING 360°): In close combat, the KILLERS may be attacking from all sides. The shooter may not have time to constantly change his position to adapt to new situations. The purpose of the crouching or kneeling traverse 360° is to fire in any direction without moving the feet. The shooter remains in the crouch position with feet almost parallel to each other. The following instructions are for a right-handed shooter. The two-hand grip is used at all times except for over the right shoulder. Turning will be natural on the balls of the feet.

Over the Left Shoulder: The upper body is turned to the left, and the weapon points to the left rear with the elbows of both arms bent. The left elbow will naturally be bent more than the right elbow.

Traversing means to be moving such as traversing in any specific way or direction.

Traversing to the Left: The upper body turns to the right, and the right firing arm straightens out. The left arm will be slightly bent.

Traversing to the Front: The upper body turns to the front as the left arm straightens out. Both arms will be straightforward.

Traversing to the Right: The upper body will turn to the right as both elbows bend. The right elbow will naturally bend more than the left.

Traversing to the Right Rear: The upper body continues to turn to the right until it reaches a point that it cannot go further comfortably. Eventually, the left hand will have to release itself from the fist grip, and the firer will be shooting to the right rear with the right hand.

Kneeling 360° Traverse: The following instructions are for right-handed shooters. The hands are in a two-hand grip at all times. The unsupported kneeling position is used. The rear foot must be positioned to the left of the front foot.

Traversing to the Left Side: The upper body turns to a comfortable position toward the left. The weapon is aimed to the left. Both elbows are bent with the left elbow naturally bent more than the right elbow.

Traversing to the Front: The upper body is turned to the front, and a standard unsupported kneeling position is assumed. The right firing arm is straight, and the left elbow is slightly bent.

Traversing to the Right Side: The upper body turns to the right as both arms straighten out.

Traversing to the Rear: The upper body continues to turn to the right as the left knee is turned to the right and placed on the ground. The right knee is lifted off the ground and becomes the forward knee. The right arm is straight, while the left arm is bent. The direction of the kneeling position has been reversed.

Traversing to the New Right Side: The upper body continues to the right. Both elbows are straight until it reaches a point that it cannot comfortably go further. Eventually, the left hand must be released from the fist grip, and the shooter will be firing to the right with the one-hand grip.

Training Methods

This method can be taught anywhere without a weapon by the shooter, simulating a two-hand grip. The shooter should be familiar with firing in all five directions.

Combat Reloading Techniques: Reloading was an overlooked problem for many years until it was discovered that soldiers were being killed due to dropping of magazines, shaking hands, placing magazines in backward, and placing empty magazines back into the weapon. The state of stress induced by a life-threatening situation *even causes soldiers to do things they would not otherwise do*, so remember that YOU need more attention to the matter than you might not normally think you need. Consistent, repeated training is needed to avoid such mistakes.

Develop a consistent method for carrying magazines for semiautomatic pistols or speed loaders for revolvers in the magazine carriers or ammunition pouches. All magazines should face down with the bullets facing forward and to the center of the body. Some revolver users prefer to carry speed strips as an alternative to speed loaders. With speed strips, you have to insert the bullets one at a time as compared to dropping in a full load and disengaging the rounds. Dropping in the speed loaders full load all at once is much faster but more difficult to carry due to the outer diameter as compared to a flat speed strip that you might have in your pocket.

Knowing How the Magazine Works Properly or Causes Malfunctions: Take your fully loaded magazine and hold it firmly in your strong hand, gripping it upright firmly around its body. Using your support palm give the magazine a sharp tap on the bottom while watching the top round to see what it does. If the magazine is hit too hard, the top round will jump half way out of the magazine as if it is being stripped out and chambered by the slide of your gun. If it doesn't, repeat the step over and over until it does so that you can see how much pressure it takes to make the round jump half way out. Note that if the magazine is in the gun and you hit the bottom with your support hand to lock it into the gun and the bullet jumps half way out of the magazine, it may cause the slide to jam on the half-fed round, and the round that is half out of the magazine will act like a lock, preventing the magazine from dropping out of the gun due to the round being half out of the magazine above the magazine well. Once this happens inside the gun, sometimes racking the slide will chamber the round. Once you understand this problem, then it becomes quite easy to understand when the gun doesn't fire; the first thing to do is to TAP the bottom of the magazine to lock it into the gun, then RACK the slide to eject a defective round if there is one, or chamber a new round from the magazine now that it is locked into the gun and then SHOOT. In other words, TAP—RACK-SHOOT.

What if The Magazine Won't Come Out: After tapping the magazine and then finding that the round might be half way out and the magazine is locked in by the partially fed round, in an emergency you will have to literally pull the magazine out and replace it with a fresh one in case you bent the lips on the magazine while pulling it free. Your magazine didn't suddenly go bad like some people say, it is the half fed round that caused your problem. Now you understand the reason for practice so you can adjust to the sequence.

Know When to Reload: When possible, count the number of rounds fired. However, it is possible to lose count in the stress of close combat. If this happens, there is a distinct difference in recoil of the pistol when the last round has been fired. Change magazines when two rounds may be left, one in the magazine and one in the chamber. This prevents being caught with an empty weapon at a crucial time. Reloading is faster with a round in the chamber since time is not needed to rack or release the slide!

Obtain a firm grip on the magazine. This precludes the magazine being dropped or difficulty in getting the magazine into the weapon while gripping as much of the magazine as possible. Place the index finger high on the front of the magazine when withdrawing from the pouch. Use the index finger to guide the magazine into the magazine well. Know which reloading procedure to use for the tactical situation. There are three systems of reloading: rapid, tactical, and one-handed. Rapid or emergency reloading is used when the shooter's life is in immediate danger, and the reload must be accomplished quickly. Tactical reloading is used when there is more time, and it is desirable to keep the replaced magazine because there are rounds still in it, or it will be needed again. One-handed reloading is used when there is an arm injury.

Tip: Remember, some model sidearms such as the 1911 have numerous custom parts available such as an extended slide release for one-handed operation in releasing the slide and also a beveled magazine well where the magazine is inserted to assist in fast reloads.

Rapid or Emergency Reloading: Place your hand on the next magazine in the ammunition pouch to ensure there is another magazine. Withdraw the magazine from the pouch while releasing the other magazine from the weapon. Let the empty magazine drop to the ground while the new magazine is passing it in the air and insert the replacement magazine, guiding it into the magazine well with the index finger. Release the slide, if necessary. Pick up the dropped magazine (ONLY) if it doesn't endanger you. Place it in your pocket, not back into the ammunition pouch, where it may become mixed with full magazines and you may otherwise end up pulling an empty one when you need a fully reloaded one, which just may get you killed. I personally have no concern for the empty magazine if I'm in a gunfight—a simple sacrifice to guarantee no mix-ups or distractions—thereby increasing the chance of saving my life. If I live through the confrontation, then I can always come back to retrieve it after the emergency is over.

Tactical Reloading: This is reloading when your gun is not necessarily empty but time permits. It will assure you of having a full magazine if the need to shoot presents itself, even if it's only a three-round difference because just one of those three might be your lifesaver! Place your hand on the next magazine in the ammunition pouch to ensure there is a remaining magazine. Withdraw the magazine from the pouch. Drop the used partially loaded magazine into the palm of the non-firing hand, which is the same hand holding the fully loaded replacement magazine. Insert the replacement magazine, guiding it into the magazine well with the index finger. Release the slide, if necessary. Place the used magazine into a pocket since it may contain unused rounds. Do not mix it with full magazines. If you accidentally drop one of the two magazines, insert the one left in your hand to assure that you're having a loaded weapon while reassessing the ability to recover the dropped magazine since it still has live rounds available.

One-hand Reloading (with the Right Hand): Push the magazine release button with the thumb. Depending on the type of pistol you have, place the safety ON with the thumb if the slide is forward and the gun is cocked. Place the weapon backward into the holster. Note that if placing the weapon in the holster backward is a problem, place the weapon between the calf and thigh to hold the weapon, or under the other arm, but placing backward in the holster will prevent you from dropping the gun in an emergency. Insert the replacement magazine. Remove the weapon from the holster. Remove the safety with the thumb if the slide is forward or push the slide release if the slide is back.

One-hand Reloading (with the Left Hand): Push the magazine release button with the middle finger. Depending on the type of pistol you have, place the safety ON with the thumb if the slide is forward and the gun is cocked. With the .45 caliber pistol, the thumb must be switched to the left side of the weapon. Place the weapon backward into the holster. Note that if placing the weapon in the holster backward is a problem, place the weapon between the calf and thigh to hold the weapon, or under the other arm, but placing backward in the holster will prevent you from dropping the gun in an emergency. Insert the replacement magazine. Remove the weapon from the holster. Remove the safety with the thumb if the slide is forward or push the slide release lever with the middle finger if the slide is back.

Under Poor Visibility Firing: THIS IS A GOOD USE FOR LASER SIGHTS TO TAKE OVER WHERE BOTH THE NORMAL IRON SIGHTS ARE NOT CLEAR ENOUGH AND THE NIGHT SIGHTS DO NOT APPEAR SUFFICIENTLY ILLUMINATED.

Coaching: Throughout preparatory marksmanship training, the coach-and-pupil method of training should be used. The proficiency of a pupil depends on how well his coach performs his duties. The coach assists the shooter by correcting errors, ensuring he takes proper firing positions and ensuring he observes all safety precautions. The criteria for selecting coaches are a serious responsibility; coaches must have experience in pistol marksmanship above that of the student shooter. Duties of the coach during instruction practice and record firing include the following:

1. Checking that the—

   (a) Weapon is cleared.
   (b) Ammunition is clean.
   (c) Magazines are clean and operational.

(2) Observing the shooter to see that he—

   (a) Takes the correct firing position.
   (b) Loads the weapon properly and only on command.
   (c) Takes up the trigger slack correctly.
   (d) Squeezes the trigger correctly.
   (e) Calls the shot each time he fires (to develop proper shooting skills).
   (f) Holds his breath correctly.
   (g) Lowers his weapon and rests his arm when he does not fire a round within 5 to 6 seconds.

(3) Having the shooter breathe deeply several times to relax if he is tense.

Storing Your Gun in an Unattended Vehicle

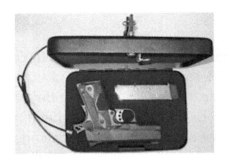

They make gun safes for vehicles that are a lock box with a cable attached that loops around the leg of the seat and locks to keep your gun safe while you're out of the vehicle and cannot carry your gun into a prohibited area. Some have a key lock while some have finger button combinations.

Accessories

While we already know about lasers and flashlights, we have rail lights and combination laser/rail light. The LED (light emitting diode) flashlights are rated in lumens, and the higher the number of lumens, the brighter the light. In other words, if the lumens are 125, it wouldn't be as bright as 500 lumens, but the higher the brightness, the higher the price. If I were to ever use a rail light, I would prefer the strobe light flashlight to simulate freeze frame movement for targeting my assailant. A word of caution: a few people including police officers use rail lights attached to the rail and trigger guard; when they attempt to turn on the flashlight, they discharge the sidearm, so beware and study your plan of defense before you buy this expensive equipment.

Shooting gloves are available in dozens of designs, configurations, and colors and are quite handy to keep a good grip on your sidearm and also give comfort during heavy recoil.

The spotting scope is handy to see where you're hitting your target downrange. Many use a shooting partner as a spotter. While there are many fine firearms cases available, there are soft cases and hard cases. If you have a polymer receiver, or a scoped firearm, I would recommend a hard case for transporting the firearm to avoid twisting the scope or bending the barrel against the receiver.

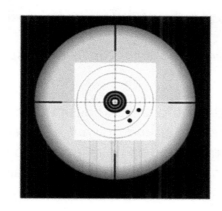

A SHOOTING BUDDY CAN SPOT FOR YOU

BESIDES BEING HELPFUL IT CAN BE FUN TIMES

Shooting Your Killer

Back to the center mass! When you use a silhouette target or any target, picture an imaginary triangle or even draw one until you can mentally visualize it by centering above the chin and extending down and across and about 2 inches beneath both nipples. If you can place your rounds at the center mass or even through the neck up to the chin, you disrupt or sever the spinal cord from the brain, the control center; it's like taking the battery out of your computer to shut it down.

While military snipers use a system from an imaginary vertical line from the center of the body, by extending it out to the ear, they call it a favor, and by extending it out to the elbow, they call it a hold. Declaring right or left obviously tells you where they are shooting—right or left of the body center (facing the target). By using an imaginary space from ear to ear downward to the waist, you stand a good chance of shutting him down, even at the edge of the breast bone, sternum in the center of the chest, although a few inches higher to the major blood vessel highway to the body and lungs would be more ideal, but the main blood vessels run vertically down the center of the body also, in front of the spine, so a center hit, no matter where, is more advantageous than to either side.

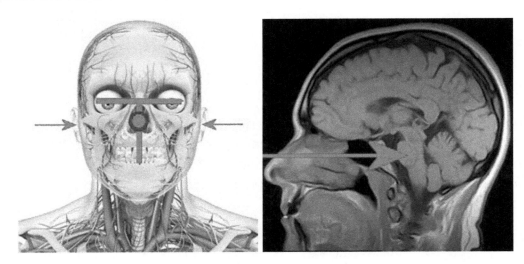

From the front, the Fatal-T, and, from the side, the center of the ear canals to the spinal cord and brain connection will stop the threat immediately.

Another place favored by military snipers to consider if the KILLER doesn't shut down is what they call the Fatal-T. This is visualizing a *T* across both eyes and down the center of the nose, but I extend it to the mouth since the inside of the mouth offers no resistance to the incoming round, offering a more powerful blow to the spinal cord. A hit anywhere in the Fatal-T will disrupt the brain or spinal cord. An excellent clear path is available through this *T*, including through the hollow internal space behind the nose and through the mouth with very little bullet deformation or energy loss until the bullet reaches the central nervous system and possibly (or probably) severs the spinal cord from the brain, dropping the KILLER where he'll most likely be dead before he hits the ground. The many articles mentioning the brain living for so long still allowing the killer to function may not work the way many seem to write it, since a strangle or sleeper hold will render the KILLER unconscious quickly by stopping the blood and oxygen supply to the brain, so do your best by a carefully placed shot and disrupting the communication link, spinal cord, or the blood and oxygen supply to the brain from wherever your round hits. A shot to the spinal cord and brain connection is through the center of the nose or center of the ear from the side. A shot through the side of the head is a better brain shot than from the front because a front shot will pass through one hemisphere of the brain as compared to a side shot which will pass through both hemispheres of the brain and most likely bring the KILLER to a halt immediately. In targeting these specific locations, if you're unsure of the exact distance, and your ability to make an effective shot due to your hands and body shaking from fear and the stress of what's happening, if it were me and I was unsure of the distance I would allow a marginal area and aim about 4 inches above the nipple line (but dead center) of the body's vertical centerline. This way, if you hit low, you get a good center-mass hit, and if you hit high, you stand to sever the spinal cord in the neck, but by staying dead center of the body's vertical centerline, you stand a very good chance of an effective hit and stopping your KILLER before he KILLS you. An imaginary centerline gives you a chance to hit any of the vertebrae in the spinal column.

Any shots to the killer in the back other than his turning around while you're shooting will make your claim of a deadly encounter in a jury situation almost cut and dried. If the KILLER starts to flee and runs from you, your pursuing him further makes YOU aggressive and subject to jail time for shooting your poor victim. Believe it! If you shoot him in the back and he dies, you may find yourself being charged with serious time in the pokey and maybe much worse; it's just the same as the situation where you rendered him unconscious and then shot him, because he'd no longer have been a deadly threat once down, and it would allow you time to flee the scene. It's always a one-way law because the KILLER will definitely KILL you, no matter what the circumstances are, but you are required by law to stop your counterattack once the threat is apparently over, but beware and never trust a KILLER! If in the midst of a confrontation and he just so happens to move in any way that gives me the shot, he's going down because I don't know what's on his mind, but since he attacked me, and I don't know anything other than he wants to KILL me, I have to shoot to survive. Knowing as to whether a killer is going to run and flee in the other direction is something we won't be able to know unless it's obvious, so don't get yourself killed because he happened to turn around in the middle of gunfire under whatever circumstances. Another set of circumstances develop when you're in a vehicle with the windows closed and the KILLER points his gun in your face and says he's going to KILL you. I'd open fire *through the windows* with multiple shots: the first one will shatter the glass and the next two follow-ups to stop my killer. If you can remember, while firing from the confines of a vehicle, try to open your mouth to equalize the pressure on your eardrums. Study your state laws, and once you know your local laws, then use commonsense.

Disconnecting Your Killer from His Attack

In modern times, everyone wants to learn the most effective way to stop a deadly threat so they may live on to enjoy their own life, but in all the information people find available to study, the author always discusses the possible shutdown of your KILLER by damaging the heart or damaging the brain. Most people know how to use computers now, so they know what happens when you pull the plug. While damaging the heart or the brain is always beneficial, pulling the power plug completely in your killer's anatomy will shut him down the very same way it does your computer. There are many situations where a bullet passes through the brain and the person lives on; it's just the same as a bullet-damaged heart generally has ¾ of the heart remaining in operation. By studying where to disconnect the superhighway of body functions, you stand a very good chance of shutting the attack down completely, which includes the brain, the heart, and the rest of the body in its entirety.

HEART: The heart is a muscular organ about the size of a fist, located just behind and slightly left of the breastbone. Too many people think the heart is so much larger due to numerous artists' renderings that illustrate the heart in various sizes, depending on who drew it, but it's very small and might be difficult to hit, especially on the move. The heart pumps blood through the network of arteries and veins called the cardiovascular system. While everyone always takes the center-mass shot first to try to stop and incapacitate the KILLER, this first center-mass shot will usually assure at least one hit (if you hit), but there's more to taking this particular shot that will definitely help you bring down your assailant. While you practice at the shooting range, it's most important to always try to place your shot in the median line, that is, down the center of the assailant, *dead center* as an imaginary line in front of his spine. If you can manage to place your shot dead center of the body, and even in elevation with the armpits where the arms join the chest area, then you should get a very good hit into the main highway of blood vessels attached to the top of the heart. While everyone always wants to stop the heart, a bullet-damaged heart may falter somewhat, but understand that while the heart has 4 chambers, one somewhat damaged chamber may still allow three of them to keep it working.

Here's how the heart works. The right atrium on the left of the heart while facing your target receives blood from the veins and pumps it to the right ventricle on the same side. The right ventricle receives blood from the right atrium and pumps it to the lungs, where it is loaded with oxygen. The left atrium on the right of the heart while facing your target receives oxygenated blood from the lungs and pumps it to the left ventricle on the same side. The left ventricle, being the strongest chamber, pumps oxygen-rich blood to the rest of the body, including to the heart's own muscles to keep it functioning. The left ventricle's vigorous contractions create our blood pressure. The aortic arch is where all the blood vessels come into and out of the heart itself at the very top of the heart to allow all the blood vessel connections to supply the entire body including to the lungs, brain and heart muscle too. If you hit the aortic arch then you disrupt and (disconnect the blood supply from the heart), and not only *starve* the heart, but also starve the body of its hydraulic fluid in essence, that it needs to energize and allow the body to work, *brain included*. This sudden deprivation of blood will cause the body to go into hypovolemic shock, which is a lack of oxygen to the body, but a good hit in this location may cause an abrupt loss of blood pressure, unconsciousness, and death. While the brain keeps the heart functioning, the heart supplies the brain to keep the brain functioning. The aortic arch is the main supply line to everything, and smaller blood vessels that immediately branch off the arch into the smaller *coronary arteries* provide the heart muscle itself with what it needs to keep the body functioning. In other words, the heart may continue to function considerably even after it is damaged. But even a perfect heart is worthless if it is disconnected from the blood vessels because the body will completely shut down in seconds and never function again. I personally prefer disconnecting the heart if such a shot or two can be had, rather than to damage it and possibly get KILLED anyway by that very man who may get his damaged heart repaired for free before they send him to prison for killing me. I know one particular situation where a very complicated heart, functioning on only one ventricle with a hole between the two atriums, kept the person alive and functioned for 13 months while 13 seconds could very well get you KILLED. So if you're facing your target, try hard to place your shot either dead center or to the right of center in the hopes that if you miss the blood vessel and aortic arch connection on the top of the heart, you have a chance to damage the left ventricle so that it cannot supply the body. While the brain normally operates the heart, the brain needs the freshly oxygenated blood supply *from the heart* to function so that it can keep the heart going, but if the heart cannot supply the brain due to the aortic arch and other blood vessels being ripped out, then the brain cannot function nor can it operate the heart. If you're quite skilled in your shooting abilities, the aortic arch would be a very good first and second shot that can certainly result in a total shutdown.

Nearly all gunshot wounds penetrating the heart are fatal, but nearly means there are still those that are not. "Large caliber and high velocity" penetrating trauma to the heart cause too much damage to allow a quick repair! An occasional victim, shot from a great distance or with a small- caliber weapon, will likely survive. The heart shielded by the skin, muscles, and bone of the chest is surrounded by pericardium, a tough, slick sack that protects, lubricates, and holds the heart in position. A puncture of the pericardium is not fatal, and the bullet can usually be found in the pericardial fluid or partially embedded in the heart muscle, the myocardium. Any amount of bleeding from a perforation of the heart muscle or great vessels (aortic arch) rapidly fills the pericardium with blood and compresses the heart itself, preventing it from filling. Again, this causes an abrupt loss of blood pressure, unconsciousness, and death.

Heart and Lung Cross Section

In the illustration below, you'll see the heart's actual location. By placing your shot straight at the dead center of the imaginary median line down the center of the body, if you miss the aortic arch and blood vessels, you can see where it's still possible to hit the heart or the spine or even the main blood vessels running vertically down the front center of the spine to the legs. You can also visualize the possibility of your being able to take a side shot into the same highway of heart and blood vessels through the lungs. A local policeman died this way last year when a criminal shot him from the side and it went exactly through his heart.

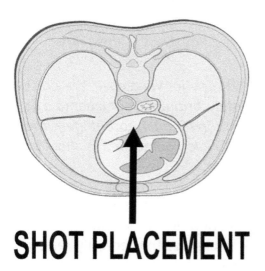

SHOT PLACEMENT

Further below is a frontal view of the human heart and the aortic arch, showing the way it's assembled on the top. Note the left and the right carotid arteries that branch off the aortic arch and go up the neck to supply the brain. Looking to the heart itself, the left and the right coronary arteries branch from the same aorta at the bottom or the ascending aorta to provide blood to allow the heart itself to function. If the blood vessels are severed in this area, then the brain has no blood supply and shuts down along with the entire body. The pulmonary arteries carry deoxygenated blood to both lungs. Veins are always illustrated in blue and carry deoxygenated blood already used by the body; while arteries are always shown in red and are blood vessels that carry oxygenated blood away from the heart to supply the body.

Arteries are much stronger than the veins because while veins return all the oxygen-depleted blood to be replenished (the return lines), the arteries supply the entire body with freshly oxygenated blood (the pressure lines). While any hit into the heart would be very acceptable with a large-caliber, high-velocity round, devastating the aortic arch and vessels in the cluster stops feeding blood to everything in the body, including the heart itself and the brain. Total shutdown! The average adult male has 5 liters of blood in the body. Typically, blood pressure begins to drop when 20-30% is lost. Death can occur when 40% of blood loss occurs and the volume is not replaced.

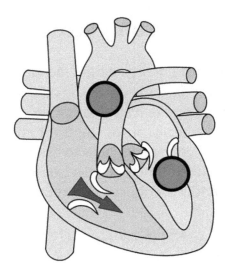

If you hit the dot on the aorta and superior vena cava, the pressure and return blood flow will be stopped and bleed down immediately, bringing your killer to a halt, and if the heart isn't damaged, it could be a possible transplant option for an innocent life. Otherwise, the dot on the left ventricle provides the body with the blood to keep going so this should help bring it to a halt. Stopping a killer is your most important concern.

There are hundreds of artists who make renderings; that is, they draw, sketch, or paint the heart and lungs for medical books and numerous other reasons. But they all see things in *their own* perspective, so if you look into a dozen medically related books "to try to determine the actual size and the exact location of the heart," you'll find the heart is of so many various sizes, locations, and angles, being too high in the anatomy and too far to one side in the anatomy or wherever that particular artist seems to think it should be while too many are also totally out of proportion. Since I try to be very accurate in my pursuit of survival, for the purpose of teaching you in my book, I modified a human x-ray to show its true location in the thoracic cavity (the chest cavity) in line with the spine illustrated by the green line, our median line, and in elevation with the armpits shown with the double-ended red arrow, with an approximation of the nipples illustrated in pink. While some anatomies will vary a little here and there, the heart will still be where the x-ray shows it to be. I've put two red dots, defensive aiming points, at the top of the heart where the aortic arch intertwines with the other vessels. Although hearts will vary slightly in size, an approximation of a large fist will suffice. The male nipples illustrated in pink average about a full hand's width from the fold of the armpit shown by the double ended arrow, and you'll use this same technique, no matter whether your killer is a male or a female due to their varied breast sizes, which may differ from the actual nipple location.

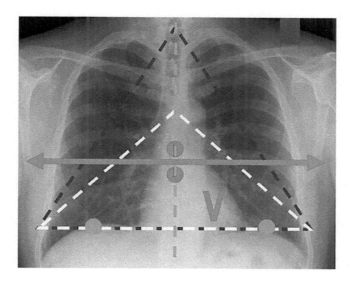

The two-dot aiming points are located at the top of the heart and blood vessel connection while the V shows the left ventricle (on his left, but on your right) while facing him. Remember, the left ventricle is responsible for providing the blood supply to the entire body. If you're not comfortable with trying to shoot for the top of the heart connection, by viewing the x-ray, it should help you determine the best spot you feel you need to be shooting for. The vertical space between the double ended arrow and the nipples is about a full width of a large hand. The very large image all across the bottom is the diaphragm, which is at the bottom of the heart.

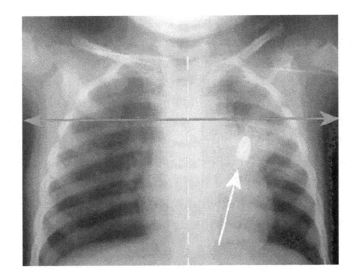

Penetration: While everyone has their own preferences for their preferred caliber, the small calibers that develop much less velocity may give very little penetration. There have been many gunshot wounds to the chest that never got deep enough to even penetrate the heart. In the x-ray above, it shows one such incident where the bullet lodged in the chest, but it didn't get deep enough for any significant penetration or damage, so understand that this is one of those incidents you hear about when they say that he was shot in the heart and kept coming! While it sounds like this guy is rough and tough, the problem is lack of ballistic or kinetic energy. This bullet wasn't even a hollow point, so the damage is very minimal, and even though you might have shot your killer, he still might kill you since the brain and the heart are both still fully functional. If you're using a small caliber, it's best to place the shot where it can do the most damage, that is, very little muscle to have to penetrate so a brain shot might be preferred. A large-caliber, high-velocity round would have done its job!

BRAIN: While everyone always says that the brain is the most critical shot that will shut down the attack, many people go for a brain shot if they think they can get one, but even a brain shot which is assumed to be a very probable shutdown may or may not stop the KILLER, but it may even allow him to still KILL YOU and even survive the confrontation that he had started while you just might be dead. Look at the illustrations.

Brain damage varies by bullets path: Recovering from a bullet wound through the brain depends on where it entered and areas it passed through.

Damage from a bullet crossing through the brain: A bullet that stays on one side of the brain, missing the central region, generally is less devastating. A bullet that crosses into both sides, or hemispheres, usually does more damage and often proves fatal.

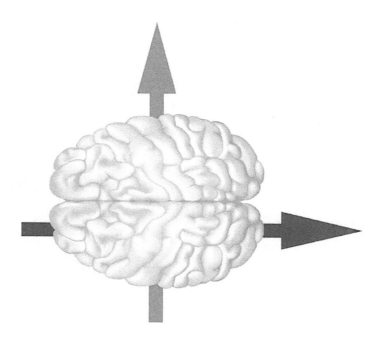

The best way to shut down the attack in a brain shot is the disconnection method once again where a direct shot through the center of the nose, and dead center in elevation of the center of the ear canal in either of the two ears, will disconnect the brain from the spinal cord in addition to the spine and skull connection being there. While I learned years ago in martial arts that it only takes about 8 pounds to break bones, the shock from a large-caliber, high-velocity round placed here should do its job! This may cause neural communication dysfunction in its entirety and completely shut down the central nervous system. The cerebellum is a region or lower part of the human brain located at the brain—spinal cord connection we're shooting for and is the part of the brain that is responsible for integration of human movement, coordination, motor control, and sensory perception. By using this disconnection method, you don't have to spend weeks studying the brain and the parts that control certain actions, but just practice your own effectiveness at placing this emergency shot. If you make the shot as recommended, it may also destroy the cerebellum located at this junction, but no matter how devastating your actual shot is, it just may render your target disoriented and/or unconscious, similar to a blow to the back of the neck-skull connection, or even dead. While a partially damaged brain may still allow the rest of the brain to function, if we succeed in disconnecting it or devastating the connecting communication highway of spine, spinal cord, and vertebrae, the threat will be shut down before he hits the ground. If you get the shot through the mouth, then as long as you're centered on the body, you'll still get pretty much the same spot, just a bit lower, but either way, you also stand a good chance of taking out the spinal-cord-to-brain connection and possibly the cerebellum. Any shot into this area should shut it down completely.

PELVIS/HIP: If we're having great difficulty stopping the threat in a gunfight, it's obvious that you're not able to get a preferred shot off. If you're able to get a shot to the pelvis where the femur bone pivots in the hip, the jointed location is the best place to try to get an effective shot because if the leg-to-body connection is broken, then the assailant will drop to the ground with probably no ability whatsoever to be mobile, but beware that this still allows him to function in full capacity in his ability to shoot you and take you out, especially if you've already taken him down where he knows that the only probable way to survive now is to definitely get you. Remember that a downed victim will experience desperation under stress for last-minute survival, refining and disciplining the KILLER to call on his instinctive skills to prevent his own death or to take you out with him.

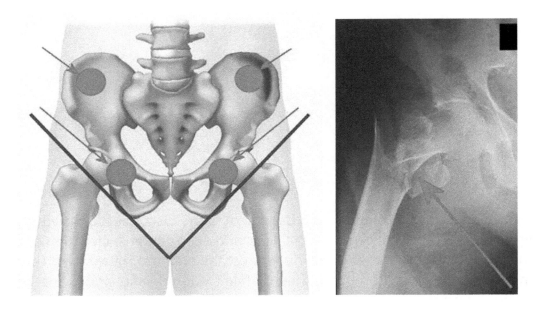

If the bone, socket, or joint is broken in any way whatsoever, your killer will lose his mobility, which gives you the opportunity to call the police and wait behind the safety of cover that his bullets cannot penetrate.

Center of Body: Always practicing an imaginary median line down the center of the body will help you develop instinctive shooting to better stop your killer. In the above brain shot, center is necessary, and in the heart shot to the super-highway of blood vessels in the aortic arch, center is necessary, but if you miss either shot by going high or low of either one, by being in the center median, you still stand a good chance of hitting the spinal cord through the spine or the major blood vessels going down from the heart vertically to the legs or a somewhat critical part of the brain that may allow you to stop the aggression anyway. In the illustration below, it shows the main blood vessels running down in front of the spine, so a center shot always has the option to hit either one or both of these and shut down his mobility. Practice is always necessary!

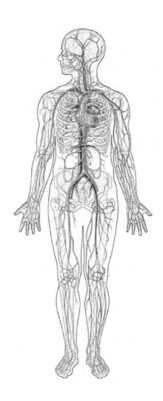

From the heart or diaphragm down to the navel, as long as your shot is center of the body median, where your imaginary center of body line is, you stand a chance of hitting one of these two major blood vessels and shutting down your killer's mobility. The aorta is the pressure line and the one we want to break; however, if you need to make this shot, then dead center or just a hair to your right of center may very well hit home. Center of body is always the best practice, especially on the move with moving targets because if you hit right or left, you are still within the body width.

Criminals' Choice of Firearms

Here's a listing of the top 10 guns used in the committing of a crime as reported by the BATFE (Bureau of Alcohol Tobacco Firearms and Explosives) back in 1993. Although this release was years ago, it gives a general idea as to what the thugs were carrying in their pockets, not to mention that since that time so many lightweight and effective handguns have been developed and obtained by so many of the criminals, but they will still continue to carry much of the same thing. Another report on the top 10 guns in crime in 2000 was just about identical even 7 years later. The television always shows the criminals carrying .45s and bigger ones, including machine guns, but in reality, they really carry anything and everything because they never know what they are going to be able to steal or buy illegally or whatever the owner of the house or car they rob seems to like, but mostly they carry whatever they can easily conceal and pull on their victim easily. However, the #1 and #2 gun of their choice according to this previous report shows that at that time, the .38 Special and the .357 magnum revolver were their main preference, but the .45 ACP is now moving in. While the reports list so many, they seem to miss some of those that are occasionally reported on the evening news, which are usually larger .45 calibers lately, but the point is to be ready to react to prevent being shot. Always assume the KILLER has the biggest, the meanest, the fastest, and the most effective gun made, so you'll never make the mistake of ever wondering what kind of gun he might have. It makes no difference! You need to be able to respond to the deadly threat as effectively as you can, no matter what gun he has. When it's pointed at you, a .22 is as mean and scary as a .45. While the reports named each make of the firearm, I removed the manufacturers' names.

1. .45 Caliber semiautomatic pistols
2. 9mm semiautomatic pistols
3. .38 Special and .357 magnum revolvers
4. .25 Caliber pistols
5. .380 Caliber pistols
6. .22 Caliber pistols
7. 12 gauge shotguns

Finally Selecting Your Firearm

With all the facts that I've provided, you should have enough knowledge now to make a proper decision or to at least get you out looking for the right concealed carry gun to suit YOU specifically. If you should decide to buy a .22 for cheaper target practice, it would be very advisable to rent one of your choosing and try it out on the range like I do, but beware that some .22s may even sell for $1,000 as compared to others for a few hundred. Just because they are expensive or cheap doesn't necessarily make them a good firearm or a bargain either, although the higher priced is most probably of much higher quality while you don't need to spend as much on your practice gun, but again, the choice is yours.

Every firearm has to be fully functional with the proper dexterity for you specifically while the balance and the weight must coincide with your anatomical features such as hand and finger size and your capabilities so that the gun can be used most effectively for YOU, if you want to be able to rely on it to save your life. You obviously wouldn't roll a baseball down a bowling alley if you planned to be the winner, just the same as making sure your defensive firearm is properly matched to your own circumstances so the opposing attorney cannot think up any ridiculous claims against you. Be careful, be properly trained, and study and do your homework! Take your time and don't be ashamed of being a beginner, and, by all means, don't be rushed. You need to learn and develop a coordinated sequence and plan to be effective, and as you challenge yourself, the speed will come your way, but the most important thing to remember is to be able to get your sidearm out and present properly to save yourself, no matter how fast or slow you seem to be. Don't be forced to any specifics; you need to be comfortable with your own desires and abilities to use whatever you finally decide on.

Self-defense Insurance

While defending yourself and firing bullets downrange, we all know they're all going somewhere, so while we also know that we have to try to assure they will most probably go where we intend for them to be, there's also personal defense liability insurance available for the concealed carry license holder to cover legal expenses that will pile up quickly if you are forced to fire in self-defense. This insurance covers criminal defense attorney fees to defend you if you are forced to shoot in defense of your life as well as civil suit defense fees to protect against the so-called victim's family from being able to ruin you financially, which very well can happen, even though you may be the rightful defender, but the courts are starting to ban certain actions in some states such as being able to sue in a civil court if the so-called victim got himself killed due to his being at fault. The NRA (National Rifle Association) offers this personal insurance as well as others like the USCCA (United States Concealed Carry Association). I have this insurance personally; so if I'm ever forced to shoot in defense of my life, I'll never have to worry about the legal expenses piling up because I'll certainly be able to hire the proper attorney since the funds will be there. This will also help those who fear carrying their sidearm due to possible financial ruin, but dead is dead, and that's what we're trying to prevent, so you might want to get this self-defense insurance and carry your sidearm.

It doesn't do any good at home in the drawer when you're staring down the end of a KILLER'S muzzle. The NRA self-defense insurance offers $250,000 in the form of liability insurance toward your legal defense for a few hundred dollars per year, but since things change, call for the actual cost. The USCCA offers $300,000 for criminal and civil defense for a few hundred dollars a year, but with the USCCA, you can combine membership with what they call Self-defense Shield.

1. NRA   (877) NRA-2000 (http://www.NRA.org)
2. NRA Liability Insurance   (877) 672-3006
3. USCCA   (877) 677-1919
   (http://www.USConcealedCarry.com)
4. USCCA Self-defense Shield   (877) 987-7443

Guidelines If You're Forced to Fire in Defense of Your Life

Call 911. "I was afraid for my life and was forced to defend myself. Please send an ambulance right away."

When police arrive, say any one of the following:

1. "He attacked me."
2. "I'll sign a complaint."
3. "There's the evidence."
4. "I need to talk to my lawyer. I do not consent to any search."

Additional Defensive Shooting Guidelines for the Responsibly Armed Citizen:

"It has been necessary to take actions to defend innocent life. I am willing to sign a criminal complaint against the perpetrator(s). I will point out witnesses and evidence. As you may have experienced yourself, this is a stressful and traumatic experience for me. Therefore, I wish to make no further statements until I have contacted an attorney and composed myself. I also do not consent to any searches. I will cooperate fully once I have consulted with an attorney and calmed down. As a lawfully armed citizen, I ask for the same courtesy that you would show a fellow officer who was involved in a similar situation. Thank you for your understanding."

Military Surplus

If you ever find any special gear as military surplus, one important fact to know is that if it's really something used by the military, it will have a prefix of NSN before the stock number. This is a National Stock Number and used for everything the military uses, so if you find a fantastic deal on a scope, binoculars, compass, or absolutely anything you think the military uses, it's a replica made somewhere else if it doesn't have the National Stock Number! Just so you know you may be buying very cheaply made items for very high prices because they might have been advertised as the real deal! Every item the military uses has its own NSN number.

After reading this extensive information, if you buy el-cheapo and it doesn't work or you are unprepared and come close to getting your life taken away, remember by doing all the wrong things, rather than being properly prepared, is like a time bomb waiting for when and where to go off. It can happen.

Abuse

Respect the property where you go to shoot. Every time this happens, it brings one more person in to support the anti-gunners who want to take your guns away! Hundreds of signs get shot around the country among other things, so let's be responsible.

While ballistic science can get quite in depth, some of it is beyond the scope of this book, but I want to familiarize you with the way it all operates, so we're not going to address all the formulas for calculating all these interactions including the power (kinetic energy) of a bullet's impact downrange, but if you desire to take your studies even further, look for firearms ballistics information.

I've never written a book before, but I hate books that don't teach you anything, so I wanted to make sure you got your money's worth. Don't underestimate KILLERS because some are as good at what they do as you are at what you do. I tried to assemble everything you need to know, but in the shooting holds and stances including my graph on breath control, you have to learn to use the process that works the very best for YOU, depending on your specific desires, health, and/or disabilities. The gun operation and the way it all comes together with the ammunition are all facts, not assumptions or theories. This also includes the long-range shooting information for rifles and shotguns. I hope you're pleased with this book, and it could be used for teaching men, women, or young adults the way it all works as a foundation for building your or their future skills. I recommend further classes with qualified shooting instructors. Good luck and good shooting. I wish you a long and happy life, all the way through old age!

The Gadsden Flag above was the very first flag to ever be carried into battle by the Continental Marines!

Disabled veterans get a huge discount for taking a LIFE membership in the NRA!

NRA MEMBERSHIP (877) NRA-2000

I provided all the facts for your self-defense with a sidearm, but the choice is yours. Place your faith in the court system and 12 of your peers or be carried away by 6 friends.

10 Things You Should Never Do After a Self-defense Shooting

When it comes to armed self-defense, it's usually not the shooting itself that trips you up legally. More often than not, it's what you do afterward that gets you in hot water.

1. **Never** call 911 in a panic. No matter how tough you are, your body and brain will be a mess after you pull the trigger and see a body lying on your living room floor. Take a moment to breathe deeply, calm down, and get your thoughts in order before you call authorities.
2. **Never** leave the scene. Unless you're in danger, stay put. You may feel an overwhelming need to seek out friends or family or run away, but don't. That could be misinterpreted as fleeing the scene, which could give the appearance of guilt.
3. **Never** move or tamper with evidence. It's natural to want to *tidy up*, especially if you're in your home. This is unwise. Touch nothing. If there are others nearby, make sure they do the same.
4. **Never** have your gun in your hand when the police arrive. Police will be responding to a *man with a gun* or *shots-fired* call and won't know who's the good guy or who's the bad guy. They will view anyone holding a gun as a threat and will deal with you as such. In short, re-holster your gun or set it down if you don't want to get shot.
5. **Never** make a statement to police before you talk to your lawyer. Police have a job to do, and you need to be cooperative, but you don't want to say too much because anything you say will be used against you. What should you say? There are many opinions on this, but here is one formulation:

    "My gun is lying over there, and that is the gun that I used to shoot my attacker in self-defense because I feared for my life. I do not want to say anything else until I have had time to talk to my attorney. I want to cooperate with the investigation completely, but I'm very upset right now, and I need to talk to my attorney first. I hope you understand."

6. **Never** fall for good cop/bad cop while showing them respect. You think you're too smart to fall for this routine, but you're not. You'll be upset and want to talk, especially to anyone who appears sympathetic. Law enforcement officers are not necessarily your enemy, but they're not your friend either. Shut up! Talk to your lawyer before you make any statement to police!

7. **Never** try your case on the spot. Police have more than one way to get you to talk. Aside from good cop/bad cop, they might challenge your use of lethal force. You'll want to argue your case, but don't. Again, shut up! You're not a lawyer and you're not in a courtroom, not yet anyway.

8. **Never** lecture police on the law or your rights. One of the worst things you can do is get belligerent or act superior. Police are human beings and will react like anyone else if you challenge their authority, belittle their intelligence, or talk down to them. No matter what police say, even if they say or do something you believe to be incorrect, this isn't the time to get into a debate.

9. **Never** fail to use the word *sir*. Most police are good, decent people who have a difficult job. Treat them with respect. Phrases such as "Yes, sir" and "No, sir" will go a long way toward showing responding officers that you are the respectable, upstanding citizen you know yourself to be.

10. **Never** be surprised if you're treated like a criminal. It's best to assume that you will be handcuffed, placed prone on the ground, locked in the back of a cruiser, or even jailed. It takes time to sort out the truth of any shooting, and police are likely to do any or all these things. Don't take it personally. Don't resist or argue. Cooperate fully and just let it all happen.

There are so many fine firearms, sights, and accessories available, and I could assemble an entire book with another 100 pages if I listed them all, but you have access to the Internet to search out their Web sites.

The US Army devised these right-handed and left-handed shooting correction targets to diagnose and help to improve your shooting skills. While there are many configurations out there, I made a right—and left-handed and placed larger images at the end of this book for clarity and understanding.

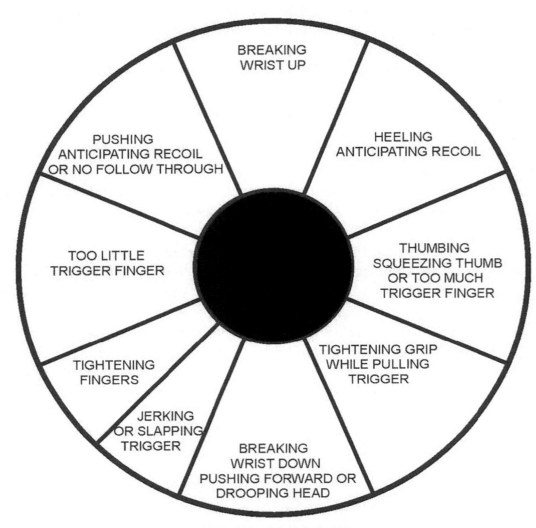

DANIEL R. ENGEL
RIGHT HAND SHOOTING GUIDE TARGET

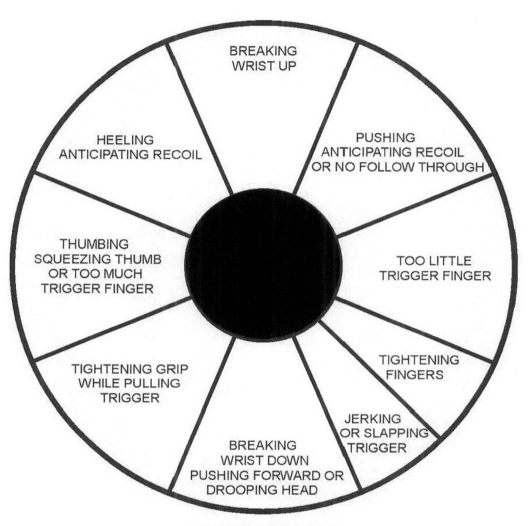

DANIEL R. ENGEL
LEFT HAND SHOOTING GUIDE TARGET

FIREARM_____ DISTANCE_____ FPS_____

WEIGHT_____

Index